A Handbook of Research Methods for Clinical and Health Psychology

A Handbook of Research Methods for Clinical and Health Psychology

Edited by

Jeremy Miles

and

Paul Gilbert

OXFORD

UNIVERSITY PRESS

OXFORD
UNIVERSITY PRESS

Great Clarendon Street, Oxford OX2 6DP

Oxford University Press is a department of the University of Oxford.
It furthers the University's objective of excellence in research, scholarship,
and education by publishing worldwide in

Oxford New York

Auckland Cape Town Dar es Salaam Hong Kong Karachi
Kuala Lumpur Madrid Melbourne Mexico City Nairobi
New Delhi Shanghai Taipei Toronto

With offices in

Argentina Austria Brazil Chile Czech Republic France Greece
Guatemala Hungary Italy Japan Poland Portugal Singapore
South Korea Switzerland Thailand Turkey Ukraine Vietnam

Oxford is a registered trade mark of Oxford University Press
in the UK and in certain other countries

Published in the United States
by Oxford University Press Inc., New York

British Library Cataloguing in Publication Data

Data available

Library of Congress Cataloging in Publication Data

Data available

Typeset by Newgen Imaging Systems (P) Ltd., Chennai, India
Printed in Great Britain
on acid-free paper by
Ashford Colour Press Ltd

ISBN 0–19–852756–X (Pbk.)   978–0–19–852756–5

10 9 8 7 6 5 4 3 2 1

Contents

Contributors

Gary Adamson
School of Psychology,
University of Ulster,
Londonderry, UK

Heather Buchanan
Department of Psychology,
University of Derby,
Derby, UK

Brendan Bunting
School of Psychology,
University of Ulster,
Londonderry, UK

David Clark-Carter
Psychology Department,
Staffordshire University,
Stoke-on-Trent, UK

Sally-Ann Clarke
Department of Psychology,
University of Sheffield,
Sheffield, UK

Neil Coulson
Department of Psychology,
University of Derby,
Derby, UK

Graham C. L. Davey
Psychology Group,
University of Sussex,
Brighton, UK

Christine Eiser
Department of Psychology,
University of Sheffield,
Sheffield, UK

Robert Elliott
Department of Psychology,
University of Toledo,
Toledo OH, USA

Eamonn Ferguson
School of Psychology,
University of Nottingham,
Nottingham, UK

Andy P. Field
Psychology Group,
University of Sussex,
Brighton, UK

Chris Fife-Schaw
Department of Psychology,
University of Surrey,
Guildford, UK

Kate Freshwater
Psychological Health Services,
Tees and North East Yorkshire
NHS Trust,
Hartlepool, UK

Fiona Fylan
Department of Health Sciences,
University of York,
York, UK

Paul Gilbert
South Derbyshire Mental Health Trust,
Kingsway Hospital,
Derby, UK

Susanne Hempel
Centre for Reviews and Dissemination,
University of York,
York, UK

Rick H. Hoyle
Department of Psychology,
Duke University,
Durham NC, USA

Chris Irons
South Derbyshire Mental Health Trust,
Kingsway Hospital,
Derby, UK

Jo Lawford
Department of Psychology,
University of Sheffield,
Sheffield, UK

Chris Leach
Department of Psychological Services,
South West Yorkshire NHS Mental
Health Trust,
Halifax, UK

Jeremy Miles
Department of Health Sciences,
University of York,
York, UK

Bruce Napier
Institute of Medical and Social Care
Research,
University of Wales,
Bangor, UK

Darcy A. Santor
Department of Psychology,
Dalhousie University,
Halifax, Nova Scotia, Canada

Linda Sheppard
Department of Psychology,
University of Sheffield,
Sheffield, UK

Mark Shevlin
School of Psychology,
University of Ulster,
Londonderry, UK

Elizabeth H. Stokoe
Department of Social Sciences,
University of Loughborough,
Loughborough, UK

Ladislav Timulak
Department of Psychology,
University of Trnava,
Trnava, Czech Republic

Kav Vedhara
MRC Health Services Research
Collaboration,
University of Bristol,
Bristol, UK

Peter Watson
MRC Cognition and Brain
Sciences Unit,
Cambridge, UK

Mark A. Wetherell
MRC Health Services Research
Collaboration,
University of Bristol,
Bristol, UK

Sally Wiggins
Psychology Division,
Department of Social Sciences,
Nottingham Trent University,
Nottingham, UK

Sue Wilkinson
Department of Social Sciences,
Loughborough University,
Loughborough, UK

Introduction

Jeremy Miles and Paul Gilbert

We compiled this volume as a practical guide for those carrying out research in health and clinical psychology. So we have brought together authors who are both expert in their fields, but also have practical experience of solving common problems of research in health and clinical psychology.

Chapter 1, by Gilbert and Irons, covers the issues and dilemmas encountered when considering and beginning to engage the research process. They look at why we should value research as a special way of answering questions, how a research question is formulated, and the many different ways our questions can be answered. Chapters 2 and 3, by Buchanan and Coulson, and Napier, consider some of the *unique* practical problems for health and clinical psychologists – that of obtaining our sample(s), and obtaining ethical guidance and clearance. They provide examples from their own and others' experience that help to steer you through what can seem like a maze of procedures and permissions required. One area that can be especially challenging (and rewarding) is working with children – because this area comes with a special set of challenges all of its own, Clarke, Lawford, Sheppard, and Eiser cover this issue in Chapter 4.

The following four chapters examine some of the different ways that we may measure characteristics of our participants. In Chapter 5, Wetherell and Vedhara consider physiological measurements – they look at both the reasons that we may be interested in such measurements, and the methods by which they may be taken. These responses may be observational, e.g. heart rate or blood pressure, or may involve sampling from either blood or saliva. On a rather different tack are the methods described by Fylan, Wilkinson and Santor, in Chapters 6, 7, and 8 – these consider different methods for measuring responses from participants by 'asking them'. Although people cannot tell you what specifically they are suffering from (we need objective measures to do that) much of health and clinical psychology is about people's subjective experience – what they feel and think. To obtain valid information requires appropriate methods. Fylan provides advice on, and examples from, semi-structured interviewing; Wilkinson considers focus groups, and Santor looks at how to use and select appropriate psychometric measures.

In Chapters 9 and 10 Ferguson, and Leach and Freshwater, consider two methods in which the data collection and the analysis are inextricably linked. Ferguson (Chapter 8) examines the use of diaries to collect data, considering the kind of questions this approach can be used to answer, the different approaches to collecting this type of data, and the analyses that can be carried out. Leach and Freshwater, in Chapter 9, focus on repertory grid techniques, used in case studies to explore people's individual 'construct systems' that give personal meaning and prediction. For both of these techniques, the researcher is required to modify and adapt statistical methods that are described in most textbooks of statistics in psychology.

In Chapters 11 and 12, Elliott and Timulak, and Stokoe and Wiggins, consider qualitative approaches to data analysis. Elliott and Timulak provide an overview of different qualitative approaches, and Stokoe and Wiggins have a more in-depth look at one of the most important approaches – discourse analysis.

Chapters 13 and 14, by Field and Davey, and Clark-Carter, are concerned with research design. Field and Davey emphasise the importance of experimental research in answering questions about causality and provide examples of situations in which use of purely correlational (or observational) research may lead researchers to fallacious conclusions. Clark-Carter discusses the sample size considerations, which are being recognised as increasingly important in planning research. Whilst researchers may see these as daunting and forbidding, Clark-Carter demystifies and clarifies the various techniques which can be employed.

The final section of this volume covers a range of methods for carrying out statistical analysis. In Chapter 15, Hempel considers the meaning and use of reliability in measurement. She considers the assessment of reliability in both psychometric measurement, and in data obtained from external raters. The theme of the next three chapters, by Fife-Schaw, Miles, and Watson, is to explore approaches to analysing *different types* of data. Fife-Schaw describes techniques for the analysis of categorical data, while Miles describes the general linear model framework of multiple regression, and shows how this framework expands into the generalised linear model, to encompass ordinal data, categorical data and count data. Watson describes survival analysis, for data in which our outcome is the time to an event; this technique is widely used in medical research, but is considerably less well known in psychology.

In Chapter 19, Shevlin looks at the use of factor analysis – both exploratory and confirmatory factor analysis – and explains how the oft-stated distinction between the two is false. He also shows how each type can and should be used. Hoyle, in Chapter 20, builds on Shevlin's chapter to describe structural equation modelling, a very broad and flexible approach, which can be used to test a wide range of hypotheses. Adamson and Bunting, in Chapter 21, focus on longitudinal research: they show the limitations of conventional analyses of this type of data, and describe methods to answer questions of these data.

Last but not least Chapter 21, by Field, covers that statistical technique increasingly used for making treatment recommendations by NICE and other bodies – meta-analysis. Meta-analysis is different from other forms of analysis, as it is a way of combining the results of a number of studies which have set out to answer the same (or similar) questions.

We hope that this selection of chapters will offer the reader an overview of an increasingly diverse and rich field of research methodologies. For many clinicians it is not so important to know how to 'do' a specific project or 'statistical test' – for here we advise seeking advice from those who are trained in these approaches. Rather it is important for clinicians to understand the range of various options available for exploring their questions. We hope this book will offer a quick and relatively easy overview to what might be involved. We are very grateful to all contributing authors for their clarity of exposition and efforts to meet our goals.

Chapter 1

Thinking about research
Issues and dilemmas

Paul Gilbert and Chris Irons

Research can often seem daunting and rather removed from what practitioners need to know for everyday practice. Moreover, research requires formulating *questions*, understanding of *methods*, trying to gather and analyse *data* – to answer the questions that have been set. Even if you do not intend to do much research this is still an important process to go through because it will alert you to a *way of thinking* about clinical and other issues in health care. Indeed, this can be even more important than any specific methods that are learnt. As the authors of this book describe, there are many ways of deciding on your research question and then deciding what types of data and what methods you will need. This chapter will focus on how to *think* in research terms. It is important not to get bogged down in methods or complex statistical tests that you find hard to grasp – research is not about these things. One of us (PG) has seen too many good clinicians lose interest in research because of this. Research methods are aids to your journey of discovery and exploration, not suppressors of excitement and the passion to know. Statisticians will know far more than you on such matters, and can help you with your methods and tests, but they cannot help you understand your subject area, or where the cutting edges and unknowns are – only you can do that. If you have ideas about what you want to know and how to ask 'questions' in research terms – with some understanding of different methods, then that gives you a start. Competent statisticians or those with experience may advise you on the rest (don't be ashamed to ask for help – we frequently do). Start simple before trying to be complex.

Why do research?

If we ask 'Why should we do research?' you will probably be able to think of a number of good reasons – for example, to help us improve our understanding of disorders, and/or to learn how to help people better. Or you might focus on the idea that research is used to test theories. These are good reasons, but there are others. Research helps us to *build ever more intricate models of the world and how it works*; but it also *challenges our assumptions* and makes us *look before we leap*. There are, however, social processes that should be acknowledged and thought about carefully, because they can undermine our efforts at discovery, understanding and knowing. Indeed, clinical theories and practices can develop for many reasons other than by demonstrated 'truth' or evidence.

Power: Dean (2004)has reviewed a number of key themes in how 'knowledge' and health-focused practices may be adopted because of power elites and authority. Powerful people in a profession may have evolved their own views or ways of doing things, and pass them on as facts rather than an as opinions. Skilled clinicians obviously have much to offer junior staff, but we want to try to ensure we do not simply learn their biases and prejudices. New ways of thinking or doing things (new paradigms) might spread slowly if the older members of a profession hang on to old ideas, theories or ways of doing things (Kuhn, 1962).

Who does the research can have an impact on findings. For example, a recent study found that if drug companies publish research they are four times more likely to report positive findings for their treatment than if an independent research group does the research (Lexchin, Bero, Djulbegovic and Clark, 2003). The reasons for this are of course a research question in itself.

Cultural influence on research: *What* we research, and how we research it, is often linked to socially constructed views. These views then permeate traditions, ideologies and consensus (Dean, 2004). Many feminists have long pointed out that 'science' has a masculine focus and the things women are interested in may not attract the necessary research monies or methods. It is not only gender that may influence the research focus and process – culture can also play an important role. Nisbett, Peng, Choi and Norenzayan (2001) explored the impact of different culture styles (individual vs collective) on the way people think about things, their relationships and the world around them. They compared ancient Greek and Chinese societies with more modern western and non-western societies. In societies that focus on relationships, the way of seeing the world is in terms of patterns and the interconnected nature of things. This ripples though all facets of life, from the type of medical sciences that develop (e.g., non-western medicine tends to focus on the whole body – using concepts such as yin and yang, bodily energies and flow of patterns of energies), the nature of the universe (e.g., created by sets of balancing and interacting forces/energies; dialectics); to the way research is focused and conducted with this world view. Harmony (in both social relationships and in bodily processes) is valued over competition and conflict. Healing seeks to use the body's own systems and to *balance* things that have become out of balance.

In contrast, individual-focused cultures create styles of thinking that split things into individual categories and units. Research focuses on individual processes and medicine is about *discrete* disease entities, not whole bodies. The cultural focus is on developing logic, rationality, the classification and dissecting of objects, studying smaller and smaller individual units. Individual achievement is valued; individuals are held responsible for themselves and are not (seen as) socially constructed. Competition (rather than harmony) is valued where the strongest or best (be this an individual or scientific idea) prove themselves in competition with others. Healing is more focused on knocking out/removing dysfunctional systems and killing off bacteria and viruses. The relationship between doctor and patient becomes secondary to finding the correct diagnosis and technical intervention. In an ideal world these would be seen as dialectical processes with each having benefits and drawbacks. It is when they become turned into exclusive (of the other) ideologies that biases can creep in.

What we research can often be about setting *priorities*, and this takes us back to who – powerful interest groups, professions, governments, product selling companies, respected individuals – controls these priorities. Thus, research is a process that takes place in a community of people who pursue and construct their own cultural-contextualised world views, and have various agendas – such as to pass their exams (satisfy their examiners) or gain recognition amongst their peers or even promote and protect their profession (Dean, 2004). Hence, we come to research questions as *embedded social actors*, already orientated to formulate questions in certain ways. This can make us rather culturally insensitive (Rogler, 1999). As an example, we can offer insight that we gained from our own research into shame. We were interested to see how shame operates in relationship to depression and help-seeking in an Asian community living in Derby. Our research was focused on the experience of the self. However, in our qualitative work we found that *reflected shame* (the shame one could bring to family and community) was far more of an issue than personal shame in this community (Gilbert, Gilbert, and Sanghera, 2004). We would not have thought about that without the advice of people from that community and the adoption of a particular methodology – focus groups – discussed in the chapter by Wilkinson.

As we explore the research process in more detail, try to keep these points in mind. A research way of *thinking* is not tied to any methodology per se, but seeks to challenge our ways of 'knowing' and 'doing', and asks us to be *open-minded*, *explorative* and *evidence seeking*.

Theory-making and testing

We form theories, beliefs and models of the world by making observations and then testing them out. We derive theory by trying to understand meaningful laws between phenomena. Now, where beliefs end and theory takes over is actually rather complex. For example, some people believe in God and heaven. For them this is not a theory but a fact, and hence a core belief. For others it is a theory. Freud thought that neurosis was caused by unconscious conflicts, while cognitive therapists argue that it is related to conscious thoughts. Two very different theories of the causes of neurosis (and even the mechanisms of the mind) which direct very different research questions.

A good theory is one that guides us in our thinking and directs attention to things we need to understand. But above all, a good theory can be tested and disproved. A good theory leads us to generate hypotheses about things and then set out to see if these hypotheses stand up to the searchlight of research. A hypothesis is a prediction. Suppose we have a theory that says 'people are more influenced by the personality of their doctor and his/her ability to convey caring and concern, than they are by his/her intellectual abilities or knowledge'. Now, we might arrive at this theory based on what we know about other aspects of our psychology (e.g., that we are more open and trusting of people who show they care for us, than we are of people who are stand-offish or coldly intellectual). This knowledge generates our theory. Still, we can't be sure this is the case until we test it. And when we do this we might find that the most influential doctors are those seen as caring *and* bright.

In the real world, researchers often 'play' with their data. They are guided by theory and hypothesis testing but only as aids to understanding – not straitjackets. They are alert to the unexpected and are in a constant relationship with their data, 'making friends with [their] data' (Wright, 2003), modifying their thoughts as new findings, both stumbled across by chance and from specific tests, arise. In this sense the very act of research is creative and exciting. You look at your data set and something suddenly hits you that you had not thought of before. Data drive theory as much as theories drive data gathering.[1]

As long as theories are guides then we stay open to the unexpected. However, once we take them as hard and fast beliefs then we start to close down on possibilities of new discoveries. An open, enquiring researching mind seeks to put our knowledge beyond that of opinions of the powerful, vested interests, tradition or consensus and seeks *evidence* for why we believe what we believe. That may appear straightforward but it isn't. 'What do we mean by evidence?'

Evidence

It may seem obvious that what counts as evidence speaks for itself – but it is a little trickier than that because we need to agree and have support for our 'evidence'. This is where methods can help. Suppose we have a new drug and want to know if it helps people with condition A. The first thing to decide is what would constitute an improvement – what should we measure? If we chose the symptoms of the condition, then these become our *variables*, the things we want to measure. They are called variables because they can vary. For example, if our variable is anxiety, depression, weight loss, or blood sugar, some people may have more than others. We call such variables *continuous* because they can take any value over a certain range or continuum. However, our variable could be a discrete category or class e.g., male or female, or cancer. Although a cancer might differ in severity, one either has it or not (discussed in the chapter Fife-Schaw). Other types of variables that we may wish to analyse are count variables, and ordinal variables, discussed in the chapter by Miles.

....

[1] At the same time without falling into the trap of data fishing, or data dredging. An unexpected result should be confirmed in a new dataset.

So the first question would be 'Which symptoms and their measurement are the most appropriate?' This may be more complex than it seems, as in the case when continuous variables can be turned into categories. For example, we might decide that if a person has certain number of symptoms from a list of possible symptoms they are then 'diagnosed' as having the disorder. Depression is like this – you have to have more than one symptom to have a diagnosis. Each symptom itself can vary in terms of severity. Now suppose you need (say) five symptoms to get a diagnosis of depression, and that Fred has five symptoms. We give him the drug and it improves one symptom. He now only has four symptoms and thus falls out of the class of 'depressed'. Is our drug therefore a success? This example is given to indicate that the way we *use variables* can be more complex than it that may initially appear.

Here is another example. Suppose we give our drug to 100 people, and 50 get much better and 50 don't change or get slightly worse. We add all 100 people's symptom scores together to see how the symptoms in the whole group have turned out, and we find, sure enough, there is a mean (average) change in symptom scores. Whilst this 'mean' improvement may look good, we now have a new variable – the *variability of response*. If we only look at the variable of *change scores* and not the *variability of response*, then we could bias our treatment decisions. We might think (by only looking at the average change score) that the treatment might be good for everyone, and miss the fact that 50 per cent of people did not do well on the treatment. This is a particular problem where some illnesses will get better by themselves. For example, colds and flu will get better with no treatment and some types of depression can do too. So if we are to use a new treatment then we have to show that in our group of 50 out of the 100 who appeared to improve on the drug this was not due to some of them getting better naturally. In other words, treatment research must control for the natural course of an illness. The above also raises the question of individual differences – that is, while some people might do well with a treatment others may do badly. Just as some people can enjoy getting drunk and wake up in the morning with no hangover, other people hate it and suffer badly the next day. We can react very differently to the same things and we can even react differently when we are in different physical or mental states. Group data rather washes these subtleties away. Again the point here is not to go into detail on issues of method but of *thinking*; what measures to attend to when we are doing our research.

So before we give our drug we want to know much more about it – not just whether some people improve (that give a good group score) but what are the indicators for those who may do less well on this drug. Treatment trials that give one treatment to one group and another intervention to another group (e.g., placebo or waiting list control) are plagued with these kinds of questions and concerns (Kline, 2000). Thinking in research terms means that we become aware of these kinds of issues, and analyse the data in such a way that we can discover them, as discussed in the chapter by Miles.

Consider also that some people may have worse side effects than others, and as a consequence of this, leave the research trial. Suppose you replace the people who dropped out with new patients. This was common practice in previous years but is not acceptable today. The reason that this is a problem is that over a period of time you will be excluding all those who have adverse reactions and dropped out. By the end of the trial, you may have none of your original patients (unlikely, but in theory it could happen). This means that you have biased your results to those who don't get side effects, or who haven't dropped out for other reasons, because those who dropped out are not part of the trial anymore. Today, researchers use an analysis approach called *intention to treat* – that is, the focus is on the cohort you start with and not just those you finish with. How to get around these kinds of problems requires specialist research skill, but learning about research alerts us to these questions. So next time you see data on a research trial that looks good based on mean scores you can wonder how many did well and how many did not (Chatfield, 2002).

It is partly because research on treatments is not always easy to understand, or can be biased, or poorly understood, that the government has set up The National Institute of Clinical Excellence (NICE). If you are interested in finding out more about the methods and issues on this type of clinical research them you can visit their web site (www.nice.org.uk).

Reliability and validity

There are other questions that we can raise about the *quality* of evidence we collect, and this is related to reliability and validity (see the chapter by Hempel in this volume).

Reliability: If we are going to focus on symptom change, then can we find a reliable and replicable way to measure symptoms? There are a number of different types of reliability. An example of one type would be if I were to assess a patient and measure their symptoms, and then you assessed the same patient's symptoms: would we come up with the same rating and diagnosis? This is called *inter-rater reliability*.

Suppose that it is just too costly to have two well-trained and reliable clinicians to measure all the symptoms you need to know – what then? Or suppose we are more interested in the patient's view of their symptoms. One answer may be to ask the patient to monitor their own symptoms or fill out a self-report scale on symptoms. However, the problem here is that some patients may be accurate and good at reporting their own symptoms, whereas others may be less so – or some may even lie to inflate or deny their symptom. Thus, there is agreement that self-report scales can not be used for *diagnosis* of a disorder (e.g., Beck, Steer and Garbin, 1998). However even for measuring things like self-esteem some researchers think that self-reports are unreliable and lack validity, and one needs interview methods to elicit such information (Andrews and Brown, 1993; see also Andrews 1998 and Santor, this volume). Another complication of self-report scales is that they will only allow people to report their *conscious* beliefs.

However, new work is showing that non-conscious or implicit processes are important. For example, some people may score highly on a self-esteem scale but their self-esteem can plummet if they fail at certain things; it is unstable and is called vulnerable or defensive self-esteem (Jordan, Spencer, Zanna, Hoshino-Browne, and Correll, 2003). Self-report scales do not allow us to recognise or study these important factors.

Another important form of reliability is *test-retest reliability*. This form of reliability concerns the (in)ability of our measure to be consistent over time – will people who score highly on it one week also score highly on it a week or month later? However, it is clear that it may be difficult to establish this type of reliability in some situations, and in fact, we may not want to see consistency over time. An example of this is that we are often trying to reduce people's symptomology over time, and thus we would hope in these situations that patients would be scoring lower on a measure than they did when initially seen (i.e. especially if they had been given some sort of intervention in between). In these cases, test-retest reliability may not be such an important considera-tion. Instead, we may try to look for other signs of reliability in our measure. This may involve trying to find out if the items in our scale have *internal consistency* (i.e. are they measuring the same thing to each other).

Unsurprisingly, it is very important to try to maximise reliability and validity when conducting health research. Whilst (on the surface at least) it would be great to use a questionnaire that showed that patients' symptoms were being quickly reduced when you use a certain intervention this is, of course, of no use if the questionnaire we are using is an unreliable measurement to measure symptom change in the first place.

Efficacy verses effectiveness

Where research is done, and how the findings translate for one area to another, can be important. For example, many research trials of treatment are done under strict condi-tions with careful patient selection and monitoring of the therapy. When there is evid-ence that the treatment works this is called efficacy. However, what happens if you roll the treatment out into the community where the controls are much less? For example, patients in the community might have more than one disorder which might have dis-qualified them for the trial. If a treatment works well under natural or normal condi-tions then we speak of its *effectiveness*. There are cases where treatments can have efficacy but are less effective. This is a different type of reliability relating to that of a treatment under natural conditions. There is a distinction to be drawn here between *explanatory* and *pragmatic* trials of treatment methods. Explanatory trials are more theoretically based – the main role is to further scientific knowledge. Explanatory trials try to use homogenous populations. Pragmatic trials are more practically based, and are used to evaluate treatments, as they are used 'at the coalface'. In addition, an explanatory trial will use intermediate outcomes – for example, evaluating relaxation therapy to reduce blood pressure; pragmatic trials usually try to represent the whole range of health gains – e.g., relaxation therapy will lead to reduction in blood pressure, which should lead to improvement in quality of life and reduction in the probability of a stroke (see Roland and Torgerson, 1998).

Setting research questions: What do you want to know?

We have explored some of the context for research thinking, alerting to issues of cultural bias and reliability. We will now explore in more detail thinking about questions and methods. There is no single process for coming up with a research question. For example, sometimes we simply recognise we don't know something that we need or want to know, or we might want to test the predictions of a theory. In many cases our questions and the kinds of answers we want will determine our methods. For example, you might be interested in people's feelings and beliefs about something. Here you may wish to use qualitative methods (see the chapters by Wilkinson, Stokoe, and Elliot and Timulak, this volume). These methods are very helpful when we have no preset ideas and are simply curious about the kinds of values patients themselves see as important. Kvale (1996, p. 52) suggests that qualitative methods are about 'understanding social phenomena from the actors' own perspectives, describing the world as experienced by the subjects, and with the assumption that the important reality is what people perceive it to be'. Elliott, Fischer and Rennie (1999, p. 216) have pointed out that 'qualitative research methods lend themselves to understanding participants' perspectives, to defining phenomena in terms of experienced meanings and observed variations, and developing theory for field work'. With each method there will be a set of sub-methods and questions.

On the other hand, you may want to know about the *differences* between one group and another, or the way one variable is related to another (e.g., what is the link between nurses salaries and alcoholism?). A key issue here may be the use of *quantitative* data (e.g., the scores on a questionnaire, or some other domain of measurement) which will require quantitative data analysis using various statistical techniques (see chapters by Miles, Watson, Hoyle, Shevlin, Fife-Schaw, and Bunting and Adamson, this volume). Like qualitative methods, there are different types of quantitative methods. For example, if you want to know if an intervention is effective you may start with some *single case studies*, and then conduct small *between-group studies* (e.g., looking at the outcome of a group that is given your intervention against one that is not), and then progress to large trials on the treatment or new care delivery systems.

Looking for differences

Let's look at this more closely. Suppose you have an idea that you could improve things in your service – how can you be sure that your ideas will work and that you are not simply 'of the opinion that they will'. Your question here is 'Does intervention A make a difference?' In this context, we set up *a trial* or *experiment* to see. Here you might have one group of people on whom you make your changes (intervention) and then take your measures (checked of course for validity and reliability) and test out if there are changes or differences on the measures you have chosen. This is a 'before and after' test – a change *measure* or a difference *within a group* over time.

However, it could be just a time effect (e.g., people get better over time and it is not the intervention at all). Here, we might want to control for this by comparing the changes in our group (the intervention group) with those in another group (the control group) who did not get the interventions. This would then be a measure of change over time in the two different groups. Now, the chances are there will be some differences on your measure in the intervention group and the control group because it would be very surprising if you got *exactly* the same scores. The question is then 'Is the difference between the groups meaningful?' – is it significant or is just a chance finding or random effect, and actually the intervention is useless (or even harmful). Now you will need to use quantitative methods here that will use various statistical methods to check out if any differences that might emerge could have been got by chance, or is the difference significant. Other authors in this book will illuminate some of these methods.

In this way of doing research, we also assume that there will be *no difference* – that you are wrong to assume your intervention will make a difference. This is called the *null hypothesis* – 'null' meaning without or no difference. Your intervention 'A' therefore has to show a difference above that which could be expected by chance. Nearly all major methods that are interested in quantitative differences will set out with a null hypothesis.

Looking for relationships

However, rather than *differences* between individuals, we might be interested in the type of *relationship* between things. For example, is there a relationship between low self-esteem and depression? Now, you could take a group of people with low self-esteem and a group with high self-esteem and see if the low self-esteem people were more depressed (test of difference). However, that would not necessarily tell you much about the nature and strength of the relationship between self-esteem and depression. If your question is 'How much is self-esteem related to depression?' then you will need a method that allows you to measure relationships. This is called *correlation*. A positive correlation means both variables move in the same direction. A negative correlation means that as one goes down (e.g., self-esteem) the other goes up (e.g., depression).

Many questions lend themselves to more complex analyses and designs. Where we are seeking to understand and to model a process we may need more complex designs and analyses. Ferguson (this volume) discusses the use of data collection using diary methods, and Adamson and Bunting (this volume) describe some approaches to analysing more complex longitudinal data.

Issues of causality are complex, and are discussed in the chapter by Field and Davey. One approach to seek an answer to that kind of question may mean you will have to study people over time and see if, as their self-esteem goes up or down, there is a subsequent increase or decrease in depression. These are known as longitudinal studies, and can be an important method in delineating issues of causation: however, they are not foolproof. Changes that we detect may be an epiphenomenon of an underlying process. To think about a simple example, the air pressure often drops rapidly as a storm approaches – we might measure this using our barometer. We might conclude that the barometer changing is the cause of the storm, because it precedes the storm, but this is obviously fallacious.

Multiple models of linkage

The key theme of this chapter is not to explain how to do research as to how to think about it. So let's explore some different types of model for linkage between variables and causation. We outline a simple model in Table 1.1.

This raises some important questions about studies of association or relationships. Whilst correlation can tell us about how, and the degree to which, two things may be related, such as self-esteem and depression, it doesn't tell us other important information that might effect this relationship. It is here that we need to start thinking about how *other variables* may also contribute to or account for the relationship between self-esteem and depression. One thing to think about is what *other factors* may also be related to increases in depression, and whether these factors are also related to self-esteem. For example, we know that being bullied is associated with the increased likelihood of depression and also the reduction in self-esteem (Schuster, 1996). However, people who have secure relationships with their friends and family are less likely to be depressed, and are also less likely to have low self-esteem or to be bullied (Arbona and Power, 2003; Troy and Sroufe, 1987). Now, whilst we can show that each of these may be significantly related to (correlated with) depression, and they are also related to each other, correlation does not take into account how the *shared* relationships between variables may affect the nature of their relationship to (in this case) depression.

To do this, we need to use a statistical procedure called *multiple regression* (Miles and Shevlin, 2001; Miles, this volume). This statistical test allows us to take into account the *interrelationship* between variables. In this case this is between self-esteem, being bullied and having secure relationships and their link to depression. Importantly, multiple regression allows us to: (1) to assess how well these variables contribute together in predicting depression, and (2) how well each variable on its own (i.e. controlling for the interrelationship with the other variables) relates to depression. This is the underpinning of many more complex modules for data analysis – including structural equation modelling (see Hoyle, this volume).

Therefore, we know that these variables (e.g., attachment relating, bullying and self-esteem) are related to each other and to depression. However, they can have different types of relationship with each other. This may also be something we want to know. For example, we might be interested in looking at how different *amounts* of self-esteem may influence the relationship between attachment relationships and depression. It

Table 1.1 Relationship between variables

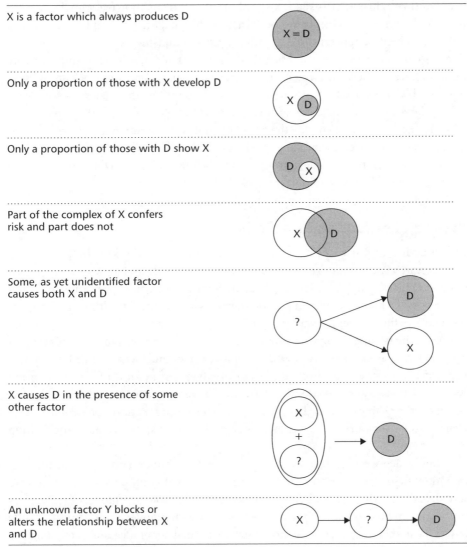

X is a factor which always produces D	
Only a proportion of those with X develop D	
Only a proportion of those with D show X	
Part of the complex of X confers risk and part does not	
Some, as yet unidentified factor causes both X and D	
X causes D in the presence of some other factor	
An unknown factor Y blocks or alters the relationship between X and D	

Adapted from Gilbert 1992

may be that those people with insecure attachments, who also have low self-esteem, are the people who will have the highest level of depression symptomology (see Table 1.1). In comparison, those people with insecure attachments who have high self-esteem may not report high depression symptomology. In this case, we may consider that self-esteem may be a *moderator* of the relationship between insecure attachments and depression. A moderator variable, also called an interaction, can be described as a variable that affects the strength or direction of the relationship between two other variables (see Baron and Kenny, 1986).

Looking at another type of relationship, it may be that self-esteem is part of the process through which insecure attachment relationships are translated into increased depression symptomology. In other words, rather than the amount of self-esteem being important in determining the relationship between insecure relationships and depression, it might be that insecure attachment relationships actually result in lower self-esteem, which in turn leads to higher depression symptomology. Thus, in this case self-esteem is said to *mediate* (account for) the relationship between insecure attachments and depression symptomology.

Whilst these are only examples, the point is that it is important to have an open mind in thinking about research findings. Whilst it may be obvious that both 'X' and 'Y' are related to 'D', careful consideration needs to be taken about how the relationship between 'X' and 'Y' may be important in explaining 'D'.

Beyond questions and methods

We would like to finish our brief introduction of research thinking by considering other research issues. One obvious issue is that our research should follow the strictest of ethical guidelines. It is important that patients are not harmed by our research, and where possible patient advice and patient groups can be involved in the planning of research (see the chapter by Napier on ethics).

There is increasing recognition that when researchers are seeking information on how patients may experience a disorder, or process associated with a disorder, or interventions, researcher should seek patient involvement in guiding and informing research (Goodare and Lockwood, 1999). Once patients understand what 'knowledge' is sought they can offer insights from 'the inside' (Goodare and Lockwood, 1999). Hence, given the nature of this research, we recruited the help of a local self-help group for depression.

Second, when we are researching our treatments and interventions for people it is important to see them as people and not as a collection of symptoms or problems to be solved. Sadly, this has not always been the case. For example, symptoms of epilepsy or psychosis can be controlled, but sometimes with such high levels of drugs that side effects mean that the patient's quality of life is extremely poor. Research should always keep an eye on the quality of life issue, when trying to develop new treatments and interventions.

Finally, we draw attention to an issue we touched on earlier, which is related to the cultural context of health research (Rogler, 1999). There is increasing concern that single process research can be limited and needs to be incorporated into a biopsychosocial model. Such models not only take into consideration the relationship between social factors and health (e.g., poverty, communal violence, sexual behaviour, drug use), but also alert us to key health priorities for research. Johnson (2003) has recently given a major overview of these issues. In this context, there is increasing interest in interdisciplinary and multidisciplinary research. This is not just about multiple data gathering from research projects but also requires detailed thinking through this type of research during planning. It is now recognised that different disciplines bring quite different views and skills to health problems (Nissani, 1997).

Conclusion

Research is a fascinating and exciting activity that can easily turn to disillusion by an over-focus on methods and statistics. We are of the view that it is more important for researchers to understand research questions and to be able to think about the interrelationship between process and phenomena than it is to know how to 'do research'. Increasingly, the doing of research requires sophisticated understanding of statistical models and computer software, which can be daunting to students who intend to work as clinicians. We hope, however, that the future will provide greater opportunities for clinicians and competent methodologists and data processors to work together. To do this, clinicians will need training in research and statistical thinking. The chapters in this book on statistics (such as Clark-Carter on Power, Miles on general linear models, Fife-Schaw on categorical data analysis) attempt to show how a person can think statistically, and usefully employ techniques – they are not attempts to turn the reader into an expert user of those techniques.

Acknowledgements

The authors would like to acknowledge the extensive help given by Jeremy Miles over a number of years on research and statistical matters and whose advice and input for this chapter was greatly appreciated.

References

Andrews, B. (1998). Methodological and definitional issues in shame research. In P. Gilbert and B. Andrews (eds) *Shame: Interpersonal Behaviour, Psychopathology and Culture*, pp. 39–54. New York: Oxford University Press.

Andrews, B. and Brown, G. W. (1993). Self-esteem and vulnerability to depression: The concurrent validity of interview and questionnaire measures. *Journal of Abnormal Psychology*, 102, 565–572.

Arbona, C. and Power, T. G. (2003). Parental attachment, self-esteem, and antisocial behaviors among African-American, European American, and Mexican American adolescents. *Journal of Counseling Psychology*, 50, 40–51.

Baron, R. M. and Kenny, D. A. (1986). The moderator-mediator distinction in social psychology. *Journal of Personality and Social Psychology*, 51, 1173–82.

Beck, A. T., Steer, R. A. and Garbin, M. G. (1998). Psychometric properties of the Beck depression inventory: Twenty-five years of evaluation. *Clinical Psychology Review*, 8, 77–100.

Chatfield, C. (2002). Confessions of a pragmatic statistician. *The Statistician*, 51, 1, 1–20.

Dean, K. (2004). The role of methods in maintaining orthodox beliefs in health research. *Social Science and Medicine*, 58, 4, 675–685.

Dennett, D. (2003). *Freedom Evolves*. London: Allen Lane.

Elliott, R., Fischer, C. T. and Rennie, D. L. (1999). Evolving guidelines for publication of qualitative research studies in psychology and related fields. *British Journal of Clinical Psychology*, **38**, 215–229.

Gilbert, P. (1992). *Depression: The Evolution of Powerlessness*. New York: Guilford.

Gilbert, P., Gilbert, J. and Sanghera, J. (2004). A focus group exploration of the impact of izzat, shame, subordination and entrapment on mental health and service use in South Asian women living in Derby. *Mental Health, Religion and Culture*, **2**, 109–130.

Goodare, H. and Lockwood, S. (1999). Involving patients in clinical research: Editorial. *British Medical Journal*, **319**, 724–725.

Haidt, J. (2001). The emotional dog and its rational tail: A social intuitionist approach to moral judgment. *Psychological Review*, **108**, 814–883.

Johnson, N. G. (2003). Psychology and health: research, practice and policy. *American Psychologist*, **58**, 670–677.

Jordan, C. H., Spencer, S. J., Zanna, M. P., Hoshino-Browne, E. and Correll, J. (2003). Secure and defensive high self-esteem. *Journal of Personality and Social Psychology*, **85**, 969–978.

Kline D. F. (2000). Flawed meta-analyses comparing psychotherapy with pharmacotherapy. *American Journal of Psychiatry*, **157**, 1204–1211.

Kuhn, T. (1962). *The Structure of Scientific Revolutions*. Chicago: University of Chicago Press.

Kvale, S. (1996). *Interviews: An Introduction to Qualitative Research Interviewing*. Newbury Park: Sage.

Lexchin, J., Bero, L. A., Djulbegovic, B. and Clark, O. (2003). Pharmaceutical industry sponsorship and research outcome and quality. *Systematic Review*, **326**, 1167–1170.

Miles, J. and Shevlin, M. (2001). *Applying Regression and Correlation: A Guide for Students and Researcher*. London: Sage.

Nisbett, R. E., Peng, K., Choi, I. and Norenzayan, A. (2001). Culture systems of thought: Holistic versus analytic cognition. *Psychological Review*, **108**, 291–310.

Nissani, M. (1997). Ten cheers for interdisciplinarity: the case for interdisciplinary knowledge and research. *The Social Science Journal*, **34**, 201–216.

Rogler, L. H. (1999). Methodological sources of cultural insensitivity in mental health research. *American Psychologist*, **54**, 424–433.

Roland, M. and Togerson, D. (1998). Understanding control trials: What are pragmatic trials? *British Medical Journal*, **316**, 285.

Schuster, B. (1996). Rejection, exclusion, and harassment at work and in schools. *European Psychologist*, **1**, 293–317.

Troy, M. and Sroufe, L. A. (1987). Victimisation among preschoolers: role of attachment relationship history. *Journal of the American Academy of Child and Adolescent Psychology*, **26**, 166–172.

Wright, D. B. (2003). Making friends with your data: improving how statistics are conducted and reported. *British Journal of Educational Psychology*, **73**, 123–136.

Chapter 2

Sampling in health and clinical psychology research

Heather Buchanan and Neil Coulson

Overview

This chapter will focus on gaining access to samples and how this impacts on sampling. We will be considering the reality of gaining access to your sample, as this is often fraught with practical difficulties that may not be immediately obvious even at the planning stage of your research. In identifying some potential problems we shall also offer some advice on how to make the process of gaining access to samples as problem-free as possible. We will also be considering how this impacts on sampling, as there are clear guidelines for how we should sample but few guides as to how this translates into reality. We will be briefly focusing on different research settings to give you a variety of examples of how this may work and some of the points you need to consider.

Gaining access

Securing access to a sample often involves more than the actual sample itself. Rather, there can be many other stakeholders (i.e. people who have a vested interest in your research) who may be relevant to the research study you are aiming to conduct. In this section we will look broadly at each of the potential stakeholders in the research process and how they may play a part in gaining access to your sample. We have mostly focused on clinical samples though many of these points will be relevant no matter who your sample are.

The researcher

Gaining access and sampling will, in the real world, depend on where you are in your research career. If you are, for example, an undergraduate psychology student you may have less time than a doctoral psychology student or established researcher to gain access to a sample simply due to when you begin your research project and how much time you can dedicate to it. This may also impact on the types of research questions you can realistically investigate with your sample, for example, it may be less realistic to do a longitudinal study as an undergraduate psychology student.

The participant

Obviously the most important people in the research process are the participants themselves. In an ideal world, each participant will happily take part in your research project. However, there are some potential problematic issues that should be taken into consideration when designing your study.

Participants belong to a frequently studied group

If you have interesting research questions to investigate regarding a specialist sample, you can bet you are not the only one. This may mean there is competition to gain access to these potential participants. For example, you may be interested in investigating the role of social support in coping with HIV, using patients from a specific HIV clinic. As HIV is a relatively rare condition these patients will often be involved in, or have been approached to be involved in, several research projects. Hence, it may well be the case that they do not want to take part in another study, or you may encounter difficulties being allowed to approach them. Indeed, Ethics Committees may want to be reassured that patients were not being 'over-researched', particularly if they are from a vulnerable group. Participating in too many studies – whether simultaneously or one after the other – would be considered burdensome to the participants and may also affect the study results. Therefore, it is sometimes a good idea to have an alternative plan to fall back on if you are unable to gain access to such participants.

The potential sample is small

If the participants you are interested in have, for example, a relatively rare condition/disorder (e.g., patients with Huntington's Disease; children with chronic fatigue syndrome) then the population you want to sample from will be small. Bear this in mind when you are considering the required sample size you need to investigate your research questions.

Potential participants are geographically diverse

Sometimes a sample may be spread far and wide across a particular town, city, region or even country. Depending on the nature of your study, this may increase the amount of time, travel or expenditure involved in conducting the study.

Handy hints

Some investigation and communication with the sample in the initial stages may alert you to any problems. By finding out as much as you can about your participants in the earliest stages of your research, potential problems can be addressed and solutions found.

The gatekeeper

What do we mean by the 'gatekeeper'? The gatekeeper can be an individual or group of individuals who are the first point of contact en route to your sample. For example, they may be the head teacher of a school, the manager of a nursing home or the consultant in charge of a hospital clinic.

Sometimes you may be in a situation where you have the opportunity to draw upon the services of a personal contact in facilitating access to your sample. If you don't have a personal contact, there are of course other ways that you can identify the gatekeeper (e.g., try the web, the phone book, or ask your supervisor or colleagues). Whichever area you are working in, and whether you have a personal contact or not, it is important that you then correctly identify who is the person that is ultimately in charge of your sample, and so is the gatekeeper to your sample. For example, if you know a teacher in a primary school you would like access to it is not enough to get permission from them, you must also get permission from the head teacher. If you don't, this could (in extreme circumstances) lead to you not gaining access to your sample and may cause unnecessary friction. The Case of Amanda (see Case Study 1) illustrates that this is not always clear-cut – alas, often the case in health and clinical psychology.

Case Study 1

The case of Amanda

Amanda is an MSc student studying health psychology. For her thesis she is interested in investigating 'burnout' in cervical screeners. She approaches several cervical screening departments, has a meeting with each manager and gives them a copy of her proposed protocol. At one hospital's cervical screening department the manager is happy for her to conduct the study and so with his support she goes through an external ethics committee. Two weeks before the study is due to start (and two months before her thesis is due to be submitted) Amanda gets a very irate phone call from the pathologist who is in overall charge of the cervical screening department as well as others. He is extremely annoyed that he has not been consulted about this study and refuses to let the study go ahead. He also phones and reprimands Mr B.

When should I contact the gatekeeper?

At what point should you contact the gatekeeper to your sample? Should you contact them before you have formalised your idea? After external ethical approval has been sought? In some ways, this presents the classic chicken and egg problem – you don't want to do a great deal of work gathering and reading literature and working out a design based on a specialist sample if there is no hope of gaining access. However, in order to gain access, the gatekeepers of the sample will want to see a well thought-out study with achievable research aims. So, what should you do? First, for all research proposals it is a very good idea to check your research idea (the feasibility of your study, research design, research questions etc.) with your supervisor, manager or colleagues, before you approach anyone externally. If they are happy then it generally makes sense to put your proposed idea onto paper and then consider approaching the gatekeeper to your sample.

There are no hard and fast rules as to when you should make initial contact regarding your sample, as it will partly depend on whether you need external ethical approval (through either a Local Research Ethics Committee or Multicentre Research Ethics Committee if you need access to multiple sites; see Napier, this volume). There are some pointers, outlined below, that may stand you in good stead depending on the type of ethical approval you need.

'I only need internal ethical approval'

It may not necessarily be the case that you will need to make contact regarding your sample before you go for internal ethical approval as internal ethics committees do differ. First, check with your supervisor, or your colleagues, and the Committee (you can usually approach the chairperson informally). It may well be the case that they prefer you to gain ethical approval for your study before you go on to approach anyone about gaining access. This sometimes helps you when you are approaching the gate-keeper to your sample, as you will be able to demonstrate that your research idea has gained ethical approval.

'I need external ethical approval'

If you are using a sample that will involve external ethical approval (see Box 1.1 and Napier, this volume, for further discussion) you should, in the majority of cases, approach the gatekeeper of your proposed sample before you put in your ethics application. This is because you will need to indicate where you will be carrying out the proposed study, and who has given you permission to approach your potential particip-ants. The key here, therefore, is to make initial contact as early as possible. This will enable you to establish whether you are able to gain access to your sample and then set about putting together your ethics application (which can be a very lengthy process) for the relevant committee. It will also enable you to try another avenue for gaining access to your sample if the first attempt was not successful. As we have continued to say throughout this chapter timing is essential – leave it too late and you'll lose out!

Box 1.1 **Central Office for Research Ethics Committees (http://www.corec.org.uk/)**

This is an extremely important web site if you want to undertake a research study in the UK and are unsure whether you need external ethical clearance for your research study. Once you have established that you do, it is invaluable for all the latest forms, procedures, committee deadlines etc. There is also an email address for enquiries about the ethics process. We would strongly advise you consult this web page even if you have gone through this process before, in order to check for any changes in forms, regulations etc.

Establishing good rapport

Once you have established who to contact and when to contact them, it is generally important to build rapport with the gatekeeper to your sample. This person (or group of people) may be the important contact in your research because it is up to them whether you get access to your sample. There are several things to take into account when contacting the gatekeeper to your sample.

◆ Assume that the gatekeeper is very busy – this will nearly always be the case. Take this into account when pitching your study (make the overview of your proposal brief and pertinent to them) and also what you expect them to do. Remember that no matter what your study involves it will normally involve some time and effort on the part of the gatekeeper and you need to make this seem worthwhile.

◆ It goes without saying that you should be as polite and professional as possible. You need to demonstrate that you are an efficient and capable researcher who appreciates the time the gatekeeper has taken to speak to you and/or reading and responding to your request to gain access to your potential participants.

◆ The type of expertise the gatekeeper has will depend on how you pitch your study. Don't use a lot of psychological jargon if they are not a psychologist.

◆ The gatekeeper to the sample will mostly be interested in the role they will play and what you are expecting of the participants. For example, will the gatekeeper be expected to give out the questionnaires (if this forms part of your study)? How much time will take it take for participants to take part? Will they be expected to participate during work/school/clinical hours? Will results be anonymous?

◆ The gatekeeper may well be interested in how the results will be of practical relevance to them and the participants. Make sure you make this clear (and be realistic about it) within both your written protocol and any meetings.

◆ It may be likely that you will need the help of the gatekeeper for external ethical clearance (if your study needs this) albeit briefly. For example, you may need their signature. Make this clear to the gatekeeper in advance and make sure that this is as hassle-free for them as possible i.e. mark out exactly what they have to do and make sure it is passed on to them in plenty of time for the application to be processed.

◆ If your study does not need external ethical clearance, it will still need internal ethical clearance (check with your supervisor or colleagues as to the relevant committee you need to go through). It is usually worth asking the gatekeeper to your sample to sign a document saying that they are happy for you to approach your potential participants (although this does not mean that these people have to participate in your study).

◆ Make it clear that you will write a brief report on your findings once you have completed the study (and make sure you do this).

Your research supervisor

If you are being supervised for your research project, your supervisor plays a significant role in your project. It is generally a good rule of thumb to check with them before you make any contact with external agencies or submit any ethics applications. They can often help secure you access to your sample by simply advising you the best way to pitch a research idea to the gatekeeper to your sample, or reviewing your ethics forms before they are submitted (to cut down on revisions later, hence saving precious time).

Sometimes it is easier to gain access to a specialist sample if you have an established research record within this research area. However, this is often not possible early on in your research career, which can pose a problem. The research record of your supervisor or colleagues can often overcome this, though. If this is the case, then make sure you emphasise this to the gatekeeper of your sample and include this within your ethics application.

The External Ethics Committee

External ethics committees serve a purpose by upholding standards of ethical practice in research (see Napier, this volume for more details) and their approval may facilitate easier access to your sample.

Time factor

One of the biggest issues you need to consider when putting together a study is the amount of time it will take you to get to the point of data collection. You must consider this in relation to the amount of time you have to complete the study (see Box 1.1 for information on where you can check on timescales and forms). The ethics forms will take time to complete and will need several signatures. You need to give time for the committee to respond and then be prepared to make changes. These will all take a considerable amount of time and effort and this may ultimately affect gaining access to your sample, because things may change in the interim period. For example, between contacting the gatekeeper to your sample and getting ethical approval:

+ The gatekeeper may no longer be able to accommodate your request for access.
+ The gatekeeper may have changed so you will need to restart negotiations for access.
+ There may no longer be the number/type of participants available.

Handy hints

Remember to inform the gatekeeper to your sample that there will be a time lapse between you initially approaching them and hoping to start the study. In addition, take into account the nature of your sample – how might their situation be different in, for example, four months time? Case Study 2 illustrates how long it can take to get to the point of data collection even when it appears you have a substantial period of time to carry out the study.

Case Study 2

The case of Michael

Michael is an undergraduate psychology student who hopes to investigate depression and anxiety in NHS dentists. His project start date is in March and it is due in at the end of the following January. Michael focuses on getting good grades in his May exams then contacts his supervisor in June. With help from a contact of his supervisor's he secures access to his sample over the summer period. He then goes through the process of applying for external ethical clearance. His original proposal is accepted with some amendments to be checked by the committee Chair before he can go ahead. By the time Michael gets his letter of approval there is one month left before his project is due in and several of the dental practices he has access to are closing for an extended period over Christmas and New Year.

Settings for research

In this section we shall examine a number of common settings for health and clinical psychology research. In each we shall explore the distinctive features of that setting and provide an overview of some of the more common pitfalls in gaining access to your sample and how this may impact on sampling and ultimately your results.

Schools

Conducting research in schools may be easier than other modes of research for simple reasons of practicality. It is often possible, if one is conducting a questionnaire study for example, that the researcher can obtain large sample sizes in a matter of days. However, other forms of research may be a much slower process and require careful planning and a longer timescale. Regardless of the nature of your research there are a number of common issues to consider and we shall take a look at some of these.

When trying to negotiate access to a school the first person with whom you should *formally* discuss your research is the head teacher of the school. This person will prove crucial in facilitating your access to your sample. It is worth bearing in mind that this person is likely to be extremely busy, so it may be useful to send in advance an outline of your study (including relevant materials) and then follow up with a phone call (if appropriate). This important gatekeeper can also advise you on whether he or she will (or can) act *in loco parentis* or whether you will need to gain additional approval from parents.

If additional approval is recommended by the head teacher you must carefully consider how you will go about gaining this. If you send letters home via pupils they may not all be delivered successfully. Moreover, should you require parents to 'opt in' then your response rate may be insufficient to meet the demands of the study. If you adopt an 'opt out' (i.e. where parent must withdraw their child) then this may increase your sample size.

One other issue to consider include working with children. Is a Criminal Records Bureau Disclosure (police) check required and if so how long will this take? You will not be allowed to be alone with a group of children if you do not have a CRB check (see www.disclosure.gov.uk).

Depending on the nature of your research questions, ensuring participation may be relatively straightforward (e.g., everyone in a class completes a questionnaire) or may be more complicated (e.g., conducting focus groups). As noted in earlier sections of this chapter, the gatekeeper is an important figure who may help facilitate participation. In this case, the head teacher may facilitate access but it is likely to be individual class teachers who you will interact with more when trying to gain access to and recruit willing participants to your study.

It is worth bearing in mind that teachers are incredibly busy people and so a study which places limited demands on their time is likely to be more positively received. If you intend to conduct a questionnaire study you must decide whether you are going to be present and oversee the process or whether you will ask teachers to undertake the questionnaire administration on your behalf. If it is the latter then you must ensure that all teachers have been trained to sufficient levels of expertise that a standardised process can be ensured.

Internet

In recent years the Internet has become an increasingly popular medium through which to conduct health and clinical research. Indeed, there are many features of the Internet that make research opportunities more attractive. Online research may transcend temporal or geographical limitations of face-to-face research. Moreover, it may be possible to reach a larger sample or indeed a population that has typically been more difficult to access (e.g., individuals affected by very rare conditions).

Despite these obvious benefits, there are a number of distinctive and unique challenges of conducting research online, which should be taken into account when planning your research. From the perspective of the researcher, online technology may be used in a variety of ways to gain access to your sample. For example, you may choose to email participants or access a chat room or you may decide to create an online questionnaire. Whilst using email or accessing a chat room are relatively easy things to do more specialist knowledge and skills may be required should you choose to create a web page with interactive features. It is worth considering the specialist knowledge requirements of your research at the outset so that any training needs can be identified or specialised knowledge accessed.

The challenges of online technology, however, are not restricted to the researcher. For participants themselves, a certain degree of computer literacy is required to participate in certain types of online research. For example, individuals who may have only very rudimentary technical skills or low literacy levels may feel reluctant to participate. It is always helpful for the researcher or the online gatekeeper to place a welcome message reassuring those who may feel reluctant to participate that these are not problems.

When accessing an online sample it is important to identify the gatekeeper involved, for example, an email discussion group moderator. Advice should be sought on how best to introduce yourself to potential participants and explain the nature of your study and their likely contribution to it. It may be the case that the gatekeeper serves as a go-between and will make contact with potential participants on you behalf or it may be the case that they give you permission to make contact yourself. Whichever the precise means through which contact is made, it is no less important to consider the ethical issues raised through this mode of research as compared with more traditional types.

The subject matter is likely to be influential in attracting participants to your study. Moreover, the way in which you conduct yourself online may have important implications for your recruitment and retention of your sample. It is worth familiarising yourself with the rules of etiquette on the Internet (sometimes called 'netiquette').

In many research studies there is often an incentive or reward given to the participant in acknowledgement of their contribution. In the case of Internet research, one could argue that this is no less important but may be slightly more difficult to arrange, though not impossible. For example, it may be possible to offer a financial reward or equivalent to participants.

One of the most common issues to face researchers when using the Internet to gain access to and recruit study participants is the problem of sampling. In many instances it may not be possible to recruit a truly representative sample. Rather, individuals who participate in studies online may be self-selected (e.g., those who have more IT skills).

Clinical

You may want to pose specific research questions to a clinical sample. For example, you may be interested in the link between depression and physical illness, and for this you may want to gain access to a sample of clinically diagnosed depressed patients. Alternatively, the clinical sample you may want to access could be health professionals working in a clinical environment e.g., doctors, dentists, community psychiatric nurses. As well as the points discussed earlier, attention must be given to ensuring participation such that you retain your sample for the duration of the study. First, make sure that you show respect for your sample; if they have physical or mental health problems you need to ensure that you have taken any specific problems or issues related to this into account. Second, highlight the relevance of your research, though be realistic about this (don't, for example, make grand claims regarding possible results of your project). Third, make it clear that choosing not to participate will not affect their treatment/job in any way.

As gaining access to your sample may involve considerable effort, and because of the problems in gaining access to clinical participants, in reality this may impact on your sampling. However, this is often recognised in the literature and there are many studies published in journals that have sampling limitations. Although major problems with sampling are not acceptable, you can get over some sampling limitations by assessing and discussing how generalisable your results are and acknowledging any limitations in sampling. For example, Johansson *et al.* (2003) conducted an interesting study to investigate how hospital patients in Finland perceive and evaluate the patient education they receive. The survey comprised 754 patients from 63 of the University hospital's 100 wards during a randomly selected week in spring 2001. Patients were given a questionnaire to complete on their own. The authors acknowledge that the results cannot be generalised to other types of hospitals though they can be generalised to other University hospitals as they claim that these hospitals are all similar in Finland, and the patients were representative of the university hospital's patient population. However, they also recognise that their sampling criteria would exclude very ill patients as the questionnaires were to be completed by the patients themselves.

Community

There are many different types of community sample that you can choose to investigate and to illustrate the point we've briefly included different examples throughout this section (though these are by no means exhaustive). Surveys are often used to invest-igate community samples and this can sometimes reduce biases in sampling. For ex-ample, it may be fairly easy to send out a community postal questionnaire on dental anxiety and oral health behaviour to randomly selected households (although note that this would not be a random sample, because some households are more mobile, and are more likely to be missed: in addition, non-response may bias the sample). There can also be problems with ensuring participation. If you are conducting a postal questionnaire study (going back to the dental anxiety and oral health example) then return rates can be both slow and low – 20–30 per cent can be typical for postal ques-tionnaires. There may be many reasons for this. It may be the case that if participants don't see you face-to-face they may be less likely to take part; think hard about how inclined *you* would be to complete a questionnaire sent to your house from someone you have never heard of. Then consider the chances of that questionnaire actually making it to the post box? It may also be the case that participants mistake your questionnaire for junk mail.

There are strategies you can adopt to increase your response rate, however. Return rates will be highest when the questionnaire has a 'personal touch' and when it requires minimum effort on behalf of the participant. In addition, if you do get a low response rate then be proactive about ways to address this. When designing the study think about how you will identify non-responders in order to send reminder letters, without compromising confidentiality. Further, there are other points to consider if your study is large-scale. These include:

+ Who is going to pay for the postage to send these out and pre-paid envelopes for participants to reply?
+ If you get an initial low response rate, will the follow-up letters push this out of the funding budget?
+ How are you going to calculate the response rate you think you need to make your study viable?
+ How much time do you have to conduct this study? Do you need to build in time for sending out reminder letters and waiting for replies?

The research questions you are posing, and the community sample you wish to investigate, will often have a bearing on your sampling. For example, Herek, Cogan, Gillis and Glunt (1997) investigated internalised homophobia and its correlates among a community sample of gay men and lesbians. They recruited 75 gay men and 75 lesbians at a booth of a gay/lesbian/bisexual street fair in Sacramento, California. Thus, the type of community sample that the authors are investigating impacts on their sampling (that is, this is a convenience sample) and therefore the generalisability of their results. Indeed the authors acknowledge that this sample may not be representative of a larger population. As the event was celebrating the gay community, those individuals taking part in the study were probably higher in self-acceptance and community involvement than many other lesbian and gay men.

How might sampling community members impact on your results?

People may be far more likely to take part if they know someone with the problem or health interest you are investigating, so this may result in response bias. Response bias is a threat to the representativeness of a sample: a carefully selected probability sample may become a non-probability sample – a convenience sample in which individuals' availability and willingness determine whether they are participants. If so, the claims you can make about your data may be limited. In addition, if your response rate is still low this will also have an effect on your results.

An example from the research literature is shown below. It is an interesting, well-designed study which nevertheless demonstrates some of the advantages and disadvantages of employing a large-scale survey design with a community sample.

Sampling in Practice: Example from the research literature

Knibb *et al.* (2000) investigated the consequences for lifestyle, welfare and dietary practices of perceived food intolerance, in a community sample. People with and without perceived food intolerance (PFI) were recruited by questionnaires enquiring about adverse symptoms attributed to foods and other agents sent to randomly identified householders (from the electoral roll) in the Birmingham area of England. Out of a total of 5,013 questionnaires mailed there were 2,081 individual replies, representing 1,003 households; a total household response rate of 20 per cent. Within this, there were 489 PFI individuals. On the questionnaire, respondents were asked if they would be willing to take part in further research of which there were 300 PFI respondents and 529 non-PFI respondents (control group). Interviews were conducted with the PFI respondents in order to elicit further information about their allergy and lifestyle/dietary changes. It was not practical to interview the controls requiring health behaviour and medical history information (the latter part of the interview with PFI individuals) so a questionnaire was sent out asking these details.

Summary and conclusions

In an ideal world, there would be no problems with gaining access to participants, ensuring their participation, and thus employing the sampling technique of choice. However, as research takes place in the real world it is highly likely that the type of participant you are trying to gain access to will impact upon your sampling and so your results. You need to ensure that, as far as possible, your sample is representative of the population, and that when writing up your research you address any limitations. In addition, it is imperative that you are realistic when interpreting and generalising your results.

References

Herek, G. M., Cogan, J. C., Gillis, J. R. and Glunt, E. K. (1997). Correlates of internalised homophobia in a community sample of lesbians and gay men. *Journal of the Gay and Lesbian Medical Association*, 2, 17–25.

Johansson, K., Leino-Kilpi, H., Salantera, S., Lehtikunnas, T., Ahonen, P., Elomaa, L. and Salmela, M. (2003). Need for change in patient education: a Finnish survey from the patient's perspective *Patient Education and Counseling*, 51(3), 239–245.

Knibb, R. C., Booth, D. A., Platts, R., Armstrong, A., Booth, I. W. and MacDonald, A. (2000). Consequences of perceived food intolerance for welfare, lifestyle and food choice practices, in a community sample. *Psychology, Health and Medicine*, 5(4), 419–430.

Chapter 3

Ethical research is better research

Bruce Napier

Introduction

This chapter sets out the reasons why paying attention to ethical issues and seeking ethical scrutiny leads to better research, as well as satisfying the more obvious needs to feel that you are taking care of the rights of your participants, and to feel secure from any challenge as to your conduct of the project.

Its structure is as follows: we start by examining some general principals of ethical conduct, take a brief look at the history of research ethics scrutiny in the second half of the twentieth century, and then get down to the practicalities of surviving and benefiting from the scrutiny process, whether that is internal to your institution, or statutorily required, or a condition of your sponsor's funding.

Finally, a couple of typical scenarios are described which involve ethical dilemmas. Some thoughts are set out for the resolution of these, but there are no answers to them in the back of this (or any other) book.

Some basic principles

A full discussion of the principles that underlie ethical or moral conduct is beyond the scope of this book. There is, after all, an entire academic discipline, moral philosophy, dedicated to these issues. However, a short outline of the keys to right conduct is in order, and interested readers are referred to the extensive literature for discussion in greater depth. For psychologists, Francis (1999) is a good starting point, and contains an extensive bibliography. A specifically North American equivalent is Koocher and Keith-Spiegel (1998).

It is useful to distinguish between legal conduct, moral conduct and ethical conduct. Normally, all three will lead to the same behaviour, but there are circumstances when this may not be so. *Legal conduct* is that which obeys the law, both the statute law laid down by Parliament or other legislature, and common law established by the precedent of court decisions. The law may, however, not appear to meet moral or ethical standards (for example, if it promotes apartheid, or prescribes capital punishment) and hard decisions may have to be made by the citizen subject to such a law.

Moral conduct is defined by the social mores of the group. Actions may be legal but immoral (for example, a rich person in public life using a threat of court action to prevent the publication of discreditable information about themselves), or they may be moral but illegal (refusing to be conscripted to fight an unjust war).

Ethical conduct is defined as that which complies with some code of conduct, and as such has an aspirational rather than prescriptive tone. Thus, the law establishes a minimum standard below which one's conduct must not fall, at risk of penalty, whereas an ethical code describes the ideal conduct to be striven for in the relevant domain. This is not to say that Codes of Conduct such as that published by the British Psychological Society (hereafter BPS) may be ignored with impunity. All those who join the BPS sign an undertaking to comply with the Code of Conduct, and one may be removed from membership if it is proved that one has failed to do so in a non-trivial way. Francis (1999) observes 'the author has seen more careers damaged by bad ethics than by professional ignorance'.

What then should be the touchstone for ethical (and indeed moral) conduct? I believe that it may be summed up as *respect for the individual*. If you never lose sight of the fact that each and every one of your research participants (and, indeed, your collaborators) is a human being with all the rights and legitimate aspirations which come with that status, then you will not go far wrong in the ethics of your research designs.

In all aspects of the practice of psychology, whether research, teaching or application to the improvement of the human condition, there are four headings to be borne in mind. These are the four Cs of *Consent*, *Confidentiality*, *Competence* and *Conduct*.

Consent

Each and every one of your participants must have given, and continue to give, a valid consent to engage in the project. This means that they understand (within the limits of their capacity to do so) what is proposed, what they are expected to do, what are the likely outcomes, and what are the risks (if any) that they bear in taking part. They must particularly understand that they have the right to withdraw at any time from their participation, and that they do not have to give a reason for so doing.

Confidentiality

It must be made clear to the participants at the outset what information will be recorded about them, to what purpose it will be applied, and assurances given that it will be kept securely, that any publication will avoid identifying individual participants, and that all aspects of the Data Protection Act and other relevant legislation will be complied with.

Competence

The research team taken together must possess all the competences required to undertake the project, analyse the information obtained and disseminate the outcome. Inadequately designed, conducted or analysed projects are *ipso facto* unethical projects. The commandment here is 'Thou shalt not waste thy participants' time.' To do so is not only a breach of that fundamental right to respect, it also potentially reduces the available pool of participants for yourself or the next researcher. For this reason, ethical scrutiny legitimately includes consideration of issues such as the power of the design, or the likelihood of recruiting enough participants to achieve the aims of the project.

Conduct

The project must be carried out in compliance with the relevant codes (in the UK, the BPS Code of Conduct already referred to, together with its extensions for research, *Ethical Principles for Conducting Research with Human Participants*, and *Guidelines for the Use of Animals in Research*), and in accordance with the protocol that has been scrutinised by an ethics committee or internal review mechanism. Once again, treating participants with respect is the key to success. A useful test for the acceptability of any piece of conduct is to ask oneself, 'Suppose my partner (child, parent, dog) underwent this procedure, and I found out about it, how would I feel?'

Having set out these principles in brief, how do you go about striving to comply with them, and indeed to demonstrate that you have done so? Disinterested third party review of your proposal is indispensable here. Every reputable research institution has its own procedures for so doing, but in the field of health and clinical research there will almost certainly be a statutorily established committee to do so, and to undertake the project without the approval of the relevant committee will not only be unethical, but illegal.

Ethics Committees, such as the UK's Local Research Ethics Committees (hereafter LRECs) and Multi Centre Research Ethics Committees (MRECs), are often perceived as a terrifying and unnecessary hurdle to be surmounted. A colleague with whom I was discussing this chapter said, 'the LREC is there to try and stop any research at all from going on in their hospital'. I hope that I convinced her that this is a long way from the truth, and I discuss below the way in which LRECs in particular can form a valuable part of the research design process, but there is no doubt that they represent a substantial response cost in the process of conducting research in a health care setting, and so it is worthwhile briefly considering why all civilised countries see the necessity for some such structure.

A brief history lesson

Events in Germany in the 1930s and 1940s are powerful evidence for the impact of social mores and political creeds on supposedly objective scholarship. This is not the place to discuss the way in which the medical profession enthusiastically espoused the National Socialist eugenic creed; the reader is referred to Hanauske-Abel (1996) for a full account.

We are here concerned with the revelations that emerged at the post-war Nuremberg trials about medical research that had been undertaken on the hapless victims of the Nazi regime incarcerated in concentration and death camps. These included surgical interventions to change eye colour to Aryan blue, and genetic breeding experiments with male Aryans and women of other, supposedly lesser, races.

At the conclusion of the Nuremberg medical trials, the judges formulated the Nuremberg Code for the purpose of the establishment and maintenance of minimum ethical standards for the conduct of medical research (Mitscherlich and Mielke, 1947). Subsequently, the World Medical Association ratified the Declaration of Helsinki, which sets out in detail the principles sketched out in the earlier code, has been systematically updated and amended over the following fifty years, and remains the international standard for such research. The code can be found at the WMA website – www.wma.net/e/policy/b3.htm.

Independent scrutiny of proposed projects is the cornerstone by which compliance with the Declaration is obtained.

Lest a feeling of smugness overwhelms the non-Germans amongst my readers, it should be pointed out that no country has entirely clean hands in these matters. American and British conduct of research into the health impact of nuclear explosions frequently breached the rights of the service personnel of those countries, for example, and Tim Madge, in his stimulating account of the social history of cocaine use abuse, *White Mischief*, describes CIA covert experiments, within the American mainland, of the value of LSD as an aid to interrogation (Madge, 2001). These experiments took place in the 1950s and 1960s, well after the ratification of Helsinki. Truly is eternal vigilance the price of freedom and democracy.

When wrestling with the complexities of your local ethics scrutiny form, therefore, bear in mind that the consequences of the alternative, of unbridled research, unmonitored and unreported, would be, and has been, infinitely worse.

Designing ethics

Ethicists and statisticians alike have one complaint above all others – that those who design research projects fail to take account of the needs of their specialty at a sufficiently early stage of the process.

Just as it is far easier to analyse data gathered by a project for which the statistical issues were considered at the outset, so is it far easier to obtain the approval of an ethics scrutiny process if the ethical issues have been so considered. Experienced researchers, of course, develop a feel for these things through long practice, but all need to be aware that the next study may involve some novel feature that invalidates the previously successful procedure. It is prudent, therefore, to use some form of checklist, linked to the requirements of the local code, as part of the design process. Such a checklist is set out below, grouped under the four Cs already described. I have had UK standards and codes in mind in its preparation, but they are of general application and modification to take account of what are almost invariably differences of detail for other jurisdictions should be straightforward.

Consent

- What will the participant actually be asked to do?
- Does the Participant Information Sheet (hereafter PIS) describe this clearly?

- Does the PIS give an adequate, readable and non-technical account of the background and purpose of the study?

- Does the PIS make clear that there is no compulsion to participate in the study, and that having agreed to participate, the participant may withdraw at any time, without giving a reason?

- If the study is a clinical trial of alternative treatments, does the PIS make clear that choosing not to participate, or to withdraw having commenced participation, will have no effect upon the quality of care that the participant receives?[1]

- What means is to be used to obtain and record consent? Is it appropriate to the level of understanding or the status of the participant?

- If the participant is a minor, or subject to some limitation of intellectual or physical ability, do the consent procedures adequately protect him or her, if necessary by reference to an appropriate guardian, carer or advocate?

- Where the participant is subject to one of the limitations just described, what procedures are in place to detect a withdrawal of consent, even if not verbally expressed?

- If a reward is to be offered for participation, is its value appropriate and proportionate to the effort required, or could it be deemed to be an excessive inducement to participate?

Confidentiality

- Is all the information to be collected necessary to the project?

- How will it be stored?

- What measures are in place to protect the privacy and anonymity of the participants?

- Do these measures comply with data protection legislation, and are they covered by the institution's data protection licence?

- If aspects of the project are blinded in some way, what procedures are in place to unblind a specific participant in an emergency?

- When preparing material for dissemination, what procedures are in place to ensure that participants cannot be identified from the published material? (Note that reliance on aggregation of data and simple anonymisation of participants may not be enough if the project concerns rare conditions, or the members of a numerically

---

[1] There is in fact a concealed ethical dilemma here. If participation or non-participation in a treatment trial did not affect clinical outcome, placebo arms or treatment-as-usual arms would be unnecessary, and it would be sufficient to compare the experimental treatment with ordinary clinical outcomes for the condition. In fact, a number of studies have shown that participation in a trial, even in the control arm, leads to better outcomes for all participants, presumably as a result of observer effects. However, the *intention* must be to treat the patient as well outside the trial as within it.

small group, either because of rurality or some unusual social feature such as membership of a small religious sect.)

◆ Are adequate procedures in place to identify and supply a participant with all the data held about them, should they request it?

Competence

◆ What is the range of skills required to undertake this study?

◆ Which members of the team possess these skills, or from whence outside the team are they to be supplied?

◆ Have all training needs for novel procedures been identified, and what courses or supervisors are available to meet them?

◆ In particular where psychometric tests are to be used, which member(s) of the team hold the relevant test user status to purchase and use them?

Conduct

◆ Which codes apply to this study, and are all members of the research team familiar with their provisions?

◆ What aspects, if any, of the study procedures present a dilemma or potential non-compliance with the relevant code?

◆ Can these problems be resolved by redesign of the study, or, failing that, how can they be justified to the ethics scrutineer or committee?

◆ In particular, if the study involves temporary deception of the participants, is this essential, or could the study be redesigned?

◆ What arrangements are in place to debrief the participants, and to provide them with information about the final outcomes of the project should they wish it?

◆ If a participant shows distress during the study procedure, what arrangements are there in place to help them?

◆ If participants experience distress after the conclusion of their participation, have they been advised about sources of assistance?

◆ Should a participant wish to complain about the conduct of the study, does the PIS indicate their first source(s) of remedy, such as the name and address of the Head of Department?

The Ethics Committee can be your friend

In one sense, this should be obvious by now: independent ethical scrutiny is vital to protect you from allegations of improper practice. Just as financial audit procedures exist to protect those who have the handling of other peoples' money, by demonstrating that they are complying with imposed procedures to prevent fraud, so ethical scrutiny protects you by demonstrating that you have objective evidence that your study complies with the relevant codes.

Nonetheless, only the most hard-bitten and experienced researchers view appearance before an ethics committee with anything other than trepidation. For the rest of us (including the present author), a stress management strategy is required. Mine has four components, of which the first element is the checklist just given.

The next is to see the world through the eyes of a member of the committee. A typical LREC will deal with between eight and ten applications in a meeting. It follows that careful attention to your submission form, so that it is as clear and easy to follow as possible, will reduce any potential negative halo effects.

LREC members are (largely) intelligent clinicians and researchers, with a small number of lay people. They are experienced in the issues posed by randomised controlled trials, but may well be less familiar with typical psychological designs, especially where these involve qualitative methodologies. Although you will normally be asked to attach a full protocol, most members will only read what you put in the form itself, together with the information sheets and consent forms. Do not, therefore, try to save time by writing 'see protocol' all over the form, unless you fancy practising anger management strategies when you appear before the committee.

Good LREC members aim to think through the protocol in terms of the experience of the participant, so try to structure your submission with this in mind.

Part three of my strategy is to hold in mind that this is an opportunity for a fresh look at what is by now probably becoming an over familiar set of ideas and concepts. It really is helpful to find out that your proposed participant recruitment strategy has a poor record of success in the area, or that the words 'left-sided neglect' conjure an image of a semi-tramp in most people's minds, not a neurological syndrome.

Finally, presenting your work at the meeting: not all LRECs, and no MRECs, allow this opportunity, but if yours does, it should be welcomed as a chance to avoid silly misunderstandings. Be prepared to give a concise account of your proposal, from the participant's viewpoint, and then to take questions. Be a psychologist! You are trying to influence the behaviour of a small group of people, so don't expect total rationality. Be unfailingly polite, and don't lose your temper. Practice phrases like 'That is a very helpful suggestion, to which we will give careful consideration', even if the suggestion makes it clear that your interlocutor has totally failed to understand the aim of the research.

LRECs and other ethical scrutineers are there to protect the public from incompetent and dangerous research. Your research is neither, of course, so all you have to do is to listen out for the misunderstandings that may suggest that it is – and to be prepared to hear about the hazards you had not foreseen! Better an awkward moment in an Ethics Committee meeting than a long and painful cross-examination in the County Court.

Two dilemmas

In conclusion, two case studies are here presented, as exercises in the kind of reasoning required to resolve ethical dilemmas in research design.

1 Accessing old information

Scenario: A Child Care Social Services team has been trying out a new care needs assessment that the team leader was trained to use at a conference he went to. They believe that it improves the quality of the decisions they make about the children referred to them. They would like to compare the outcomes of the cases taken onto their caseload in the next six months, having started to use the assessment tool, with those of the corresponding six months the year before.

Take a moment to identify the main potential problems here. They concern the two proposed samples in different ways. First of all, the prospective sample: there are at least two kinds of participant, the children and their parents or guardians. Indeed, it could be argued that other professionals involved in caring for the children are also participants, and should be consented, especially if they are to be asked to complete instruments assessing the outcomes of the care team's decisions. All of these groups need a particular approach to the consent process.

Next, there is the retrospective sample. Some of these participants will no longer be available, and none, of course, supplied clinical information with this research purpose in mind. In the UK, the Caldicott Report (Department of Health, 1997) sets out the circumstances in which clinical information gathered for one purpose (usually the immediate care of the person) may be used for another (such as this kind of research). Each Health Authority and NHS Trust must have a senior person identified as the Caldicott Guardian, and he or she has the final say about the way in which patient-identifiable information may be used. Detailed guidance is available on the Department of Health website at http://www.doh.gov.uk/ipu/confiden/index.htm

In this case, much will depend on the decisions to be made about what information is needed to make an effective comparison between the two samples, and on the level of resource available to undertake the study. If it is to be done within the resources ordinarily available to a Trust, then the design sketched out may be the only feasible one, but it is never going to have the power of a prospective trial, perhaps using cluster randomisation, so that some teams within an area (or even across the UK) continue with the original assessment scheme, and others adopt the new strategy.

If the 'quick and dirty' approach has little chance of effectively answering the question, should it even be attempted? On the other hand, not every service research question can be turned into a multicentre trial costing of the order of a million pounds.

2 Consent and the impaired participant

Scenario: A Dementia Care Service is investigating carer stress in the context of severe Alzheimer's Disease, and its alleviation by structured care planning. They want to undertake a controlled trial of two methods of designing and monitoring care programmes, and systematically measure the stress experienced by the informal carers. This means that the patients will be randomly allocated to Method A or Method B.

Again, think about the issues presented by this topic: the following questions were the ones that came to my mind:

- To what extent should the patients be consulted about their participation in this project? (The carers will be consented in the usual way, obviously.) How disabled will these patients be (remembering that the effects of dementia vary from mild memory problems to catastrophic personality loss)?

- To the extent that consent can be obtained from the patients, how should this be recorded? Are witnesses needed, and who should they be?

- To what extent or under what circumstances can the carer give consent on behalf of the patient? This is an area full of incorrect assumptions and beliefs, which could take an entire chapter of its own.

Summary

- Good research is ethical research: unethical research is not.

- Ethical issues should be considered from the outset, as part of the process of working up the research design.

- Only by submitting research protocols to independent review can the ethical standards of the work be assured.

- Although submission to formal ethical scrutiny may feel threatening, it should be welcomed as an opportunity to improve the design, and for the protection it affords to the investigator in the event of ethical challenge.

References

British Psychological Society (2000) *Code of Conduct, Ethical Principles and Guidelines*. Leicester: British Psychological Society.

Department of Health (1997) *The Caldicott Committee: Report on the review of patient-identifiable information*. London: HMSO.

Francis, R. D. (1999) *Ethics for Psychologists*. Leicester: BPS Books.

Hanauske-Abel, H. M. (1996) Not a slippery slope or sudden subversion: German medicine and national socialism in 1933. *BMJ*, **313**(7070), 1453–63.

Koocher, G. P. and Keith-Spiegel, P. (1998) *Ethics in Psychology*. New York: Oxford University Press.

Madge, T. (2001) *White Mischief: a cultural history of cocaine*. Edinburgh: Mainstream Publishing.

Mitscherlich, A. and Mielke, F. (1947) *Doctors of Infamy: the story of the Nazi medical crimes*. New York: Schuman.

Chapter 4

Research with children

Sally-Ann Clarke, Jo Lawford, Linda Sheppard
and Christine Eiser

Research with children in health contexts

Compared with later life, children should be fit, well and healthy. Indeed, in developed
countries with established health services, this is usually the case, and certainly significant improvements have been achieved in terms of reducing neonatal and infant mor-
tality and morbidity. At the same time, new treatments have resulted in increased
survival of children with previously life-threatening or chronic conditions such as
cancer or diabetes. However there is no absolute cure for these conditions, and
children need continued medical care. At the same time, changes in diet and reduced
exercise are contributing to an epidemic of children who are much less healthy than
previous generations. Type 2 diabetes, previously found only in adult patients, is
increasingly seen to be a problem for children in developed countries (Drake1, Smith,
Betts, Crowne1 and Shield, 2002). Children, then, are significant users of health
services and pose unique problems for clinicians.

In health contexts, doctors typically ask parents, most usually mothers, for information
about their child's health. Clinic staff have often operated on a 'children should be seen
and not heard' principle. At best, they might ask children about their problem, but
diagnostic and treatment information is usually directed predominantly at parents
(Pantell, Stewart, Dias, Wells and Ross, 1982; Tate and Meeuwesen, 2001). Before and
during the 1960s, doctors did not think it was appropriate to discuss illness with their
child patients, on the assumption that information might make them anxious or
unnecessarily worried (Plank, 1964).

A more open approach has emerged slowly over time. This has been in part the result
of a growing demand from patient groups for more honest discussions between adult
patients and their doctors. Second, there were indications that children were more
distressed when they had no information than when they were told the truth. Thus,
a child diagnosed with diabetes without any explanation was reported to be afraid of
'dying of betes'. Most children unavoidably pick up information on their own accord
(Gray Deering and Jennings Cody, 2002) and exposure to contextual information such
as regular hospital visits and medical procedures outweigh parents' efforts to conceal

information (Claflin and Barbarin, 1991). Kendrick *et al.* (1986) showed that children with cancer asked other children and sometimes cleaning staff for information about their illness. Third, and most recently there has been a series of pieces of legislation requiring that children are given access to information, and allowed to make decisions about their own care whenever possible. Thus, issues about how children understand medical treatment and how to involve them in medical research are now more topical than ever.

A first question relates to why children are a special case. Why not extrapolate findings from work with adults rather than precipitate a separate body of research? In this chapter, we argue first that issues of working with children are unique. There are differences in the kinds of diseases that affect children, and critically in their abilities to answer questions and take part in research generally. Second, we describe some of the special considerations that need to be made when working with children, focusing on the advantages and disadvantages of using interviews, questionnaires or observational studies. Third, we identify some key points for work with children in the future.

Why are children a special case?

Diseases

Diseases that affect children are qualitatively different from those that affect adults. Some diseases affect children and not adults at all. For example, many more adults are diagnosed with cancers of the breast or lung, while leukaemia and brain tumours are more prevalent in children. Some conditions, for example, cystic fibrosis or muscular dystrophy, are not seen in adults at all.

Differences in understanding of disease/treatment

Children differ in their understanding of disease, its cause and prognosis compared with adults. A number of authors have described developmental changes in children's understanding of illness that parallel those seen in children's understanding of physical concepts such as space or time (Bibace and Walsh, 1981). Although recent work has challenged details of this schema (Carey, 1985), there is no doubt that information about illness to children needs to be sensitive to their concerns.

Ethical issues

While it may be desirable to inform children about their illness and involve them as far as possible in decisions about their health, a number of obstacles have emerged. Notably, relatively large differences between children and their parents in reports about the effects of illness have been identified. It is well established that parents are less reliable when rating the child's internalising behaviours (e.g. emotional responses such as sadness or anxiety) compared to rating externalising behaviours (e.g. acting out or aggression) (Quay and La Greca, 1986). In health contexts, parents typically report that illness has a more negative consequence than the children themselves (Eiser and Morse, 2001). Parents are less able to judge accurately the impact of disease on the social and emotional aspects of their child's quality of life compared to physical domains (Eiser and Morse, 2001).

These differences in perceptions of the impact of illness may have several explanations. First, it is possible that parents' awareness about their child's quality of life is situation-specific. They have no direct experience of their child's activities in the world outside the immediate family environment (e.g. at school or other times when they are not with the child). Second, parents may inadvertently bias their judgements based on their own adult experience. For example, parents may anticipate the impact of illness on work, fertility or their child's general health in the future, whilst children might focus on the immediate consequences of the illness, such as missing friends at school or not being able to keep up a favourite hobby (Eiser *et al.*, 2003).

Parents' views may further be biased and influenced by their own mental health (Tarullo *et al.*, 1995), perceptions of the child's vulnerability to health problems (Dolgin *et al.*, 1990), and the extent to which they experience illness stressors associated with the care of the child's disease and treatment (Chesler and Barbarin, 1987). For example, parents may be responsible for many aspects of medical care at home. Seriously ill children need daily medication. In some cases (for example cystic fibrosis), parents must perform daily physiotherapy to clear the child's lungs. These tasks can add to their daily workload and can be made much more difficult where children refuse medication or are fearful of treatments.

Due to the considerable differences between children's and parents' views about the effects of illness, information needs to be taken from the children themselves whenever possible. Relying on information from adults alone may result in an incomplete assessment and fail to address children's subjective experiences and perceptions of their own quality of life. In response to recent legislation changes, the Department of Health (2002) advocate the need to obtain data from the child's point of view whenever possible, and recent research concludes that any assessment of quality of life should include information from both the child and caregiver (Eiser and Morse, 2001).

When a child is too ill or disabled to provide information, or too young to read and respond to questionnaires, there may be no other alternative but to ask parents their views. Limitations in attention span, language skills, and a limited understanding of conventional rating scales may also create difficulties for obtaining quality of life ratings from children (Eiser and Jenney, 1996; Spieth and Harris, 1996). In these cases parents and sometimes teachers can be an invaluable source of additional information.

In an experiment by Weithorn and Campbell (1982), young adults aged 14 years or older demonstrated a level of competence to make ethical decisions equivalent to that of adults. Nine-year olds were less competent in terms of understanding or giving rational reasons for the research, but did not differ from adults in understanding treatment choices or reasonable outcome alternatives. Nevertheless, the way in which children and adolescents make decisions in hypothetical situations may be very different from the choices they make when faced by real life treatment dilemmas. Unfortunately moral and ethical objections mean that real-life decision-making is particularly difficult to study, and evidence as to how well children are able to understand the concept of a clinical trial, or make rational decisions about their own treatment is scarce.

Children have been shown to be most knowledgeable about concrete information (freedom to ask questions, time involved to take part in the study and possible benefits of participation) and least knowledgeable about abstract information (scientific vs. therapeutic benefits of the study and alternative treatments) (Susman, Dorn and Fletcher, 1992).

Young children's ability to respond to self-report items

Self-report measures have traditionally been presented using a written format, which requires respondents to read the items themselves and then give their answers on paper (i.e. the questionnaire method). Researchers cannot assume that young children (i.e. below eight years) are able to respond to items presented within self-report measures, or that they have the skills necessary to communicate their thoughts and feelings.

Children below eight years can communicate and understand much more than has been previously thought, but there are still various communication and language barriers that can influence their replies. First, most questionnaires designed for adults require an advanced level of literacy and good reading ability. Young children have much less experience with everyday language, and possess a smaller vocabulary than adults. Consequently, they can easily misunderstand words or the context in which these words are used. Reverse wording, often used as a way to balance items, may also cause problems for young children, as they may interpret negatively worded items differently to positively worded items (Benson and Hovecar, 1985; Marsh, 1986).

Second, young children are less experienced in the rules of conversation and communication, and therefore may not fully understand the pragmatics of language. This may mean children misinterpret the meaning behind researchers' questioning. For example, young children may not respond well to repeated questioning, as they may feel that they are being told that their first answer was incorrect and change their response as a result of this uncertainty.

Third, there is an imbalance of power inherent in any interactions between 'adult' researchers and 'child' respondents. Researchers need to be aware that children may feel intimidated or anxious during interview situations, and this may hinder their ability to report accurately on their feelings and thoughts. Children may also assume there is a 'right' answer, and therefore seek to give the answer they think is required rather than what they really think.

Researchers have made various recommendations to help overcome these language and communication problems. There is a need to establish an environment where children feel safe and comfortable to express themselves freely without fear of rejection. Pictures, cartoons or props can be used to help engage and maintain children's attention. Readability formulas may also be useful to help judge the lower age limit for given measures.

Young children's ability to understand and use traditional response scales

Traditionally, authors of child self-report measures have employed quantitative response scales to represent the response choices to respondents for their items. However, there are a variety of measurement concerns that arise when using such response scales with young children.

First, due to their developmental status, young children may lack the cognitive skills needed to process the question, retrieve the relevant information from memory, and then translate their response onto the given response scale. Second, young children may also be more prone to various response biases that can lead to inaccurate responding. Researchers have provided evidence that young children are more likely to produce extreme responses (Chambers and Johnston, 2002), and to acquiesce to questions (Warren *et al.*, 1991; McBrien and Dagenbach, 1998). Third, the type of response scale used and the number of response options chosen can influence the way children self-report. Different response scales convey different meanings (for example a bipolar scale indicates that the question is bipolar to like either feeling happy or sad, while a unipolar scale indicates rating of a frequency of one given attribute). Essentially, the meaning conveyed by the scales used should match with the types of items being rated (McLaughlin, 1999). Fourth, the type of anchors used and whether children understand these can have a strong influence on the scaling properties of measures. Schwartz and Sprangers (1999) have argued that researchers should avoid vague quantifiers such as 'frequently' or 'occasionally', which can be interpreted in different ways for different types of behaviours.

Researchers have suggested a variety of techniques to help overcome children's difficulties in understanding and using conventional response scales. These suggestions range from using creative ways to represent response scales (such as ladders or coloured shapes), to using a specific time recall period for items, and a training period to help children become familiar with the rating task.

Collecting information from families at home – some practical and ethical issues

We have argued that it is important to elicit information directly from children, and indeed that there are circumstances where children's views provide an entirely different perspective from those of parents. However, collecting data from children is more challenging than from adults.

Formal assessments of memory, intelligence or cognition involve strict procedures and guidelines about how to get the appropriate responses from children. In other information gathering situations (especially those that take place in the home) the procedures are less clear and may rely more on researcher experience than formal guidelines. In these circumstances the apparent lack of formality allows researchers to obtain richer and more diverse information from children and their parents, but at the same time requires careful thought and planning. Multiple methods of data collection (interviews, questionnaire completion and formal IQ assessment) may be employed during one session and researchers can face the challenge of moving smoothly between different methodologies in the family's home environment.

In this section, we discuss issues concerned with developing good practice in conducting home-based research studies. It is not possible to anticipate every difficulty that may arise, but we hope issues raised here will minimise disruptions or misunderstandings, and encourage rapport between researchers and families. These potential problem areas will naturally be familiar to more experienced researchers, but will hopefully increase awareness of newer researchers and assist in developing good practice. All of the suggestions here are given in addition to the guidelines offered in the British Psychological Society's publications *Code of Conduct, Ethical Principles and Guidelines* and *Professional Practice Guidelines (Division of Clinical Psychology)*, both available from www.bps.org.uk, and the recommendations of the Medical Research Council's publication *The Ethical Conduct of Research on the Mentally Incapacitated* (see the Ethics and Best Practice page on www.mrc.ac.uk). For a full guide to children's rights under the law, the 1989 Children Act should be referred to.

Clear communication between families and researchers is essential; if parents and children are well informed they should feel comfortable about participating in research and encourage other families to contribute in the future. It is important that the purpose of the study is appropriately outlined with clearly written information sheets provided. Dissemination of research findings, storage of personal information or results and how participants are identified (e.g. as groups, individuals, numbers or initials) are issues that require clarification. It is also important to be clear about the role of the researcher. Sometimes families believe that participating in research can directly influence their child's well-being, education or medical treatment. Misunderstandings may arise when people confuse academic researchers with more familiar health care or educational professionals. If parents ask for information from the study to be made available to other professionals, it is important that the nature and context in which the information was collected is clear.

Building rapport with parents and children is important. Thinking about simple, easy to answer questions can sometimes help put both children and parents at ease. It is often the case that siblings want to join in and can be disruptive. Giving them something to do at the same time, or telling them they can try when their brother or sister is finished also helps. It is clear that some children wish their parents to be present, whilst others prefer to work alone with the researcher. In either event, it is good practice to raise these issues before beginning data collection (especially in the case of IQ assessment or questionnaire completion with children).

Creating a child-friendly environment and one that is free from distraction is not always practically possible, however it helps to check the immediate environment for obvious distractions (television, CD players, computer games etc.) and to ask (politely) for them to be turned down a little (or off). It can be useful to identify any items that cue or prompt particular answers (magazines, books or games lying around). Working with children at the same physical level is a practical way of putting children at ease. If possible it is desirable to work at a table or on the floor, unless formal procedures state otherwise. Parents should be asked at the outset not to answer questions or prompt their children, no matter how tempted they are (this may be minimised if the researcher sits behind the child). During procedures it is important to remember to check regularly if the child or parent wishes to stop.

Occasionally conflicts arise between parents and children around participation. Sometimes parents are very keen for their children to participate when children are clearly reluctant. In these situations it is best to allow the child to set the pace: if they don't feel pressurised they are more likely to feel comfortable about changing their minds later. In addition, children sometimes feel more at ease after they've observed their parents interacting comfortably with a researcher or they have had a little time to interact with the researcher themselves.

It is also important to be aware that children or adults may sometimes feel intimidated with researchers and may not feel able to say what they want for fear of being impolite or wrong. In particular, other types of behaviour in children should be also be observed e.g. misbehaving, not answering or gradually falling silent, looking around or physically walking out of the room, etc. Maintaining regular eye contact and using the child's name intermittently can help draw attention back to the task in hand, but physical contact should not be encouraged. It is also important that formal clearances for researchers are conducted before contacting participants (in the UK Criminal Records Disclosure Certificates should be obtained from the Criminal Records Bureau: information can be found at www.crb.gov.uk).

In instances where children or parents become distressed, it is always important to stop, allow them time to recover and ask if they wish to continue. Providing the families are happy to continue and clearly state this, their wishes may be adhered to. In the event that children are distressed but state a wish to continue, this should be discussed with parents present. Any unresolved issues or uncertainties should be resolved through discussion with the study's principle investigator.

If researchers are asked for advice or help it is usually appropriate to refer families to their local family practitioner (GP) or the appropriate health or educational professional. For more general information web sites or addresses of voluntary associations or charities are useful to pass on. Although rare, a parent or child may disclose difficulties of a more serious nature (e.g. bullying, child abuse or domestic violence). Again, it is important to know what institutional policy is or make contact with relevant organisations to clarify lines of referral or appropriate action.

Working with children and parents in their own home can sometimes be a challenge and on occasion, require a great degree of ingenuity and diplomacy on the part of researchers.

Conclusions

Working with children is far more challenging than working with adults. It is vital to try to understand the mind of the child and to be aware that given their limited experience, children are likely to view the purpose of the study and the researcher's role very differently. It is difficult to overcome the implicit power relationship between researcher and child. Even a novice researcher is an authority to a child and great skill is required to establish the child's ease. When this is achieved, working with children can be a delight and very satisfying.

It would be a mistake to assume that methods used routinely with adults will necessarily be as helpful for work with children. As we have seen, differences in language, cognition and emotions mean that the experience of research is likely to be very different for children compared with adults. It is vital that new methodologies are developed that take into account these differences.

Further reading

Bibace R. and Walsh M. E. (1981). *Children's conceptions of illness. New directions for child development: No. 14 Children's conceptions of health, illness and bodily functions.* San Francisco: Jossey-Bass.

Carey S. (1985). *Conceptual change in childhood.* Cambridge, MA: MIT Press.

Eiser C. (2004). *Children with cancer: The quality of life.* London: Lawrence Erlbaum.

Eiser C. and Jenney M. E. M. (1996). Measuring symptomatic benefit and quality of life in paediatric oncology. *British Journal of Cancer*, **73**, 1313–6.

Eiser C. and Morse R. (2001). Quality of life measures in chronic diseases in childhood. *Health Technology Assessments*, **5**, 1–156.

Spieth L. E. and Harris C. V. (1996). Assessment of health related quality of life in children and adolescents: An integrated view. *Journal of Pediatric Psychology*, **21**, 175–94.

References

Benson J. and Hocevar D. (1985). The impact of item phrasing on the validity of attitude scales for elementary school children. *Journal of Educational Measurement*, **22**(3), 231–40.

Bibace R. and Walsh M. E. (1981). *Children's conceptions of illness. New directions for child development: No. 14 Children's conceptions of health, illness and bodily functions.* San Francisco: Jossey-Bass.

British Psychological Society (1997). *Code of Conduct, Ethical Principles and Guidelines.* www.bps.org.uk

British Psychological Society (2001). Professional Practice Guidelines 1995 Division of Clinical Psychology. www.bps.org.uk

Carey S. (1985). *Conceptual change in childhood*. Cambridge, MA: MIT Press.

Chambers C. T. and Johnston C. (2002). Developmental differences in children's use of rating scales. *Journal of Pediatric Psychology*, **27**(1), 27–36.

Chesler M. A. and Barbarin O. A. (1987). Childhood cancer and the family: Meeting the challenge of stress and support. New York: Brunner/Mazel.

Claflin C. J. and Barbarin O. A. (1991). Does "telling" less protect more? Relationships among age, information disclosure, and what children with cancer see and feel. *Journal of Pediatric Psychology*, **16**(2), 169–91.

CRB (Criminal Records Bureau), P. O. Box 165, Liverpool, ML69 3JD.

Department of Constitutional Affairs, Justice, Rights, and Democracy (1989). *Children Act*. London: HMSO.

Department of Health (2002). *Department of Health action plan. Core principles for the involvement of children and young people. Listening, hearing, and responding*. London: DOH.

Dolgin M. J., Phipps S., Harow E. and Zeltzer L. K. (1990). Parental management of fear in chronically ill and healthy children. *Journal of Pediatric Psychology*, **15**, 733–744.

Drakel A. J., Smith A., Betts P. R., Crownel E. C. and Shield J. P. H. (2002). Type 2 diabetes in obese white children. *Archives of Disease in Childhood*, **86**, 207–208.

Eiser C. and Jenney M. E. M. (1996). Measuring symptomatic benefit and quality of life in paediatric oncology. *British Journal of Cancer*, **73**, 1313–16.

Eiser C. and Morse R. (2001). Quality of life measures in chronic diseases of childhood. *Health Technology Assessment*, **5**, 1–156.

Eiser C., Vance Y. H., Horne B., Glaser A. and Galvin H. (2003). The value of the PedsQLTM in assessing quality of life in survivors of childhood cancer. *Child: Care, Health and Development*, **29**(2), 95–102.

Gray Deering C. and Jennings Cody D. (2002). Communicating with children and adolescents. *American Journal of Nursing*, **102**(3), 34–41.

Kendrick C., Culling J., Oakhill T. and Mott M. (1986). Children's understanding of their illness and its treatment within a paediatric oncology setting. *Association of Psychology and Psychiatry (Newsletter)*, **8**, 16–20.

Marsh H. W. (1986). Negative item bias in ratings scales for preadolescent children: a cognitive-developmental phenomenon. *Developmental Psychology*, **22**(1), 37–49.

McBrien C. M. and Dagenbach D. (1998). The contributions of source misattributions, acquiescence, and response bias to children's false memories. *American Journal of Psychology*, **111**(4), 509–28.

McLaughlin M. E. (1999). Controlling method effects in self-report instruments. *Research Methods Forum*, **4**. Available at www.aom.pace.edu/rmd/1999_RMD_Forum_Method_Effects_in_Self_Reports.htm.

Pantell R. H., Stewart T. J., Dias J. K., Wells P. and Ross A. W. (1982). Physician communication with children and parents. *Pediatrics*, **70**, 396–402.

Plank E. (1964). Death on a children's ward. *Medical Times*, **92**, 638–644.

Quay H. C. and La Greca A. M. (1986). Disorders of anxiety, withdrawal, and dysphoria. In: H. C. Quay and J. S. Werry (eds) *Psychopathological disorders of childhood*, 3rd edn, pp.73–110. New York: Wiley.

Schwartz C. E. and Sprangers M. A. G. (1999). Methodological approaches for assessing response shift in longitudinal health-related quality-of-life research. *Social Science and Medicine*, **48**, 1531–1548.

Spieth L. E. and Harris C. V. (1996). Assessment of health related quality of life in children and adolescents: An integrative review. *Journal of Pediatric Psychology*, **21**, 175–194.

Susman E. J., Dorn L. D. and Fletcher J. C. (1992). Participation in biomedical research: The consent process as viewed by children, adolescents, young adults, and physicians. *Journal of Pediatrics*, **121**(4), 547–52.

Tarullo L. B., Richardson D. T., Radke-Yarrow M. and Martinez P. E. (1995). Multiple sources in child diagnosis: Parent-child concordance in affectively ill and well families. *Journal of Clinical Child Psychology*, **24**, 173–183.

Tates K. and Meeuwesen L. (2001). Doctor-parent-child communication: a (re)view of the literature. *Social Science and Medicine*, **52**, 839–851.

Warren A., Hulse-Trotter K. and Tubbs E. C. (1991). Inducing resistance to suggestibility in children. *Law and Human Behavior*, **15**(3), 273–85.

Weithorn L. and Campbell S. (1982). The competency of children and adolescents to make informed treatment decisions. *Child Development*, **53**, 1589–98.

Chapter 5

The measurement of physiological outcomes in health and clinical psychology

Mark A. Wetherell and Kav Vedhara

Researchers are interested in the physiological outcomes of psychological events for two reasons:

1　Do psychological experiences result in physiological changes, and if so, what are the behavioural and physiological outcomes of this change?

2　To provide further information on the nature and consequences of individual's response to a psychological event, which, when combined with the individual's report of the event, provide a comprehensive measurement of response.

This chapter details techniques that allow for the measurement of the major physiological systems that react to psychological stimuli, i.e., the nervous, endocrine and immune systems. These core systems are discussed in relation to their function in response to psychological stimuli, and appropriate measurement techniques for each of the systems are explained.

The nervous system

When a stimulus is detected by one of the five sensory systems, a message is sent to the brain. The brain interprets the stimulus before deciding what action must be taken to deal with it. The brain then responds to the stimuli via the nervous system – a network of nerves allowing communication between the brain and the body. The nervous system is divided into two main parts; the *central nervous system* (CNS) comprising the brain and spinal cord, and the *peripheral nervous system* (PNS) comprising the network of nerves that spread across the body and organs. The brain is constantly interpreting stimuli; however, we would be overloaded if we were consciously aware of all of these stimuli, or the actions that they evoke. As such, the PNS is further divided into the *somatic nervous system*, which receives information from sensory systems and controls movement of muscles, and the *autonomic nervous system* (ANS). The ANS is so named because it is automatic and controls the involuntary activities of the body without conscious awareness. The ANS therefore deals with the multitude of stimuli that we encounter, and creates reactions in smooth muscle, cardiac muscle and glands accordingly. Some of these reactions are excitatory, whilst others are inhibitory: as such, the ANS comprises two branches, *the sympathetic branch*, and *the parasympathetic branch*. In the main the sympathetic branch is responsible for preparing the body to deal with a stimulus (e.g., it speeds up heart rate, increases arterial pressure, increases sweat production and dilates the iris). In contrast, the parasympathetic branch works to reverse these reactions (e.g., it slows down heart rate, reduces arterial pressure and constricts the iris), as well as other important functions such as increasing the flow of saliva and other bodily secretions.

Nervous system measures

Many nervous system reactions can be easily measured and provide markers of ANS activity. Some of these reactions are observable, for example, when faced with a stressor SNS activity causes a dilation of the pupils and whitening of the face as blood is redirected to major organs. Some of these reactions are immediately obvious, others are more ambiguous. For example, flushing of the face is readily apparent, but the measurement of pupil dilation requires complex equipment.

Such reactions can provide basic information regarding the effects of a stimulus upon an individual. More objective measures of nervous system activity are also available. A summary of the most frequently used measures is provided below.

Cardiovascular measures

Heart rate

We have all experienced environmental changes in heart rate – an increase during a sudden stressful event, and a slower heart rate during relaxation. Heart rate therefore provides one of the more obvious measures of nervous system activity, which can be measured very simply through a main pulse point (e.g., in the neck or wrist) or using more sophisticated measurement and recording equipment. The resting heart rate of a healthy adult is between 60 and 80 beats per minute (bpm). Table 5.1 shows changes in heart rate following various acute psychological and physiological stressors. Note that, in general, acute stressors increase heart rate: however, different reactions will occur depending on the type and effect of the stimulus. For example, watching a video of surgical procedures (Bosch *et al.*, 2003) evokes a passive coping response resulting in a decrease in heart rate. In contrast, the likely cause of the reduced heart rate following the carbon dioxide (CO_2) challenge test (Wetherell *et al.*, 2004) is a result of the direct vagal action of CO_2.

Further considerations: maximal heart rate

Heart rate increases immediately following physical exertion or in response to a stimulus; however, safe maximum heart rates reduce with age. To ensure that the stimulus is not

Table 5.1 Selected examples of studies demonstrating basal and stress-related changes in cardiovascular parameters

	Stressor type	Duration	Time of sample	Baseline	Stress
Willemsen et al., 2000	Serial arithmetic of digits ranging from 1–9	8 min	7 min		
Heart rate				65.01	71.50
SBP				121.19	129.19
DBP				66.69	76.88
Bosch et al., 2003	Memory task where Ps must identify characters from a previous list of 6	11 min	10 min		
Heart rate				69.6	77.6
SBP				115.2	133.1
DBP				68.2	79.7
Bosch et al., 2001	Observing a video of surgical procedures	11 min	11 min		
Heart rate				68.6	65.8
SBP				114.3	118.3
DBP				65.7	68.3
Willemsen et al., 2002	Cold pressor task where Ps keep their hand immersed in 10°C water	4 min	4 min		
Heart rate				64.7	63.5
DBP				124.5	133.3
SBP				73.7	81.4
Wetherell et al., 2004	CO_2 test where Ps must inhale a single breath of 35% carbon dioxide	1 min	1 min		
Heart rate				73.9	65.7
SBP				115.4	126.8
DBP				66.1	70.1

SBP = Systolic blood pressure; DBP = Diastolic blood pressure; CO_2 = Carbon dioxide, Ps = Participants.

> ### Box 5.1 **Maximal heart rate by age**
>
> $208 - \text{Age} \times 0.7$
> e.g. $208 - 28 \times 0.7 = 188.4$ (189 to be safe!)
> Therefore, for a 28-year old participant, the maximum heart rate should not exceed 189 beats per minute (Tanaka *et al.*, 2001).

putting the participant under undue strain, maximal heart rates, based on participant age can be calculated (see Box 5.1).

Heart rate variability

The rate at which the heart beats is dynamic – via the sympathetic and parasympathetic branches of the nervous system, the heart is instructed to either speed up or slow down in response to frequent changes in the environment. Simple measurements of heart rate usually give an average number of heartbeats over a given period – usually beats per minute. However, there may be a lot of variation in heartbeat to achieve an average heart rate of 80 bpm, e.g., for part of the minute the heart may beat at 100 bpm, but for another part it may beat at 60 bpm. It is considered healthier to have greater variability in heart rate as this implies greater flexibility and the capacity to respond quickly to changes in demand. The measurement of this variation is called *heart rate variability* (HRV). This procedure involves complex equipment and even more complex analyses and can therefore be quite an expensive measurement technique. As such, this technique is not discussed in great detail here. For a more extensive review of heart rate variability see Kop, Krantz and Baker (2001).

Blood pressure

Traditionally, the measurement of blood pressure was an invasive technique that required a needle being inserted into the artery. This method provides a very accurate measure of blood pressure; however, its appeal is reduced owing to its invasive nature. Fortunately, reliable measures of blood pressure can be obtained non-invasively using a sphygmomanometer. This involves an inflatable cuff being placed around the upper arm. The cuff is inflated to a higher pressure than the pressure of the heart when contracting resulting in occlusion of the brachial artery, and then the pressure is released. These measurements can now be obtained using automated machines, which can be set to take measurements at given time periods and record all data. This technique provides a measure of the heart at rest (diastole) when the ventricles relax and fill with blood, and during contraction (systole) when the ventricles pump blood into the pulmonary artery or aorta, as measured by mm/hg. This measurement produces two figures; the first figure is always the largest and is the systolic pressure (SBP), the second, and smaller figure is the measure of diastolic pressure (DBP). The two figures are usually presented as in Box 5.2. Like heart rate,

Box 5.2 **Average blood pressure reading in a healthy adult**

Average blood pressure (approximately) $^{120}/_{80}$
High blood pressure (greater than) $^{140}/_{90}$
Low blood pressure (less than) $^{90}/_{60}$

blood pressure changes in quickly in response to stimuli. Examples of changes in blood pressure following physiological and psychological stressors are shown in Table 5.1.

Problems with cardiovascular measurement

Cardiovascular reactivity is sensitive and even non-invasive methods of measurement can be influenced by factors other than the study variables. For example, 'white-coat hypertension' is a well-known medical phenomenon that describes increases in blood pressure and heart rate that occur as a result of a medical practitioner taking the measurement. Regardless of the quality of your bedside manner, this phenomenon may also affect your measurements. Therefore, always allow a lengthy rest period (about 15 minutes) prior to collecting any cardiovascular data. It is also a good idea to ask the participants to refrain from any physical exercise, smoking, or drinking caffeine immediately before coming to the laboratory.

Electrodermal activity: the galvanic skin response

The skin helps to maintain the body's water balance and core temperature in two ways; (1) through the constriction and dilation of blood vessels, and (2) through the secretion of moisture (sweat) by sweat glands. These glands are present almost all over the body; however, they are most abundant on the palms of the hands and soles of the feet. These glands make the skin's surface a good conductor of electricity. According to Edelberg's (1972) delightfully named 'sweat circuit model', sweat ducts on the skin act as electrical resistors. When these ducts are filled with sweat the resistance is reduced and electrical conductance is increased. Sweat secretion is controlled by the SNS and changes in response to external stimuli, for example, the experience of sweaty palms prior to and/or during an interview. *The galvanic skin response* (GSR) measures the electrical resistance of the skin to a small electrical current being passed across electrodes attached to the fingers. The greater the sympathetic activation the more you sweat, the more you sweat the lower your skin conductance and the higher your GSR. For a more in-depth look at electrodermal activity of the skin see Endelberg (1972).

The endocrine system

The endocrine system is an important mediator of the effects of psychological factors upon physiological health outcomes. One direct route is the effect of the sympathetic-adrenal-medullary (SAM) and hypothalamic-pituitary-adrenal (HPA) axes. The SAM axis is responsible for the body's immediate response to stress – sometimes called the fight-flight response. The SNS signals the release of catecholamines from the adrenal medulla. These catecholamines (adrenaline and noradrenaline) are then released as hormones into the bloodstream and neurotransmitters in the brain, where they create reactions that enable an individual to cope with an initial threat. For example, greater blood flow to major organs, such as the liver, and muscles is achieved through increasing heart rate, and increasing blood flow through major vessels. This ensures a greater supply of oxygen to the parts of the body that need it most, e.g., the muscles to enable mobilisation, and the liver where glycogen is broken down into glucose to provide readily available energy.

At the same time the HPA axis is also mobilised, however, this process prepares the individual for the longer-term effects of a threat, and therefore the process takes a little longer. The reaction starts with the release of corticocotrophin-releasing hormone (CRH), which signals the release of adrenocorticatropic hormone (ACTH) from the pituitary gland. ACTH then signals the release of corticosteroids (cortisol in humans) from the adrenal cortex. This end product is produced about 15–20 minutes after the initial threat and enables the continuation of the responses initiated by the SAM axis. Cortisol has many responsibilities: first, it signals the breakdown of muscle protein-releasing amino acids, which are then used by the liver to continue the production of glucose. Second, cortisol stimulates the release of fatty acids, which are used as an energy source for the muscles. Cortisol also suppresses immune system activation in order that energy can be redirected to systems considered more important in dealing with the event. Finally, cortisol is responsible for turning off the HPA stress response. When cortisol levels become excessive (in relation to the perceived threat) a negative feedback system signals to the hypothalamus and pituitary gland to stop the release of CRH and ACTH, therefore preventing further release of cortisol.

The endocrine system is therefore a key-player in the physiological stress response, and as such, the products of the SAM and HPA axes provide the opportunity to assess the effects of external stimuli on the stress process. Laboratory studies have demonstrated that catecholamines and cortisol increase following a variety of acute physiological (e.g., cold pressor, inhalation of carbon dioxide) and psychological stressors (e.g., multi-tasking stress, public speaking). The functions of these axes place these findings into context – increases in these hormones enable the body to cope with the immediate, short-term effects of the event. Similarly, chronic stress is associated with increases in catecholamines and cortisol. Sustained production of these hormones provides the resources required to deal with the longer-term effects of an event, or indeed the cumulative effects of lots of stressful events. However, this continued production is not desirable. Under normal circumstances the stress response is successful – enough resources to deal with the threat will be provided, the threat will be dealt with and stress hormones will return to normal levels. However, if for whatever reason, the event is not resolved, levels of stress hormones will remain elevated. This results in a continuous state of physiological arousal/tension and can cause many secondary problems with regard to the cardiovascular and immune systems, as well as the endocrine system itself.

Measuring the endocrine system response

Methods of sampling

Many endocrine measures can only be effectively sampled in blood or urine. In the same way as white coat hypertension can be a nuisance variable when assessing cardiovascular changes to stress or external stimuli, the taking of blood can also be a stressful experience. The stress experience will obviously be magnified in anyone with a phobia of needles and as such, lengthy acclimatisation periods must follow the insertion of a needle to ensure that responses can be attributed to the manipulated variable. Whilst some research may only require a single blood sample (e.g., for measurement of immunity) some studies may require you to take blood on more than one occasion, for example, baseline and several post-stress measurements may be required if assessing the effects of an acute stressor. In such cases it is far easier to cannulate the vein. This involves the insertion of a needle and a cannula (like a plastic sheath) into a vein (usually in the arm). Once inside the vein the needle is removed, the cannula is secured and a valve is fitted so that blood can be removed whenever necessary.

Whilst blood or saliva are the most convenient vehicles for collecting samples following acute changes, the collection of multiple urine samples allows for average estimates of endocrine activity over extended periods of time (e.g., 24 hours). There are two main problems, however, with this technique. The first, and probably the most obvious, is that of participant adherence. Although not invasive, 24-hour urine collection requires the collection of all urine samples during the collection period in order that periods of activation and relative inactivity are accounted for in the final measure. Second, urinary catecholamines are quickly broken down if left at room temperature. The collection procedure is therefore made more troublesome; because in order to avoid this breakdown, participants are asked to keep their sample refrigerated, or to add a preservative.

In some cases endocrine activity can be measured using saliva. Saliva is collected using salivette collection tubes that consist of small cotton rolls inside a sealed plastic tube. The participant collects saliva by placing a cotton roll in their mouth and chewing on it until it becomes saturated with saliva. The sample is then placed into the tube and frozen before analysis.

Hypothalamic-pituitary-adrenal (HPA) axis

HPA activity can be assessed through the measurement of any of the HPA hormones (i.e., CRH, ACTH or cortisol). Data regarding all CRH, ACTH and cortisol may well provide information regarding regulation of the system and the effects of specific stimuli on the stages of HPA activation. However, as CRH and ACTH can only be sampled in blood, this section will focus on the end product of HPA activation, namely cortisol.

Cortisol

Cortisol is often sampled in blood (total plasma cortisol); however, it can also be measured in saliva (free cortisol, cortisol that is not bound to a cortisol-binding-globulin). Concentrations of cortisol in saliva are indicative of levels in the blood (although levels in plasma are considerably higher). Saliva collection is less intrusive than blood collection and as such, the measurement of cortisol in saliva has become a popular method of physiological assessment in psychobiological research. Although salivary cortisol is relatively stable, the samples must be refrigerated quickly after sampling. Samples can be stored in domestic fridges, which makes sampling in homes more convenient, before being transferred to the lab. As a rule, samples should be analysed with six months of collection. Table 5.2 shows changes in cortisol (cortisol reactivity) in response to three different sorts of acute psychological stressor. These stressors are administered in the laboratory; under the assumption that observed changes are indicative of the changes that would be expected when encountering stressors in everyday life. More recently, studies have explored the moderating effects of psychosocial variables upon the diurnal cortisol profile and the effects of this profile on health. Flatter profiles (i.e., less of a decline throughout the day) have been associated with increased stress as a result of maltreatment in children (Hart *et al.*, 1996) and poorer interpersonal relationship functioning (Adam *et al.*, 2001). This profile is also associated with poorer health outcomes, for example, greater risk of death in breast cancer patients (Sephton *et al.*, 2000) and chronic fatigue syndrome (MacHale *et al.*, 1998). In contrast, a flattened profile

Table 5.2 Salivary cortisol responses to acute psychological stress

	Stressor type	Duration	Time of sample	Cortisol reactivity
Kirschbaum *et al.*, 1995	First exposure TSST: requires public speaking/mental arithmetic in front of an audience	23 min	30 min	14.3 nmol/l
Kunz-Ebrecht *et al.*, 2003	Stroop colour-word task and mirror tracing	12 min	12 min	3.45 nmol/l
Earle *et al.*, 1999	Verbal mental arithmetic under harassment	12 min	25 min	10.48 nmol/l

TSST = Trier Social Stress Test; nmol/l = nanomoles per litre of volume.

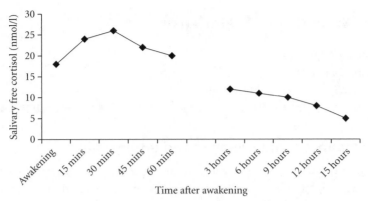

Fig. 5.1 Typical awakening response and diurnal profile of cortisol secretion.

has been associated with reduced reporting of upper-respiratory tract infections (Edwards *et al.*, 2003).

Other issues: the diurnal cycle and cortisol secretion

Cortisol secretion is influenced by a diurnal cycle with highest levels in the morning, especially in the period immediately following awakening, and a gradual decline throughout the day (see Figure 5.1). Other factors (e.g., digestion of food) can also cause temporary changes in this decline. In addition, the HPA axis is more reactive during certain periods of this cycle (e.g., when cortisol levels are lower). These factors must therefore be carefully considered when planning the timing of experiments that involve cortisol measurement. This cycle can, however, provide lots of useful information regarding normal diurnal secretion of cortisol, and therefore the effects of other factors (e.g., levels of distress, illness, personality traits etc.) on this profile. Multiple sampling is not always convenient, and can be quite expensive. However, given the significance of this diurnal profile on cortisol secretion it is wise to take as many samples as possible in order to account for changes that occur throughout the day. Short of taking samples every 30 minutes, it is essential that the important aspects of the diurnal profile be considered (e.g., the waking response and the low evening levels). Figure 5.1 details the key sampling times that capture important periods of the profile.

Sympathic-adrenal-medullary (SAM) axis

Although cardiovascular parameters can be used as markers for SAM activation, the most direct markers are the catecholamines. The catecholamines, adrenaline (also called epinephrine) and noradrenaline (also called norepinephrine) are chemically very similar and both serve to initiate and maintain (in the short-term) the body's immediate response to stimuli.

> ## Box 5.3 **Basal levels of catecholamines**
>
> Noradrenaline 410 pg/ml
> Adrenaline 50 pg/ml
> pg/ml = picograms per millilitre volume

Catecholamines (noradrenaline and adrenaline)

Catecholamine reactivity following a stimulus is very quick (e.g., within a couple of minutes). Although levels of catecholamines will remain elevated for some time after the presentation of a stimulus, in order to measure the initial catecholamine response, samples must be taken in the period immediately following the onset of a stimulus. Normal basal levels of adrenaline are lower than noradrenaline (see Box 5.3), however, any external event that elicits a SAM response, will increase catecholamine levels. For example, levels of adrenaline and noradrenaline increased in response to social stress (TSST), but unlike cortisol reactivity, catecholamine reactivity did not habituate with repeated administrations of the same test (Schommer *et al.*, 2003).

The immune system

The immune system is a complex network of organs and tissues that protect the body from potentially harmful substances, e.g., viruses, bacteria and parasites. It is made up of two main kinds of immune protection: cellular and humoral immunity, which work together in the recognition and subsequent destruction of foreign agents. A fully efficient response requires the involvement of both cellular and humoral responses.

Measurements of the immune system can be of two kinds: enumerative, i.e., levels or numbers of immune cells (cell counts), or functional, i.e., the functional ability of these cells. These measurements can be made *in vivo*, meaning in the body, or more commonly, *in vitro* (sometimes called *ex vivo*) meaning that measurements are made on cells extracted from the body. In most cases, immune assays must be conducted on blood samples, so unless stated otherwise, assume that the following immune measurements are typically sampled in blood. Many acute stimuli elicit temporary changes in immune parameters. This may not represent an actual change in cell proliferation and/or activity, but movement of these cells as a result of activation of the nervous system. For example, acute stressors such as multi-tasking stress (Wetherell *et al.*, 2004) and mental arithmetic (Bosch *et al.*, 2001) temporarily increase the secretion of secretory immunoglobulin A (S-IgA). More chronic stimuli, e.g., chronic stress, usually result in a reduction in immune activity. This reduction is, in part, brought about by the immunomodulatory effects of the endocrine system (e.g., cortisol). For example,

Table 5.3 Differential effects of acute and chronic stress on immune parameters

	Psychological variable	Immune parameter	Findings
Glaser *et al.*, 1985	Exam stress	Lymphocyte proliferation	↓ Lymphocyte proliferation to PHA and Con A during exam period
Kiecolt-Glaser *et al.*, 1986	Exam Stress	NK activity	↓ NK activity during exam period
Bosch *et al.*, 2001	Mental ar.ithmetic and viewing video of surgery	S-IgA	↓ S-IgA to surgical video ↑ S-IgA to mental arithmetic
Deinzer *et al.*, 2003	Exam stress	S-IgA	↓ S-IgA up to 14 days after in exams
Wetherell *et al.*, 2004	Acute multi-tasking stress	S-IgA	↓ S-IgA in Ps who perceived greatest task workload ↑ S-IgA in Ps who perceived least task workload
Glaser *et al.*, 1985	Exam stress	Latent virus titers	↑ EBV and HSV titers during exam period
Burns *et al.*, 2002	Levels of stress and Coping style	Hepatitis B vaccination	↓ antibody titers in Ps with greater number of stressful experiences
Vedhara *et al.*, 1999	Chronic stress in caregivers	Influenza vaccine	↓ IgG response to flu vaccine in caregivers
Marucha *et al.*, 1998	Exam stress	Wound healing	Slower wound healing during exam period

PHA = phytohaemaglutinin; Con A = Concanavalin A; S-IgA = Secretory immunoglobulin A; EBV = Epstein–Barr Virus; HSV = Herpes-Simplex Virus; IgG – Immunoglobulin G; NK = Natural Killer (cell).

the stress associated with examination periods are associated with decreases in S-IgA (Deinzer, 2003) and reduced natural killer cells (Glaser *et al.*, 1985). The differential effects of acute and chronic stress on a variety of immune parameters are shown in Table 5.3.

Measures of cellular immunity

Lymphocyte enumeration

Sufficient numbers of appropriate immune cells must be present in order that the immune system can recognise and eradicate foreign bodies. One measurement of immune status is therefore to count the numbers of cells in circulation. Cell numbers are measured using a technique called *flow cytometry* where blood flows through a detection device that is capable of differentiating between and counting cells in the blood sample. These cell-counts are, however, limited in their interpretation, i.e., what do high or low numbers of certain cells mean in clinical terms? First, enhanced or depleted numbers of cells do not necessarily indicate enhanced or depleted cell function. Second, a variety of factors unrelated to the immune system per se, can influence cell counts (e.g., diurnal rhythms). As such, enhanced or depleted cell numbers are unlikely to be indicative of an actual rise or fall in cell numbers, but moreover, a product of redistribution of cells throughout the immune system.

Lymphocyte proliferation

The majority of circulating lymphocytes are in a state of inactivity until a novel stimulus is encountered, whereupon the lymphocytes will begin to proliferate. The proliferative response, therefore, provides an indication of the functional status of the immune system, i.e., the ability of inactive cells to mount a response to a stimulus. Stimuli can be specific or non-specific. Specific stimuli will stimulate specific cells (e.g., influenza antigens will stimulate cells which respond only to influenza antigens). In contrast, non-specific cells will activate a broader range of cells. Non-specific cells are typically synthetic products such as the plant proteins concanavalin A (Con A) and phyto-haemaglutinin (PHA).

Natural killer (NK cells)

NK cells are also lymphocytes, however, unlike B and T-lymphocytes they do not need to recognise a specific stimuli before being activated. Instead they target and destroy some but not all, tumour cells as well as some virus-infected cells by attaching to the target and releasing a chemical that produces holes in the target cell's membrane. Like lymphocytes, both numbers and functional status of NK cells can be measured. The latter involves the incubation of NK cells with a radioactively labelled target cell, which is selected on the basis of its susceptibility to being destroyed by NK cells. When a target cell is attacked, the radioactive label is released providing a quantifiable marker for NK activity. One drawback of this technique concerns the possible presence of other non-specific cytotoxic cells in the assay. The presence of other cells capable of destroying the target cells may therefore lead to erroneous conclusions regarding the functional capacity of the NK cells. This issue can, however, be rectified through the use of NK pure samples, i.e., samples where other cytotoxic cells have been excluded.

Humoral immunity

Humoral immunity comprises the secretion from lymphoid cells of protein molecules (antibodies) to all bodily fluids, these antibodies are capable of binding to specific foreign molecules (antigens) and either neutralising them or facilitating their destruction and removal by other immune cells (e.g., cell-mediated). Either latent levels of antibody, or antibody response to an antigen can be measured.

Antibodies

There are five major immunoglobulin classes (IgM, IgG, IgD, IgE and IgA), which vary in their specificity and their role in immune defence. The specific purpose of IgD is unknown, however it is thought to aid activation of B cells following recognition of an antigen. IgM and IgG are the predominant immunoglobulin classes present in the blood and IgE is responsible for eliciting immune response to allergens and parasites. Finally, IgA is found on all surfaces of the mucosa and acts as a first line of defence on the upper respiratory, urino-genital and gastrointestinal tracts by preventing antigens attaching to epithelial surfaces. The majority of antibodies can only be sampled in blood, however, as IgA can be sampled in more accessible secretions, greater detail will be given regarding this immune parameter and the issue involved in its measurement.

IgA

IgA is the predominant antibody in human secretions (e.g., saliva, tears and breast milk). When found in secretions, IgA is referred to as secretory IgA (S-IgA). These molecules are structurally different to those found in serum as they contain a secretory component, which is thought to protect the IgA molecule from enzymatic breakdown. S-IgA sampled from saliva, the most accessible of the bodily secretions, provides information about the entire mucosal system and therefore can provide a broad measure of immune status. The ability to measure S-IgA in saliva makes it a very accessible and a relatively cheap immune parameter. However, there are several important issues that are essential to the accurate measurement of this antibody.

Other issues: total or specific IgA?

There are two different ways to measure the S-IgA antibody: total S-IgA antibody levels or levels of specific S-IgA. Total S-IgA is a measure of all S-IgA secreted regardless of its antigenic variance, whereas specific S-IgA is a measure of S-IgA that binds to a specified antigen (e.g., rabbit albumin). The issue of which of the two measures to use is a source of much controversy (see Stone *et al.*, 1987; Jemmott *et al.*, 1989), however, they should be looked upon as measuring distinct aspects of the immune response. That is, the measurement of total S-IgA provides an indicator of general immune status, whilst specific S-IgA provides an in-vivo model of immune function.

The effect of saliva volume

When attempting to observe S-IgA change in response to a stimulus, it is difficult to determine whether changes in S-IgA concentration occur as a result of the manipulated stimulus, or whether they exist as an artefact of the amount of saliva produced. For example, increases in S-IgA may be observed following exposure to a stressor. However, if the same stressor also decreases the secretion of saliva, then S-IgA increases cannot be solely attributed to the stressor, but to the reduction in saliva volume and the

Box 5.4 **The calculation of S-IgA secretion rate**

S-IgA secretion rate (μg/min)

$$\frac{\text{S-IgA concentration } (\mu g) \times \text{flow rate of saliva } (\mu l)}{\text{Total collection time}}$$

μg = micro-grams, μl = micro-litres, μg/min = micro-grams secreted per minute of time

apparent inflation of S-IgA within the sample. The specific relationship between S-IgA concentration and saliva volume is dependent upon the effects of the manipulated stressor upon saliva volume. Although it is clear that a range of psychosocial variables can alter saliva flow, and can, therefore, influence measures of S-IgA, it is likely that different stressors will exert differential effects upon saliva production and secretion. As such, saliva flow rate should be included when reporting S-IgA concentrations. The most common method of controlling for saliva volume is to calculate the S-IgA secretion rate (see Box 5.4). Most studies assess salivary flow via the collection of unstimulated saliva over a given time period: usually between 2 and 6 minutes. It is possible to stimulate saliva flow either through sucking a citric sweet, or using cotton rolls impregnated with citric acid. Whilst this might appear beneficial, especially if the stressor reduces saliva flow and the participant has difficulty producing a sample, some saliva glands may be stimulated more than others resulting in a artificial elevation of S-IgA in the sample.

Saliva is usually collected in one of two ways:

1 Drooling: Saliva is allowed to accumulate in the base of the mouth and the participant spits it out into a pre-weighed tube every 60 seconds.

2 Swab/salivette tubes: Saliva is collected (absorbed) by a pre-weighted cotton roll in the mouth for a timed period. For the collection of S-IgA via salivette, it is imperative that the participant refrains from moving the jaw or chewing during the collection period as chewing differentially activates the major glands in the mouth – these glands excrete varying concentrations of S-IgA and as such, can produce erroneous results.

Antigen-specific antibodies

Latent virus titres

Some viruses are always present but kept under control by the immune system (e.g., *Herpes Simplex virus* (HSV), responsible for cold sores and *Epstein–Barr virus* (EBV), responsible for glandular fever). For the majority of time, these viruses are dormant in the body until they become activated. This activation could occur as a result of the immune system being compromised in some way, thus preventing the adequate control of the virus. When the viruses are activated, antibodies will be released into circulation thus providing a measurement of the antibody control of the virus. Unlike many other immune parameters where it can be assumed that higher levels are indicative of greater immunity, in the case of latent virus titres, higher levels occur in response to increased viral activity and are therefore indicative of poorer immune function.

Response to viral challenge (vaccination response)

Vaccinations against hepatitis B are routinely administered to health care professionals and influenza vaccines are given to the elderly and other groups at greater risk of influenza. Taking advantage of these routine vaccination programmes can provide important information regarding the effects of psychological factors (e.g., chronic stress) on the responsiveness of the immune system. This immune measurement is similar to that of antibody measurement, however, the vaccination paradigm allows for the measurement of *in vivo* immune responses.

Wound healing

A relatively new area of measurement involves studying the wound healing process. This process may take advantage of naturally occurring wounds (e.g., following surgery) or may involve the study of experimentally induced wounds (e.g., Marucha *et al.*, 1998). The latter procedure typically involves making a small puncture wound (often on the forearm or the hard palate in the mouth) and monitoring the healing process over subsequent days/weeks. Like vaccination studies, wound healing allows for the study of external factors upon an *in vivo* response.

Conclusions

In this chapter we have attempted to make the reader aware of existing measurements of physiological stimuli, the strengths and weaknesses of these techniques and examples of how these techniques have been utilised in psychological research.

Information regarding the functioning and activity of these systems can be obtained individually; however, when these systems are measured together, a detailed profile of the physiological response to stimuli can be obtained.

Further reading

Evans, P., Hucklebridge, F. and Clow, A. (2001). *Mind, Immunity and Health: The Science of Psychoneuroimmunology*. Free Association Books: London.

Herbert, T. B. and Cohen, S. (1993). Stress and immunity in humans: A meta-analytical review. *Psychosomatic Medicine*, **55**, 364–379.

Van Rood, Y. R., Bogaards, M., Goulmy, E. and Hoiwelingen, H. C. (1993). The effects of stress and relaxation on the in-vitro immune responses in man: A Meta-analytical study. *Journal of Behavioural Medicine*, **16** (2), 163–181.

Vedhara, K., Fox, J. D. and Wang, E. C. Y. (1999). The measurement of stress-related immune dysfunction in humans: An introduction to psychoneuroimmunology. *Neuroscience and Biobehavioral Reviews*, **23**, 699–715.

References

Adam, E. K. and Gunnar, M. R. (2001). Relationship functioning and home and work demands predict individual differences in diurnal cortisol patterns in women. *Psychoneuroendocrinology*, **26**, 189–208.

Bosch, J. A., De Gues, E. J. C., Kelder, A., Veerman, E. C. I., Hoogstraten, J. and Nieuw Amerongen, A. V. (2001). Differential effects of active verus passive coping on secretory immunity. *Psychophysiology*, **38**, 836–846.

Bosch, J. A., De Gues, E. J. C., Veerman, E. C. I., Hoogstraten, J. and Nieuw Amerongen, A. V. (2003). Innate secretory immunity in response to laboratory stressors that evoke distinct patters of cardiac autonomic activity. *Psychosomatic Medicine*, **65** (2), 245–258.

Burns, V. E., Carroll, D., Ring, C., Harrison, L. K. and Drayson, M. (2002). Stress, coping and hepatitis B antibody status. *Psychosomatic Medicine*, **64**, 287–293.

Deinzer, R., Kleineidam, C., Stiller-Winkler, R., Idel, H. and Bachg, D. (2000). Prolonged reduction of salivary immunoglobulin A (sIgA) after a major academic exam. *International Journal of Psychophysiology*, **37**, 219–232.

Earle, T. L., Linden, W. and Weinberg, J. (1999). Differential effects of harassment on cardiovascular and salivary cortisol reactivity and recovery in women and men. *Journal of Psychosomatic Research*, **46** (2), 125–141.

Edwards, S., Hucklebridge, F., Clow, A. and Evans, P. (2003). Components of the diurnal cortisol cycle in relation to upper respiratory symptoms and perceived stress. *Psychosomatic Medicine*, **65** (2), 320–7.

Endelberg, R. (1972). Electrical activity of the skin: Its measurement and uses in psychophysiology. In N. S. Greenfield and R. A. Steinbach (eds) *Handbook of Psychophysiology*, pp. 367–418. New York: Holt.

Glaser, R., Kiecolt-Glaser, J. K., Speicher, C. E. and Holliday, J. E. (1985). Stress, loneliness, and changes in herpesvirus latency. *Journal of Behavioral Medicine*, **8**, 249–260.

Hart, J., Gunnar, M. and Cichetti, D. (1996). Altered neuroendocrine activity in maltreated children related to symptoms of depression. *Developmental Psychopathology*, **8**, 201–214.

Jemmott, J. B. and McClelland, D. C. (1989). Secretory IgA as a measure of resistance to infectious disease: Comments on Stone, Cox, Valdimarsdottir, and Neale. *Behavioural Medicine*, **15** (2), 63–71.

Kiecolt-Glaser, J. K., Glaser, R., Strain, E. C., Stout, J. C., Tarr, K. L., Holliday, J. E. and Speicher, C. E. (1986). Modulation of cellular immunity in medical students. *Journal of Behavioral Medicine*, **9**, 5–21.

Kirschbaum, C., Prussner, M. S., Stone, A. A., Federenko, J. G., Lintz, D., Schommer, N. and Hellhammer, D. H. (1995). Persistent high cortisol responses to repeated psychological stress in a subpopulation of healthy men. *Psychosomatic Medicine*, **57**, 468–474.

Kop, W. J., Krantz, D. S. and Baker, G. (2001). Measures of blood pressure and heart rate variability in behavioral research on cardiovascular disease. In A. Vingerhoets *Assessment in Behavioral Medicine*. Taylor and Francis: New York.

Kunz-Ebrecht, S. R., Mohamed-Ali, V., Feldman, P., Kirschbaum, C. and Steptoe, A. (2003). Cortisol responses to mild psychological stress are inversely related with proinflammatory cytokines. *Brain, Behavior and Immunity*, **17** (5), 373–383.

MacHale, S. M., Cavanagh, J. T. O., Bennie, J., Carroll, S., Goodwin, G. M. and Lawrie, S. M. (1998). Diurnal variation of adrenocortical activity in chronic fatigue syndrome. *Neuropsychobiology*, **38**, 213–217.

Marucha, P. T., Kiecolt-Glaser, J. K. and Favagehi, M. (1998). Mucosal wound healing is impaired by examination stress. *Psychosomatic Medicine*, **60** (3), 362–365.

Schommer, N. C., Hellhammer, D. H. and Kirschbaum, C. (2003). Dissociation between reactivity of the hypothalamus-pituitary-adrenal axis and the sympathetic-adrenal-medullary system to repeated psychosocial stress. *Psychosomatic Medicine*, **65** (3), 450–460.

Sephton, S., Sapolsky, R., Kraemer, H. and Spiegel, D. (2000). Diurnal cortisol rhythm as a predictor of breast cancer survival. *Journal of the National Cancer Institute*, **92**, 994–1000.

Stone, A. A., Cox, D. S., Valdimarsdottir, H., Jandorff, L. and Neale, J. M. (1987). Evidence that secretory IgA is associated with daily mood. *Journal of Personality and Social Psychology*, **52** (5), 988–993.

Tanaka, H., Monahan, K. D. and Seals, D. R. (2001). Age-predicted maximal heart rate revisited. *Journal of the American College of Cardiology*, **37**, 153–156.

Vedhara, K., Cox, N. K., Wilcock, G. K., Perks, P., Hunt, M., Anderson, S., Lightman, S. L. and Shanks, N. M. (1999). Chronic stress in elderly carers of dementia patients and antibody response to influenza vaccine. *Lancet*, **353** (9153), 627–31.

Wetherell, M. A., Hyland, M. E. and Harris, J. E. (2004). Secretory immunoglobulin A reactivity to acute and cumulative acute multi-tasking stress: Relationships between reactivity and perceived workload. *Biological Psychology*, **66**, 257–70.

Wetherell, M. A., Kaye, J., Vedhara, K. and Lightman, S. L. (2004). HPA axis, cardiovascular and psychosomatic responses following 35% CO_2: Stability over six months. *Proceedings of the British Psychological Society*, **12** (1) Feb.

Willemsen, G., Carroll, D., Ring, C. and Drayson, M. (2002). Cellular and mucosal immune reactions to mental and cold stress: Associations with gender and cardiovascular reactivity. *Psychophysiology*, **39**, 222–228.

Willemsen, G., Ring, C., McKeever, S. and Carroll, D. (2000). Secretory immunoglobulin A and cardiovascular activity during mental arithmetic: effects of task difficulty and task order. *Biological Psychology*, **52**, 127–141.

Chapter 6

Semi-structured interviewing

Fiona Fylan

Interviewing is one of the most enjoyable and interesting ways to collect data. As a psychologist, you probably have an interest in the way that people think and feel. During interviewing, particularly semi-structured interviewing, you get to talk to people in order to find out about what they have experienced and what they think and feel about something that you are interested in.

And this, some people say, is work.

In this chapter I hope to give you a useful and easy-to-follow guide about how to conduct effective semi-structured interviews; before we start, let's examine that statement in more detail.

- By *useful* I mean that this is a practical guide to semi-structured interviewing – we will not explore the various theoretical frameworks within which you can conduct and analyse your interviews. There are various texts, for example Lindlof and Taylor (2002) if you want to read more about theoretical perspectives.

- By *easy to follow*, I mean that I have kept the text brief, and have included examples and tips to remember.

- By *effective* I mean that you should be confident that the results you obtain are a reasonably accurate representation of what your participants think, feel and have experienced, and that the participants you have selected to interview are sufficiently diverse for you to have developed a good understanding of your topic.

This chapter describes the methods that I use to conduct interviews so that they're enjoyable rather than onerous. I hope it works for you too.

What are semi-structured interviews?

Semi-structured interviews are simply conversations in which you know what you want to find out about – and so have a set of questions to ask and a good idea of what topics will be covered – but the conversation is free to vary, and is likely to change substantially between participants. They contrast with structured interviews, in which there is a predetermined list of questions that are covered in the same order for each person: you can think of these as questionnaires that are administered verbally. They also contrast with unstructured interviews, in which the area of investigation is delineated, but there is no assumed order to the questions, and very little predetermined boundaries as to the topics that should be covered.

This being said, semi-structured interviews vary tremendously. At one extreme, the questions are very simple and the order of questions easily adhered to. At the other, the questions can be very open, and the conversation can take many directions before all the areas you want to address are covered. The amount of structure you use will depend on the research question being asked – more complex questions generally need less structured formats. You should also bear in mind the method you are using to analyse the data. Less structured formats are well suited to social constructionist paradigms, whereas if you intend to use a coding frame, your semi-structured interviews should contain more structure. (See Elliott and Timulak, this volume.)

Why use semi-structured interviews?

The starting point is to look at your research question and decide whether semi-structured is the right approach. Semi-structured interviews are great for finding out *Why* rather than *How many* or *How much*. For example, if you want to find out whether or not people buy vitamin supplements, and how much per month they spend on them, this is a 'how many, how much' question and probably better answered using a questionnaire or a structured interview. If, on the other hand, you want to know why some people, but not others, buy vitamin supplements, and why they spend a particular amount, then you're on the right track with a semi-structured interview.

The flexibility of semi-structured interviews makes them so well suited to answering a 'why' question. By changing the questions and the areas discussed during the interview we can address aspects that are important to individual participants, and by doing so we can gain a better understanding of the research question. For example, imagine that we want to find out about why people choose to wear contact lenses rather than glasses. Our semi-structured interview would have a list of questions – a schedule – that cover the main areas we think will be important. Our list might include reasons for wearing contact lenses or glasses when socialising, when working, when playing sport, and when going on holiday. Our schedule wouldn't have a long list of detailed questions that our participants would respond yes or no to (e.g. Would you prefer wearing contact lenses to glasses when going to a bar? What about the cinema? And to work?) — this would be a structured interview. And not every question would be relevant to every participant – for example not everybody plays sports, and not everybody works. Instead, we would talk around the area with the participant, and find out from him or her about what is important, and why. Therefore, you can use semi-structured interviews to explore more complicated research questions.

Because the semi-structured interview is such a versatile means of collecting data, you can also use it to develop a much deeper understanding of the research question by exploring contradictions within your participants' accounts. Now I know I began by saying that this chapter would be practical rather than theoretical, but if you take a social constructionist perspective, a participant's attitudes would not be fixed and pre-determined, but would emerge as part of the interview. If you identify contradictions within their conversation, you can explore these in more detail by careful (not confrontational) questioning.

Another reason to use semi-structured interviews is that they provide a more appropriate format for discussing sensitive topics. For example, in the UK the British Psychological Society Codes of Conduct for Psychologists (available from http://www.bps.org.uk) requires us to ensure that

> Where research may involve behaviour or experiences that participants may regard as personal and private the participants must be protected from stress by all appropriate measures, including the assurance that answers to personal questions need not be given.
>
> (p. 12)

If we were to administer a postal questionnaire about a potentially sensitive area, e.g. loneliness, childlessness, or illness, we could not be sure that participants realise that they do not have to answer all (or any) of the questions, or that completing the questionnaire won't cause participants to dwell on the topic and become more unhappy as a result of taking part in our survey. While taking part in an interview is likely to be equally uncomfortable/distressing – the fact that we can talk through the topic with the participant, debrief them afterwards, and answer their questions about why we are doing the research, and stop at any point means that we can be much more confident that at the end of the interview they are not any worse off emotionally than they were before.

Preparation

Many first-time interviewers underestimate the amount of planning required to conduct semi-structured interviews. Because the similarities of interviews and conversations are often highlighted, many people assume that they can throw together a few questions and, recording equipment in hand, go and do some interviews. Don't be tempted – preparation is so important – it should not be overlooked.

The first stage is to undertake a thorough literature review and evaluate previous work – both the methods and the findings. How can you use this previous work as a foundation from which to develop your research question? Similarly, are there relevant theories that you can use to guide the questions you will ask? For example, if you are interested in why people take vitamin supplements, there are several theories of health-related behaviours (for example Ajzen and Madden, 1986) that will give you a starting point from which to develop an interview schedule.

Next, you should identify who you are interested in talking to. Who is your population? There are various methods you can use to identify a sample from your population, but given the short time frame of many projects, I recommend a purposive sample (or course, you may have the luxury of sufficient time and money to be able to take a larger, random sample – if this is the case, you are in a minority). A purposive sample involves identifying the characteristics of interest along which your population is likely to vary, and choosing people who will give you the maximum variation, regardless of the relative frequency at which the characteristics occur within the population. For example, consider the contact lenses vs. glasses question. A purposive sampling schedule would include people who have never worn contact lenses, those who always wear them, and those who sometimes do. For each of these characteristics you should select at least one male and one female older and younger participant, and people with a range of occupations and hobbies. The reason for including such a range of different participants is that you are trying to find out *why*. Therefore, you want people to have lots of different beliefs, values and behaviours to explore.

Armed with knowledge of what has been done in this area before, some relevant theories of behaviour, and a clear idea of your sampling frame, you are ready to start developing your interview schedule. The interview schedule is simply a list of questions that you will address during the interview. The exact form of the schedule will differ between research questions, and researchers prefer different amounts of detail. Here are my own preferences.

- **Keep it brief**: your schedule should usually contain around five broad questions. Any more than that and it becomes difficult to keep track of which areas you have covered.

- **Differentiate the processes you are interested in**: a useful division for psychology research is cognitions, emotions and actions. You would want participants to talk about all of these – what they *thought* about an event, how they *felt*, and what they *did* in response to it.

- **Ensure the question order is logical**: try to make the questions flow so that they arise naturally as the interview progresses. While you would not expect to keep to the order in the schedule, there's no point starting with something that doesn't make sense.

- **Develop a series of prompts**: these can be used to provide examples of what you might expect participants to talk about. But bear in mind that these are prompts, to be used only if the participant needs help. Berg (2001) provides an entertaining analogy of interviewing with theatre – and in this framework, prompts should be used as a last resort, only when the actor (i.e. the participant) has a blank and cannot move on. Last resort or not, your prompts should be sensible and should help the participant explore the area of discussion without supplying leading questions.

◆ **Know the schedule**: there is never ever any excuse for going into an interview without knowing the schedule – backwards and forwards, inside and out. A successful semi-structured interview is a conversation with the participant and you cannot do this if you are constantly looking through your schedule to check whether an area has been covered already. This is one more reason for keeping your schedule brief.

So, by now you should have short but perfectly formed interview schedule that notes the research questions you will ask, the different aspects you are interested in, and some prompts to keep the conversation moving. The next stage is to pilot the schedule to find out if it needs changing. Conduct at least two pilot interviews with different types of participant and find out how well it works. And not just from your point of view. Seek feedback from participants about the questions you asked:

◆ Where they easy to understand?

◆ Did they seem to make sense?

◆ Did the questions enable participants to talk about all the areas that they thought were important?

While it's never easy to find out that something you've done isn't perfect, if your participants found any of the questions difficult to understand, then it's the *questions* that are at fault and not your participants. Make the changes, or there was no point doing the pilot. If you don't make the changes then the interviews will be more difficult to conduct, and if there are misunderstandings, your data will be less valid and you will be less confident in the conclusions you draw.

Conducting the interview

Equipment

Having done all of the preparation, we are ready to start conducting the interviews – this is the part I enjoy the most. First, you need to think about practicalities – where the interview will take place, and the equipment that you will need. The room should be reasonably quiet and comfortable. The interviews should be recorded if at all possible – with the participant's consent of course – so you'll need a power socket or recording equipment that runs on batteries (make sure you have spare batteries too). I usually take a power extension lead with me so that I can be sure that I can get to the power. It's also worth investing in a good microphone. Around £20 will buy you a good surround microphone suitable for both interviews and focus groups (see Wilkinson, this volume). A good microphone (for example, the Sony ECMF8 condenser microphone) improves the quality of the recording and thereby makes transcribing the interview much easier.

The room

When you arrive for the interview, the first thing you should do is check the layout of the room. Both you and the participant need to feel at ease, so arrange the chairs and table (if there is one) so that your participant can sit and talk comfortably. Chairs should be placed fairly close together, but not so close that your participants feel uncomfortable, and placing them at a slight angle will help you make eye contact without feeling as if you are staring at the participant. It's also a good idea to have access to tea and coffee so that you can take a break, or continue to talk over refreshments.

The opening

When your participant arrives, make them welcome. The interview should begin with a briefing – you need to tell your participant enough about the interview to enable them to provide informed consent to participate. This is important not only for the ethics of the study, but also because your participants will try to make sense of the interview process and your motivation for conducting the interview – it is better that they have an accurate understanding of this rather then misunderstanding the purpose, which could lead them to provide biased responses. You then need to negotiate terms, such as whether they agree to the interview being audio recorded. Hopefully, your participant will agree to this – particularly if you point out that it's just to make sure you don't have to keep stopping so that you can write down what they say. Place the recorder somewhere unobtrusive so that the participant does not focus on it. Follow the British Psychological Society Code of Conduct for Psychologists on confidentiality and anonymity. Tell your participants who will have access to the data.

It is worth repeating that a good semi-structured interview is like a conversation rather than a series of questions and answers. So it helps to begin the interview with a general conversation, such as getting to the interview, e.g. public transport or parking. Then you can guide your participant around to questions from your research schedule. This initial conversation can give you valuable insight to interpreting the responses your participant provides later, and help you identify important areas to pursue later in the interview. For example, consider this opening exchange during an interview about factors influencing a person's decision about taking part in a clinical trial to diagnose knee problems:

I: Thanks for coming in today to talk to me. It's good of you to give up your morning.
P: Monday mornings, I never like those anyway.
I: I know what you mean, the weekends go so quickly.
P: They fly by.
I: Did you do anything over the weekend?
P: I went to the football – I go every week for the home matches, and when I can make if for the away ones.
I: Which is your team?
P: Manchester, the proper one [sorry, United fans, he's talking about Manchester City]
I: Oh yes?

P: It was a brilliant game, although the referee we had was a disgrace, sent off xx. Mind you, when he went off, I was ranting and raving. Actually it's quite good because it's a good stress buster and it gets the adrenaline going. I used to play: for 20 years, 30 years I played football. I used to be the goalkeeper, so I was diving around here, there, everywhere.

This opening conversation revealed that the participant (*P*) is a football fan and used to play a lot of football, but now has stopped doing so. This information was used by the interviewer (*I*) to contextualise a subsequent interview question about the effect of his knee injury on leisure activities.

Moving through the interview schedule

Once you are ready to start, move onto the first question on the interview schedule. Often the conversation drifts naturally from the initial briefing and exchange onto one of the questions from the interview schedule. This is fine – don't stick rigidly to asking the first question on your schedule – you should aim to let the interview develop naturally. In the above example, the first question on the interview schedule was about when the knee injury occurred, but because of the opening exchange we drifted straight into a discussion about the effects of having to stop playing sports. We immediately developed a rapport, and the interview was much richer because of the flexibility offered by a semi-structured format.

The ease with which participants talk expansively varies tremendously from one participant to another. Some participants talk at length about events, feelings and actions, while others require more help. When you think your participant has more to say, use a series of probes. As the name suggests, probes are simply tools for deeper exploration of a topic. The verbal probes that we use can be either simply encouragements, such as:

- Really?
- Yes?
- Tell me more about that
- What happened next?
- What did you do?
- Why did you do that?
- How did you feel about that?

You can also use non-verbal probes such as nodding. Don't forget your body language right the way through the interview. Crossing your arms and looking away will inhibit your participants from speaking further. So nod, smile appropriately, and make eye contact (without, of course, staring). Don't over-use probes, though. Many inexperienced interviewers describe how they use probes or prompts to fill silences because they feel uncomfortable during silences. At first, it may feel awkward to sit in silence – a few seconds can seem like hours. But it is perfectly acceptable to give participants enough time to collect their thoughts. They may be thinking of examples or trying to remember an event or feeling.

The other extreme is a participant who talks very easily and extensively. You need to focus their conversation and make sure it addresses the topics you are interested in. This requires you to steer the interview skilfully.

Steering the interview

The major difference between a conversation and an interview is that you, as interviewer, control the situation. While conducting interviews is a great deal of fun, especially if you enjoy listening to people, you always need to remember the purpose of the interview – what you are trying to find out – and steer the conversation in that direction.

There is often a fine line between what is of interest and what is not. Particularly with participants who talk readily, you may begin by thinking that a topic is not going to help you answer your research question, but find out after a few minutes that the topic being discussed is very relevant to your participant, it was simply that the link wasn't obvious to you at first. The following example is taken from an interview which was part of a study to explore women's experiences of colposcopy (examination of the cervix) following the result of an abnormal cervical (Pap) smear result. The following extract explores whether women would prefer to have their colposcopy in their family doctor's surgery rather than hospital.

I: So would you choose to have this done at your family doctor's surgery, if it were available there?

P: Erm, no, I don't think I'd want that. I'd rather come here.

I: Why's that?

P: Oh, I don't know, really, I just would.

I: So have you been to the same family doctor for a long time?

P: About ten years.

I: Where were you before that?

P: Well I wasn't based anywhere, really, I used to travel about a lot.

I: That sounds interesting, where did you go?

P: Oh, all over the place. I used to work on a cruise ship, I was a dancer, so we went all over the world, really. We all had such a great time. It was work, but it was like a huge holiday at the same time. You had your groups of friends, as you do at home, and we just went around together and enjoyed it. We mainly worked in the evening so we had all day to do what we wanted.

I: That sounds brilliant!

P: Oh, it was, but then you can't do it forever, so I settled back home again, but people talk.

I: About what?

P: Well, you know, that it's an unusual job, you haven't just stayed at home. And that, you know, you might not be respectable.

I: Oh, I see.

P: So that's why I'd rather come here, really, because I wouldn't want anybody to know I've had this done.

This example shows how, although the participant's previous job did not initially appear relevant, it allowed her to reveal the reasons behind her preference for having her colposcopy at the hospital. She thought that if she went to her family doctor's surgery, there would be more chance of somebody finding out that she had received an abnormal cervical smear result – she feared that she might be labelled as sexually promiscuous, and believed that her previous job might make this labelling more likely. Of course, receiving an abnormal cervical smear result does not mean that the person is sexually promiscuous, but this participant believed this to be the case. Allowing her to digress meant that her reasoning became clear.

The trick is to know how long to let your participant talk about something that seems unrelated to your research question, and then steering them back to a topic you want to find out about. There is no fixed time for this – to some extent it depends on how long has been scheduled for your interview. If your participant is expecting the interview to last for only half an hour, then you must be a lot more focused. If, on the other hand, they have dedicated a couple of hours, then you can afford to talk about seemingly unrelated topics for longer. Bringing the interview topic back on course requires skill. You can't just tell your participant you want them to talk about something else – they will be a lot more guarded about what they talk about for the remainder of the interview, and they may feel resentful – that you're not interested in them or what they have to say, and that you don't value their experiences. So your steering should be very light. Done skilfully, the participant will not notice that you have shifted the topic of the interview because it will have appeared as a normal conversation. Some techniques you can use are:

- Introduce an example or experience of your own that is more closely aligned to what you want to find out about.

- Mention something the participant had talked about earlier, and get them to expand on it.

- Provide prompts in the form of "some other people I've talked to suggested this". Is that something you've ever come across, or not?

- Break the interview by suggesting refreshments, and then resume with a different topic.

If all else fails, simply tell your participant that their experiences are very interesting, and so you'd appreciate their thoughts on a few different topics before the interview ends, so can they tell you about their experiences of the new topic.

But beware – you should steer the interview, not guide it. Never ever ask leading questions, unless it's a topic you need a definite opinion on. One example of this is as follows: a researcher was conducting a practice interview about the experiences of being a patient on an intensive care unit. The interview was progressing very well, until she asked: 'did the tubes make you feel tied down?' The participant had not talked about this, and by introducing such a leading question she ran the risk of making the patient believe that this was important, and in so doing biasing the interview.

Another topic that can be very difficult for the novice interviewer to handle is that participants sometimes become emotional, particularly when talking about a sensitive or traumatic topic. As with the rest of this chapter, my advice relates to what has worked best for me over many years of interviewing. I recommend acknowledging the emotion and assuring the participant that it is OK to become tearful or cry – keeping a box of paper tissues close by can be useful. Encourage the participant to keep talking, if they want to, but tell them that they can take a break if they prefer. Don't ignore the emotion and continue the interview as if nothing were happening. This is confusing and unpleasant for the participant, and they may well avoid sensitive topics for the rest of the interview. In contrast, don't force participants to keep talking about the topic, and explore their feelings deeper if they would rather not. You should aim to create an atmosphere in which participants feel comfortable enough to talk about emotional topics, but not one in which they feel coerced into doing so. If, at the end of the interview, the participant is still upset, don't just leave. Stay with them for a cup of tea or coffee to enable them to unwind out of the interview mode and feel their usual self again.

Debriefing

Every interview should end with you summarising what you have talked about. Don't turn your recording equipment off just yet, as participants often provide valuable information at this point – and it provides evidence that you've debriefed in line with ethical requirements. Seek feedback from the participant about whether you have interpreted what they said correctly – this provides a useful check for validity. Ask if there is anything else they think is important that you haven't already talked about – your participants will sometimes have further experience that your schedule hasn't covered and yet is important to them. For example, the following extract from an interview with a university student about what they would like to change about their accommodation:

I: Ok, well I think we've covered everything that I wanted to. But is there anything else that you think is important that we haven't yet talked about?

P: No, I don't think there's anything else that's important, oh, except that maybe we haven't talked about that they don't give you the option to leave your stuff in your room over the holidays. That's really annoying. I know that they rent the rooms out to conference people...

And so on. The participant then talked more about how having to empty their room meant that it felt less 'homely'. Once this conversation had finished, the interviewer then summarised the main points and checks that they have been interpreted correctly.

I: Right, I'll summarise the main points of what we've talked about, and if I've missed any, or got anything wrong, please tell me. We talked about the size of the room as being most important, and that if you could leave your stuff in there over the holidays it would make it feel more like your own space. The facilities in the kitchen are OK, but it would be better if there were table and chairs so that you could sit down to eat together with the other people in the flat, rather than taking your food back to your room. You said that it would also be nice if there were a living area with a sofa or comfy chairs that you could put a TV in. You like the shops on campus but would prefer it if they opened later, and you like the social atmosphere in the bar. Have I got that right?

P: Yes, that's it exactly.

You should then ask participants if they have any questions about the interview. Finally, thank them for having taken part. I always ask participants if they would like a summary of the results of the study when you have finished. Some do, and some don't, but it helps them feel a valued part of the research. This may not benefit you directly, but they may be more willing to volunteer for other research projects in the future, or provide feedback to their friends that taking part in research interviews is enjoyable. I usually provide a contact telephone number or email address so that participants can contact me again in the future if they think of any questions they want answering. Very few people tend to get in touch, but it gives them, and me, piece of mind.

Reflexivity: acknowledging your effect on the interview

You have a tremendous effect on the way in which the interview unfolds, and the quantity and quality of what your participant talks about. It's worth examining the way in which you affect the interview for two reasons: first, to identify how you can improve your interview technique; second, to consider how you might have affected what the participant talked about, and so how you influenced the results obtained.

First, let's consider the ways in which you can examine your behaviour with the aim of improving your technique. Participants will generally talk more, and more genuinely, when they have a rapport with the interviewer. Hence you must make the participant feel relaxed, and chat to them – genuinely – at the start of the interview to put them at their ease and convince them that you're interested in what they have to say.

You must also build an atmosphere of trust – tell participants that you are interested in their thoughts and feelings and experiences and that there are no right or wrong answers. Assure them of the confidentiality of what they say (but be honest about who will have access to the transcripts).

Once you have developed a trusting relationship and a good rapport with the participant, don't ruin it by being judgemental about what they tell you. It is likely that in the course of your interviews that people tell you things that you don't agree with, or you don't approve of. You must not show them how you feel about what they say. Always maintain an atmosphere of encouragement. And beware of conveying your feelings by facial expressions or body language. This is not to say that you should be poker-faced throughout, or not to show any feelings to your participants – you need to let your personality show through in order to build a rapport. But you mustn't influence what your participant tells you by overt approval or disapproval of their story.

We've already touched upon asking leading questions – don't do it. Probe those areas you are interested in – and if you have a specific topic you want to explore, then ask specific questions, but do so without suggesting the answers you anticipate. A good interviewer acts as a conduit through which the participant tells their story. Make sure you tell the participant's story, and not the one you expect or hope to hear.

Top tips

Tell the participant the purpose of the interview
Know the interview schedule
Keep the questions simple
Steer the interview subtly
Don't ask leading questions
Silences aren't scary
Ask the participant if there is anything else you should talk about

Further reading

Arksey H. and Knight P. (1999) *Interviewing for social scientists: an introductory resource with examples*. London: Sage Publications.

Gillham B. (2000) *The research interview*. London: Continuum.

Holstein J. A. and Gubrium J. F. (2003) *Inside interviewing: new lenses, new concerns*. London: Sage Publications.

Keats D. M. (2000) *Interviewing: a practical guide for students and professionals*. Buckingham: Open University Press.

Wengraf T. (2001) *Qualitative research interviewing; biographic narrative and semi-structured methods*. London: Sage Publications.

References

Ajzen I. and Madden T. J. (1986) Prediction of goal-directed behavior: attitudes, intentions and perceived behavioral control. *Journal of Experimental and Social Psychology*, **22**, 453–74.

Berg B. L. (2001) *Qualitative research methods for the social science*s, 4th edn, p. 85. Needham Heights: Allyn and Bacon.

Lindlof T. R. and Taylor B. C. (2002) *Qualitative communication research methods*, 2nd edn. London: Sage Publications.

Chapter 7

Using focus groups
Exploring the meanings of health and illness

Sue Wilkinson

Seven women, linked by a shared diagnosis of breast cancer, meet over coffee one evening. Their conversation ranges across 'finding the lump', cone biopsies, a friend's death from breast cancer, the insensitivity of medical professionals, the experience of radiotherapy, partners' reactions to mastectomy scars, and the merits – or otherwise – of 'stick-on nipples'. They tell stories, crack jokes, argue, support one another, and talk over each other. This is a typical focus group scenario, drawn from my own research. A focus group is – at its simplest – 'an informal discussion among selected individuals about specific topics' (Beck *et al.*, 1986, p. 73). Focus group research generally involves organising and running a series of small, focused group discussions, like the one described above, and analysing the resulting data using a range of conventional qualitative techniques.

The invention of focus groups is usually attributed to sociologist Robert Merton and his colleagues (in the 1940s); however, prior to the 1970s most focus group research was in the field of business and marketing (Goldman and McDonald, 1987). The contemporary 'resurgence of interest' (Lunt and Livingstone, 1996, p. 79) in focus groups has generated research across the social sciences, particularly within the fields of health (e.g. Harrison and Barlow, 1995); communication/media studies (e.g. Lunt and Livingstone, 1996); education (e.g. Vaughn *et al.*, 1996); and feminist research (Wilkinson, 1998a, 1999). Health researchers pioneered the use of focus groups in social action research, particularly family planning and preventive health education (e.g. Folch-Lyon *et al.*, 1981; Schearer, 1981; Suyono *et al.*, 1981); focus group research on health and illness in now conducted within nursing studies, social policy and sociology, as well as within clinical and health psychology.

Centrally, the focus group method involves one or more group discussions, in which participants focus collectively upon a topic or issue, most commonly presented to them (either verbally or in written form) as a set of questions – although sometimes as a film, a collection of advertisements, cards to sort, a 'game' to play, or a vignette to discuss. Focus group participants (usually 6–8) may be pre-existing clusters of people (such as family members, friends or work colleagues) or they may be drawn together specifically for the research. An increasingly common use of focus groups is to bring together 'a group of people who have experienced the same problem, such as residents of a deteriorating neighbourhood or women in a sexist organization' (Rubin and Rubin, 1995, p. 139). Discussions between group participants, usually audiotaped (sometimes videotaped) and transcribed, constitute the data, and conventional techniques of qualitative analysis are then employed. This most commonly entails some variety of content analysis or thematic analysis (sometimes computer-assisted with the use of programs such as NUD.IST or THE ETHNOGRAPH) – as typically employed in analysing other forms of qualitative data, such as that generated in one-to-one interviews. Additionally, some researchers have used rhetorical, discursive, and conversation analytic techniques (e.g. Agar and McDonald, 1995; Frith and Kitzinger, 1998).

There is an extensive methodological literature on the practical details of conducting focus groups (e.g. Bloor *et al.*, 2001; Krueger and Casey, 2000; Morgan, 1997; Morgan and Krueger, 1998; Wilkinson, 2003a, b), so I will not rehearse such details here. As many of these commentators on focus group method emphasise, the method is distinctive, not for its mode of analysis, but rather for its *data-collection* procedures. Crucially, focus groups are characterised by the interaction of group participants *with each other* as well as with the researcher/moderator, and it is the collection of this kind of interactive data which distinguishes the focus group from the one-to-one interview (cf. Kitzinger, 1994a; Morgan, 1988), as well as from procedures which use multiple participants but do not permit interactive discussions (cf. Stewart and Shamdasani, 1990).

In clinical and health psychology, increasing interest is being directed toward participants' *own meanings* of health and illness, 'the patient's view' (Armstrong, 1984). Such meanings are seen as essential in understanding (for example) coping behaviour, psychosocial well-being, and adaptation to negative life events, as well as offering important insights into people's phenomenological lifeworlds (cf. Fife, 1994). For those researchers with an interest in accessing participants' own meanings, focus groups provide a valuable research tool.

I will briefly overview the main uses of focus groups in health research; and then illustrate my key argument – that focus groups are an ideal method for gaining access to participants' own meanings – with examples from health-related research, including my own current work on breast cancer.

Focus groups in health research: a brief overview

An extensive range of topics central to health and illness has been studied using focus groups. Such topics include: the experience of specific disorders and diseases; reproductive issues; violence and abuse; living with chronic illness or disability; health care practices and procedures; health-related behaviours; and broader factors which mediate health and illness (see Wilkinson, 1998b for references). Across these topics, focus groups have been used in five main theoretical and/or practical ways:

Studies of lifeworlds and health beliefs

There is a tradition of health-related research that uses focus groups to explore people's own meanings of health and illness. Some of this work seeks to develop in-depth under-standings of individuals' lifeworlds: e.g. women's experiences postpartum (DiMatteo et al., 1993); the experiences of mothers with physical disabilities (Prilleltensky, 2003); the experience of living in a nursing home (Brody, 1990); or the experience of living with multiple sclerosis (Lyons and Meade, 1993) or with the rare chronic condition, scleroderma (Joachim and Acorn, 2003). Other studies broadly in this tradition seek to develop more specific understandings of individuals' health beliefs or models: e.g. about HIV/AIDS (Irwin et al., 1991), heart attacks (Morgan and Spanish, 1985), or nutrition (Crockett et al., 1990). As Hoppe et al. (1994, p. 118) point out, focus groups are 'a use-ful method for learning about the vocabulary and thinking patterns of a population within its social context'; and, in addition, as a relatively naturalistic method, which enables relatively spontaneous interaction between people, focus groups increase the likelihood of 'gaining deeper insights than might arise with individual structured inter-views or questionnaires' (Ritchie et al., 1994, p. 97). Focus groups have been used to study, for example, the knowledge and beliefs of elementary school children about AIDS (Hoppe et al., 1994); the beliefs of blue collar workers about coronary risk behaviours (Ritchie et al., 1994); and the traditional beliefs of black women in relation to breast cancer (Duke et al., 1994) and AIDS (Flaskerud and Rush, 1989).

Assessment of health status and health care needs

Focus group research has also been used to obtain an index or measurement of indi-viduals' state of health, or health care needs, including assessments of 'quality of life': e.g. in relation to breast cancer (Wyatt et al., 1993) or asthma (Hyland et al., 1991) or 'quality of care': e.g. in relation to migraine (Cottrell et al., 2003) or multiple sclerosis (Defriez et al., 2003). Other such indices derived from focus group research include individuals' satisfaction with their health status or with health care services on offer to them, such as general practice (Murray et al., 1994), or community health services (Collins et al., 1991). In some of these studies, focus groups are used on a stand-alone basis to assess individuals' needs or attitudes. In others, they are used as an initial data-gathering tool to inform the later development of surveys (O'Brien, 1993) or scales (Hyland et al., 1991). One major advantage of this, as O'Brien (1993) notes, in report-ing the use of focus groups to develop an instrument to survey the social relationships of gay and bisexual men at risk for AIDS, is that focus groups enable the investigator to identify concepts and practices central to the respondents, and so to construct more appropriate survey items. Further, using material derived from focus groups, the inves-tigator can design a questionnaire using respondents' own words or phrases, thereby enhancing their understanding of the research questions. Focus groups may also be used as an exploratory technique to generate hypotheses meriting further qualitative or quantitative investigation.

Health education and health promotion

A great deal of focus group research focuses around health education and health promotion. Key areas where focus groups have been used include: the US National High Blood Pressure Education Program (cf. Basch, 1987); take-up of cervical screening facilities, particularly among ethnic minority women (Dignan et al., 1990; Naish et al., 1994); prevention of teenage pregnancy (Kisker, 1985; Okonofua, 1995); and sex education, particularly the promotion of safer sex in the context of HIV/AIDS (Kline et al., 1992; Lupton and Tulloch, 1996). Used in the context of health education, focus groups are particularly useful in identifying obstacles or objections which prevent or discourage individuals from (say) using contraception or practising safer sex (e.g. Strange et al., 2003). There is also a substantial body of focus group work on individuals' understanding of, and responses to, health-related media messages (e.g. Aitken et al., 1986; Freimuth and Greenberg, 1986; Kitzinger, 1990; Philo et al., 1994). Health education messages have often been proposed, or modified, on the basis of focus group research which has assessed their likely effectiveness. For example, following focus group research in which men spoke of their sense of responsibility, the message 'protector of the family' was designed to encourage condom use (Kline et al., 1992, p. 455); and another focus group study on compliance in taking medication led to the extension of the health promotion message 'Do It For Them' to include 'doing it for oneself' (Basch, 1987, p. 424).

Participatory and social action research

Focus groups have been used extensively in planning and developing health-related social action programmes. Examples of such programmes include: smoking prevention (Bush et al., 2003; Heimann-Raitan et al., 1985); worksite nutrition (Mullis and Lansing, 1986); malaria and child survival (Glik et al., 1988); residential aged care (Lindeman et al., 2003); and – notably – family planning (Folch-Lyon et al., 1981; Knodel et al., 1984; Suyono et al., 1981). Some focus group researchers (e.g. Plaut et al., 1993) suggest that the method is particularly useful for accessing the views of those who have been under-represented in, or poorly served by, traditional research. Others suggest that focus groups can be used radically in participatory or action research 'to empower and to foster social change' (Johnson, 1996, p. 536). For example, Jean Orr's (1992) project on well women clinics encouraged participants to view their problems as deriving from social structure rather than personal inadequacy and offered 'support to members in changing aspects of their lives' (p. 32) via the community health movement. Similarly, Annie George (1996), conducting participatory research on sexuality with poor women in Bombay, ran focus groups in collaboration with a NGO aiming to help separated or deserted women in regularising their legal status. 'The focus group meetings', she says, 'were a means in the process of analysing the various forces which were bottlenecks in their search for greater autonomy' (p. 128). Other examples of the use of focus groups in feminist action research on health issues may be found in Brems and Griffith (1993) and de Koning and Martin (1996).

Evaluation and marketing of products and services

This tradition of focus group research draws on the early development of the method in the context of business and marketing, in a number of ways. First, focus groups are used as a means to evaluate the success of health promotion, disease prevention, early intervention or social action programmes (see Basch, 1987, for a review). Basch argues for the value of focus groups in both 'formative' evaluation (i.e. monitoring programmes during their development and use) and 'summative' evaluation (i.e. making final judgements about their worth). Second, focus groups are used in service evaluation and public relations exercises. Typically, health care 'consumers' are asked to give their views on the services available to them; more rarely, 'providers' are asked to reflect on consumer views, or on their relations with consumers. Examples include the evaluation of mental health services (Richter *et al.*, 1991); abortion services (Flexner *et al.*, 1977); cancer screening services (Hamilton and Barlow, 2003; McFall and Hamm, 2003); cancer patient information (Moumjid *et al.*, 2003); public health care in the community (Loevy and O'Brien, 1994); and hospital administration (Hisrich and Peters, 1982). Third, focus groups are used to facilitate the marketing of health care services and products. Focus group studies have been used, for example, to increase the acceptability of contraceptive implants (Zimmerman *et al.*, 1990), and to maximise the impact of TV advertisements for spermicidal foaming tablets (Freimuth and Greenberg, 1986).

Exploring the meanings of health and illness

I now move on to show the ways in which focus groups are an ideal method for the study of people's own meanings of health and illness. I will consider five specific mechanisms through which focus groups encourage the elicitation and elaboration of participants' own meanings.

Enhancing disclosure

Contrary to the common assumption that people will be inhibited by the presence of other group members, the group context *facilitates* openness and disclosure. Focus group participants often assist the researcher by asking questions of each other (perhaps more searching than those the researcher might have dared ask); by contradicting and disagreeing with each other (in a manner which, coming from the researcher, might have seemed authoritarian); and by pointing to apparent contradictions in each others' accounts (often in a manner which the 'empathetic' and 'sensitive' researcher might feel to be inappropriate coming from her). The effect of these questions, disagreements and challenges from other group members is generally to produce enhanced disclosure, as people answer questions, resolve disagreements and defend their views against attack.

This enhanced disclosure is especially evident when sensitive issues are under discussion. Many focus group researchers report that when research participants share common experiences – in particular, painful or emotionally intense experiences (such as domestic violence, a stigmatising illness, or a sudden bereavement) – individuals typically offer considerable detail about such aspects of their lives, particularly when their contributions are reinforced and their concerns legitimated by other group members (Zeller, 1993). It is commonly found that the less inhibited members of the group 'break the ice' for shyer participants, and that one person's revelation of 'discrediting' information encourages others to disclose similar experiences. According to Kissling (1996), for example, it is easier for young people to talk freely about menstruation in a group context than in a one-to-one interview with an adult researcher: the 'solidarity among friends' seems to 'decrease their discomfort with the topic'. Similarly, Kitzinger (1994a, p. 111) cites data in which interaction between female focus group members enables one of them to talk about oral sex, and she describes this as an example of the *facilitation* of the expression of difficult or taboo experiences in a group context.

In particular, social desirability may be less of a problem in focus groups than in one-to-one interviews. Several researchers have noted that, compared with interviews, group discussions tend to generate the expression of more 'socially undesirable' opinions and emotions. In a focus group study of lovers of people with AIDS, for example, the researchers found that there were more angry and emotional comments about their treatment by the medical profession than are generally found in individual interviews (Geis *et al.*, 1986). Similarly, researchers have found that women whose babies are delivered healthy are generally unwilling to express dissatisfaction, in one-to-one interviews, with the practices and procedures of childbirth. In focus groups, by contrast, the 'supportive environment' of other women also talking about their birth experiences facilitates women's ability to be critical of the management of the birth process (DiMatteo *et al.*, 1993).

Providing access to participants' own language and concepts

The relatively free flow of discussion and debate between members of a focus group offers an excellent opportunity for hearing 'the language and vernacular used by respondents' (Bers, 1987, p. 27). Focus group researchers have seen the method as providing an opportunity for 'listening to local voices' (Murray *et al.*, 1994); for learning the participants' own language instead of imposing the researcher's language upon them (Freimuth and Greenberg, 1986; Mays *et al.*, 1992); and for gaining an insight into participants' conceptual worlds, on their own terms (Broom and Dozier, 1990).

Listening in on focus group discussions – or 'structured eavesdropping' (Powney, 1988) – enables the researcher to become familiar with the way research participants habitually talk, the particular idioms, terminology and vocabulary they typically use, the ways in which they joke, tell stories, construct arguments, and so on. In listening to participants' talk in the social context of a focus group, the researcher is able to observe a (sub)cultural argot in use. Focus group interactions reveal not only shared ways of talking, but also shared experiences, and shared ways of making sense of these experiences. The researcher is offered an insight into the commonly-held assumptions, concepts and meanings which constitute and inform participants' talk about their experiences.

In particular, focus groups can enable researchers 'to observe people who may be very different from themselves' (Bers, 1987, p. 26). Such respondents may use very different language from the researcher to describe their experiences or convey their opinions (see also Wilkinson and Kitzinger, 1996).

Enabling participants to follow their own agendas

As focus group researchers have pointed out, the researcher's influence is 'diffused by the very fact of being in a group rather than a one-to-one situation' (Frey and Fontana, 1993, p. 26) and focus groups place 'control over [the] interaction in the hands of the participants rather than the researcher' (Morgan, 1988, p. 18). Compared with a one-to-one interview, it is much harder for the researcher to impose her or his own agenda in the group context. Indeed, reduced researcher influence is seen as a *problem* in much of the focus group literature, which typically offers the researcher a range of techniques for constraining participants and reasserting control (e.g. Krueger, 1988; Stewart and Shamdasani, 1990; Vaughn *et al.*, 1996).

However, reduced researcher influence can be seen as a *benefit* of focus group research for researchers who are primarily interested in participants' own meanings, and who encourage participant-directed interaction, rather than constraining it. Reduced researcher control gives focus group participants much greater opportunity to set the research agenda, and to 'develop the themes most important to them' (Cooper *et al.*, 1993). These may diverge from those identified by the researcher and participants may challenge – or even undermine – the researcher, insisting on their own interpretations and agendas being heard in place of the formal requirements of the research project. For example, one researcher changed her analytic focus to include social class as well as gender after the insistence of young women in her focus groups in talking about this issue (Frazer, 1988).

One particular benefit of focus group participants' increased role in setting the research agenda is to provide researchers with new information, or to draw their attention to previously-neglected or unnoticed phenomena: for example, researchers running a focus group with former LSD-using adolescents uncovered the possible use of Robitussin (a strong cough medicine) as a substitute for LSD (Agar and McDonald, 1995, p. 80).

Encouraging the production of elaborated accounts

Focus group interactions also encourage individuals to develop and elaborate their accounts – in response both to *agreement* and to *disagreement* from other group members. For example, bolstered by the support of others, one or more group members may enthusiastically extend, elaborate or embroider an initially sketchy account. Through the consensual piling up of fine detail – the height of shoe heels, the size of buttons, the fastening mechanisms of jewellery, and the dangers of beauty appliances – focus group participants who shared the diagnosis of multiple sclerosis conveyed a consensual sense of what it is like to live with the disease on a mundane and daily basis (Lyons *et al.*, 1995, pp. 24–25). Such a jointly elaborated account offers the researcher a far more detailed and in-depth insight into their shared lifeworld – and direct evidence that it *is* a shared lifeworld – than could one-to-one interviews.

However, as Kitzinger (1994b, pp. 170–171) points out, participants do not just agree with each other: 'they also misunderstand one another, question one another, try to persuade each other of the justice of their own point of view and sometimes they vehemently disagree'. These challenges and disagreements between participants are also effective in provoking the development and elaboration of accounts. In the British-based AIDS Media Research Project, which ran focus groups based on pre-existing social groups (e.g. colleagues, friends), participants often challenged each other on contradictions between what they *claimed* to believe and how they actually behaved: e.g. 'How about that time you didn't use a glove while taking blood from a patient?'; 'What about the other night when you went off with that boy at the disco?' (Kitzinger, 1994a, p. 105). Challenges like these, in forcing people to defend and justify their actions or beliefs, often lead to the production of more elaborated accounts.

Providing an opportunity to observe the co-construction of meaning in action

Finally, focus groups are an ideal approach for researchers interested in exploring participants' own meanings, because they offer a unique opportunity to observe the co-construction of meaning in action. People's health beliefs, their ideas about what causes a disease, or what cures an illness, the meanings they attribute to different parts of their bodies or to different medical procedures are not generated by individuals in splendid isolation. Such beliefs are forged and shaped in everyday social contexts: in discussions between family members in the home; in conversations with others at school or in the workplace; in exchanges with medical professionals or members of self-help groups. People build their ideas, beliefs, understandings and world views *in interaction* with others, in a *social context*: as Radley and Billig (1996, p. 223) say, 'thinking is a socially shared activity'. I am using the term 'co-construction of meaning' to refer to the interactive processes through which individuals collaboratively construct their meanings of health and illness in a social context. A focus group is itself a social context; its participants are members of a social group in interaction; and it is this social interaction among participants which constitutes the primary data.

Focus groups are not, of course, entirely 'naturalistic'; and a researcher running a focus group (unlike a researcher engaged in participant observation) is not witnessing a 'naturally occurring' event, in the sense that focus groups constitute part of a research enterprise, and are not part of participants' everyday social contexts. Such everyday social contexts are not, however, always easily accessible to the researcher. For example, although Morgan and Spanish (1984), in studying how people collectively make sense of heart attacks, would have liked to observe 'informal discussions of friends' and acquaintances' heart attacks', such discussions are – of course – relatively rare events. By using focus groups, rather than participant observation of naturally occurring discussions, they were able to collect far more data. And although, as they point out, the focus group discussions 'lacked the "Oh my God, not Harry" quality of a lunch table group first hearing about one of their number's heart attack' (Morgan and Spanish, 1984, pp. 258–259), these data do nevertheless share many of the features of ordinary social interaction. Focus group data reflect everyday social process of communication, such as arguing, joking, boasting, teasing, persuasion, challenge and disagreement. Focus groups may, like those run by Robin Jarrett (1993, p. 194), have 'the feel of rap sessions with friends'. Crucially, then, focus groups offer an opportunity for researchers to observe how people interactively construct the meanings attributed to health and illness: how opinions are formed, expressed, defended and (sometimes) modified within the context of discussion and debate with others.

I will illustrate how the co-construction of meaning can be explored through focus group research using an example drawn from my own data: a focus group in which three women talk about their experience of breast cancer. 'Anne' had had a mastectomy a year before; 'Carol' a lumpectomy some weeks ago; and Barbara, who arrived for the focus group looking tense and nervous, a mastectomy only a few days before.

Within about ten minutes of the start of the focus group, Anne asks Barbara whether she is wearing a prosthesis (artificial breast), and Barbara explains that, because her mastectomy is so recent, she has 'only a little soft comfie' (a lambswool puff – typically given to women until the scar heals sufficiently for them to be fitted for a silicone prosthesis). Anne responds by reflecting on the difference in size between 'your bosom' and 'my bosom', and then offers to show Barbara (who has never seen a prosthesis before) what hers looks like. As Barbara hesitates, Anne reaches inside her bra, pulls out her prosthesis, and passes it around the table:

Anne: Would you like to see my prosthesis?
         The **size** of it?
Barbara: [Laughs] Well, mine's only really tiny
         [Laughs]
Anne: Excuse me [Pulls out breast prosthesis
         and passes it around the table].
         Feel the weight
Carol: [Gasps]
Anne: You don't, you don't feel it though, once it's
Carol: My friend's, though, isn't as,
         it doesn't seem as **heavy** as that

Anne: [To Barbara] Pick it up. Look at it
Barbara: No, I've had-
Carol: [Cuts in] It's **very heavy**
Several: [Raucous laughter, voices indistinct]
Carol: It's ra- [Collapses into laughter]
Several: [More laughter]
Carol: It's **rather heavy**, isn't it?
Anne: You can imagine **my** scar
Barbara: Do you want to see my scar?
Several: [More laughter and clamorous voices
          overlapping].
          Look at **my** scar. Look at **my** scar
          [More raucous laughter, voices indistinct]
Barbara: [Picks up prosthesis] My goodness, it feels
          so nice. It even feels warm [Laughs]

Various features of this brief interaction (it lasts only a few minutes of a focus group totalling over two hours in all) point to the advantages of focus groups in studying the co-construction of meaning. Anne, Barbara and Carol are sharing information in a relatively naturalistic way: it is possible to imagine that similar interactions might take place, for example, in a self-help group discussion, or among friends. Through this sharing of information, Barbara's ideas about her post-mastectomy experience are being actively constructed. She is learning not only what a prosthesis looks and feels like, but also a socially acceptable *attitude* to it – that it is something which can be shown to and explicitly discussed with others, something about which women with breast cancer can laugh, joke (and even brag!). She is also being socialised into the conventional belief that a prosthesis (however small) is an essential part of post-mastectomy life: this group is typical in that prostheses are taken for granted. The possibility of *not* wearing one is rarely discussed in my focus groups – and then only as an oddity.

Barbara's attitude to prostheses can be observed changing over the course of this interaction. At the beginning of the extract, she deflects Anne's question about whether or not she would like to see the prosthesis (perhaps she doesn't take the question seriously – in any event, she sounds embarrassed and awkward). The group interaction then shifts to Anne and Carol, who compare and contrast prostheses they have known, while Barbara sits stunned, unable to look at or to touch the prosthesis, although Anne specifically encourages her to do so: 'No . . .', she says. Various other group members juggle the prosthesis from hand to hand, crack jokes (sadly, inaudible on tape), talk excitedly over each other, and laugh together. Finally, Barbara relaxes and joins in, holding the prosthesis and saying with surprise and laughter in her voice, 'My goodness, it feels so nice.' For researchers interested in people's own understandings of health-related issues, this extract offers the opportunity to observe the co-construction of the *meaning* of a prosthesis. It shows how Barbara, in the social context provided by the focus group, responds to the collaborative construction of a prosthesis as something publicly to be joked about, and begins to incorporate this benign image into her own understandings.

Conclusion

As I have shown, then, focus groups are widely used in health research; and they are – in particular – an ideal method for eliciting people's own meanings and understandings of health and illness. This makes the method well-suited to those researchers concerned with 'the patient's view', or who are approaching health-related research from theoretical perspectives in which 'meanings', 'folk theories', 'lay representations', 'common-sense beliefs', and so on are crucial. Given this apparently good fit between focus group method and the aims of phenomenological, experiential or narrative researchers, it is surprising to find how rare it is for such researchers to see focus groups as an appropriate method: one-to-one interviews are far more commonly used.

Moreover, it is also surprising that to find that in a great deal of published focus group research, the interaction between participants – i.e. precisely that feature of focus groups which makes them such a good method for eliciting meanings – is neither reported nor analysed. It is rare to find reports which concentrate on the analysis of group interactions and, indeed, very few which include any data extracts showing participants' interactions. Focus group data are most commonly presented as if they were one-to-one interview data.

Finally, it should be noted that focus group method is flexible in terms of the analytic frameworks within which it can be used. It is possible, as I have indicated, to use the focus group method within a traditional essentialist framework (such as in some versions of cognitive psychology and some types of research on health beliefs and attitudes). It is also possible to use focus groups within the alternative (social construc-tionist) framework offered by the 'turn to language' in health psychology (e.g. Radley and Billig, 1996; see also Stokoe and Wiggins, this volume). For those health researchers working within an essentialist framework, focus groups offer a valuable way of study-ing 'the individual in social context' (Goldman, 1962; Rubin and Rubin, 1995, p. 95) and provide insights both into the content of cognitions and into the processes through which such cognitions are formed and modified. For those health researchers working within a social constructionist framework, focus group data offer a route to studying the construction and negotiation of health-related talk; the social functions served by different accounts or discourses; and the ways in which aspects of health and illness are produced and perpetuated through talk.

In this chapter, I have shown that focus group method can be used flexibly across a wide range of health-related research contexts, to address a wide range of research questions central to the study of health and illness. I have argued that the method is of particular value to those researchers (e.g. phenomenological, experiential or narrative researchers) interested in exploring individuals' own meanings of health and illness because focus group interactions facilitate access to such meanings. Health researchers were pioneers in the early use of focus groups and we have continued to make extensive use of the method in our research. If we are able fully to exploit the analytic potential of group interactions in exploring the meanings of health and illness, the focus group method offers researchers in clinical and health psychology a major opportunity for the future.

Acknowledgement

An earlier – longer – version of this chapter was published in the *Journal of Health Psychology* (1998).

Further reading

I would particularly recommend the following:

Wilkinson, S. (1998) Focus group methodology: A review. *International Journal of Social Research Methodology*, **1** (3), 181–203. Good brief introduction to the method and the range of ways in which it has been used in various disciplinary contexts.

Barbour, R. and Kitzinger, J. (eds) (1999) *Developing Focus Group Research: Politics, Theory and Practice*. London: Sage. A recent edited collection, issue-based, and with a wider range of examples than most anthologies of this type.

Krueger, R. A. and Casey, M. A. (2000) *Focus Groups: A Practical Guide for Applied Research*, 3rd edn. Thousand Oaks, CA: Sage. One of the two best introductions to doing focus group research, very practical. The second edition of this text – Krueger (1994) – is also very useable.

Morgan, D. L. (1997) *Focus Groups as Qualitative Research*, 2nd edn., Newbury Park, CA: Sage.

The other best introduction to doing focus group research, covers key issues as well as practical details.

Wilkinson, S. (2000) Women with breast cancer talking causes: Comparing content, biographical and discursive analyses. *Feminism and Psychology*, **10** (4), 431–460. Useful for more examples of different types of data analysis, with extensive discussion of their implications.

References

Armstrong, D. (1984). The patient's view. *Social Science and Medicine*, **18** (9), 737–744.

Agar, M. and MacDonald, J. (1995). Focus groups and ethnography. *Human Organization*, **54** (1), 78–86.

Aitken, P. P., Leathar, D. S. and O'Hagan, F. J. (1986). Monitoring children's perceptions of advertisements for cigarettes. In D. S. Leathar, G. B. Hastings, K. O'Reilly and J. K. Davies (eds) *Health Education and the Media II*, pp. 155–161. Oxford: Pergamon.

Barbour, R. and Kitzinger, J. (eds) (1999). *Developing Focus Group Research: Politics, Theory and Practice*. London: Sage.

Basch, C. E. (1987). Focus group interviews: A underutilized research technique for improving theory and practice in health education. *Health Education Quarterly*, **154**, 411–448.

Beck, L., Trombetta, W. and Share, S. (1986). Using focus group sessions before decisions are made. *North Carolina Medical Journal*, **47** (2), 73–74.

Bers, T. H. (1987). Exploring institutional images through focus group interviews. In R. S. Lay and J. J. Endo (eds) *Designing and Using Market Research*, pp. 19–29. San Francisco, CA: Jossey-Bass.

Brems, S. and Griffiths, M. (1993). Health women's way: Learning to listen. In M. Koblinsky, J. Timyan and J. Gay (eds) *The Health of Women: A Global Perspective*, pp. 255–273. Boulder, CO: Westview Press.

Bloor, M., Frankland, J., Robson, K. and Thomas, M. (2001). *Focus Groups in Social Research.* London: Sage.

Brody, C. M. (1990). Women in a nursing home: Living with hope and meaning. *Psychology of Women Quarterly*, **14**, 579–592.

Broom, G. M. and Dozier, D. M. (1990). *Using Research in Public Relations: Application to Program Management.* Englewood Cliffs, NJ: Prentice Hall.

Bush, J., White, M., Kai, J., Rankin, J. and Bhopal, R. (2003). Understanding influences on smoking in Bangladeshi and Pakistani adults: Community based, qualitative study. *BMJ*, **326** (7936), 962.

Collins, C., Stommel, M., King, S. and Given, C. W. (1991). Assessment of the attitudes of family caregivers toward community services. *The Gerontologist*, **31**, 756–761.

Cooper, P., Diamond, I. and High, S. (1993). Choosing and using contraceptives: Integrating qualitative and quantitative methods in family planning. *Journal of the Market Research Society*, **35** (4), 325–339.

Cottrell, C., Drew, J., Waller, S., Holroyd, K., Brose, J. and O'Donnell, F. (2003). Perceptions and needs of patients with migraine: A focus group study. *Headache: The Journal of Head and Face Pain*, **43** (4), 128.

Crockett, S., Heller, K., Merkel, J. and Peterson, J. (1990). Assessing beliefs of older rural americans about nutrition information: Use of the focus group approach. *Journal of the American Dietetic Association*, **90**, 563–567.

Defriez, M., Griffiths, D., Millett, C., Thakrar, D. N. and Winterbotham, M. (2003). The perception of the current provision of care for multiple sclerosis sufferers in the community. *Primary Health Care Research and Development*, **4** (3), 233–243.

de Koning, K. and Martin, M. (eds) (1996). *Participatory Research in Health: Issues and Experiences.* London: Zed Books.

Dignan, M., Michielutte, R., Sharp, P., Bahnson, J., Young, B. and Beal, P. (1990). The role of focus groups in health education for cervical cancer among minority women. *Journal of Community Health*, **15**, 369–375.

DiMatteo, M. R., Kahn, K. L. and Berry, S. H. (1993). Narratives of birth and the postpartum: Analysis of the focus group responses of new mothers. *Birth*, **20** (4), 204–211.

Duke, S. S., Godon-Sosby, K., Reynolds, K. D. and Gram, I. T. (1994). A study of breast cancer detection practices and beliefs in black women attending public health clinics. *Health Education Research*, **9**, 331–342.

Fife, B. L. (1994). The conceptualization of meaning in illness. *Social Science and Medicine*, **38** (2), 309–16.

Flaskerud, J. and Rush, C. (1989). Traditional health beliefs and practice of black women related to AIDS. *Nursing Research*, **38**, 210–215.

Flexner, W. A., McLaughlin, C. P., and Littlefield, J. E. (1977). Discovering what the consumer really wants. *Health Care Management Review*, **1**, 43–49.

Frazer, E. (1988). Teenage girls talking about class. *Sociology*, **22** (3), 343–358.

Freimuth, V. S. and Greenberg, R. (1986). Pretesting television advertisements for family planning products in developing countries: A case study. *Health Education Research*, **1** (1), 37–45.

Frey, J. H. and Fontana, A. (1993). The group interview in social research. In D. L. Morgan (ed.) *Successful Focus Groups: Advancing the State of the Art*, pp. 20–34. Newbury Park, CA: Sage.

Frith, H. and Kitzinger, C. (1998). 'Emotion work' as a participant resource: A feminist analysis of young women's talk-in-interaction. *Sociology*, **32** (2), 299–320.

Folch-Lyon, E., de la Macorra, L. and Schearer, S. B. (1981). Focus group and survey research on family planning in Mexico. *Studies in Family Planning*, **12**, 409–432.

Geis, S., Fuller, R. and Rush, J. (1986). Lovers of AIDS victims: Psychosocial stresses and counselling needs. *Death Studies*, **10**, 45–53.

George, A. (1996). Methodological issues in the ethnographic study of sexuality: Experiences from Bombay. In K. de Koning and M. Martin (eds) *Participatory Research in Health: Issues and Experiences*, pp. 119–129. London: Zed Books.

Glik, D., Gordon, A., Ward, W., Kouame, K. and Guessan, M. (1988). Focus group methods for formative research in child survival: An Ivoirian example. *International Quarterly of Community Health Education*, **8**, 297–316.

Goldman, A. E. (1962). The group depth interview. *Journal of Marketing*, **26**, 61–68.

Goldman, A. E. and McDonald, S. S. (1987). *The Group Depth Interview: Principles and Practice*. Englewood Cliffs, NJ: Prentice-Hall.

Hamilton, E. and Barlow, J. (2003). Women's views of a breast screening service. *Health Care for Women International*, **24** (1), 40–48.

Harrison, K. and Barlow, J. (1995). Focused group discussion: A 'quality' method for health research? *Health Psychology Update*, **20**, 11–13.

Heimann-Ratain, G., Hanson, M. and Peregoy, S. (1985). The role of focus group interviews in designing a smoking prevention program. *Journal of School Health*, **55**, 13–16.

Hisrich, R. D. and Peters, M. P. (1982). Focus groups: an innovative marketing research technique. *Hospital and Health Services Administration*, **27** (4), 8–21.

Hoppe, M. J., Wells, E. A., Wilsdon, A., Gilmore, M. R. and Mortison, D. M. (1994). Children's knowledge and beliefs about AIDS. Qualitative data from focus group interviews. *Health Education Quarterly*, **21** (1), 117–26.

Hyland, M. E., Finnis, S. and Irvine, S. H. (1991). A scale for assessing quality of life in adult asthma sufferers. *Journal of Psychosomatic Research*, **35**, 99–110.

Irwin, K., Bertrand, J., Mibandumba, N., Mbuyi, K., Muremeri, C., Makolo, M., Munkolenkole, K., Nzilambi, N., Bosenge, N., Ryder, R., Peterson, H., Lee, N. C., Wingo, P., O'Reilly, K. and Rufo, K. (1991). Knowledge, attitudes and beliefs about HIV infection among healthy factory workers and their wives, Kinshasa, Zaire. *Social Science and Medicine*, **32**, 917–930.

Jarrett, R. L. (1993). Focus group interviewing with low-income minority populations: A research experience. In D. L. Morgan (ed.) *Successful Focus Groups: Advancing the State of the Art*, pp. 184–201. Newbury Park, CA: Sage.

Joachim, G. and Acorn, S. (2003). Life with a rare chronic disease: The scleroderma experience. *Journal of Advanced Nursing*, **42** (6), 598–606.

Johnson, A. (1996). 'It's good to talk': The focus group and the sociological imagination. *The Sociological Review*, **44** (3), 517–538.

Kisker, E. E. (1985). Teenagers talk about sex, pregnancy and contraception. *Family Planning Perspectives*, **17**, 83–90.

Kissling, E. A. (1996). Bleeding out loud: Communication about menstruation. *Feminism and Psychology*, **6** (4), 481–504.

Kitzinger, J. (1990). Audience understandings of AIDS media messages: A discussion of methods. *Sociology of Health and Illness*, **12**, 319–335.

Kitzinger, J. (1994a). The methodology of focus groups: The importance of interaction between research participants. *Sociology of Health and Illness*, **16** (1), 103–121.

Kitzinger, J. (1994b). Focus groups: Method or madness? In M. Boulton (ed.) *Challenge and Innovation: Methodological Advances in Social Research on HIV/AIDS*, pp. 159–175. London: Taylor and Francis.

Kline, A., Kline, E. and Oken, E. (1992). Minority women and sexual choice in the age of AIDS. *Social Science and Medicine*, **34**, 447–457.

Knodel, J., Havanon, N. and Pramualratana, A. (1984). Fertility transition in Thailand: A qualitative analysis. *Population and Development Review*, **10**, 297–328.

Krueger, R. A. (1988). *Focus Groups: A Practical Guide for Applied Research*. Newbury Park, CA: Sage. (2nd edition, 1994).

Krueger, R. A. and Casey, M. A. (2000). *Focus Groups: A Practical Guide for Applied Research*, 3rd edn. Thousand Oaks, CA: Sage.

Lindeman, M., Black, K., Smith, R., Gough, J., Bryce, A., Gilsenan, B., Hill, K. and Stewart, A. (2003). Changing practice in residential aged care using participatory methods. *Education for Health: Change in Learning and Practice*, **16** (1), 22–31.

Loevy, S. S. and O'Brien, M. U. (1994). Community based research: The case for focus groups. In A. J. Dan (ed.) *Reframing Women's Health*, pp. 102–110. Thousand Oaks, CA: Sage.

Lunt, P. and Livingstone, S. (1996). Focus groups in communication and media research. *Journal of Communication*, **42**, 78–87.

Lupton, D. and Tulloch, J. (1996). 'All red in the face': Students' views on school-based HIV/AIDS and sexuality education. *The Sociological Review*, **44**, 252–271.

Lyons, R. and Meade, D. (1993). The energy crisis: Mothers with chronic illness. *Canadian Woman Studies*, **13** (4), 34–37.

Lyons, R. F., Sullivan, M. J. L., Ritvo, P. G. with Coyne, J. C. (1995). *Relationships in Chronic Illness and Disability*. Thousand Oaks, CA: Sage.

McFall, S. and Hamm, R. M. (2003). Interpretation of prostate cancer screening events and outcomes: A focus group study. *Patient Education and Counseling*, **49** (3), 207–218.

Mays, V. M., Cochran, S. D., Bellinger, G., Smith, R. G., Henley, N., Daniels, M., Tibbits, T., Victorianne, G. D., Osei, O. K. and Birt, D. K. (1992). The language of black gay men's sexual behavior: Implications for AIDS risk reduction. *The Journal of Sex Research*, **29** (3), 425–434.

Morgan, D. L. (1988). *Focus Groups as Qualitative Research*. Sage University Papers, Qualitative Research Methods Series, No. 16. London: Sage.

Morgan, D. L. (1997). *Focus Groups as Qualitative Research*, 2nd edn. Newbury Park, CA: Sage.

Morgan, D. L. and Krueger, R. A. (1998). *The Focus Group Kit*. Newbury Park, CA: Sage.

Morgan, D. L. and Spanish, M. T. (1984). Focus groups: A new tool for qualitative research. *Qualitative Sociology*, **7** (3), 253–270.

Morgan, D. L. and Spanish, M. T. (1985). Social interaction and the cognitive organisation of health-relevant knowledge. *Sociology of Health and Illness*, **7** (3), 401–422.

Moumjid, N., Morelle, M., Carrere, M-O., Bachelot, T., Mignotte, H. and Bremond, A. (2003). Elaborating patient information with patients themselves: Lessons from a cancer treatment focus group. *Health Expectations*, **6** (2), 128–139.

Mullis, R. M. and Lansing, D. (1986). Using focus groups to plan work-site nutrition programs. *Journal of Nutritional Education*, **18**, 532–534.

Murray, S. A., Tapson, J., Turnbull, L., McCallum, J. and Little, A. (1994). Listening to local voices: Adapting rapid appraisal to assess health and social needs in general practice. *British Medical Journal*, **308**, 698–700.

Naish, J., Brown, J. and Denton, B. (1994). Intercultural consultations: Investigation of factors that deter non-English speaking women from attending their general practitioners for cervical screening. *BMJ*, **309**, 1126–1128.

O'Brien, K. (1993). Using focus groups to develop health surveys: An example from research on social relationships and AIDS-preventive behavior. *Health Education Quarterly*, **20**, 361–372.

Okonofua, F. E. (1995). Factors associated with adolescent pregnancy in rural Nigeria. *Journal of Youth and Adolescence*, **24**, 419–438.

Orr, J. (1992) Working with women's health groups. In P. Abbott and R. Sapsford (eds) *Research into Practice: A Reader for Nurses and the Caring Professions*, pp. 23–38. Buckingham: Open University Press.

Philo, G., Secker, J., Platt, S., Henderson, L., McLaughlin, G. and Burnside, J. (1994). The impact of the mass media on public images of mental illness: Media content and audience belief. *Health Education Journal*, **53**, 271–281.

Plaut, T., Landis, S. and Trevor, J. (1993). Focus groups and community mobilization: A case study from rural North Carolina. In D. L. Morgan (ed.) *Successful Focus Groups: Advancing the State of the Art*, pp. 202–221. Newbury Park, CA: Sage.

Prilleltensky, O. (2003). A ramp to motherhood: The experience of mothers with physical disabilities. *Sexuality and Disability*, **21** (1), 21–47.

Powney, J. (1988). Structured eavesdropping. *Research Intelligence: Journal of the British Educational Research Foundation*, **28**, 10–12.

Radley, A. and Billig, M. (1996). Accounts of health and illness: Dilemmas and representations. *Sociology of Health and Illness*, **18** (2), 220–240.

Richter, M., Bottenberg, D. and Roberto, K. D. (1991). Focus groups: Implications for program evaluation of mental health services. *Journal of Mental Health Administration*, **18**, 148–153.

Ritchie, J. E., Herscovitch, F. and Norfor, J. B. (1994). Beliefs of blue collar workers regarding coronary risk behaviours. *Health Education Research*, **9**, 95–103.

Rubin, H. J. and Rubin, I. S. (1995). *Qualitative Interviewing: The Art of Hearing Data*. Thousand Oaks, CA: Sage.

Schearer, S. B. (1981). The value of focus groups for social action programs. *Studies in Family Planning*, **12**, 407–408.

Stewart, D. W. and Shamdasani, P. N. (1990). *Focus Groups: Theory and Practice*. London: Sage.

Strange, V., Oakley, A. and Forrest, S. (2003). Mixed-sex or single-sex sex education: How would young people like their sex education and why? *Gender and Education*, **15** (2), 201–214.

Suyono, H., Piet, N., Stirling, F. and Ross, J. (1981). Family planning attitudes in urban Indonesia: Findings from focus group research. *Studies in Family Planning*, **12**, 433–442.

Vaughn, S., Schumm, J. S. and Sinagub, J. (1996). *Focus Group Interviews in Education and Psychology*. Thousand Oaks, CA: Sage.

Wilkinson, S. (1998a). Focus groups in feminist research: Power, interaction and the co-construction of meaning. *Women's Studies International Forum*, **21** (1), 111–125.

Wilkinson, S. (1998b). Focus groups in health research: Exploring the meanings of health and illness. *Journal of Health Psychology*, **3** (3), 329–348.

Wilkinson, S. (1999). Focus groups: A feminist method. *Psychology of Women Quarterly*, **23**, 221–244.

Wilkinson, S. (2003a). Focus groups. In J. A. Smith (ed.) *Qualitative Psychology: A Practical Guide to Research Methods*. London: Sage.

Wilkinson, S. (2003b). Focus groups. In G. M. Breakwell (ed.) *Doing Social Psychology*. Oxford: Blackwell.

Wilkinson, S. and Kitzinger, C. (eds) (1996). *Representing the Other: A 'Feminism and Psychology' Reader*. London: Sage.

Wyatt, G., Kurtz, M. E. and Liken, M. (1993). Breast cancer survivors: An exploration of quality of life issues. *Cancer Nursing*, **16** (6), 440–8.

Zeller, R. A. (1993). Focus group research on sensitive topics: Setting the agenda without setting the agenda. In D. L. Morgan (ed.) *Successful Focus Groups: Advancing the State of the Art*, pp. 167–183. Newbury Park, CA: Sage.

Zimmerman, M., Haffey, J., Crane, E., Szumowski, D., Alvarez, F., Bhiromrut, P., Brache, V., Lubis, F., Salah, M., Shaaban, M., Shawky, B. and Sidi, I. P. S. (1990). Assessing the acceptability of NORPLANT implants in four countries: Findings from focus group research. *Studies in Family Planning*, **21**, 92–103.

Chapter 8

Using and evaluating psychometric measures
Practical and theoretical considerations

Darcy A. Santor

Psychometric scales and measures are one of the most pervasive and influential technologies used in virtually every basic or applied discipline investigating human behaviour, development and health. As a technology, psychometric measurements achieve an important scientific and clinical goal – they streamline how information is managed and simplify how decisions are made. However, with an ever-growing number of available scales, the manner in which scales are selected and evaluated has become increasingly difficult. In the first part of this chapter, I will draw on the extensive literature on the assessment of depression to illustrate many of these theoretical and practical issues, common to most areas of research, that require consideration in selecting and evaluating psychometric measures. In the second and third sections, I will highlight several issues in evaluating the performance of psychometric measures.

Theoretical foundations: towards a theory of symptoms and signs

Several issues must be considered in selecting a psychometric measure, including both (a) the assessment objective (assessing the severity of a condition or screening for the presence of a disorder) and (b) the unique differences and special needs of the particular individual or population being assessed (assessing depression in children, adults or the elderly). Choosing the best measure available depends on knowing how well a specific measure performs relative to any and every other measure available for the given assessment goal and specific population being assessed. Evaluating the relative performance of a number of psychometric measures depends on the appropriateness of the analytic model used to compare the performance of one test to any other (i.e., internal reliability coefficients versus test characteristic curves) and the performance of any given test will be influenced by the manner in which constructs are operationalised into specific test questions or indicators, which should be determined by the definition of that construct. Depression, for example may be viewed as a mood state, as a number of diagnostic and non-diagnostic symptoms, or as a specific syndrome).

Historically, the manner in which symptoms are believed to be related to the underlying depression has remained largely implicit, expressed primarily through the analytic models imposed on the data and the nature and number of the questions that comprise the scale. Ideally, in designing or evaluating a psychometric measure, the researcher should articulate a theory of symptoms that formally answers a number of questions. These include:

- what the ontological status of the construct being assessed is (i.e., is depression a continuous or categorical entity, a simple mood state or a specific syndrome),
- what symptoms, signs and associated conditions should and should not be included,
- how those symptoms are related to the underlying illness and combined to derive an index of severity,
- how many and what type of questions should be used to operationalise each of the symptom domains being assessed, and
- how those symptoms are expressed differently in different groups, whether the groups are differentiated with respect to age, gender, culture, co-morbid condition or any other characteristic.

Ontological status

One of the most important conceptual distinctions that must be addressed in selecting and evaluating a psychometric measure, concerns whether the condition or illness should be viewed as a category, as a single, unidimensional construct on a continuum with other normal and pathological phenomena, or as a multidimensional construct. Whether depression is more appropriately viewed along a continuum or as a category constitutes one of the most contentious debates in the literature on depression (Coyne, 1994; Flett, Vredenburg, and Krames, 1997; Kendall and Flannery-Shroeder, 1995; Tennen, Hall and Affleck, 1995a, b; Vrendenburg, Flett, and Krames, 1993; Weary, Edwards, and Jacobson, 1995). Viewing depression as a continuum implies that individuals can be ordered on the basis of the severity of their symptoms and that any score on a measure of depressive severity is determined only by the severity of their depression. This assumption serves as the foundation for research studies using college students, who score high on measures of depression but who have not been formally evaluated for a depressive illness. Viewing these participants as analogues assumes that a high score on a measure of depression in a non-depressed individual is similar to a high score in a depressed person.

In contrast, viewing depression as a discrete category or syndrome implies that depression is defined by a set of symptoms which tend to manifest themselves together, which occur for a particular period of time and which are, according to most diagnostic criteria, by definition impairing (American Psychiatric Association, 1987). Viewing depression as a distinct category also implies that the validity of 'analogue' studies will be limited. High scores in non-depressed individuals are not equivalent to high scores in depressed individuals. Although originally developed for use in depressed patients, measures such as the Beck Depression Inventory (BDI) (Beck, Steer, and Brown, 1996) and The Hamilton Rating Scale for Depression (HRSD) (Hamilton, 1960) have been used to assess severity in both patient and non-patient populations. However, there is good evidence to show that the HRSD functions differently in both depressed and non-depressed individuals (Santor and Coyne, 2001) and that the BDI may be less discriminating of differences in college samples compared to other measures such as the CES-D (Centre for Epidemiological Studies Depression Scale) (Santor, Zuroff, Ramsay, Cervantes and Palacios, 1995).

Symptoms, signs and associated conditions

A theory of symptoms should also state what symptoms should be assessed in order to gauge the severity of depression and how many questions or indicators are to be used to assess a specific symptom domain. This includes stating explicitly what symptoms are core symptoms and what symptoms are peripheral or associated with various symptoms and difficulties. Santor, Gregus and Welch (2002) showed that the number of test items assigned to symptom domains varied significantly, with most measures of depression allocating more test items to cognitive symptoms. Whether these subtle differences are important is an empirical question which has rarely been investigated explicitly.

However, the symptoms that are used to assess severity are not necessarily synonymous with those symptoms used to diagnose the presence of a disorder (inclusionary symptoms) or rule out a related condition (exclusionary symptoms). Indeed, there may be a number of symptoms which are good indicators of severity but which are not necessarily specific to a diagnosis of depression. For example, social withdrawal is experienced by many depressed people. However, social withdrawal strictly speaking is a not a symptom diagnostic of a depressive disorder, unless it is interpreted broadly as indicative of a feature of anhedonia. This view implies that measures designed to assess the presence or absence of a disorder or measures which are constructed strictly from diagnostic criteria may not be the most valid or effective tools for assessing severity.

Relation of symptoms and signs to the underlying illness

A theory of symptoms should also state how various symptoms relate to depressive severity and how symptoms should be combined to derive an index of severity. Very little theorising exists on how individual symptoms of depression might relate to overall depressive severity or how symptoms should be combined. Typically, item scores are summed to produce a composite score reflecting the individual's overall level of depressive severity. However, there are a number of potential difficulties associated with evaluating overall depressive severity in this manner. Aggregating symptom scores assumes (a) that symptoms are equally informative about how depressed an individual is, (b) that symptoms are uniformly informative at all levels of depressive severity, (c) and that the manner in which symptoms are expressed does not vary from one population to another. Many of these assumptions are unlikely to be valid. How symptoms are expressed at different levels of depressive severity and in different populations is ignored. The likelihood of a clinician rating any symptoms of depression may vary across symptoms, across measures of depression, and across levels of depressive severity.

There is little reason to believe that all symptoms of depression should be equally effective as indicators of depressive severity or should be equally related to depressive severity throughout the entire continuum of depressive severity. Indeed, symptoms may be related to overall severity in a number of ways. First, some symptoms of depression may be atypical and may only be observed in a minority of depressed individuals. For example, few depressed individuals report weight gains. Second, other symptoms may be present only in depressed individuals but not necessarily related to the severity of depression. Some symptoms may discriminate depressed from non-depressed individuals, without necessarily being related to depressive severity. Third, some symptoms, like weight loss, are likely to be influenced by a number of psychological and physiological factors, which may or may not be related to the severity of depression. As a result, the relation between depressive severity and weight loss is likely to be weak. Finally, symptoms may be related to depressive severity only within certain levels of depressive severity; there may be a discrete threshold at which certain symptoms of depression are no longer related to depressive severity, just as there may be a certain threshold of depressive severity at which some symptoms of depression are only first noticed. This view implies that many diagnostic symptoms might not be good measures of severity if they do not change with increases in the severity of illness and as such should be disregarded in deriving a measure of severity.

Operationalising symptoms

A theory of symptoms should also state how symptoms should be operationalised, that is specify how symptoms are turned into questions, how many questions are used to assess a single symptom, the format of those questions, who responds to questions, as well as the period of time over which questions should be answered. For example, it is well known that the Centre for Epidemiologic Studies Depression Scale (Radloff, 1977), is completed with respect to the past week, the Beck Depression Inventory (Beck, Steer and Brown, 1996) the past two weeks, and the Youth Self Report Form, 'now or anytime in the past 6 months' (Achenbach, 1991). Despite the many different possibilities, there has been little systematic investigation concerning the manner in which symptoms are operationalised and their effects on the measures overall performance. Research does suggest that some scales do function differently, even though they purportedly assess the same underlying construct, i.e., depression.

Results of a number of studies have suggested that the most frequently used clinician-rated and self-report measures of depression, the HRSD and BDI, do not correlate strongly, just 0.58 (Sayer *et al.*, 1993). Optimistically, one could argue that these scales show convergent validity. More critically, one might note that the measures share only one third of their variance. The factors underlying these differences are likely to be numerous, including differences in item content (more somatic symptoms versus more cognitive symptoms), scaling (items on the HRSD are scored on scales with varying ranges) and different reporting formats (clinician-rated versus self-report).

Measures also differ with respect to their response format. The BDI for example requires individuals to rate the severity of symptoms with respect to a series of uniquely worded options that differ in severity (i.e., are graded response options) with respect to the past two weeks. In contrast, the CES-D asks about the frequency of symptoms in the past two weeks, without asking about the severity with which those symptoms are expressed.

Finally, symptoms may be assessed either via global judgements (i.e., eating and appetite is disturbed) or by quantifying disturbance (i.e., weight loss exceeding 10 lbs). Currently, both approaches have been used. However, it is not clear whether quantifying disturbances in concentration, appetite, or sleep is superior to patient or clinician judgements of severity in predicting symptom severity.

Assessing the performance of severity measures

In general, most scales have been developed for the purpose of differentiating individuals with respect to the severity of symptoms or conditions, which is typically achieved through a composite score derived by summing the scores assigned to individual items and options. Differentiating individuals on the basis of their total score implies that individuals can be ordered along a continuum and that the difference or interval between 30 and 35 on a measure of depressive severity is similar to the interval between 5 and 10. Summing individual items to yield a total score also implies that items are *equally* informative, assigning no priority to any specific subset of symptoms. Both the extent to which scores reflect an interval scale and the equal importance of items are indeed assumptions that should be verified directly. A variety of analytic models have been used to evaluate scale performance.

Internal consistency

Traditionally, scale performance has been evaluated with global measures of internal consistency (e.g., Cronbach's α; see Hempel, this volume) and validity (e.g., item-total correlations) that summarise the performance of the scale for the entire sample. Scale performance is generally improved by deleting items that diminish the internal consistency of the scale and which do not correlate strongly in the anticipated direction with the scale's total score. Historically, most measures of depression have shown adequate to good internal consistency. What may be considered the first psychometric measure of depression, Woodworth's personal data sheet (Woodworth, 1918) showed a remarkably high internal consistency score ($\alpha = 0.90$), achieved without the aid of sophisticated analytic models such as exploratory and confirmatory factor analysis (see Shevlin, this volume).

Given that virtually every *published* measure of depression will have adequate to good internal consistency, performance measures, such as internal consistency, will not be the most useful means by which scales can be compared. Moreover, direct comparisons of scales, on the basis of internal consistency, are not easily achieved given that differences may reflect a range of factors, such as sample variation, which is not determined by the quality of the items themselves. In summary, internal consistency coefficients themselves have not been useful in a practical sense to assist researchers in selecting which tools are most useful.

Variance–covariance models

Scale developers have come to rely more and more on confirmatory and exploratory factor analysis to construct, evaluate, and in particular guide the revision of psychometric measures (see Shevlin, this volume). Both exploratory and confirmatory factor analysis evaluate the relation of individual items to an underlying dimension of variation (or factor). Items which load strongly (i.e., >0.30) on just one factor are considered good indicators of the underlying dimension of variation. Confirmatory factor analysis differs from exploratory factor analysis in the degree to which the investigator is able to impose a structure on the data, namely by (a) specifying the number of components or latent constructs believed to account for the variation in responses that individuals make to items, as well as (b) the manner in which constructs are related, and (c) the way in which items are believed to be associated with those constructs. Whether item responses are best characterised as multidimensional or unidimensional is determined on the basis of a variety of fit statistics that compare the observed variance–covariance matrix to the variance–covariance matrix implied by the paths and path coefficients (see Shevlin, this volume).

With the development of user-friendly statistical software packages, confirmatory factor analysis has been used more and more frequently to examine the underlying components of variation in item responses. However, there are concerns with the use of both the exploratory and confirmatory factor analytic approaches in both the evaluation of full scales and the development of short-forms and revisions. For example, research on the subcomponents of the Center for Epidemiologic Studies for Depression Scale (CES-D) (Radloff, 1977) has identified between three and five components of variation in a variety of samples that have been replicated across both samples and sites (Clark *et al.*, 1981; McCallion and Kolomer, 2000; Radloff, 1977; Verdier-Taillefer, Gourlet, Fuhrer and Alperovitch, 2001; Wong, 2000), which implies that the scale is not unidimensional. With any substantial departure from unidimensionality, estimates of depressive severity and decisions about individuals will become more complex.

One concern with many of these studies is that the statistics by which restricted models (i.e., one-factor models) are rejected in favour of more flexible models (i.e., two or more factor models) have been evaluated with a test-statistic which does not capture the extent to which level one factors can be subsumed under a second-order factor. Marsh and Hocevar (1985) have advocated the use of a *target coefficient* to summarise the relation between the first-order model and the second-order model. The target coefficient is the ratio of the chi-square of the first-order model to the chi-square of the second-order model. It provides a measure of optimum fit for the higher order model and is bounded by zero and one. A target coefficient of 1 suggests that relations among the first-order factors could be entirely accounted for by a more restrictive second-order model. In this way, the target coefficient has the advantage of distinguishing a lack of fit at the second-order level from a lack of fit in the first-order model.

More recently, investigations have suggested that although there are a number of components of variation in the CES-D, these components are generally highly correlated and are well captured by a single higher order factor (Hertzog *et al.*, 1990; Sheehan *et al.*, 1995). In retrospect, the finding that variation in item responses may be best captured by a single higher-order factor under which a set of highly correlated subcomponents are subsumed should not be surprising. Given that items for the majority of depression scales constructed in the past 80 years were selected to maximise internal consistency (i.e., unidimensionality), large subcomponents of variation should not be anticipated. Indeed, any subcomponents that are identified should be strongly intercorrelated. As a result, identifying subcomponents of variation as a measure of evaluating scale performance or suitability is unlikely to be very productive, unless the focus of the investigation is on between-group factor invariance.

Exploratory or confirmatory factor analysis has also become the primary tool for revising psychometric measures. However, these types of analysis may not be ideally suited to the task of reducing the number of items measuring a construct while preserving the psychometric properties of the original scale. For example, several short forms of the Depressive Experiences Questionnaire (DEQ) (Blatt, D'Afflitti, and Quinlan, 1976) have now appeared (Bagby, Parker, Joffe, and Buis, 1994; Viglione, Lovette, and Gottlieb, 1995; Welkowitz, Lish, and Bond, 1985), the majority of which have been developed with the use of confirmatory or exploratory factor analyses to identify and retain items loading strongly (>0.30) on their constituent factors. Interestingly, short-forms developed in this manner have failed, without exception, to reproduce the degree of orthogonality observed between the original Dependency and Self-Criticism scales (Santor, Zuroff and Fielding, 1997).

Fine-grained analyses examining the correlation between subscales of Dependency and Self-criticism and a variety of criterion measures showed that the psychometric properties of the original scales were only preserved after including about 30 items, many of which had a factor loading of less than 0.30 (Santor, Zuroff and Fielding, 1997). Selecting items on the basis of factor loadings greater than ±0.30 ignores the incremental contribution of individual unit-weighted items to the psychometric features of the original scores, and the factor loadings themselves do not provide any information showing how items are related to the original scores and therefore to other measures with which the original scales were validated. Results of this kind illustrate how selecting items solely in terms of their relationship to an underlying dimension of variation may not necessarily preserve all of the psychometric properties of the original scale.

Item response models

In contrast to exploratory and confirmatory factor analysis, which were initially designed to examine components of variation among individual items, item response models were designed to model how responses to individual items (or options) vary as a function of some underlying ability or condition, such as depression (Lord, 1980; van der Linden, and Hambleton, 1997). Performance is characterized by an option (OCC) or item characteristic curve (ICC), which are presented for both the Depressed Mood and Weight Loss items from the BDI in Figure 8.1.

Adopting an item response model acknowledges that the performance of an option, item or the entire scale, will vary within a group of individuals. Ideally, a scale should consist of a set of indicators (i.e., items and options) that are likely to be endorsed at different levels of depressive severity, as is the case for the Item 1 (Depressed mood) from the BDI. Failure to discriminate among individuals at some level of depressive

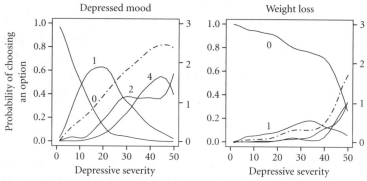

Fig. 8.1 Option characteristic curves (solid lines) and item characteristic curves (broken lines) for two items from the Beck Depression Inventory plotted as a function of depressive severity. Results show that the expected item scores increase smoothly throughout the range of depressive severity for Depressed Mood but only begin to change in the most severe region of depressive severity for Weight Loss.

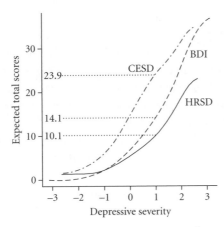

Fig. 8.2 Test Characteristic Curves for the CESD, BDI and HRSD plotted as a function of depressive severity expressed as standard normal scores. Horizontal dashed lines equated expected total scores at a similar level of depressive severity. The slope of the curves in the region −3 to 0, shows that the CESD is more discriminating of differences in severity than the BDI or HRSD.

severity, as is observed for Item 19 (Weight loss) from the BDI, will produce a restricted range of scores and consequently reduce the power of any statistical test, thereby requiring investigators to involve more individuals to increase the power of the study.

Item response models are able to address a number of questions concerning the performance of scales, such as how effective tests and test items are at assessing differences in depressive severity (item, option and scales discriminability) and whether certain groups of individuals endorse items differently (differential item functioning). Results of item response analyses have shown (a) differential item functioning between men and women on the BDI (Santor, Ramsay and Zuroff, 1994) and between individuals with and without a formal diagnosis of depression on the HRSD (Santor and Coyne, 2001), (b) differences in the relative effectiveness of the BDI and CES-D at discriminating individual differences in depressive severity in both clinical and nonclinical samples (Santor *et al.*, 1995), and (c) evidence for the appropriateness of response option weights assigned to the BDI (Santor, Ramsay and Zuroff, 1994).

The advantages that item response models offer over traditional performance measures are considerable. By modelling items as a function of depressive severity, individuals, specific groups, and even different tests themselves can be compared at different levels of severity. In this regard, item response theory offers a means of comparing different tests, either for the purpose of identifying the best test for a specific population or for the purpose of translating scores on one test to scores on another.

Comparing severity measures

One of the most important issues in selecting a psychometric measure is to determine which measure is the most effective in discriminating among individual differences in severity. Determining which of a number of scales is most discriminating requires that test scores be plotted and compared along a common dimension of depressive severity, which can be achieved by computing and plotting test characteristic curves. Test characteristic curves are plotted as a function of standard normal quantities in Figure 8.2 for three measures of depression. These test characteristic curves show the extent to which a one-unit increase in depression is expressed by actual test scores. A one-unit change in depressive severity is captured by a broader range of test scores on the CES-D and BDI than on the HRSD. In this sense, the CES-D and the BDI are more discriminating than the HRSD (i.e., greater range of scores). The test characteristic curves also show how to translate a score of 15 on the HRSD to a score (of 30) on the CES-D and to a score (of 35) on the BDI.

Given the impracticality of comparing a large number of measures of depressive severity directly, there is a need for the routine administration of an anchor measure by which scales can be equated and compared. Although choosing an anchor measure may be difficult, progress in understanding the strengths and weaknesses of different measures depends on it. Indeed, it is essential to preserving the continuity of knowledge.

Assessing the performance of screening measures

In addition to differentiating individuals with respect to the severity of some disorder or condition, psychometric measures are frequently used to facilitate the detection of some illness or condition. A cut-off score is selected above and below which individuals are designated as depressed or non-depressed. The performance of the cut-off score is evaluated with respect to its sensitivity, specificity and both positive and negative predictive values, which are defined as follows.

Sensitivity   (# of depressed persons with positive test scores) *divided by* (# of depressed persons)

Specificity   (# of non-depressed persons with negative test scores) *divided by* (# of non depressed persons)

Positive predictive value   (# of persons with positive test scores who are actually depressed) *divided by* (# of persons with positive test scores)

Negative predictive value   (# of persons with negative test scores who are not depressed) *divided by* (# of persons with negative test scores)

Sensitivity, specificity and predictive values serve as measures of efficiency. High sensitivity is important when the clinician or researcher wants to minimise the number of depressed people who are not identified. Generally, the sensitivity of a measure can be increased by lowering the cut-off point so that more cases are detected. However, the cost of lowering the cut-off point to improve the sensitivity of the measure is often a corresponding increase in the number of false-positives, or the number of individuals who are identified as depressed but are in fact not depressed.

A receiver operator curve (ROC) is frequently used to identify the 'optimal' cut-off point for the test (Metz, 1978). The ROC shows the relationship of the probability of a positive test, given no disease (1 – Specificity) to the probability of a positive test given the disease (Sensitivity). Cut-points chosen with respect to the receiver operator curve will maximize the probability of a true positive (Sensitivity) relative to the probability of a false alarm (1 – Sensitivity).

In contrast, the positive predictive value of a cut-off point associated with a psycho-metric test concerns the probability that a person actually is depressed, given a positive test result. It is important to note that the predictive value is a probability rather than a ratio of probabilities, as is the ROC. A high positive predictive is important when the clinician or researcher is making inferences about the prevalence of depression in a sample or is concerned about the cost and feasibility of following-up a first stage screening with structured or semi-structured interviews. Studies that have examined the positive predictive value of the CES-D suggest that it can be quite low. In some instances, as few as 11 per cent of individuals identified as depressed using standard cutoff scores may be actually diagnosed as depressed (Roberts *et al.*, 1991). Two major reviews focussing on screening measures for adult depression (US Preventive Services Task Force 1996, 2002) have challenged the utility of these tests.

Although the ROC is theoretically independent of the base rate of illness in the sample, the predictive validity of the test is not. Understanding the relation among sensitivity, specificity and predictive values is important in selecting and evaluating a measure given that the performance of a test will be influenced by the base rate of the cases in the popu-lation or study sample. Figure 8.3 illustrates the impact of different base rates on positive predictive value for different levels of sensitivity and specificity. Only recently has the US Preventive Services Task Force (2002) reversed its position on the utility of screening

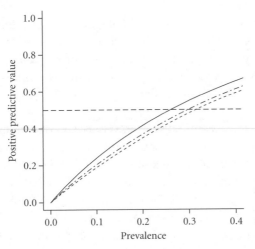

Fig. 8.3 Positive Predictive Value plotted as a function of Prevalence or Base Rate in a sample for Sensitivity values of 0.85, 0.70, and 0.65 holding specificity constant at 0.70. Results show that even with good Sensitivity and adequate Specificity, Predictive Value is strongly influenced by prevalence or base rate.

tests, concluding that first line screening for adult depression in a physician's office was warranted, where the base rate of cases of depression was sufficiently high. Where base rates are low (i.e., in adolescents), no high level of specificity or sensitivity will make a test work adequately as a screening device. Figure 8.2 also illustrates the importance of evaluating the performance of scales in samples that are representative of the base rate in the population of interest (cf. Santor and Coyne, 1997).

Improving the performance of screening tests

Without exception, attempts to improve most screening instruments have focused on adjusting the cut-off scores rather than on identifying effective items, and the appropriateness of cut-off points have generally been evaluated primarily with respect to some measures of efficiency, like sensitivity and specificity, with correspondingly less attention to other measures of efficiency like positive or negative predictive values. With the benefit of hindsight, the inability of measures like the CES-D to accurately ascertain the diagnostic status of individuals should not be surprising. The CES-D was originally developed to assess severity of depressive symptoms in adults residing in the community and was validated with respect to which the mean total score in a group of clinically depressed individuals differed from the mean total score in non-clinical groups (Radloff, 1977). Detecting the presence or absence of a depressive disorder was never the criterion against which individual items and response options were included or excluded from the scale (cf. Radloff, 1977). As result, it is unlikely that both objectives – accurately classifying individual cases of depression and assessing the extent to which individuals differ along a continuum of distress – are compatible. It is therefore crucial to identify options or combinations of options that differentiate individuals as depressed or non-depressed, irrespective of the absolute amount of distress reported by both groups of individuals (Santor and Coyne, 1997). There is good evidence to show that screening tests with as few as two carefully chosen items can still function well.

Results of the US Preventive Services Task Force (2002) highlight the importance of an adequate base rate where screening is desired. However, it is important to differentiate the prevalence of the illness from the base rate in a specific setting. This distinction is important since it acknowledges that the efficiency of screening programs may be improved if the base rate of illness in the screening context could be increased.

The US Preventive Services Task Force (1996, 2002) also acknowledged that the poor performance of screening tools may also reflect the fact that measures failed to discriminate among different types of mood disorders. This implies that the efficiency of screening tools might be improved if the target of screening was left broad (i.e., any mood disorder) versus narrow (i.e., a specific mood disorder) and underscores the importance of developing brief, first stage screening measures which are sensitive to illness and dysfunction in general rather than just discrete diagnostic syndromes.

Comparing screening measures

Determining which of a number of screening scales is most effective requires that performance indices for two measures be compared. However, direct tests examining the degree to which two measures differ statistically on all measures of performance, specificity, sensitivity, predictive values, ROCs have been rare (cf. LeBlanc, Almudevar, Brooks and Kutcher, 2002).

Summary

What we know about a disorder and what decisions we make about an individual's condition depends greatly on the quality of the tests and measures we use. There are numerous theoretical and practical issues to address in selecting and evaluating psychometric measures. A clear understanding of the goal and conceptual definition of the disorder with which the measure was designed, the manner in which symptoms were included and operationalised, and the appropriateness of the analytic model on the basis of which the test was evaluated are essential to making clear and useful decisions.

Further reading

Allen, Mary J. and Yen, Wendy M. (2001). *Introduction to Measurement Theory*. Long Grove, Ill: Waveland Press Inc.

Bollen, K. A and Lenox, R. (1991). Conventional wisdom on measurement: A structural equation perspective. *Psychological Bulletin*, **110**, 305–314.

Cronbach, L. J. and Meehl, P. E. (1955). Construct validity in psychological tests. *Psychological Bulletin*, **52**, 281–302.

DeVellis, R. F. (2003). *Scale Development: Theory and Applications*, 2nd edn. Sage Publications.

Embretson, S. E. (1996). The new rules of measurement. *Psychological Assessment*, **8**, 341–349.

Loevinger, J. (1957). Objective tests as instruments of psychological theory. *Psychological Reports*, **3**, 635–694. Monograph Supplement 9.

Michell, J.l (2002). Stevens's theory of scales of measurement and its place in modern psychology. *Australian Journal of Psychology*, **54**, 99–104.

Nunnally, J. C. and Bernstein, I. H. (1994). *Psychometric Theory*, 3rd edn. New York: McGraw Hill.

Santor, D. A. and Ramsay, J. O. (1998). Progress in the technology of measurement: Applications of item response models. *Psychological Assessment*, **10**, 345–359.

Shavelson, R. J., Webb, N. M. and Rowley, G. L. (1989). Generalizability theory. *American Psychologist*, **44**, 922–932.

Wainer, H. and Braun, H. I. (1988). *Test Validity*. Hillsdale, NJ: Lawrence Erlbaum.

References

Achenbach, T. M. (1991). *Manual for the Youth Self Report Form*. Burlington, VT: University of Vermont.

American Psychiatric Association (1987). *Diagnostic and Statistical Manual of Mental Disorders DSM-IV*. Washington, DC: American Psychiatric Association.

Bagby, R. M., Parker, J. D. A., Joffe, R. T. and Buis, T. (1994). Reconstruction and validation of the Depressive Experiences Questionnaire. *Assessment*, **1**, 59–68.

Beck, A. T., Steer, R. A. and Brown, G. K. (1996). *Beck Depression Inventory II*. London: Psychological Corporation.

Blatt, S. J., D'Afflitti, J. P. and Quinlan, D. M. (1976). Experiences of depression in normal young adults. *Journal of Abnormal Psychology*, **85**, 383–389.

Clark, V. A., Aneshensel, C. S., Frerichs, R. R. and Morgan, T. M. (1981). Analysis of effects of sex and age in response to items on the CESD scale. *Psychiatry Research*, **5**, 171–181.

Coyne, J. C. (1994). Self-reported distress: Analog or ersatz depression? *Psychological Bulletin*, **116**, 29–45.

Flett, G. L. Vredenberg, K. and Krames, L. (1997). The continuity of depression in clinical and non-clinical samples. *Psychological Bulletin*, **121**, 395–416.

Hamilton, M. (1960). A rating scale for depression. *Journal of Neurology, Neurosurgery, and Mental Science*, **105**, 985–987.

Hertzog, C., Van Alstine, J., Usala, P. D., Hultsch, D. F. and Dixon, R. (1990). Measurement properties of the Center for Epidemiological Studies Depression Scale (CESD) in older populations. *Psychological Assessment*, **2**, 64–72.

Kendall, P. C. and Flannery-Schroeder, E. C. (1995). Rigor, but not rigor mortis in depression research. *Journal of Personality and Social Psychology*, **68**, 892–894.

LeBlanc, J., Almudevar, A., Brooks, S. and Kutcher, S. (2002). Screening for Adolescent Depression: comparison of the Kutcher Adolescent Depression Scale with the Beck Depression Inventory. *J Child Adolesc Psychopharmacol*, **12**(2), 113–26.

Lord, F. M. (1980). *Applications of Item Response Theory to Practical Testing Problems*. Hillsdale, NJ: Erlbaum.

Marsh, H. W. and Hocevar, D. (1985). Application of confirmatory factor analysis to the study of self-concept: first- and higher order factor models and their invariance across groups. *Psychological Bulletin*, **97**, 562–582.

McCallion, P. and Kolomer, S. R. (2000). Depressive symptoms among African American caregiving grandmothers: The factor structure of the CES-D. *Journal of Mental Health and Aging*, **6**(4), 325–338.

Metz, C. E. (1978). Basic principles of ROC analysis. *Sem Nuc Med*, **8**, 283–298.

Radloff, L. S. (1977). The CES-D scale: A self-report depression scale for research in the general population. *Applied Psychological Measurement*, **1**, 385–401.

Roberts, R. E., Lewinsohn, P. M. and Seeley, J. R. (1991). Screening for adolescent depression: A comparison of scales. *Journal of the American Academy of Child Adolescent Psychiatry*, **30**, 1, 58–66.

Santor, D. A. and Coyne, J. C. (1997). Shortening the CES-D to improve its ability to detect cases of depression. *Psychological Assessment*, **9**, 233–243.

Santor, D. A. and Coyne, J. C. (2001). Evaluating the continuity of symptomatology between depressed and nondepressed individuals. *Journal of Abnormal Psychology*, **110**, 216–225.

Santor, D. A., Gregus, M. and Welch, A. (2002). Eight decades of measurement in depression. Manuscript under review.

Santor, D. A., Ramsay, J. O. and Zuroff, D. C. (1994). Nonparametric item analyses of the Beck Depression Inventory. Examining item bias and response option weights in clinical and nonclinical samples. *Psychological Assessment*, **6**, 255–270.

Santor, D. A., Zuroff, D. C. and Fielding, A. (1997). Analysis and revision of the DEQ: Examining scale performance as a function of scale length. *Journal of Personality Assessment*, **69**, 145–163.

Santor, D. A., Zuroff, D. C., Ramsay, J. O., Cervantes, P. and Palacios, J. (1995). Examining scale discriminability in the BDI and CES-D as a function of depressive severity. *Psychological Assessment*, 7, 131–139.

Sayer, N. A., Sackhein, H. A., Moeller, J. R., Prudic, J., Devanand, D. P., Coleman, E. A. and Kiersky, J. E. (1993). The relations between observer-rating and self-report of depressive symptomatology. *Psychological Assessment*, 5, 350–360.

Sheehan, T. J., Fifield, J., Reisine, S. and Tennen, H. (1995). The measurement structure of the Center for Epidemiologic Studies Depression Scale. *Journal of Personality Assessment*, 64, 507–521.

Tennen, H., Hall, J. A. and Affleck, G. (1995a). Depression research methodologies in the *Journal of Personality and Social Psychology: A review and critique. Journal of Personality and Social Psychology*, 68, 870–884.

Tennen, H., Hall, J. A. and Affleck, G. (1995b). Rigor, Rigor Mortis, and Conspiratorial Views of Depression Research. *Journal of Personality and Social Psychology*, 68, 895–900.

United States Preventive Services Task Force (1996). *Guide to Preventive Services. Second Edition.* Baltimore, MD: Williams and Wilkins.

van der Linden, W. J. and Hambleton, R. K. (1997). *Handbook of Modern Item Response Theory.* New York: Springer.

Verdier-Taillefer, M.-H., Gourlet, V., Fuhrer, R. and Alperovitch, A. (2001). Psychometric properties of the Center for Epidemiologic Studies – Depression Scale in multiple sclerosis. *Neuroepidemiology*, 20, 262–267.

Viglione, D. J., Lovette, G. J. and Gottlieb, R. (1995). Depressive Experiences Questionnaire: Exploration of the underlying theory. *Journal of Personality Assessment*, 65, 91–99.

Vredenburg, K., Flett, G. L. and Krames, L. (1993). Analog versus clinical depression: A clinical reappraisal, *Psychological Bulletin*, 113, 327–344.

Weary, G., Edwards, J. A. and Jacobson, J. A. (1995). Depression research in the *Journal of Personality and Social Psychology*: A reply. *Journal of Personality and Social Psychology*, 68(5), 885–891.

Welkowitz, J., Lish, J. D. and Bond, R. N. (1985). The depressive experiences questionnaire: Revision and validation. *Journal of Personality Assessment*, 49, 89–94.

Wong, Yin-Ling, I. (2000). Measurement properties of the Center for Epidemiologic Studies – Depression Scale in a homeless population. *Psychological Assessment*, 12, 69–76.

Woodworth, R. S. (1918). *Dynamic Psychology.* New York: Columbia University Press.

Chapter 9

The use of diary methodologies in health and clinical psychology

Eamonn Ferguson

Introduction

Psychology, epidemiology and the behavioural sciences have devoted considerable research effort and resources into sampling people and variables but relatively less into sampling time and daily experiences. However, there is now a growing body of research exploring daily experiences and temporal patterns (see Bolger, Davis and Rafaeli, 2003). These techniques are particularly important for clinical and health psychology as many of the phenomenon (e.g., fluctuations in symptoms) and theories (e.g., transactional model of stress) have a strong temporal component or relate to daily experiences (e.g., the nature of social interactions). These daily and temporal experiences need to be examined to develop theory and inform practice (e.g., Tennen, Affleck, Armeli and Carney, 2000).

In an attempt to explore these issues researchers have turned increasingly to the use of diary methods (e.g., Aitken *et al.*, 1994; Thiele, Laireiter and Baumann, 2002). Diary methods basically involve sequentially collecting data on individuals within a temporal framework such as a day (Breakwell and Wood, 1995). Therefore, diaries allow for behaviour to be explored *in situ*, as close as possible to its actual occurrence, and thus, to an extent, reduce retrospective biases (Reis and Gable, 2000). Reis and Gable (2000) further argue that diaries have an important role to play in theory development and the generation of novel hypotheses.

Typically, diaries are also used to explore:

1   The frequency with which a particular phenomenon occurs,

2   The temporal (or causal) structure of events and

3   Assess the efficacy of interventions in clinical trials (cf. Thiele *et al.*, 2002).

This chapter will examine the methodological and statistical issues as well as problems associated with diary research and conclude with examples of how diaries can be used in health/clinical research and practice.

Methodological issues

Types of diaries

Thiele *et al.* (2002) suggest that diaries may be described and characterised by four types of registration:[1]

1 object,

2 mode,

3 trigger and

4 distance.

The object is the theoretical or therapeutic focus of the diary (e.g., pain). The mode is the method of data collection (e.g., pencil and paper). The trigger is either (1) the occurrence of a particular event or (2) specified time interval or (3) a signal from the researcher (e.g., bleeper). Finally, distance refers to whether or not the registration of the behaviour is immediate or delayed. Wheeler and Reis (1991) distinguished three main diary types by combining triggers and distance.

Event contingent

Event contingent diaries require the participant to make their responses every time a specific predefined event (e.g., social interaction) occurs, over the specified duration of the study. This technique is especially suited to the study of infrequent and well-defined events (e.g., smoking), and can be used to estimate event prevalence (see Reis and Gable, 2000; Thiele *et al.*, 2002). The trigger here is the event and the registration is immediate.

Interval contingent

Interval contingent diaries maybe fixed (e.g., the same time a.m. and p.m. every day) or random (e.g., two time intervals each day) occasion diaries and require the individual to record their behaviours and cognitions over a particular specified time period. For example, with a fixed time interval of a day, participants would be asked at the end of each day to complete the diary form. This would be repeated each day for a number of days or weeks. Therefore, some retrospective bias may be present. Wheeler and Reis (1991) argue that the extent of this bias is related to the nature of the phenomenon being studied as well as the time interval between the occurrence of the phenomenon and its registration, with the problem being reduced the more often ratings are provided. Indeed, using interval-contingent diaries participants can record their current behaviours at pre-specified intervals. In this case the intervals are often of shorter durations (e.g., hours).

This diary design is especially useful for behaviours that: (1) are frequent, (2) do not have definitive start and end points and (3) may be either continuous or sporadic, such as mood.

---

[1] Registration refers to registering cognition or behaviours in the diary.

Signal contingent

Signal contingent diary designs require the individual to respond and register their immediate ongoing behaviours every time a signal (usually a bleeper) is given. The trigger is again temporal but the registration is immediate. The sequence of signals is preset by the experimenter. As individuals are reporting their immediate behaviours, retrospective bias is reduced, as are biases that may occur due to completing the diary at a fixed point in the day (e.g., feeling more tired in the evening: Wheeler and Reis, 1991). However, this method is somewhat intrusive, especially as a random signal may go off at times when completing the diary is not convenient. This method is especially suited to recording data on the distribution, frequency and duration of events (see Thiele *et al.*, 2002).

Measurement techniques

Three types of measurement technique are generally used in diary studies: (1) open-ended, (2) rating scales and (3) checklists (Reis and Gable, 2000; Thiele, *et al.*, 2002). These techniques can be used in combination. For example, it is possible to have participants provide free responses for a particular class of event (e.g., odours) and then rate this for duration and intensity using rating scales (see Ferguson, Cassaday and Bibby, 2004). Similarly, checklists can be used to identify which of a series of events or behaviours has occurred and then to provide additional quantitative ratings of these. For example, the presence or absence of symptoms may be noted and then these may be rated for the severity to which they were experienced (cf. Ferguson, Cassaday, Erskind and Delahaye, 2004).

The duration–frequency decision

How long should the diary study last (duration) and how often (frequency) should behaviours be sampled? In one sense this is dictated by the pragmatics of the study, such as financial and personnel resources as well as participant burden. However, theoretical and methodological considerations should also inform this decision.

Theoretically, the nature of the phenomena under study should be considered. For example, shorter intervals may be more appropriate for studying mood and performance (e.g., Stone, Smyth, Pickering and Schwartz, 1996), with longer intervals for stress and health (David and Suls, 1999). It has also been recommended that intervals, which are logically intuitive and that participants may use to describe their behaviour (e.g., days), should be also considered (see Reis and Gable, 2000). Statistical issues of power (see Hox, 2002 and below) and choice of analytic procedure (see West and Hepworth, 1991) should be considered. Finally, more basic research to identify the natural cycles and temporal organization in diary data over different time intervals and for different constructs (e.g., mood, symptom reporting) would help to inform such design decisions (cf. Affleck *et al.*, 1999).

Participant motivation

Completing diary protocols can be very burdensome on participants. As such, time should be spent with the participants explaining their role in the research programme, why their cooperation is important, and frequent contact maintained with participants through out the study (e.g., researcher present, emails, telephone calls) (Reis and Gable, 2000). Financial or other incentives may also help.

Reactivity

Reactivity refers to the general phenomenon whereby repeated assessments of behaviours or events alters the participants experience of those behaviours or events (see Affleck et al., 1999; Reis and Gable, 2000). The problem is inherent in all repeated measures studies, including experimental studies (Keren, 1993). Reis and Gable (2000) suggest that the problem is minimal, citing studies showing that those who keep diaries do not have different retrospective reports to those that do not keep diaries (see also Affleck et al., 1999; Litt, Cooney and Morse, 1998). However, researchers can check data to see if reactivity is present. One method is to test the data for trends over the course of the diary. If trends are absent then this may, in part, be taken as evidence that reactivity did not occur (e.g., over the course of a study on symptom reporting the participants did not become more aware of their symptoms). However, Affleck et al. (1999) point out that absence of a trend may reflect other 'biases' that work against reactivity (e.g., participant boredom and fatigue, individual differences). Methodologically, reactivity may be reduced somewhat by ensuring that diaries are returned after each entry or computer files are locked to prevent participants reviewing previous responses.

Power

There is a wide range of sample sizes (N) used in diary studies ranging from numbers in the low tens to the low hundreds, as well as a variety of sampled (1) time intervals (T: days, weeks, months) and (2) frequency of assessments within those intervals. Thus issues of power and reliability are complex questions with respect to diary studies. Hox (2002) provides a detailed discussion of the issues and there is useful advice available in Snijders and Bosker (1999). There is also a piece of free software (PINT: Power in two level models) for power calculations that can be found at http://stat.gamma.rug.nl/snijders/multilevel.htm.

There are many pragmatic reasons why large samples may be difficult to achieve. For example, certain clinical groups may be rare, difficult to access or due to the nature of their problems find completing diaries more burdensome. In such cases, a strong theoretical model from which specific hypotheses can be derived is a useful guard against spurious results. Also in such cases, especially where the theoretical basis is less strong, replication is important (e.g., two distinct but small samples).

Methods of data collection

There are a number of ways of recording diary data (see also Bolger *et al.*, 2003). The relative strengths and weaknesses of the four most common methods are discussed briefly.

Pencil and paper

The main advantage here is the participant's familiarity with the method. The main disadvantage is confirming accurate compliance.

Palm top computers

The main advantages include: (1) economic storage and downloading of data, (2) accuracy in timings (i.e., the computer records the time of data entry). The main disadvantages with this approach include: (1) the high levels of technical support needed (in case of damage), (2) time spent training the participants to use the computers, (3) the frequent contact needed between participants and researchers and (4) matching the participant's computer skills to the task (cf. Feldman-Barrett and Barrett, 2001; Thiele *et al.*, 2002).

Computer disks

This is becoming a more popular and important technique and involves the participants being provided with a computer diskette, which contains the files for each interval of the diary (e.g., Nezlek, 2002). Participants complete each file separately (e.g., at the end of each day) and the computer logs the time and date of completion. The file can then be automatically locked so that the participant cannot view (or alter) their previous responses. A number of the issues associated with the palm top computers also apply here, as do the advantages. However, this technique is limited to people with computer access and as such wider scale population or clinical studies (at present) have not used this technique. However, this will possibly become an increasingly important methodology in the future.

Email/Internet/mobile phones

The increased use of email, the Internet and mobile phones means that it should be possible to collect diary data using these means. For example, in a daily diary study, participants could be emailed the daily response sheet(s) at the end of each day and asked to email their responses back. As such, timings could be checked for accuracy. At present, many of the technical issues for palm top and PC methods apply here, but again with time these should start to disappear. Specific disadvantages here are the possibility that systems may crash, emails be lost and that not all populations have access to this digital technology (cf. Bolger *et al.*, 2003).

Compliance and causality

Diary methods are particularly useful for helping to infer causality when observing systems that cannot be directly manipulated (see West and Hepworth, 1991). That is, like other sciences such as astronomy, where only observation is currently possible, evidence for causality may be inferred between X and Y if (1) either linear or non-linear relationships exist, (2) temporal precedence between X and Y is shown and (3) confounding with spurious variables is eliminated (Kenny, 1979). Therefore, it is important that participants keep to the diary protocol, completing the assessments when they are instructed to do so (i.e., show compliance).

For example, it has been recommended in relation to fixed interval daily diary studies, that data are returned at the end of each day (see Reis and Gable, 2000). However, some researchers have had returns scheduled bi-weekly (Gunthert, Choen and Armeli, 1999). Others allow the participants to keep the diary and return it at the end of the study (e.g., David, Green, Martin and Suls, 1997; David and Suls, 1999; Fuligni, Yip and Tseng, 2002). However, it is worth noting that when different return protocols are used (daily versus end of study), in general similar patterns of results are reported (e.g., Gable, Reis and Elliot 2000; Marco and Suls, 1993).

What is the effect of non-compliance on results? Gable *et al.* (2000) showed the same pattern of results across three studies when non-compliance was not controlled and when it was controlled in different ways (removing non-compliant participants or non-compliant days). More specific studies are needed the effects of compliance on patterns of results. However, when the aim of the research is to infer causality then temporal compliance is required. When this is not possible, for example because of sampling constraints, it should be acknowledged. With fixed interval daily diaries daily returns are an important way to index compliance and with event and signal contin-gent diaries electronic palm top computers are essential (cf. Stone and Shiffman, 2002).

What is the extent of non-compliance? Recent empirical work has shown that partic-ipants overestimate their compliance compared to post-diary interviews (Litt *et al.*, 1998) and computerised records (Stone, Shiffman, Schwartz, Broderick and Hufford, 2002). The Stone *et al.* (2002) study showed that with a paper and pencil diary making four fixed interval assessments each day the reported compliance was 90 per cent and the actual compliance was 11 per cent. Based on daily return rates compliance is higher for single fixed interval daily diary (see Gable *et al.* 2000). Therefore, while these stud-ies mark an important start in studying compliance, future work needs to explore factors (design and motivational) that might influence compliance (cf. Bolger *et al.*, 2003). For example, is compliance better for paper and pencil diaries when multiple assessments made within a day are returned daily rather than returned bi-weekly or weekly? Are certain groups (e.g., patients) more motivated to provide accurate data than other groups (e.g., healthy students)?

Researchers could also incorporate design parameters to try and increase compliance. One possibility might be to use a 'bogus pipeline' procedure. Participants could be told that the paper diary or computer disk has a chip in it that records the time of entry and that this will be checked against the time they actually enter on the diary (cf. Nezlek and Plesko, 2001).

Data analysis

Hierarchies in data

Data collected in field studies (and experimental studies for that matter), due to either sampling or the nature of the study design, often conform to hierarchies (Snijders and Bosker, 1999). For example, in a daily diary study of the effects of stress on health, both measures of stress and health may be collected on a daily basis. These daily assessments are nested within each individual contributing to the diary. Information on each individual's personality, for example, can be collected. In this example the daily assessments represent what is often referred to as Level 1 variables and the personality scores to Level 2 variables. The point of any analysis is not just to understand the within subject Level 1 relationships, but how these might be modified by the Level 2 (between-subjects) variables (this has similarities with the longitudinal data analysis, described by Adamson and Bunting, this volume – the level 1 variables are the measurements, the level 2 variable is the random assignment. There are links between the methods described in this chapter, and the methods used by Adamson and Bunting: however each has its own advantages – see Raudenbush, 2001).

The data collected in diary studies has a number of features that need to be accounted for in the analytic procedures. These primarily include (1) the hierarchical nature of the data and (2) serial dependency, typically among Level 1 variables. Two techniques used to deal with these issues – multilevel modelling (MLM) and time series analysis – are described briefly below.

Multilevel modelling

This technique allows for both between subject and the within subjects observations to be treated as independent observations and analysed simultaneously. Both Affleck *et al.* (1999) and Nezlek (2001) warn that when a complete data set has both between and within subjects observation, misleading results may emerge if only one of these levels is analysed.

The basic principles of MLM

MLM produces *intercept* coefficients (i.e., the mean level of the DV at a specific level in the analysis) and *slope* coefficients (i.e., the relationship between variables within a level). These outputs at one level become the parameters that are modelled/analysed at the next level. Basically the regression coefficients from one level are treated as the DV at the next level (cf. Nezlek, 2001).

Building a MLM

Three main issues will be discussed:

1 unconditional to conditional modelling

2 centring and

3 random or fixed effects.

Raudenbush and Bryk (2002) refer to the *fully unconditional* model as one where there are no predictors at Level 1 or Level 2, only the Level 1 intercept is modelled. They distinguish this from the *unconditional Level 2* model where there are no Level 2 predictors, but both the intercept and slopes are modelled at Level 1. Finally, '*conditional*' models may be specified where relationships observed at Level 1 are 'modified' by Level 2 variables. The unconditional models allow the analyst to calculate the percentage of variance in the model accounted for by additional steps in the analysis.[2]

Another decision that has to be made refers to where the reference point for a predictor is placed. This is known as *centring*. There are three options: (1) the natural metric (no centring), (2) group mean centring and (3) grand mean centring (see Raudenbush and Bryk, 2002; Snijders and Bosker, 1999). The natural metric should be used if the variable has a meaningful zero (or is a dummy variable), and in this case the outcome variable score is the expected score when the predictor is equal to zero (cf. Raudenbush and Bryk, 2002).[3] Group and grand mean centring allow for raw scores to be adjusted relative to these means. Such that the intercepts are the expected score when the predictors are equal to either the group means or grand mean. A number of discussion on which centring option to use have been published and the interested reader is referred to these (Raudenbush and Bryk, 2002; Kreft, de Leeuw and Aiken, 1995; Reis and Gable, 2000).

Finally, the Level 1 coefficients can be modelled at Level 2 as either fixed or allowed to vary randomly. Theoretical as well as the type of inference the researcher wishes to make about the data should guide this choice. Snijders and Boskers (1999, pp. 43–45) discuss some of these issues in more detail.

For a fuller explanation of these techniques the reader should consult one of the following texts: Raudenbush and Bryk (2002), Snijders and Bosker (1999), Nezlek (2001), or Leyland and Goldstein (2001).

MLM: a brief (simplified) example

Imagine that daily diary data on appraisals of stress and symptom reporting are collected from a number of individuals over a four-day period (these are the level 1 variables). For each individual, data is also collected on neuroticism, prior to starting the diary (this is a level 2 variable). Using this hierarchical data set a number of theoretical questions can be asked. For example: 'Are daily negative appraisals of stress associated with daily levels of symptom reporting?' If the level 1 slope coefficient is significant and positive, then the answer is yes. Furthermore, this indicates that more symptoms are reported when stress in appraised more negatively.

---

[2] The difference between deviance statistics at different stages in a models development can be used to check if additional parameters add significantly to the model (see Snijders and Bosker, 1999).

[3] Un-centred variables may cause problems in terms of accurate coefficient estimation due to high correlations between intercepts and slopes.

A subsequent question might be: 'Is the relationship between appraisals and symptom reporting stronger for those individual with higher scores on neuroticism?' A positive and significant level 2 coefficient for the level 1 slope term with respect to neuroticism (referred to as a cross-level interaction) would indicate that those who score higher on neuroticism express or experience a stronger relationship between stress appraisals and symptom reporting.

Time series analysis

Time series analysis is a useful technique when the interval between assessments is equal and the number of intervals is large (50 plus) (cf. Wheeler and Reis, 1991). The basic idea of time series analysis is to build a model that describes the temporal pattern within a single variable or between two variables (cross-correlations). McDowall, McCleary, Meidinger and Hay (1980) describe the model building process as having three iterative stages.

Identification

This involves identifying the sources of variability that need to be taken account of in the time series model. These include: trends (e.g., steady upward drift over time), seasonality (e.g., variation due to time of year, month) and serial dependency (e.g., correlations between the error terms of adjacent temporal measures). Detailed description of these tools is beyond the scope of this chapter and the reader should refer to one of the following texts: Brown and Moskowitz (1998); Jaccard and Wan (1993); McDowall et al. (1980); West and Hepworth (1991).

Estimation

Based on the identification stage the analyst develops a model to try and explain the data. A good model should be parsimonious, have parameters that are statistically significant and within reasonable limits. Auto-Regressive-Integrated-Moving-Average (ARIMA) models are the most commonly used in this context.

Diagnosis

Finally, the residuals from the model can be analysed to check if they are un-correlated (i.e., random). This would indicate that the meaningful variability in the series has been accounted for.

An excellent example of the application of time series analysis to mood data can be found in Larsen and Kasimatis (1990).

Diaries in clinical and health psychology practice

Thiele et al. (2002) note that diary methods are one of the most widely used tools in behavioural therapy. In relation to interventions they suggest that diaries can be used at the start as a behavioural assessment to guide design as well as to monitor the course and outcome effectiveness of an intervention. Thiele et al. (2002) suggest that self-monitoring the behaviour may itself change the frequency of the behaviour (cf. the reactivity issue). This statement seems at odds with the comments made above on reactivity. However, diaries may work in a therapeutic setting only for certain individuals (cf. Affleck *et al.*, 1999) or when they are used as the basis of one-to-one feedback, where the participant is instructed to pay attention to their diary ratings.

Within the field of health psychology diaries are less frequently used therapeutically. However, given one of health psychology's foci is on behaviour change (e.g., smoking cessation), the use of diaries as a potential intervention should be considered. In particular, diaries may be used to identify triggers to disorders, which can subsequently be avoided (e.g., Klassen and Dooley, 2000)

Diaries in clinical and health psychology research

Within more clinically focused work, diaries have been applied to the study of

- Depression (Nezlek and Gable, 2001)
- Schizophrenia (e.g., Myin-Germeys, Krabbendam, Jolles, Delepaul and van Os, 2002) and
- Bulimia (Steiger, Gauvin, Jabalpurwala, Seguin and Stotland, 1999).

As for more traditional health, psychology diaries have been applied to issues in

- Health behaviours (Duncan, Jones and Moon, 1993)
- Cystitis (Rothrock *et al.*, 2001) and
- Diabetes (Aitken *et al.*, 1994).

Conclusions

From the above descriptions it will be apparent that diary methods are very labour intensive and time-consuming (for both researchers and participants). However, as Wheeler and Reis (1991) point out, the benefits and richness of the data should outweigh this barrier to diary research. Finally, diaries should be viewed as complementary to experimental and survey research (cf. Reis and Gable, 2000).

Further reading

These authors provide detailed further reading, developing on the points made in this chapter.

Affleck, G., Zautra, A., Tennen, H. and Armeli, S. (1999). Multilevel daily process designs for consulting and clinical psychology: a preface for the perplexed. *Journal of Consulting and Clinical Psychology*, **67**, 46–754.

Hox, J. (2002). *Multilevel Analysis: Techniques and Applications*. Lawrence Erlbaum Associates, London.

Jaccard, J. and Wan, C. K. (1993). Statistical analysis of temporal data with many observations: Issues for behavioural medicine data. *Annals of Behavioural Medicine*, **15**, 41–50.

Leyland, A. and Goldstein, H. (2001). *Multilevel Modelling of Health Statistics*. Chichester, Wiley.

McDowall, D., McCleary, R., Meidinger, E. E. and Hay, R. A. Jnr. (1980). *Interrupted Time Series Analysis*. Sage, London.

Nezlek, J. B. (2001). Multilevel random coefficients analyses of event- and interval-contingent data in social and personality psychology research. *Personality and Social Psychology Bulletin*, **27**, 771–785.

Raudenbush, S. W. and Bryk, A. S. (2002). *Hierarchical Linear Models*, 2nd edn. Sage, London.

Reis, H. T. and Gable, S. L. (2000). Event-sampling and other methods of studying everyday experiences. In H. T. Reis and C. M. Judd (eds) *Handbook of Research Methods in Social and Personality Psychology*, pp. 190–279. Cambridge University Press.

Snijders, T. and Bosker, R. (1999). *Multilevel Analysis: An Introduction to Basic and Advanced Multilevel Modelling*. Sage, London.

Stone, A. A. and Schiffman, S. (2002). Capturing momentary, self-report data: A proposal for reporting guidelines. *Annals of Behavioral Medicine*, **24**, 236–243.

Thiele, C., Laireiter, A. R. and Baumann, U. (2002). Diaries in clinical psychology and psychotherapy: a selective review. *Clinical Psychology and Psychotherapy*, **9**, 1–37.

West, S. G. and Hepworth, J. T. (1991). Statistical issues in the study of temporal data: Daily experiences. *Journal of Personality*, **59**, 609–661.

References

Affleck, G., Zautra, A., Tennen, H. and Armeli, S. (1999). Multilevel daily process designs for consulting and clinical psychology: A preface for the perplexed. *Journal of Consulting and Clinical Psychology*, **67**, 46–754.

Aitken, J. E., Wallander, J. L., Bell, D. S. and McNorton, A. (1994). A nomothetic-idiographic study if daily psychological stress and blood glucose in woman with type I diabetes mellitus. *Journal of Behavioural Medicine*, **17**, 535–548.

Bolger, N., Davis, A. and Rafaeli, E. (2003). Diary methods: Capturing life as it is lived. *Annual Review of Psychology*, **54**, 579–616.

Breakwell, G. M. and Wood, P. (1995). Diary techniques. In G. M. Breakwell, S. Hammond, and C. Fife-Schaw (eds) *Research Methods in Psychology*, pp. 293–301. Sage, London.

Brown, K. W. and Moskowitz, D. S. (1998). It's a function of time: A review of the process approach to behavioural medicine research. *Annals of behavioural Medicine*, **20**, 109–117.

David, J. P. and Suls, J. (1999). Coping efforts in daily life: Role of big five traits and problem appraisals. *Journal of Personality*, **67**, 265–294.

David, J. P., Green, P. J., Martin, R. and Suls, J. (1997). Differential roles of neuroticism, extraversion and event desirability for mood in daily life: An integrative model of top-down and bottom-up influences. *Journal of Personality and Social Psychology*, **73**, 149–159.

Duncan,C., Jones, K. and Moon, G. (1993). Do places matter? A multi-level analysis of regional variations in health related behaviour in Britain. *Social Science and Medicine*, **37**, 725–733.

Feldman-Barret, L. and Barrett, D. J. (2001). An introduction to computerized experience sampling in psychology. *Social Science Computer Review*, **19**, 175–185.

Ferguson, E., Cassaday, H. J., Erskind, J. and Delahaye, G. (2004). Individual differences in the temporal variability in medically unexplained symptom reporting. *British Journal of Health Psychology*, **9**, 219–240.

Ferguson, E., Cassaday, H. J. and Bibby, P. (2004). Odors and sounds as triggers for medically unexplained symptoms: A fixed occasion diary study of in Gulf War veterans. *Annals of Behavioral Medicine*, **27**, 205–214.

Fuligni, A. J., Yip, T. and Tseng, V. (2002). The impact of family obligation on the daily activities and psychological well-being of Chinese American Adolescents. *Child Development*, **73**, 302–314.

Gable, S. L., Reis, H. T. and Elliot, A. J. (2000). Behavioural activation and inhibition in everyday life. *Journal of Personality and Social Psychology*, **78**, 1135–1149.

Gunthert, K. C., Choen, L. H. and Armeli, S. (1999). The role of neuroticism in daily stress and coping. *Journal of Personality and Social Psychology*, **77**, 1087–1100.

Hox, J. (2002). *Multilevel Analysis: Techniques and Applications*. Lawrence Erlbaum Associates, London.

Jaccard, J. and Wan, C. K. (1993). Statistical analysis of temporal data with many observations: Issues for behavioural medicine data. *Annals of Behavioural Medicine*, **15**, 41–50.

Kenny, D. A. (1979). *Correlation and Causation*. New York: Wiley-Interscience.

Keren, G. (1993). Between- or within-subjects design: a methodological dilemma. In G. Keren and C. Lewis (eds) *A Handbook for Data Analysis in the Behavioral Sciences – Volume* 1: *Methodological Issues*. Hillsdale, NJ, Erlbaum. pp. 257–72.

Klassen, B. D. and Dooley, J. M. (2000). Chronic paroxysmal hemicrania-like headaches in a child: Response to a headache diary. *Headache*, **40**, 853–855.

Kreft, I. G. G., de Leeuw, J. and Aiken, L. S. (1995). The effect of different forms of centering in hierarchical linear models. *Multivariate Behavioural Research*, **30**, 1–21.

Larsen, R. J. and Kasimatis, M. (1990). Individual differences in entrainment of mood to the weekly calendar. *Journal of Personality and Social Psychology*, **58**, 164–171.

Leyland, A. and Goldstein, H. (2001). *Multilevel Modelling of Health Statistics*. Chichester, Wiley.

Litt, M. D., Cooney, N. L. and Morse, P. (1998). Ecological momentary assessment (EMA) with treated alcoholics: Methodological problems and potential solutions. *Health Psychology*, **17**, 48–52.

Marco, C. A. and Suls, J. (1993). Daily stress and the trajectory of mood: Spillover, response assimilation, contrast, and chronic negative affectivity. *Journal of Personality and Social Psychology*, **64**, 1053–1063.

McDowall, D., McCleary, R., Meidinger, E. E. and Hay, R. A. Jnr. (1980). *Interrupted Time Series Analysis*. Sage, London.

Myin-Germeys, I., Krabbendam, L., Jolles, J., Delepaul, P. A. and van Os, J. (2002). Are cognitive impairemnets associated with sensitivity to stress in schizopghrenia? An experience sampling study. *American Journal of Psychiatry*, **159**, 443–449.

Nezlek, J. B. (2001). Multilevel random coefficients analyses of event- and interval-contingent data in social and personality psychology research. *Personality and Social Psychology Bulletin*, **27**, 771–785.

Nezlek, J. B. (2002). Day-to-day relationships between self-awareness, daily events, and anxiety. *Journal of Personality*, **70**, 249–275.

Nezlek, J. B. and Gable, S. L. (2001). Depression as a moderator of relationships between positive daily events and day-to-day psychological adjustment. *Personality and Social Psychological Bulletin*, **27**, 1692–1704.

Nezlek, J. B. and Plesko, R. M. (2001). Day-to-day relationship among self-concept clarity, self-esteem, daily events and mood. *Personality and Social Psychological Bulletin*, **27**, 201–211.

Raudenbush, S. (2001). Toward a coherent framework for comparing trajectories of individual change. In L. M. Collins and A. G. Sayer (eds) *New Methods for the Analysis of Change*. Washington, DC, American Psychological Association. pp. 35–64.

Raudenbush, S. W. and Bryk, A. S. (2002). *Hierarchical Linear Models*, 2nd edn. Sage, London.

Reis, H. T. and Gable, S. L. (2000). Event-sampling and other methods of studying everyday experiences. In H. T. Reis and C. M. Judd (eds) *Handbook of Research Methods in Social and Personality Psychology*, pp. 190–279. New York: Cambridge University Press.

Rothrock, N. E., Lutgendorf, S. K., Kreder, K., J., Ratliff, T. and Zimmerman, B. (2001). Stress and symptoms in patients with interstitial cystitis: A life stress model. *Urology*, **57**, 422–427.

Snijders, T. and Bosker, R. (1999). *Multilevel Analysis: An Introduction to Basic and Advanced Multilevel Modelling*. Sage, London.

Steiger, H., Gauvin, L., Jabalpurwala, S., Seguin, J. R. and Stotland, S. (1999). Hypersensitivity to social interactions in bulimic syndromes: Relationship to binge eating. *Journal of Consulting and Clinical Psychology*, **67**, 765–775.

Stone, A. A. and Schiffman, S. (2002). Capturing momentary, self-report data: A proposal for reporting guidelines. *Annals of Behavioral Medicine*, **24**, 236–243.

Stone, A. A., Schiffman, S., Schwartz, J. E., Broderick, J. E. and Hufford, M. R. (2002). Patient non-compliance with paper diaries. *British Medical Journal*, **324**, 1193–4.

Stone, A. A., Smyth, J. M., Pickering, T. and Schwartz, J. (1996). Daily mood variability: From diurnal patterns to determinants of diurnal patterns. *Journal of Applied Social Psychology*, **26**, 1286–1305.

Tennen, H., Affleck, G., Armeli, S. and Carney, M. A. (2000). A daily process approach to coping. *American Psychologist*, **55**, 626–636.

Thiele, C., Laireiter, A. R. and Baumann, U. (2002). Diaries in clinical psychology and psychotherapy: a selective review. *Clinical Psychology and Psychotherapy*, **9**, 1–37.

West, S. G. and Hepworth, J. T. (1991). Statistical issues in the study of temporal data: Daily experiences. *Journal of Personality*, **59**, 609–661.

Wheeler, L. and Reis, H. T. (1991). Self-recoding of everyday life events: Origins, types and uses. *Journal of Personality*, **59**, 339–354.

Chapter 10

Analysis of repertory grids in clinical practice

Chris Leach and Kate Freshwater

This chapter's main aim is to provide an account of some of the forms of analysis of repertory grid data, illustrating strengths, weaknesses and appropriate use of the various methods currently available and commenting on the pitfalls of inappropriate analysis. A detailed analysis is presented of repertory grids completed by a client at various stages of group therapy. We also suggest computer packages to perform the analyses, providing illustrative commands in SYSTAT to allow the analyses to be replicated.

The woman whose data form the case study participated in a group for survivors of child sexual abuse facilitated by one of the authors (KF) together with a male clinical psychologist (for further details, see Freshwater *et al.*, 2001). Sarah (whose name has been changed to protect confidentiality) and the other group members completed individual repertory grids before group therapy, after therapy and at three- and six-month follow-up. For each grid, a list of elements was provided. These were Child self (CS), Self now (SN), Ideal self (IS), Mother (Mo), Father (Fa), Abuser in childhood (AC), Partner (Pa), Men in general (MG) and Women in general (WG). To rate Ideal self, group members were asked simply to consider 'myself as I would like to be'. In some settings, it may be preferable to ground this concept by saying something like 'imagine how you would like to be if everything went as well as you would like over the next two or three years'.

Sarah was asked to rate these nine elements on 7-point scales using 11 provided constructs and 3 constructs of her own, elicited using the standard triadic procedure (Bannister and Fransella, 1980). This involved selecting three of the elements at a time and asking for an important way in which any two of the three were alike and different from the third. The triads of elements were selected arbitrarily, with an attempt to control replications by using a balanced incomplete block design. For some purposes, it may be helpful to select element triads systematically, so that, for example, some comparisons involve only family members, while others cut across different groups. In some settings, different forms of elicitation might be helpful (such as the computerised elicitation procedure based on pairs of elements discussed by Keen and Bell, 1980).

The balanced incomplete block design used here to select triads was drawn from the design for selecting three items out of ten, as there is no design for selecting three items

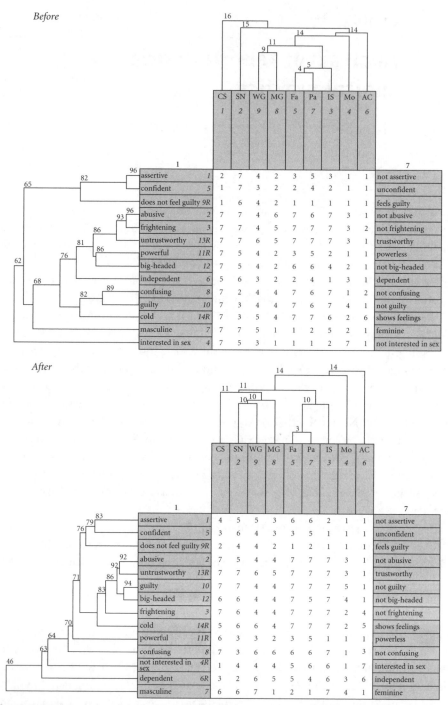

Fig. 10.1 Sarah's rearranged repertory grids before and after therapy with single link Hierarchical Cluster Analysis (HCA) trees for elements and constructs. CS = Child self; SN = Self now; WG = Women in general; MG = Men in general; Fa = Father; Pa = Partner; IS = Ideal self; Mo = Mother; AC = Abuser in childhood.

out of nine (see Cochran and Cox, 1957). The full design involves the following thirty triples:

1. *1 2 3*	6. *4 6 9*	11. *1 2 4*	16. *6 8 9*	21. *1 3 5*	26. *1 6 8*
2. *2 5 8*	7. *1 7 9*	12. *2 3 6*	17. *3 7 10*	22. *2 6 7*	27. *2 7 9*
3. *3 4 7*	8. *2 8 10*	13. *3 4 8*	18. *1 8 10*	23. *3 8 9*	28. *4 7 8*
4. *1 4 6*	9. *3 9 10*	14. *4 5 9*	19. *2 5 9*	24. *2 4 10*	29. *1 9 10*
5. *5 7 8*	10. *5 6 10*	15. *1 5 7*	20. *6 7 10*	25. *3 5 6*	30. *4 5 10*

It is called balanced because each pair appears twice in the thirty selections. For Sarah's grid, triples were selected at random from these thirty, excluding those with item 10.

For Sarah and the other group members, the same elements and constructs were used for each of the repeated grids. This makes comparison between grids simpler, but does not allow consideration of constructs added or subtracted to a client's repertoire that might happen during therapy. Sarah's constructs are shown in her before and after therapy grids in Figure 10.1.

Analysis of repertory grids – general principles

The aim of any form of analysis of repertory grid data is to make underlying patterns more apparent, as well as emphasising exceptions to these patterns, this dual aim being the key feature of all exploratory data analysis (Tukey, 1979). Table 10.1 shows the various forms of analysis illustrated in this chapter, going from analyses that preserve the full detail of the original grid (at the top) to those that provide a broader picture by blurring the details. Our main messages are:

1 The original grid keeps you closest to the client's words and meanings and is the starting point for making sense of the data;

2 Any attempt at looking for patterns involves making simplifying assumptions, not all of which can be satisfied all of the time;

3 Different forms of analysis make different assumptions, so it helps to do more than one analysis at a time, partly to provide a check on the assumptions and partly to notice different patterns emphasised by the different methods;

4 The same analyses can be used with grids using rating scales (as in our examples), dichotomous grids (e.g., Leach, 1988), or rankings of elements on constructs. In addition, despite some advice to the contrary (e.g., Fransella and Bannister, 1977), lop-sided constructs (those with just one or two elements rated on one construct pole) do not need to be excluded from the analysis, although, in some cases, care is needed with such constructs.

Over the years, most analyses of repertory grids have been determined by the availability of computer programs, the most commonly used being INGRID (Slater, 1977), which

Table 10.1 Levels of analysis of repertory grid data

Level	Data	Type of analysis	Computer programs
1 *Maximum detail*	Original grid	Clinical Skill	GRAN or FOCUS produce rearranged grid to aid interpretation
2	Similarity/dissimilarity measures for elements and constructs	Euclidean distances for elements	SYSTAT, SPSS, S-PLUS or GRAN
		Product-moment correlations for constructs	SYSTAT, SPSS, S-PLUS or GRAN
3	Analysis of elements and constructs separately	Principal Components Analysis	SYSTAT, SPSS S-PLUS
		Hierarchical Cluster Analysis	GRAN, FOCUS, SYSTAT, SPSS or S-PLUS
		Multidimensional Scaling (MDS)	SYSTAT or SPSS
4	Joint analysis of elements and constructs	Biplot	SYSTAT, S-PLUS
		Hierarchical Cluster Analysis	GRAN, FOCUS
		Unfolding Analysis	SYSTAT
		Correspondence Analysis	SYSTAT or SPSS
5 *Broad picture*	Combined analysis of several grids	Individual Differences Scaling (INDSCAL)	SYSTAT
		Unfolding Analysis	SYSTAT or SPSS

is based on a singular-value decomposition of the grid that allows elements and constructs to be plotted in the same space. Various forms of hierarchical cluster analysis have also been used to provide an alternative view of grid structure. These have been made available in programs such as GRAN (Leach, 1988) or FOCUS (Shaw and Thomas, 1978), which have the advantage of preserving the original grid, in rearranged form, as part of the analysis, making them easy to understand for those clients and clinicians with little statistical expertise. Also aimed at those with little statistical expertise are programs that attempt to simplify grid structure but end up giving misleading views (for reasons outlined below), such as GAB (Bannister and Higginbottom, 1983). In recent years, a more extensive range of multivariate statistical procedures has become available in standard statistical packages such as SPSS, SYSTAT or S-PLUS. These include biplots (e.g., Gabriel, 1971, Gower and Hand, 1996), multidimensional scaling (MDS) (e.g., Shepard, 1962a, b), unfolding analysis (e.g., Coombs, 1964) and correspondence analysis (e.g., Greenacre, 1984). These newer techniques are rarely used with grids, but can be helpful, complementary ways of exploring grid structure. We illustrate the use of some of these methods below and provide SYSTAT commands for most of the procedures illustrated. (The easiest way to use SYSTAT for anyone not familiar with the command syntax is to use the drop-down menus and then to discover the syntax implicitly used by clicking on the log tab in the Output Organiser. This can then be compared with the syntax given here.)

Other accounts of newer approaches to grid analysis are available in Shaw (1981) and Bell (1988, 1994). The availability of these methods in standard statistical packages is both a blessing and a problem – it is now easier for anyone to use these fancy statistical methods than it has ever been, but it is also easier than ever to make fundamental mistakes in analysis.

Analysis of Sarah's grids

Sarah, aged 32, was referred with problems of depression and sexual difficulties relating to childhood sexual abuse. She had three children and was living with her male partner. From the age of 9 her brother, an adult, had sexually abused Sarah. She attended a group for survivors of child sexual abuse and completed repertory grids prior to the group, immediately after the group and at three- and six-month follow-up. She also completed other questionnaires at each stage, these being the Beck Depression Inventory (BDI) (Beck *et al.*, 1961), the SCL-90R (Derogatis, 1983), the Rosenberg Self-Esteem Scale (RSE) (Rosenberg, 1965) and the Jehu Belief Inventory (Jehu, 1988). Her pre- and post-therapy BDI scores of 39 and 21 were above the cut-off for clinically significant depression, but by three-month follow-up, her BDI score had dropped to 10, below the cut-off, and dropped further to 4 by six-month follow-up. Sarah's Global Severity Index on the SCL-90R showed a similar pattern, falling from 2.41 before therapy to 1.63 after therapy, 0.50 and 0.39 at three- and six-month follow-ups. Sarah's self-esteem, indexed by the RSE, rose from 13 pre-therapy to 19 post-therapy, followed by a substantial rise to 37 and 38 at three- and six-month follow-ups. Her level of dysfunctional beliefs, measured by the Jehu Belief Inventory, fell substantially post-therapy from 65 to 15, falling further to only 1 at three-month follow-up, with a rise to 8 at six-month follow-up.

Figure 10.1 shows Sarah's complete pre- and post-therapy grids, in the rearranged form provided by the output of GRAN (Leach, 1988), which also includes marginal cluster analyses of the elements and constructs, as described further below. These grids show little separation in the ratings of men and women. Sarah's father (Fa) and partner (Pa) are rated similarly, which matches her verbal report of holding them both in high esteem. Her father was dead and she reported a tendency to idealise him, which shows in the pre-therapy grid with her father rated similarly to her ideal self. Sarah's mother (Mo) and her abuser (Ac) are both rated negatively and outside these other groupings, which is even more apparent in the post-therapy grid. This again corresponds to

Table 10.2 The two variations on Sarah's before grid used for analysis

Original grid as elicited

Original Elements / Label S	Ass	Abu	Fri	Int	Cnf	Ind	Mas	Con	Fee	Gui	Pws	Big	Tru	Sho
CS	2	7	7	7	1	5	7	7	7	7	1	7	1	1
SN	7	7	7	5	7	6	7	2	2	3	3	5	1	5
IS	3	7	7	2	2	1	5	7	7	7	6	4	1	2
Mo	1	3	3	7	1	3	2	1	7	4	7	2	5	6
Fa	3	7	7	1	2	2	1	7	7	7	5	6	1	1
AC	1	1	2	1	1	1	1	2	7	1	7	1	7	2
Pa	5	6	7	1	4	4	2	6	7	6	3	6	1	1
MG	2	6	5	1	2	2	1	4	6	4	6	2	3	4
WG	4	4	4	3	3	3	5	4	4	4	4	4	2	3

Reversed grid (= 8 − Orig)

Reversed	NAs	NAb	NFr	NIn	Unc	Dep	Fem	NCo	NFe	NGu	Pwl	NBi	Unt	Col
CS	6	1	1	1	7	3	1	1	1	1	7	1	7	7
SN	1	1	1	3	1	2	1	6	6	5	5	3	7	3
IS	5	1	1	6	6	7	3	1	1	1	2	4	7	6
Mo	7	5	5	1	7	5	6	7	1	4	1	6	3	2
Fa	5	1	1	7	6	6	7	1	1	1	3	2	7	7
AC	7	7	6	7	7	7	7	6	1	7	1	7	1	6
Pa	3	2	1	7	4	4	6	2	1	2	5	2	7	7
MG	6	2	3	7	6	6	7	4	2	4	2	6	5	4
WG	4	4	4	5	5	5	3	4	4	4	4	4	6	5

CS – Child self, SN – Self now, IS – Ideal self, Mo – Mother, Fa – Father, AC – Abuser in childhood, Pa – Partner, MG – Men in general, WG – Women in general.

Sarah's self-report of negative feelings towards her brother (the abuser) and her mother, who tended to dismiss Sarah's experiences. Closer inspection of the rearranged grids shows an important change in the Self elements, with ratings for Child self (CS) and Self now (SN) moving closer to Ideal Self (IS). This is partly due to CS and SN shifting closer to each other on constructs such as 'does not feel guilty', 'guilty', 'confusing' and 'confident' and partly because IS has shifted slightly away from her Father, Ideal self being seen as more confident, and Self now moving to a slightly more confident rating. We would expect any form of analysis to pick up such patterns, which can be noticed, with a little effort, from the raw grid.

Table 10.2 shows Sarah's pre-therapy grid in two of the forms required for use by the programs illustrated below. *Original* is the original form of the grid as elicited. It is shown in the form recommended for input to SYSTAT, with construct labels being truncated, and element labels stored in the variable *Label$*. For some analyses, a reversed form of the grid is required. This is formed by flipping the ratings of elements on the constructs, which can be achieved by subtracting each rating from 8 (the maximum rating + 1), and is shown at the bottom of Table 10.2 as *Reversed*. For other analyses, a doubled form of the grid (*Doubled*) is required, which is obtained by putting *Original* and *Reversed* alongside each other. SYSTAT commands to produce *Doubled* from *Original* and *Reversed* are as follows:

USE *Original*

SORT Label$

SAVE OrigSort

USE *Reversed*

SORT Label$

SAVE RevSort

SAVE *Doubled*

MERGE OrigSort (Label$ .. Sho) RevSort (Label$ .. Col)/ Label$

Pairwise analysis of elements

The first stage on from the raw grid is to look at how similar or dissimilar pairs of elements are rated and how similar or dissimilar pairs of constructs are rated. Care is needed at this stage, because elements and constructs need to be handled differently, since the bipolar nature of constructs means that a different similarity/dissimilarity measure is needed for elements and constructs. Some statistical packages (e.g., GAB) do not recognise this and hence give potentially misleading analyses, while the more general packages like SPSS and SYSTAT offer such a large choice of dissimilarity measures that it is easy to go wrong.

Measuring similarity/dissimilarity among elements

To assess similarity among pairs of elements, a measure is required that is unaffected by reversing the poles of any construct. Several appropriate measures can be found in most statistical packages. The most commonly used is the Euclidean distance measure. This is a simple measure of squared discrepancy between the ratings of the two elements across all constructs. Comparing CS and SN on Sarah's pre-therapy grid (using *Original* in Table 10.2), for example, gives a Euclidean distance of $(2 - 7)^2 + (7 - 7)^2 + \cdots + (1 - 5)^2$ or 156. In most packages this is normalised by dividing by a constant, this being the maximum value possible $(14 \times (1 - 7)^2$ or 504) in the case of GRAN (giving $156/504 = 0.31$ as the distance), or the number of constructs (14) in the case of SYSTAT. We use the GRAN version here, multiplied by 100 for convenience, so that identically rated elements have a distance of 0 while maximally discrepant elements are at distance 100. Notice that reversing the poles of any construct would change the ratings of the elements, but would have no effect at all on the Euclidean distance. For example, reflecting the 'confident/unconfident' construct (Construct 5) would change the rating of CS from 1 to 7 and the rating of SN from 7 to 1, but this construct's contribution to the Euclidean distance would still be $(1 - 7)^2$. So the same distances are obtained whether working from the *Original* or the *Reversed* versions. To produce Euclidean distances in SYSTAT requires that the *Original* grid first be transposed before the distances are calculated. The following commands produce a transposed grid, *Transposed*, with Elements now in columns, and a matrix of element distances, *Euclidean*:

USE *Original*

SAVE *Transposed*

TRANSPOSE

USE *Transposed*

CORR

EUCLIDEAN

SAVE *Euclidean*

Another possibility for measuring similarity between elements is the City Block measure, which is just the sum of the absolute differences between the ratings of two elements. For example, the city block distance between Sarah's Child self and Self now elements is $5 + 0 + 0 + \cdots + 0 + 4$ or 36. This places less emphasis on the very discrepant ratings than the Euclidean measure, where the squaring emphasises the discrepant ratings more than those close together. It can be calculated in SYSTAT by replacing the command EUCLIDEAN above with CITY.

Some packages (e.g., GAB) and authors (e.g., Clarke and Llewelyn, 1994) use correlational measures to assess similarity between elements, but this is misleading because it can be affected by reversing poles of constructs. For example, the product moment correlation between the ratings for Child self and Self now is -0.38 when the 'confident/unconfident' construct is as given, but -0.32 when it is reversed. The reason for this is that reversing the poles of one or more constructs changes the variance of the ratings for the elements, and this variance figures in the calculation of a correlation coefficient.

It is often helpful to compare changes in these rescaled Euclidean distances before and after therapy. Care is needed in interpreting these, however, as such comparisons assume the client uses the scales in the same way on each occasion. For example, the client may be cautiously avoiding extreme ratings on one grid but not on another. These different response styles would render the distances incomparable. With this proviso, we selected four comparisons for Sarah's four grids:

1   *Self now/Ideal self distance*. This distance is often used as a measure of self-esteem. For Sarah, this falls from 33 to 18 post-therapy, with a further fall to 12 at three-month follow-up and a slight increase to 19 at six-month follow-up. This parallels the changes in the more direct Rosenberg self-esteem questionnaire.

2   *Self now/Child self distance*. Sarah's discrepancy between child and adult self starts at 31, then reduces to 11, 8 and 19 for the three post-therapy grids. The more similar ratings of child and adult self occurred at a time when she was not showing distress on the psychometric measures. It is partly due to her more positive ratings of Child self on many of the constructs – for example, more 'confident' – and partly due to a shift of the ratings of Self now towards Child self.

3   *Men in general/Women in general distance*. This provides an index of sex role polarisation. For Sarah, there is little noticeable change throughout the four grids, going from 9 pre-therapy to 10, 6 and 9 in the post-therapy grids.

4   *Abuser in childhood/Men in general distance*. This distance starts at 14 pre-therapy, staying at 14 post-therapy, but increasing to 38 and 29 at three- and six-month follow-up, with men in general being rated as increasingly different from her abuser.

In thinking through these changes, Sarah reported having found group therapy beneficial in that it helped reduce her sense of isolation and stigmatisation regarding her childhood abuse. This then led to an increase in self-esteem, self-confidence and reduced feelings of shame and guilt. She reported having found working with a male therapist useful as it 'added a male perspective and the message that not all men are evil', but she did not feel that this had led to any changes in her relationships with men, as she reported that she had never had problems relating to men in general and that she did not tend to cast all men in the same category. However, sexually, Sarah had difficulties with flashbacks to the abuse during sex and aversion to sex, for which she entered couple therapy with her partner after the group. Although Sarah did not construe men as particularly similar to the abuser pre-therapy (Euclidean distance of 14), this distance had more than doubled at six-month follow-up, suggesting that there may have been more subtle similarities for Sarah between men in general and the abuser before therapy, perhaps relating to sex, which she had managed to separate out more at the six month measures.

Pairwise analysis of constructs

To assess the similarity/dissimilarity of pairs of constructs, a Pearson product moment correlation coefficient is usually the most appropriate measure. It applies equally well to rated, ranked or dichotomous grids, reducing to the Spearman rank correlation coefficient for ranked grids and the phi coefficient for dichotomous grids. Reversing the poles of a construct will change the sign but not the magnitude of the correlation. This does not affect the meaning of the measure, as it just determines which poles of the two constructs go together. However, it may affect later analyses that take note of the sign. For example, a cluster analysis of a set of correlations will treat a correlation of $+0.20$ as indicating greater similarity between the two constructs than a correlation of -0.99. The simplest solution when using cluster analysis is to work only with absolute correlations (i.e., ignore the sign) in subsequent analyses, as is done in GRAN. An alternative strategy, simpler in other packages such as SYSTAT, is to use the squares of the correlations. Other forms of analysis, such as principal components analysis, automatically sort out the directions of the correlations.

For Sarah's pre-therapy grid, the highest correlations between constructs are for the constructs 'abusive–not abusive' and 'frightening–not frightening' ($r = 0.96$) and the constructs 'assertive–not assertive' and 'confident–unconfident' ($r = 0.96$). Of her own elicited constructs (constructs 12–14), the highest correlation is between 'trustworthy–untrustworthy' and 'abusive–not abusive' ($r = -0.93$) and 'frightening–not frightening' ($r = -0.93$).

SYSTAT commands to produce the construct correlations are:

USE *Original*

CORR

PEARSON

Analysis of elements and constructs separately

The next stage of analysis (Level 3 in Table 10.1) is to find a method of revealing the structure in the element relationships or in the construct relationships. From the previous stage we will have a matrix of interrelationships amongst the elements (Element distance matrix) and a separate matrix of interrelationships amongst the constructs (Construct correlation matrix). At the previous level of analysis, the strategy was to pull out interesting looking individual comparisons, such as looking for pairs of constructs that correlate highly. At this stage the task is to simplify the large number of comparisons in each of these matrices by imposing some simplifying assumption that, we hope, will reveal structure without too much distortion of the rich information contained in the matrices. The choice of analyses is between those methods that give a (usually two-dimensional) plot of the elements (or constructs) in standard so-called Euclidean space (these being Principal Components Analysis or Multidimensional Scaling) and those that impose a tree-like structure in what is called ultrametric space (the various clustering methods known as hierarchical cluster analysis). All of these analyses can be done in standard statistical packages like S-Plus, SPSS or SYSTAT.

Hierarchical Cluster Analysis

We start with hierarchical cluster analysis (HCA). There are many variations to choose from, mainly distinguished by the criteria used for new elements to join already formed clusters. We use the simplest version, single link hierarchical clustering, partly because it is simple, but partly because it has desirable mathematical properties such as continuity, which means that small changes in the distances or correlations make for only small changes in the analysis (see, for example, Jardine and Sibson, 1971). This makes it fairly transparent, so that you can see easily when it is not giving a good representation of the data. Most other methods do not have this property, so small changes in the distances or correlations can result in big changes in the analysis. The joining criterion for single link clustering is that an item joins an already formed cluster when it is similar to any item in the cluster. For this reason, the method can result in clusters of items that are not compact. Other clustering methods do not have this property, which is often seen as a disadvantage (see, for example, Hands and Everitt, 1987). Our preferred strategy is to compare the results of several clustering methods. If they give similar results, you can be confident that a reliable structure has been captured; if they do not, further analysis is needed to discover the most appropriate method. A frequently used alternative to single link clustering is Ward's method (Ward, 1963), which produces compact clusters but is not continuous. SPSS, SYSTAT and S-PLUS provide both methods (and several others), while GRAN provides only the single link method.

HCA of elements

Figure 10.2 shows the results of a single link HCA of Sarah's element distance matrix for each of her four grids. The analysis on the left shows the tree (or dendrogram) resulting from the analysis of her pre-therapy grid. Each branching point or node shows a cluster of similar elements and the nodes are labelled with the distance at which the cluster is formed. For example, the most similar cluster is Father (Fa) and Partner (Pa) (joining at distance 4), confirming what we already know, that Sarah sees her father and her partner as being very similar. Ideal self (IS) joins this cluster next (at distance 5) and the cluster of women in general (WG) and men in general (MG) (linked at distance 9) joins these three at distance 11. Self now (SN) and Child self (CS) are out on a limb, joining the rest at distances 15 and 16 respectively. Level of similarity between elements in these trees is represented by the level at which they join together and not by the order in which they are written. For example, even though SN is written

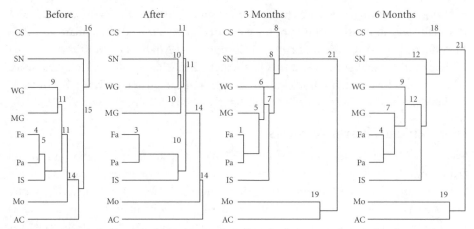

Fig. 10.2 Single link Hierarchical Cluster Analysis (HCA) of elements for Sarah's four grids. CS = Child self; SN = Self now; WG = Women in general; MG = Men in general; Fa = Father; Pa = Partner; IS = Ideal self; Mo = Mother; AC = Abuser in childhood.

close to CS, they are not similar, because they do not join together until the final level of the tree. The easiest way to interpret the trees is to see them as mobiles, which can move around without changing the cluster membership, even though the order of the elements can change. For example, CS could flip over to be next to AC and away from SN without changing the meaning of the tree.

In Figure 10.2, the elements in all four grids are written in the same order for easier comparison. It will not always be possible to do this without getting the trees twisted. While CS are SN are both isolated in the pre-therapy tree, both move closer to each other and to other elements in the post-therapy and three-month follow-up trees, although by six-month follow-up CS has moved further out. Also apparent is the increasing isolation of her mother (Mo) and brother (AC), who are seen as relatively similar to each other, but increasingly different from the other elements in the grid.

SYSTAT commands to carry out a single link HCA of the elements for Sarah's pre-therapy grid are as follows:

USE *Original*

CLUSTER

JOIN Ass .. Sho/ ROWS DISTANCE = EUCLIDEAN LINKAGE = SINGLE

Replacing LINKAGE = SINGLE with LINKAGE = WARD produces Ward's method.

HCA of constructs

A single link hierarchical cluster analysis of the constructs for Sarah's pre- and post-therapy grids is shown alongside the constructs in Figure 10.1. This was produced by

GRAN and is based on the absolute value of the correlations between constructs. The nodes are labelled with the value of the correlation at which the clusters are formed. The two trees show a similar structure for the constructs before and after group therapy, with a cluster of similarly used constructs formed by 'abusive', 'frightening', 'untrustworthy', etc., and a separate cluster formed by 'assertive', 'confident' and 'does not feel guilty'. When using HCA with the statistical packages SPSS, SSYSTAT or S-PLUS, remember to use the absolute values (or the squares) of the correlations between constructs, as these programs will automatically do the analysis with signs attached, which will give a different result. SYSTAT commands for the HCA of constructs, using squared correlations, are as follows:

USE *Original*

CLUSTER

JOIN Ass ... Sho/ COLUMNS DISTANCE = RSQUARED LINKAGE = SINGLE

As before, replacing LINKAGE = SINGLE with LINKAGE = WARD produces Ward's method.

Principal components analysis

Principal components analysis (PCA) provides a picture of the correlations between constructs in a small-dimensional plot. The basic idea is that all the construct correlations can be perfectly represented in a spatial picture in 8 dimensions (the number of elements in the grid minus 1 or the number of constructs minus 1, whichever is smaller), but it is not easy to interpret like this, so PCA finds the best-fitting straight line through this 8-dimensional space to give the first principal component, and then the next best-fitting line perpendicular to the first to give the second principal component, and so on. The analysis is usually only done in two or three dimensions for ease of visualisation. The key point is that the first component accounts for most of the variation in the data, the second accounts for the next largest amount, and so on, so that two-dimensional analyses will often suffice. The proportion of variance accounted for by the first two components also provides a simple index of how well the analysis fits the data. PCA is one of a number of forms of analysis that decompose principle components. It is available in all the general statistical packages such as SYSTAT, S-PLUS and SPSS, and similar ideas are also used in further analyses in INGRID or in Biplot analysis (see below). The following SYSTAT commands produce a PCA from the *Doubled* version of the grid:

USE *Doubled*

FACTOR

MODEL Ass ... Col

PRINT SHORT

ESTIMATE/METHOD = PCA LISTWISE CORR NUMBER = 2

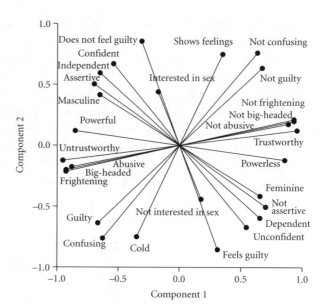

Fig. 10.3 Principal Components Analysis (PCA) of Sarah's pre-therapy grid.

Figure 10.3 shows a PCA for Sarah's pre-therapy grid, with the first component accounting for 49 per cent of the variance and the second accounting for 27 per cent, giving an adequate 76 per cent of the variance accounted for by the first two components. Similarity between constructs is shown by those with a small angular distance between them. For example, the lines representing the constructs 'Trustworthy–Untrustworthy' and 'Not abusive–Abusive' are almost parallel, showing that these constructs are highly correlated, while 'Does not feel guilty–Feels guilty' is almost perpendicular to these two, showing an almost zero correlation. The length of the axes joining the two poles of each construct together reflects the variance explained by the two components, so that 'Feels guilty–Does not feel guilty' has a large amount of variance captured by the two components, while 'Interested in sex–Not interested in sex' does not. The clusters of constructs shown in the HCA in Figure 10.1 are also apparent here.

Multidimensional scaling

Nonmetric multidimensional scaling (MDS) was developed in the 1960s by Shepard (1962a, b) and Kruskal (1964) as an alternative to PCA, making fewer assumptions. It gives a similar spatial picture of the similarities between elements (or constructs) in two or more dimensions. It has a number of measures of goodness of fit, the most commonly used being Kruskal's Stress measure; the lower the stress, the better the fit. Kruskal recommended seeking stress values of 0.05 or less, but this is now often felt to be a very conservative guide. A good introduction to MDS is Schiffman *et al.* (1981).

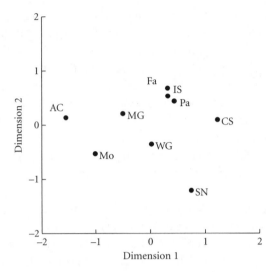

Fig. 10.4 Multidimensional Scaling Analysis (MDS) of Sarah's pre-therapy grid. CS = Child self; SN = Self now; WG = Women in general; MG = Men in general; Fa = Father; Pa = Partner; IS = Ideal self; Mo = Mother; AC = Abuser in childhood.

The following SYSTAT commands produce the two-dimensional MDS representation of the elements for Sarah's pre-therapy grid, using the *Euclidean* file containing the element distances:

USE *Euclidean*

MDS

MODEL CS . . . WG / SHAPE = SQUARE

ESTIMATE / SPLIT = MATRIX LOSS = KRUSKAL REGRESSION = MONO

Figure 10.4 shows the MDS solution in two dimensions for Sarah's pre-therapy grid, with a stress value of 0.05. The picture shows *Self now* isolated, with *Father*, *Ideal self* and *Partner* very similar. On Dimension 1, *Child self* and *Self now* are at one end while *Abuser in childhood* and *Mother* are at the other, with *Partner*, *Father*, *Ideal self*, *Men in general* and *Women in general* in the middle, a picture broadly similar to the HCA analysis in Figure 10.2, although *Child self* and *Self now* appear less isolated here. Dimension 2 isolates *Self Now*, with all the others similar, although emphasising the similarity of *Father*, *Ideal self* and *Partner* further at the other end of the scale.

Joint analysis of elements and constructs

The next level of analysis provides a joint representation of elements and constructs. The most popular of these was INGRID (Slater, 1972), but this is almost identical to biplot representations now widely available through SYSTAT and S-PLUS, so we only consider biplots here.

We also consider analyses based on the marginal hierarchical cluster analyses of elements and constructs separately, which result in a rearranged version of the raw grid as in Figure 10.1. This helps to keep our attention firmly on the original ratings and allows us to assess goodness of fit visually and pick out exceptions to the general patterns revealed by the marginal analyses. These analyses can be produced in SPSS, S-PLUS and SYSTAT, as long as you remember to analyse elements and constructs with different similarity measures (see above) and to do a cluster analysis of constructs based on absolute or squared correlations. However, the made-to-measure packages like GRAN or FOCUS do it all for you. The disadvantages of these packages are that they are less widely available, have less local support, and provide no choice in method of cluster analysis.

We also consider unfolding analysis, a variation on multidimensional scaling, developed by Coombs (1964) to analyse preference data, but equally applicable to repertory grid data. This gives a joint spatial picture of elements and constructs similar to a biplot, but with a slightly different interpretation. This is available in SYSTAT and SPSS (using ALSCAL).

Other analyses not considered here are also possible. For example, correspondence analysis (Greenacre, 1984), although developed for the analysis of contingency tables, is also applicable with slight modification to repertory grids and gives a similar picture to a biplot. This is also available in SYSTAT and SPSS (using ANACOR).

Hierarchical Cluster Analysis

Figure 10.1 shows the joint analysis produced by GRAN for Sarah's pre- and post-therapy grids. Notice that the constructs labelled R have been reversed to make the structure more apparent; this is done automatically in GRAN. In both grids, Father, Partner and Ideal self are clearly distinguished from the others, particularly Mother and Abuser in childhood, on the major cluster of constructs, getting the most extreme scores on 'not abusive', 'not frightening', 'trustworthy', 'not guilty' and 'shows feelings'. The slight change post-therapy in Sarah's view of her Child self and Self now is apparent in the changes in ratings on 'assertive', 'confident', 'does not feel guilty', with Child self shifting away from these poles and Self now shifting closer to these poles. This seems to be the main reason for Child self and Self now moving closer to the other elements and closer to each other after group therapy.

The analysis can be extended to make more apparent the internal patterns and exceptions using the marginal HCA analyses to analyse the interaction structure in the grid as shown in Leach (1980), but this is not available in any computer package, so is not included here. It is based on Hartigan's (1975) joiner-scaler algorithm, which is available in BMDP (and a variation is also provided in SYSTAT). However, these methods should not be used with grids without considerable modification (see Leach, 1980).

Biplot analysis

A biplot is basically the plot of constructs from the simple PCA shown in Figure 10.3 with the elements superimposed. The rating of an element on each construct can be estimated by finding the projection of that element on the construct axis, i.e., by dropping a perpendicular onto the construct axis from the element. SYSTAT produces a biplot from the *Doubled* grid as follows, with the LET command reversing the poles of all the constructs to get the labels the right way round on the picture:

USE *Doubled*

LET (Ass...Col) = 8 − @

IDVAR = Label$

PERMAP

MODEL Ass...Col

ESTIMATE / METHOD = BIPLOT STANDARDIZE

Figure 10.5 shows the two-dimensional biplot for Sarah's pre-therapy grid. Self now is shown as extremely 'unconfident' and 'feels guilty' but somewhere near the middle of the 'trustworthy – untrustworthy' construct. To see how close this is to the true rating, we can look at the rearranged grid in Figure 10.1, where Self now gets ratings of 7 for 'unconfident', 6 for 'feels guilty' and 7 for 'trustworthy', so the first two are accurately represented, but the third rating is distorted. As with PCA, a quick index of overall goodness of fit is given by the proportion of variance accounted for by the two components, in this case 49 per cent and 27 per cent or 76 per cent in total. This is identical to

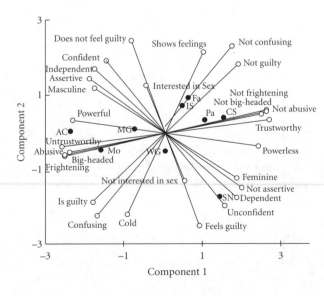

Fig. 10.5 Biplot of Sarah's pre-therapy grid. CS = Child self; SN = Self now; WG = Women in general; MG = Men in general; Fa = Father; Pa = Partner; IS = Ideal self; Mo = Mother; AC = Abuser in childhood.

the fit given by the PCA analysis shown in Figure 10.3, which it must be, as a biplot is just a PCA with element information added.

Unfolding Analysis

Figure 10.6 shows a two-dimensional unfolding analysis of Sarah's pre-therapy grid. This was produced in SYSTAT using the following commands:

MDS

USE *Original*

LET (Ass...Sho) = 8 – @

MODEL Ass...Sho / SHAPE = RECT

IDVAR = Label$

ESTIMATE / SPLIT = ROWS

The result in Figure 10.6 looks like a biplot without the lines for the constructs, but it is interpreted slightly differently. Here, the elements and the constructs are both represented as points and the rating of an element on a particular construct is reflected in how close the two are in space. Thus, Abuser in childhood (AC) is close to Mother (Mo), and both these elements are close to the construct poles 'masculine' and 'independent', while Child self (CS) and Partner (Pa) are close to each other and to the constructs 'shows feelings' and 'trustworthy'. As with MDS, Kruskal's stress measure gives an idea of goodness of fit. In this case, the fit is 0.11, not excellent but acceptable. Only one construct pole is represented here, but it is possible to use the same trick as with the biplot of doubling the grid before analysis to capture both poles. However, in the

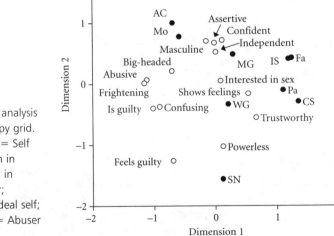

Fig. 10.6 Unfolding analysis of Sarah's pre-therapy grid. CS = Child self; SN = Self now; WG = Women in general; MG = Men in general; Fa = Father; Pa = Partner; IS = Ideal self; Mo = Mother; AC = Abuser in childhood.

case of the biplot, doubling has no impact at all on the analysis apart from adding the extra pole to the picture. With unfolding analysis, doubling the grid can have an impact on both the picture produced and its fit to the data. For this grid, doubling increases the stress value to 0.16, reducing the fit of the data.

Combined analysis of several grids

Combining several grids together takes us to level 5 in Table 10.1, the level furthest removed from the original grid data, so we can expect only a broad sweep with important details almost certain to be missed. However, the broad sweep sometimes gives insight into how the information in the grids is shifting over the course of therapy. The fuller account in Leach *et al.* (2001) gives two methods that are extensions of MDS and unfolding analysis. The MDS extension is often known as INDSCAL (for individual differences scaling). It is applicable when, as with Sarah's grids, the same elements and constructs are used on all occasions. However, its starting point is the element distance matrix for each grid, so it will be applicable also for combining grids when the elements are common but the constructs are different. The combined unfolding analysis is applicable only when elements and constructs are shared across grids. Both analyses are available in SYSTAT.

A different approach to combining grids with common elements and constructs is to treat the combined grids as one large grid, distinguishing the elements from different grids with different labels, and then analysing the combined grid in any of the ways shown above. This has not been done here, but Van der Kloot (1981) gives an illustration of the approach using MDS. A difficulty with this approach is that within and between grid variation is confounded.

Conclusions

The rich data in repertory grids can be looked at in many different ways, illustrated by the levels of analysis in Table 10.1. Quantitative comparisons, such as the Ideal self/Self now discrepancy provide a useful addition to standard psychometric measures. This chapter has also illustrated the qualitative use of repertory grids.

The available computer packages can assist in drawing out patterns from grids, although some caution is required for appropriate use. Some of the available programs are given in Table 10.1. Other packages are available at the web sites given in the Appendix. Before using any package, a good strategy is to try it out on a small well-known test grid to see if the results look sensible.

Not all of the packages are appropriate for analysis at all levels. For example, the base version of SPSS provides a principal components analysis but not an accompanying biplot. SYSTAT and S-PLUS produce both, but in different ways, with SYSTAT providing only a standardised biplot and S-PLUS providing only an unstandardised one. GRAN provides a hierarchical cluster analysis of both elements and constructs, both of which can be done in the bigger packages, but with care. To do a HCA of constructs with the bigger packages requires a choice of correlation coefficient (usually a product-moment correlation) and then a further procedure to turn these correlations into absolute (or squared) values before performing the HCA. The benefit of the bigger packages is the wider choice of HCA versions available (with single-link clustering and Ward's method being recommended). Our recommended strategy is to try out a number of forms of analysis and look for common and different features in the analysis. If several analyses produce similar results, this will increase confidence in any conclusions reached. If the methods give conflicting pictures, then further analysis is required to check which forms of analysis best fit the grid.

The broader sweep analyses (combined unfolding analysis and INDSCAL) do not prove very helpful for comparing Sarah's grids (see Leach *et al.*, 2001). Although tempting to use, this level of analysis is often too far removed from the original grids to give more than a crude comparison. Perhaps the best advice is George Kelly's typical recommendation of staying close to what the client has to say.

Acknowledgements

This chapter is a shortened and updated version of an article published in the *British Journal of Clinical Psychology* (Leach *et al.*, 2001) and is reprinted with permission of the publisher.

We would like to thank all participants in the group therapy sessions, in particular Sarah, for their cooperation. Jan Aldridge and Joanne Sunderland helped to put the original article together, which was also improved considerably by comments from Stephen Morley, Chris Evans, Richard Bell and an anonymous referee.

References

Ainscough, C. and Toon, K. (2000). *Breaking Free: Help for Survivors of Child Sexual Abuse*, 2nd edn. London: Sheldon Press.

Bannister, D. and Fransella, F. (1980). *Inquiring Man*, 2nd edn. London: Penguin Books.

Bannister, D. and Higginbotham, P. (1983). *GAB Manual*. Unpublished document, Department of Psychology, University of Leeds, LS2 9JT, UK.

Beck, A. T., Ward, C. H., Mendelson, M., Mock, J. and Erbaugh, J. (1961). An inventory for measuring depression. *Archives of General Psychiatry*, **4**, 561–571.

Bell, R. (1988). Theory-appropriate analysis of repertory grid data. *International Journal of Personal Construct Psychology*, **1**, 101–118.

Bell, R. C. (1994). *Using SPSS to Analyse Repertory Grid Data*. Unpublished report, School of Behavioural Science, University of Melbourne, Parkville, Victoria 3052, Australia.

Chambers, W. V. and Grice, J. W. (1986). Circumgrids: A repertory grid package for personal computers. *Behavior Research Methods, Instruments, and Computers*, **18**, 468.

Clarke, S. and Llewelyn, S. (1994). Personal constructs of survivors of childhood sexual abuse receiving cognitive analytic therapy. *British Journal of Medical Psychology*, **67**, 273–289.

Cochran, W. G. and Cox, G. M. (1957). *Experimental Designs*, 2nd edn. New York: Wiley.

Coombs, C. H. (1964). *A Theory of Data*. New York: Wiley.

Derogatis, L. R. (1983). *The SCL-90R: Administration, Scoring and Procedures – Manual II*. Towson, MD: Clinical Psychometrics Research.

Fransella, F. and Bannister, D. (1977). *A Manual for Repertory Grid Technique*. London: Academic Press.

Freshwater, K., Leach, C. and Aldridge, J. (2001). Personal constructs, childhood sexual abuse and revictimisation. *British Journal of Medical Psychology*, **74**, 379–397.

Gabriel, K. R. (1971). The biplot-graphic display of matrices with application to principal component analysis. *Biometrika*, **58**, 453–467.

Gower, J. C. and Hand, D. J. (1996). *Biplots*. London: Chapman and Hall.

Greenacre, M. J. (1984). *Theory and Applications of Correspondence Analysis*. London: Academic Press.

Hands, S. and Everitt, B. (1987). A Monte Carlo study of the recovery of cluster structure in binary data by hierarchical clustering techniques. *Multivariate Behavioral Research*, **22**, 235–243.

Hartigan, J. A. (1975). *Clustering Algorithms*. New York: Wiley.

Jardine, N. and Sibson, R. (1971). *Mathematical Taxonomy*. London: Wiley.

Jehu, D. (1988). *Beyond Sexual Abuse: Therapy with Women who were Childhood Victims*. Chichester: John Wiley and Sons.

Keen, T. R. and Bell, R. C. (1980). One thing leads to another: A new approach to elicitation in the repertory grid technique. *International Journal of Man-Machine Studies*, **13**, 25–38. Reprinted in M. L. G. Shaw (ed.) *Recent Advances in Personal Construct Technology*. London: Academic Press, 1981.

Kruskal, J. B. (1964). Multidimensional scaling by optimizing goodness of fit to a nonmetric hypothesis. *Psychometrika*, **29**, 1–27.

Leach, C. (1980). Direct analysis of a repertory grid. *International Journal of Man-Machine Studies*, **13**, 151–166. Reprinted in M. L. G. Shaw (ed.) *Recent Advances in Personal Construct Technology*. London: Academic Press, 1981.

Leach, C. (1988). GRAN: A computer program for the cluster analysis of a repertory grid. *British Journal of Clinical Psychology*, **27**, 173–174.

Leach, C., Freshwater, K., Aldridge, J. and Sunderland, J. (2001). Analysis of repertory grids in clinical practice. *British Journal of Clinical Psychology*, **40**, 225–248.

Mackay, N. (1992). Identification, reflection and correlation: Problems in the bases of repertory grid measures. *International Journal of Personal Construct Psychology*, **5**, 57–75.

Rosenberg, M. (1965). *Society and the Adolescent Self-Image*. New Jersey: Princeton University Press.

Schiffman, S. S., Reynolds, M. L. and Young, F. W. (1981). *Introduction to Multidimensional Scaling: Theory, Methods and Applications*. New York: Academic Press.

Shaw, M. L. G. (ed.) (1981) *Recent Advances in Personal Construct Technology*. London: Academic Press.

Shaw, M. L. G. and Thomas, L. F. (1978). FOCUS on education – an interactive computer system for the development and analysis of repertory grids. *International Journal of Man-Machine Studies*, **10**, 139–173.

Shepard, R. N. (1962a). The analysis of proximities: Multidimensional scaling with an unknown distance function. I. *Psychometrika*, **27**, 125–140.

Shepard, R. N. (1962b). The analysis of proximities: Multidimensional scaling with an unknown distance function. II. *Psychometrika*, **27**, 219–246.

Slater, P. (1977). *The Measurement of Intrapersonal Space by Grid Technique*, Vol. 2. London: Wiley.

Tukey, P. A. (1979). *Exploratory Data Analysis*. New York: Addison Wesley.

van der Kloot, W. A. (1981). Multidimensional scaling of repertory grid responses: Two applications of HOMALS. In Bonarius, H., Holland, R. and Rosenberg, S. (eds) *Personal Construct Psychology: Recent Advances in Theory and Practice.* London: Macmillan.

Ward, J. H. (1963). Hierarchical grouping to optimize an objective function. *Journal of the American Statistical Association,* **58**, 236–244.

Appendix

Repertory grid analysis – resources

Statistical packages

S-PLUS is available from Insightful UK, 5th Floor, Network House, Basing View, Basingstoke, Hampshire RG21 HG, UK. Their web address is www.insightful.com

SPSS 12.0 is available from SPSS(UK) Ltd, 1st Floor, St Andrews House, West Street, Woking, Surrey GU21 1EB, UK. Their web address is www.spss.com/UK

SYSTAT 10.0 is available from Statistical Solutions, 8 South Bank, Crosse's Green, Cork, Ireland. Their web address is www.statsol.ie

University computing laboratories are likely to have one or more of these and may be able to offer cheaper licence rates for staff and student copies. Other packages not mentioned also do similar analyses – for example BMDP and SAS.

The Help files for these big programs are quite limited unless you have very specific queries. More useful are the manuals that come with some programs. For example, the SYSTAT and S-PLUS manuals offer good worked examples for most procedures.

Purpose-built grid analysis programs

GRAN is available from the first author on a copyleft basis – i.e., it can be used and copied for others as long as it is not changed or used for profit. Support is very limited. It is written in QBASIC and only available in a DOS version for PCs.

Other DOS programs are GRIDSTAT.EXE and GRIDSCAL.EXE, both written by Richard Bell.

FOCUS has been incorporated into an interactive web site (WebGrid II) by Brian Gaines and Mildred Shaw, which allows online grid elicitation and analysis, available at http://gigi.cpsc.ucalgary.ca/. It has also been updated as a Mac program (RepGrid II).

Other resources

More information about grid analysis programs and other information about personal construct theory is well-represented on the web. A good starting point is the site mounted by Chris Evans at www.psyctc.org/grids/. This provides good links to other sites, as well as downloadable copies of some of the programs mentioned in this article. Most of these are free, although support is limited. Also at this site is a set of programs that do the same analysis as INGRID and incorporate Biplot displays.

Chapter 11

Descriptive and interpretive approaches to qualitative research

Robert Elliott and Ladislav Timulak

Qualitative research methods today are a diverse set, encompassing approaches such as empirical phenomenology, grounded theory, ethnography, protocol analysis and discourse analysis. By one common definition (Polkinghorne, 1983), all these methods rely on linguistic rather than numerical data, and employ meaning-based rather than statistical forms of data analysis. Distinguishing between measuring things with words and measuring them in numbers, however, may not be a particularly useful way of characterising different approaches to research. Instead, other distinctive features of qualitative research may turn out to be of far greater importance (Elliott, 1999):

- emphasis on understanding phenomena in their own right (rather than from some outside perspective);
- open, exploratory research questions (vs. closed-ended hypotheses);
- unlimited, emergent description options (vs. predetermined choices or rating scales);
- use of a special strategies for enhancing the credibility of design and analyses (see Elliott, Fischer and Rennie, 1999); and
- definition of success conditions in terms of discovering something new (vs. confirming what was hypothesised).

Space limitations preclude a complete survey of this rapidly growing field of research methods. Instead, we will focus on what are today regarded as established, well-used methods within the descriptive–interpretive branch of qualitative research. (In particular, we will not cover discourse analysis, e.g., Potter and Wetherell, 1987; Stokoe and Wiggins, this volume, or ethnography.) These methods came into their own in the 1970s and 1980s, and have become mainstream in education, nursing, and increasingly in psychology, particularly in non-traditional or professional training schools. Because there is now an extensive history with these methods, standards of good research practice have emerged (e.g., Elliott *et al.*, 1999).

Descriptive–interpretive qualitative research methods go by many 'brand names' in which various common elements are mixed and matched according to particular researchers' predilections; currently popular variations include grounded theory

(Henwood and Pigeon, 1992; Strauss and Corbin, 1998), empirical phenomenology (Giorgi, 1975; Wertz, 1983), hermeneutic-interpretive research (Packer and Addison, 1989), interpretative phenomenological analysis (Smith, Jarman, Osborn, 1999), and Consensual Qualitative Research (Hill, Thompson, Williams, 1997). Following Barker, Pistrang and Elliott (2002), we find the emphasis on brand names to be confusing and somewhat proprietary. Thus, in our treatment here, we take a generic approach that emphasises common methodological practices rather than relatively minor differences. It is our hope to be able to encourage readers to develop their own individual mix of methods that lend themselves to the topic under investigation and the researchers' preferences and style of collecting and analysing qualitative data.

In the approach to qualitative research we present here, we begin with the formulation of the research problem, followed by a discussion of issues in qualitative data collection and sampling. We will then go on to present common strategies of data analysis, before concluding by summarising principles of good practice in descriptive–interpretive qualitative research and providing suggestions for further reading and learning.

Formulating the problem

Previously, some qualitative researchers believed that it was better to go into the field without first reading the available literature. The reason for this position was the belief that becoming familiar with previous knowledge would 'taint' the researcher, predisposing them to impose their preconceptions on the data and raising the danger of not being sensitive enough to allow the data speak for themselves in order to reveal essential features of the phenomenon. It is our view that this approach is somewhat naive. For one thing, it is now understood that bias is an unavoidable part of the process of coming to know something and that knowledge is impossible without some kind of previous conceptual structure. Far from removing the researcher's influence on the data, remaining ignorant of previous work on a phenomenon simply ensures that one's work will be guided by uninformed rather than informed expectations.

For this reason, the formulation of the research problem in qualitative research is similar in many ways to that in quantitative research. As a consequence, before commencing data collection, researchers carefully examine available knowledge and theory, carrying out a thorough literature search that includes up to date information on the topic of investigation. Strauss and Corbin (1998) refer to this as 'theoretical sensitivity' quoting Pasteur's motto, 'Discovery favours the prepared mind'.

An important feature of this initial phase, however, is that the researcher should become as aware of possible of the nature of their pre-understandings of the phenomenon, as these are likely to shape the data collection, analysis and interpretation. At the same time, the researcher should regard their expectations lightly, in a way that is open to unexpected meanings.

The formulation of research problem is guided by the traditional questions: e.g., What do we know about the phenomenon? Why is it important to know more? What has influenced previous research findings (methodology, social context, researcher theory)? What do we want to make clearer by the new study? Note that the problem formulation itself may not imply a need for a qualitative approach. Therefore, the researcher should not prejudge the question of whether they will use qualitative methods for the study. Instead, use of a qualitative strategy should emerge as a means to answer the particular research questions (Elliott, 1995, 2000).

The research questions leading to employing qualitative data collection and analysis strategies are usually open-ended and exploratory in nature. Barker *et al.* (2002) suggest that exploratory questions, suitable as the base for qualitative inquiry are typically used when: (a) there is little known in a particular research area; (b) existing research is confusing, contradictory, or not moving forward; or (c) the topic is highly complex. As to the aim of exploratory questions, Elliott (2000) sees the following types:

♦ *Definitional*: What is the nature of this phenomenon? What are its defining features? (e.g., What does it mean for patients with metastatic breast cancer to experience help in this existential support group treatment?)

♦ *Descriptive*: What kinds or varieties does the phenomenon appear in? What aspects does it have? (e.g., In what ways do adolescent patients in a cognitive behavioural treatment for diabetes self-care change?)

♦ *Interpretive*: Why does the phenomenon come about? How does it unfold over time? (e.g., What is the story or sequence of patients' improvement in a post-surgery cardiac rehabilitation programme? What changes led to what other changes?)

♦ *Critical/action*: What's wrong (or right) about the phenomenon? How could it be made better? (e.g., What complaints do patients have about a specialist sleep disorder clinic?)

♦ *Deconstruction*: What assumptions are made in this research? Whose social or political interests are served by it? (e.g., What are the cultural and sociopolitical implications of the way in which patient outcome has been measured in behavioural medicine research, such as focusing on pathology as opposed to health?)

Data collection

While the formulation of the research problem does not distinguish sharply between quantitative and qualitative research traditions, data collection often differs dramatically. There is a difference in the format of the data, but also in the general strategy for obtaining the data. As to the format, simply stated, qualitative inquiry looks for *verbal* accounts or descriptions in words, or it puts observations into words (occasionally it also uses other forms of description, e.g., drawings by children with leukaemia). Another major difference is that it uses open-ended questions. However, more importantly, it also uses an *open-ended strategy* for obtaining the data. By 'open-ended' we mean not only that participants are encouraged to elaborate on their accounts, or that observations are not restricted to certain pre-existing categories. Rather, open-endedness refers to the general strategy of data gathering. It means that inquiry is flexible and carefully adapted to the problem at hand and to the individual informant's particular experiences and abilities to communicate those experiences, making each interview unique.

There are several methods of obtaining information for qualitative inquiry. Qualitative interviews are the most common general approach, with semi-structured and unstructured interview formats predominating. In these forms of interview, participants are asked to provide elaborated accounts about particular experiences (e.g., tell me about a time when your asthma was particularly severe). The interviewer should have basic skills plus additional training in open-ended interviewing; such interviews are very similar to the empathic exploration found in good person-centred therapy (Mearns and Thorne, 1999). Good practice is to develop an interview guide that helps the interviewer focus the interview without imposing too much structure. Hill *et al.* (1997) recommend providing interviewees with a list of questions before the interview.

Variant formats

Self-report questionnaires are used much less in qualitative research, because they typically do not stimulate the needed level of elaboration sought by the qualitative researcher. However, given time and space constraints, questionnaires may be used as well. In that case they naturally consist of open-ended questions and ask respondents for elaboration, examples, etc. A good practice is to build in the opportunity to follow-up on questionnaires by phone interview (Hill *et al.*, 1997) or email correspondence, as responses often do not provide enough elaboration to understand the respondents' point.

A popular alternate form of qualitative interview is the focus group (see Wilkinson, this volume, for more information), a group format in which participants share and discuss their views of a particular topic (e.g., needed services for teenagers with spina bifida), allowing access to a large number of possible views and a replication of naturalistic social influence and consensus processes. A special form of qualitative interview, used, for example, in research on helping processes (e.g., between breast cancer patients and their partners; Barker, Pistrang and Rutter, 1997), is tape-assisted recall. Here, a recording of an interaction is played back for the interviewee so that they can recall and describe their experience of particular moments (Elliott, 1986). Finally, think-aloud protocols (McLeod, 1999) are special forms of interview in which the participant is asked to verbalise their thought processes as they deal with a problem (e.g., managing an episode of high blood sugar).

When observational methods are used in qualitative research they typically make extensive use of field notes or memos. These notes are primarily descriptive and observational but may also include the researcher's interpretations and reactions, as long as these are clearly labelled as such. Qualitative observational methods often use non-interview archival data, such as tape recordings and associated transcripts of doctor–patient interactions. (Projective techniques can also be used as methods of data collection in qualitative research but are rarely seen, especially in clinical and health psychology.)

There are three key aspects typical of the data collection in descriptive/interpretive qualitative research worth mentioning at this point:

First, despite the fact that data collection in qualitative research generally does not use pre-existing categories for sorting the data, it always has a focus. The focus is naturally driven by the specific research questions. (At the same time, however, the general research approach encourages constructive critique and openness to reassessment of the chosen focus, if the data begin to point in a different direction.)

Second, qualitative interviews are distinguished by their deliberate giving of power to respondents, in the sense that they become co-researchers. The interviewer tries to empower respondents to take the lead and to point out important features of the phenomenon as they see it. For example, respondents may be encouraged not only to reveal aspects of their experiences that were not expected by the researcher, but also to suggest improvements in the research procedure.

Last but not least, a *triangulation* strategy is often used in this kind of research, with data gathered by multiple methods (e.g., observation and interviewing). This strategy can yield a richer and more balanced picture of the phenomenon, and also serves as a cross-validation method.

Specifics of sampling

Sampling in qualitative research, as in the quantitative tradition, is focused on the application of findings beyond the research sample. However, we cannot talk about generalisability in a traditional sense of stratified random sampling. Qualitative research does not aim at securing confidence intervals of studied variables around exact values in a population. Instead, qualitative research typically tries to sample broadly enough and to interview deeply enough that all the important aspects and variations of the studied phenomenon are captured in the sample – whether the sample be 8 or 100! Generalisability of specific population values or relationships is thus replaced by a thorough specification of the characteristics of the sample, so that one can make judgements about the applicability of the findings. As to the sample size, qualitative research does not use power analysis to determine the needed n, but instead mostly commonly uses the criterion of *saturation* (Strauss and Corbin, 1998), which means adding new cases to the point of diminishing returns, when no new information emerges. Obviously, given the nature of the data collected, and the time-consuming nature of analysis (see below) the size of the samples is usually much lower than in quantitative research.

In order to satisfy the saturation criterion, the most common sampling strategy used in qualitative research can be labelled as *purposeful sampling* (Creswell, 1998). That is, if the study aims to depict central, important or decisive aspects of the investigated phenomenon, then sampling should assure that these are covered. In the grounded theory tradition, where the result of the study is a complete theory of the phenomenon, the preferred sampling strategy is referred to as *theoretical sampling*. This kind of sampling is driven by the need of the researchers to cover the relevant aspects of developing theory. Obviously then, sampling in qualitative research can and should be flexible and should reflect the research problem, ranging from sampling for maximum variation to focusing in-depth on a single exceptional case (see sampling strategies in Miles and Huberman, 1994).

Data analysis in descriptive/interpretive qualitative research

Qualitative research also requires *flexibility* during the analysis phase as well, with procedures developing in response to the ongoing analysis. *Critical challenge* is a key but sometimes overlooked aspect of qualitative data analysis, as the researcher uses constant critical (but not paralysing) self-reflection and challenging scepticism with regard to the analysis methods and the emerging results. We could say that all steps of the analysis are taken prudently with much reflection. *Checking* and *auditing* all steps of the analysis is natural part of the qualitative research, as well as careful archiving of each step of the analysis for later checking. The analysis has also to be *systematic* and *organised*, so the researcher can easily locate information the data set and can trace provisional results of the analysis back to the context of the data.

However, in spite of cherishing flexibility, qualitative research often employs a general strategy that provides the backbone for the analysis. In grounded theory, this strategy is referred to as *axial coding* (Strauss and Corbin, 1998); in consensual qualitative research (Hill *et al.*, 1997), it takes the form of a set of general *domains* that are used to organise the data (e.g., context → illness onset → coping → outcome).

We provide here a general framework for descriptive/interpretive qualitative research. We use this framework in our own work (e.g., Elliott *et al.*, 1994; Timulak and Elliott, 2003) and note that it is similar to and influenced by comparable frameworks used by other researchers (e.g., Hill *et al.*, 1997). Even in our own research work, however, it is just a general structure that we use flexibly and, as appropriate, modify or add to.

Data preparation

The first step of analysis is data preparation. The data are usually obtained in the form of notes and tape recordings. In case of tape recordings, the data are first transcribed verbatim. In case of the combination of researcher observational notes and transcribed recordings, the notes are usually interwoven with the transcripts, often using different fonts, so that the researcher's voice can be clearly distinguished from the informant's voice in the data. During this stage of the analysis, it is worthwhile to read the whole data set, so that the researcher can get the whole picture of the studied phenomenon. During this initial reading, insights and understandings begin to emerge and are written down as memos. This is a kind of pre-analysis that can influence future steps of the analysis because the first relevancies start to unfold.

During or after the initial reading an initial editing of the data often takes place. Obvious redundancies, repetitions, and unimportant digressions are omitted. One must, of course, be sure that the deleted data do not constitute important and relevant aspects of the phenomenon. Checks in the form of independent and challenging auditing processes by either the main analyst or others can be applied here also.

Delineating and processing meaning units

Next, we start to divide the data into distinctive *meaning units* (cf. Rennie, Phillips and Quartaro, 1988; Wertz, 1983). Meaning units are usually parts of the data that even if standing out of the context, would communicate sufficient information to provide a piece of meaning to the reader. The length of the meaning unit depends on the judgement of the researcher, who must assess how different lengths of meaning unit will affect the further steps of the analysis and who also should adopt a meaning unit size that is appropriate to their cognitive style and the data at hand. Generally, the longer the meaning unit is the bigger number (variety) of meanings it contains but the clearer its contextual meaning will be.

As we delineate the meaning units, we can shorten them by getting rid of redundancies that do not change the meanings contained in them. For example, in a study of significant events in cognitive therapy with a diabetic patient, the data might read: 'What was important for me was that the therapist verbalised exactly how I feel about my diabetes. The words she used helped me to be more aware of the things about it that I am having trouble with.' A shortened version of this, which we would use in the further analysis, might then look as follows: 'T verbalised exactly how P felt about her illness – it helped P to be more aware of what aspects of it P is having trouble with.' (T stands for the therapist and P for the patient.)

The meaning units are the units with which we do the analysis. However, it is good to be able to trace them back to the full data protocol, in case we need to be able clarify something from the context. For that reason it is a very good idea to assign a consecutive code (in numbers and letters) to each meaning unit. The code should localise the unit in the original protocol. For example, if for each case we use different letter, we immediately know where meaning unit H82 came from. This procedure facilitates auditing.

Finding an overall organising structure for the data

Naturally, different sets of meaning units describe different aspects of the phenomenon. From their pre-research understanding of the phenomenon and their first reading of the data the researcher already has some ideas about some very broad headings for organising the phenomenon into different processes or phases, referred to as *domains*. In fact, the researchers often introduce this structure into the data from the beginning via the interview question themselves. Nevertheless, the researcher typically waits until they finally sit down to code the data before developing a formal version of this organising framework in relation to the first one or two data protocols. Consistent with this practice, Hill *et al.* (1997) recommend sorting the data into domains that provide a conceptual framework for the data, referred to in grounded theory as *axial coding* (Strauss and Corbin, 1998). As noted, this framework for meaningfully organising the data should be flexible and tested until it fits the data. It is important that the researcher always be open to using the data to restructure the organising conceptual framework. Critical auditing and testing out different possible frameworks are both useful strategies here.

In studies reported in the literature, it is possible to find various kinds of relationship between domains, including temporal sequence (these things happened before these things), causes (this influenced this), significations (that is what this thing means now), etc. We typically find a variety of different types of structuring. Sometimes the domains may also mirror the different sources of the data, e.g., different kinds of observation, different kinds of self-report. If it is conceptually meaningful or in cases when the researcher is not sure about the structuring the data for the moment, it is possible to assign some data to more than one domain.

Generation of categories

Next, the meaning units are *coded* or *categorised* within each of the domains into which they have been organised. The categories evolve from the meanings in the meaning units. The word *category* refers to the aim of discerning regularities or similarities in the data (Glaser and Strauss, 1967). Creation of categories is an interpretive process on the part of the researcher (or in many cases the team of researchers, cf. Hill *et al.*, 1997), in which the researcher is trying to respect the data and use category labels close to the original language of participants. On the other hand, ideas for categories also come in part from the researcher's knowledge of previous theorising and findings in other studies. Categorising is thus an interactive process in which priority is given to the data but understanding is inevitably facilitated by previous understanding. It is a kind of *dialogue with the data*. (In grounded theory this step is referred to as *open coding*.)

The initial label for a category may come from the first occurrence of the meaning in some meaning unit; however, during the analysis it is typically refined as similar meanings are incorporated from subsequent meaning units. This evolving refining of categories means that some meaning units may eventually need to be reassigned to different categories.

In this process, the meaning units are *constantly compared* (Glaser and Strauss, 1967) to each other and to the emerging categories, until all the data are sorted. At this point the analysis may contain thin or undeveloped categories or groups of categories lacking differentiation or multiple examples (i.e., not adequately saturated). The researcher reflects whether these will be left out of the findings as not contributing sufficiently to the understanding of the phenomenon. Our position is that no data should be left out in this step, because idiosyncratic aspects of the phenomenon can inform the study in interesting ways. After all, qualitative research is interested in the different aspects of the examined phenomenon; therefore, it should not discard some of them just because they are infrequent.

The next step in creating the categories is often categorising the categories. In this process we would be looking for similarities and regularities between the already established categories. Thus, we typically establish categories of the first order that categorise meaning units, categories of the second order that categorise the categories of the first order, and so on leading to a hierarchy of categories, with the bottom level including the meaning units and more and more abstract categories evolving (e.g., Rennie, 1990, who created a taxonomy of clients' experiences in therapy sessions).

In some studies, it is meaningful to do the categorisation separately for each case from the sample (e.g., if we have a lot of data for each case, or if we expect variance within the cases). In that situation, the categorisation of the data for each case is followed by the cross-case analysis (Elliott *et al.*, 1994; Hill *et al.*, 1997) examining similarities and dissimilarities across cases.

A key aspect of the categorisation is a delineation of the relationships between the categories. These relationships usually respect the structure of the domains but they may also evolve their own structure, if the data suggest it. The relationships among categories are often pictured in the form of figures or diagrams.

Abstracting the main findings

The generation of categories usually ends with a taxonomy that describes and interprets the whole phenomenon as it was contained in the gathered data. As qualitative analysis is a very complex endeavour and deals with many details, the taxonomies that result from it are often overwhelming and do not convey directly the essence of the phenomenon. The essence of the phenomenon is, however, the aim of the analysis, so it is very important for the researcher avoid the temptation to stop with a set of categories and not take the next step of abstracting the main findings from the category structure. This abstracting follows the rule of *essential sufficiency*, which means that we are looking for the simplest way to fully depict the phenomenon. We are looking for what constitutes the main findings contained in the categorisation or taxonomy, so that we can communicate them clearly to the reader. Thus, we may also ask of our results, What categories are required to communicate the essence of the phenomenon?

This part of the analysis usually employs graphs, diagrams, figures, tables, and narratives (e.g., the typical story of recovering from an eating disorder). It is a step aiming at grasping the essence of the phenomenon. This step, too, is carefully documented so that it can be tracked back to the data.

We can think of this part of the analysis as about the ultimate categorisation of the categorisation, or as about marketing what we found, or as about *abstracting the results* of our work. (In grounded theory this step is referred to as *selective coding*.)

Validity of analysis

The validity of the analysis is assessed throughout the study, as previously noted. To accomplish this, a *constructively sceptical* process of independent auditing is recommended. Although it is best for researchers to employ careful internal auditing throughout the analysis, the major auditing step typically occurs after a complete draft analysis has been produced.

In addition, there are several other useful validation strategies. *Validation by research participants* is common, and involves presenting the results to the original informants or others like them in order to obtain feedback and correction. Another strategy, *triangulation*, involves comparing data collected by different methods (including quantitative). *Collection of more cases* may also be useful, particularly is auditing identifies problems with inadequate saturation of categories. Finally, *resonation with the reader* of the research paper is an essential form of validation in qualitative research. To facilitative this, the qualitative study should ground the findings in many illustrative examples, so readers may make their own judgements.

Interpretation of the results

Although categorisation of data uses interpretive strategies, one should not confuse this with the interpretation and discussion of the findings, which is done in qualitative research as in any other kind of research, after the findings are presented. As in quantitative research, it is important to place one's qualitative findings within a context of previous theory and research findings. We can do this partly by reflecting thoroughly on the methodological influences and limitations shaping the results of our study (and previous studies). Probing the implications of our research can also include subjecting the existing literature to the same kind of rigorous process of analysis and categorisation as we used with our own data. In addition, it is also important to locate our findings within a socio-historical and scientific context, and to imagine useful further research.

Reviewing and critiquing qualitative research

In this chapter, we have tried to provide guidance on good practice in descriptive–interpretive qualitative research. Some of the key points of evaluation can be summed up in the following guidelines (see Elliott *et al.*, 1999, for more detail and examples of good and bad practice for each):

1 *Own your perspective*: Describe your theoretical orientation and personal interest in the research: values, interests, commitments, assumptions, expectations, and the role these played in the study.

2 *Describe your sample*: Provide relevant features of the research participants and their life circumstances (e.g., age, gender, ethnicity, social class; variations in kind of experience described).

3 *Ground categories in examples*: Provide one or two concrete examples or each category (can be brief or extended).

4 *Provide one or more credibility checks*, including checking results with the original informants or others similar to them; using multiple qualitative analysts; using an additional analytic auditor (or a review by the original analyst); comparing two or more varied qualitative perspectives; or comparing results with quantitative data or external factors.

5 *Organise categories to provide coherent understanding of how they fit together*: Provide a data-based narrative, map, framework, or underlying structure to organise the phenomenon for the reader (e.g., memorably-named core categories or figures).

6 *Accomplishing general vs. specific research tasks*: For a *general* understanding of a phenomenon, use an appropriate sampling strategy and range of instances (informants or situations). For understanding a *specific* instance, make sure it has been studied and described systematically and comprehensively.

7 Allow readers to evaluate whether your categories resonate with their first- or second-hand experience of the phenomenon: Use concrete, rich language in order to help readers judge whether it has accurately represented the phenomenon.

Conclusions

Over the past 20 years, rigorous qualitative research methods have brought a breath of fresh air to the social sciences and increasingly to the health sciences, in particular re-habilitation and nursing. While our colleagues were at first highly suspicious of these approaches, they have subsequently learned that the kinds of methods we have been describing do not pose a threat to traditional quantitative methods but rather offer a useful complement for enriching, enlivening, and illuminating quantitative results. Nevertheless, these methods remain generally under-utilised by psychologists, including health psychologists. We urge readers to take the plunge by adopting a more pluralist approach to research incorporating the methods described here along with other, more traditional approaches.

Further reading

Miles and Huberman (1994), Denzin and Lincoln (2000), and Creswell (1998) provide varied but useful general treatments each covering a range of approaches to qualitative research. The central sources for the particular version of qualitative research described in this chapter are Rennie *et al.* (1998) and Wertz (1983); see also Strauss and Corbin (1998) on grounded theory; Hill *et al.* (1997) on Consensual Qualitative Research, and

Smith *et al.* (1999) on interpretative phenomenological analysis. For a more extended survey of a broad range of qualitative approaches to studying the change process in psychotherapy, see Elliott, Slatick and Urman (2001).

References

Barker, C., Pistrang, N. and Elliott, R. (2002). *Research methods in clinical psychology: An introduction for students and practitioners*, 2nd edn. Chichester, England: John Wiley and Sons.

Creswell, J. W. (1998). *Qualitative inquiry and research design: Choosing among five traditions*. Thousand Oaks, CA: Sage.

Denzin, N. K. and Lincoln, Y. S. (eds) (2000). *Handbook of qualitative research*, 2nd edn. Newberry Park, CA: Sage.

Elliott, R. (1986). Interpersonal process recall (IPR) as a psychotherapy process research method. In L. S. Greenberg and W. M. Pinsof (eds) *The psychotherapeutic process: A research handbook*, pp. 249–286. New York: Guilford Press.

Elliott, R. (1995). Therapy process research and clinical practice: Practical strategies. In M. Aveline and D. A. Shapiro (eds) *Research foundations for psychotherapy practice*, pp. 49–72. Chichester, England: John Wiley and Sons.

Elliott, R. (1999). Editor's introduction to special issue on qualitative psychotherapy research: Definitions, themes and discoveries. *Psychotherapy Research*, **9**, 251–257.

Elliott, R., (2000). *Rigor in psychotherapy research: The search for appropriate methodologies*. Unpublished paper, Department of Psychology, University of Toledo.

Elliott, R., Fischer, C. and Rennie, D. (1999). Evolving guidelines for publication of qualitative research studies in psychology and related fields. *British Journal of Clinical Psychology*, **38**, 215–229.

Elliott, R., Shapiro, D. A., Firth-Cozens, J., Stiles, W. B., Hardy, G., Llewelyn, S. P., and Margison, F. (1994). Comprehensive process analysis of insight events in cognitive-behavioral and psychodynamic-interpersonal therapies. *Journal of Counseling Psychology*, **41**, 449–463.

Elliott, R., Slatick, E. and Urman, M. (2001). Qualitative change process research on psychotherapy: alternative strategies. In J. Frommer and D. L. Rennie (eds) *Qualitative psychotherapy research: Methods and methodology*, pp. 69–111. Lengerich, Germany: Pabst Science Publishers.

Giorgi, A. (1975). An application of phenomenological method in psychology. In A. Giorgi, C. Fisher, and E. Murray (eds) *Duquesne studies in phenomenological psychology*, Vol. 2. Pittsburgh, PA: Duquesne University Press.

Glaser, B. G. and Strauss, A. L. (1967). *The discovery of grounded theory: Strategies for qualitative research*. Chicago: Aldine.

Henwood, K. L. and Pidgeon, N. (1992). Qualitative research and psychological theorising. *British Journal of Psychology*, **83**, 97–111.

Hill, C. E., Thompson, B. J. and Williams, E. N. (1997). A guide to conducting consensual qualitative research. *The Counseling Psychologist*, **25**, 517–572.

McLeod, J. (1999). *Practitioner research in counseling*. London: Sage.

Mearns, D. and Thorne, B. (1999). *Person-centred counselling in action*, 2nd edn. Newberry Park: Sage.

Miles, M. B. and Huberman, A. M. (1994). *Qualitative data analysis: An expanded sourcebook*, 2nd edn. Thousand Oaks, CA: Sage.

Packer, M. J. and Addison R. B. (eds) (1989). *Entering the circle: Hermeneutic investigation in psychology*. Albany, NY: SUNY Press.

Pistrang, N., Barker, C. and Rutter, C. (1997). Social support as conversation: Analysing breast cancer patients' interactions with their partners. *Social Science and Medicine*, **45**, 773–782.

Polkinghorne, D. (1983). *Methodology for the human sciences*. Albany, NY: Human Sciences Press.

Potter, J. and Wetherell, M. (1987). *Discourse and social psychology*. London: Sage.

Rennie, D. (1990). Toward a representation of the client's experience of the psychotherapy hour. In G. Lietaer, J. Rombauts, and R. Van Balen (eds) *Client-centered and experiential psychotherapy in the nineties*, pp. 155–172. Leuven, Belgium: Leuven University Press.

Rennie, D. L., Phillips, J. R., Quartaro, G. K. (1988). Grounded theory: A promising approach to conceptualization in psychology? *Canadian Psychology*, **29**, 139–150.

Smith, J. A., Jarman, M. and Osborn, M. (1999). Doing interpretative phenomenological analysis. In M. Murray and K. Chamberlain (eds) *Qualitative health psychology*, pp. 218–240. London: Sage.

Strauss, A. and Corbin, J. (1998). *Basics of qualitative research: Techniques and procedures for developing grounded theory*, 2nd edn. Newbury Park, CA: Sage.

Timulak, L. and Elliott, R. (2003). Empowerment events in process-experiential psychotherapy of depression. *Psychotherapy Research*, **13**, 443–460.

Wertz, F. J. (1983). From everyday to psychological description: Analyzing the moments of a qualitative data analysis. *Journal of Phenomenological Psychology*, **14**, 197–241.

Chapter 12

Discursive approaches

Elizabeth H. Stokoe and Sally Wiggins

In this chapter, we introduce a method of qualitative analysis that focuses on exploring and explicating language in use. The discourse analytic approach we discuss has developed within psychology over the past fifteen years and is called 'discursive psychology' (DP) (cf. Edwards and Potter, 1992). We aim to provide a basic understanding of DP: its origins and foundations, its theory and approach to language, its questions and topics of investigation, its methods of data collection and analysis and, for the current purposes, its utility for clinical and health psychologists. To this end, our illustrations of the approach are drawn from a range of clinical and health contexts of interaction.

A brief introduction to discursive psychology

Discourse analysts examine, most broadly, forms of talk and text and the social actions performed within them. DP is just one of an assortment of approaches to text and interaction analysis. It is therefore important to distinguish it from other linguistic, sociolinguistic, cognitive or post-structuralist methods that all, in one way or another, analyse text and talk as social practice. DP involves the fine-grained, close-up analysis of a variety of discourse sites, including interview talk, written texts and everyday conversation. It is arguably not 'just' a method that can be deployed from a range of many different alternatives; nor is it a recipe-like discipline that can be applied in a stepwise fashion to textual data. DP is a perspective that encompasses both theoretical and analytic principles and, in its most ambitious formulation, constitutes a novel take on any psychological phenomena: a reworking of what psychology is and could be (Potter, 2003).

The term 'discursive psychology' was first coined by Edwards and Potter (1992) in their book of the same title. Its foundational writings can be found in this book and a number of other key publications: *Discourse and Social Psychology* (Potter and Wetherell, 1987); *Arguing and Thinking* (Billig, 1987) and *Common Knowledge* (Edwards and Mercer, 1987). These books can be regarded as part of a wider project following and constituting the so-called 'crisis' in social psychology (see Parker, 1989) and the 'turn to discourse' and social constructionism across the social sciences (e.g. Gergen, 1973; Harré and Gillett, 1994; Shotter, 1993).[1] These writings were,

---

[1] The term 'discursive psychology' (and subsequently 'critical discursive psychology') has also been adopted by other authors (e.g. Harré and Gillett, 1994; Parker, 2002; Wetherell, 1998).

in turn, influenced by a variety of theoretical strands in psychology, sociology and philosophy including social constructivist approaches to cognitive development (e.g. Bruner, 1986; Vygotsky, 1978), ecological work in memory research (e.g. Neisser, 1982), the language philosophy of Wittgenstein (1953) and Austin (1962), social studies of science (e.g. Gilbert and Mulkay, 1984), the ethnomethodological programme within sociology (Garfinkel, 1967) and the writings of Sacks (cf. 1992) on conversation analysis and membership categorisation analysis.

A major goal of many of these publications was to unpack, critique and respecify the topics of social, developmental and cognitive psychology and their methods of investigation. For example, in their analysis of interview talk, Potter and Wetherell (1987) illustrated the variable, carefully managed and rhetorically contingent nature of 'attitudes' as they are organised in interview talk, as well as the constitutive nature of discourse in building versions of events. With regard to memory, the focus shifts to everyday talk about memories and epistemic claims: how people talk about past events and orient to memory as a participants' concern (Edwards and Middleton, 1990). Other themes in DP include the study of sexism, heterosexism and racism (e.g. Speer and Potter, 2000; Wetherell and Potter, 1992), attribution, argumentation and accountability (e.g. Antaki, 1994; Buttny, 1993) and identity construction (e.g. Antaki and Widdicombe, 1998). Some authors are influenced, to a greater or lesser extent, by themes of social power and oppression in Foucauldian and post-structuralist theory (see Hepburn, 2003 for an overview). Recently, however, discursive psychology is increasingly influenced by the conversation analytic studies of Sacks, Schegloff and others, and we will explain this in more detail later.

There are several key features of DP. It conceives of human action in such a way as to understand discourse as *action oriented*, whereby actions are to be analysed in their situated context rather than as discrete units of activity (Potter, 2003). Discourse is both *constructed*: people talk by deploying the resources (words, categories, commonsense ideas) available to them, and *constructive*: people build social worlds through descriptions and accounts thereof (Potter, 2003; Wetherell, 2001). DP therefore examines members' *situated* descriptions of persons, categories, events and objects. It investigates, for example, how 'factual descriptions' are produced in order to undermine alternative versions, to appear objective and reasonable or weak and biased, and deal with the speaker's and others' motives, desires, intentions and interests (Edwards and Potter, 1992). DP pays attention to the persuasive and rhetorical work done in producing descriptions and accounts and the subtle inferential work that is done as objects, people and events are described *this* way rather than *that* way. There is a fundamental shift from treating psychological states (e.g. anger, intention, identity) as operating behind talk as explanations for why people say the things they do. DP embraces what Chomsky called 'performance', leading analysts away from the traditional psychological treatment of language as a channel to underlying mental processes and experimental studies of those processes. Instead, DP studies how common-sense psychological concepts (such as mental or cognitive states) are deployed in, oriented to and handled in the talk and texts that comprise social life. Thus language is not treated as an externalisation of underlying thoughts, motivations, memories or attitudes, but as *performative* (Edwards in press, a). For example, saying 'I don't remember' or 'I don't know' may or may not be 'accurate' in any kind of verifiable sense, but saying such things in the context of surrounding talk (e.g. in a courtroom, in a classroom, to one's partner) can comprise subtle discursive moves that manage the current business at hand.

In their most recent writings, Edwards and Potter (in press) set out a clear agenda and programme of work for DP, including its theoretical basis and its preferred methods for collecting, transcribing and analysing data. They identify three key overlapping strands of interest:

1 'Respecification and critique': the study of how psychological topics are 'transformed into (or rediscovered as) discourse practices' (Edwards, in press, a). In this strand of work, traditional psychological topics such as 'health attitudes' are investigate as topics of discourse and the object of discursive practice.

2 'The psychological thesaurus': the study of instances in everyday talk and interaction where psychological terminology (e.g. jealous, angry, motive) is occasioned by speakers to perform local interactional work (argue a case, construct a particular version of events).

3 'Managing psychological implications': the study of the situated, turn-by-turn orientation to, and handling of, psychological business (e.g. issues of blame, prejudice, intention, memory).

These themes in DP require a detailed analysis of talk in its interactional context. In order to explore the uptake and response to 'factual' accounts, the trajectory of inferential and persuasive rhetoric, or the way psychological business is managed, discursive psychologists must pay close attention not only to an individual speaker's turns in talk, but to the sequential organisation of entire interactions. As mentioned earlier, DP is most closely (and increasingly) related to a version of discourse analysis called *conversation analysis* (CA). CA, as developed by Sacks, Schegloff and Jefferson (e.g. 1974), is the study of naturally occurring 'talk-in-interaction': the mundane and ordinary conversations that constitute social life. It is a rigorous empirical method for studying the organisation of interaction, routine patterns and procedures and for producing 'repeatable qualitative studies of interaction' (Potter, 2003, p. 74). It examines, via turn-taking sequences, the way 'members' interpret ongoing talk and display their interpretations and commonsense reasoning in each subsequent turn. For conversation analysts, like discursive psychologists, talk performs social actions. Greetings, invitations, compliments, storytelling, complaints, and so on are achieved in talk, and analysts have found that these actions are highly ordered and routinized events. Via the micro-level analysis of transcripts, robust and generalizable patterns of social interaction have been found across an unlimited range of interactional moments. For example, in a greeting sequence, one greeting ('hello') is routinely, and thus normatively and in preference, followed by another greeting. This finding of normativity (or 'generalizability' in traditional terminology) does not require statistical analyses. It is a generalizable finding in the sense that this is what normatively happens in talk and we can see people orienting to the norm, especially when something goes wrong. When a sequence of turns does not fit the emerging pattern, we can analyse the 'deviant case'. Turns at talk set up what comes next, but this is not a deterministic 'cause-effect' relationship. It is in *breaches* that the order of social action is revealed (Garfinkel, 1967): it is not that normative patterns have been incorrectly observed.

DP's methodology: Questions, data collection and analysis

The influence of CA can be observed not only in DP's analytic approach but also in its formulation of *research questions*, its preferred choice of *data collection* and method of *transcription*. DP does not ask the cause-effect questions typical in psychology, so rather than asking 'What is the effect of X on Y?' DP asks 'How is X done?' DP questions might include 'How do doctors manage giving bad news to patients?', 'How do patients make sense of diagnoses?' or 'How might medical advice be more effectively presented?' When analysing talk itself, analysts avoid asking 'Why' questions ('Why was that thing said') but ask 'How' is it there now: 'Why that [turn at talk], in that way, right now?' (Heritage, 1984, p. 151).

DP aims to follow rigorous programme of analysis, using sophisticated technology to collect and analyse naturally occurring interactions across wide variety of contexts. Early work was based on loosely structured interviews (cf. Wetherell and Potter, 1992). However, many discursive psychologists prefer to ground their work in recordings of naturally occurring data. Studies have examined recordings of a variety of contexts including those relevant to health and clinical practice such as counselling talk (Edwards, 1995), psychiatric interviews and therapy talk (Antaki, 1999), child helpline interaction (Potter and Hepburn, 2003) and mealtime interaction (Wiggins, 2003).

Data collection therefore centres on the audio and video recording of interactions in everyday and institutional contexts. Sample size can vary depending on the aim of research. In their analysis of NSPCC helpline interaction, Potter and Hepburn (2003) have collected hundreds of calls and, from there, made systematic observations about opening sequences and other phenomena. On the other hand, Beach (2000) analyses a single brief conversation in order to make points about the way storytelling works. Data are transcribed according to a system devised for CA by Gail Jefferson (1984), and is illustrated in our later examples. This method was developed to enable a focus on talk as social interaction. It includes details such as precisely timed pauses, aspects of intonation and vocal delivery, the onset of overlapping talk and the mechanics of turn-taking.

Ethical issues around access, consent and anonymity are important when dealing with recordings of people's lives. Participants must give informed consent by, for example, signing a consent form before recording takes place or responding to the verbal delivery of an ethics 'script' at the start of an interaction. Digital recordings, which are used increasingly in preference to standard cassette tapes and dictaphones, can be manipulated to preserve anonymity. For instance, voice quality can be transformed and identifying features (such as names or places) can be reversed or erased completely. Once the recording has been anonymised, and the transcript produced, analysis proper can start, which begins in the process of transcription itself.

We noted at the start of this chapter that DP is not a recipe-like method with distinct steps to follow. It is a craft skill learnt by engaging with data sets and by reading other DP analyses (Potter, 2003). However, some authors have attempted to describe

....

[2] Transcription notation from Jefferson (1984):

Symbol	Function
1	Line number
A:	Current speaker
CAPS	Indicates louder than surrounding talk
Underlining	Indicates emphasis
(.)	Micropause
(0.2)	Timed pause to nearest tenth second
=	Latching – no pause between turns
((context))	Contextual information if necessary
Yes[I agree]	Indicates beginning and ending of overlapping talk
[yeah]	
Ye:ah	Colon indicates prolonged sound of preceding part of utterance
?	Rising intonation
!	Excited intonation
.⁻	Shift to higher or lower pitch
Wh-	Dash marks abruptly cut-off sound
.hhh and hhh	Intake of breath/exhalation
.	Periods (full stops) mark falling, stopping intonation ('final contour'), irrespective of grammar, and not necessarily followed by a pause.
,	'Continuation' marker, speaker has not finished; marked by fall-rise or weak rising intonation, as when enunciating lists
>he is<	'greater than' and 'lesser than' signs enclose speeded-up talk. Sometimes used the other way round for slower talk.
°Quiet°	Softer tone within degree signs
Heh heh	Voiced laughter. Can have other symbols added, such as underlinings, pitch movement, extra aspiration, etc
Sto(h)p i(h)t	Laughter within speech is signalled by h's in round brackets
( ), (guess)	Untranscribable, or transcriber's guess at a word
*	Croaky pronunciation of immediately following section

the basic procedures involved in an attempt to elucidate the process. DP is not a hypothesis-based project. One might begin with an interest in a particular topic (e.g. body image and dieting) and then consider the types of data that might tap that interest (e.g. tape recordings of self-help weight management groups). Alternatively, one might approach a pre-existing data set without having a particular interest and see what emerges after a thorough engagement with it. Then again, one might begin with an interest in a setting (e.g. therapy talk) and see where analysis of the data leads. After data recording and transcription, the first step in analysis requires a thorough reading and re-reading of the transcripts whilst listening to the recordings. Analysis proceeds with one or a series of 'noticings': sequences of talk that grab your attention. For instance, in a corpus of doctor-patient interaction, you might become interested in the 'diagnosis' sequences, and so the next step would be to collect together the instances of interest: both transcript excerpts and related sound files (Potter, 2003).

The next step is to look for patterns in the extracted sequences, by examining the internal organisation of individual speakers' turns and accounts, the preceding and subsequent turns, and deviant cases in emerging patterns. Phenomena found in the details of talk, such as lexical choice, speakers' self corrections, hesitations, pauses, overlaps are features that may be consequential for the interactional trajectory (Potter, 2003). Edwards (in press, a) notes that analysts should attend to the actions performed in talk and participants' concerns and orientations: the categories and concepts they make relevant to ongoing interaction. The focus is on how speakers attend reflexively to their basis for knowing things (epistemic orientations), how they seem to resist being seen as biased, motivated or emotionally involved. Edwards also instructs researchers to analyse *rhetorically*: to think about what might be being countered or what might have been said. DP also attends to the function of *variation* in accounts: the seemingly contradictory descriptions or attitudes that appear at different moments, doing different things for specific purposes (Potter, 1998). More generally, one should focus on speakers' orientations to their own and others' accountability: a pervasive feature of social action whereby people attend to own activities as rationale, objective and plausible (Potter, 2003).

Validation of discursive analysis is achieved in a variety of ways and reflects the differing concerns of the approach, which stand in marked contrast to validation procedures for conventional measurement DP studies are validated primarily through *participants' orientations*. Given that for DP and CA participants display their understanding of the interaction as they take each turn at talk, the analyst's explication is grounded in participants' sense making orientations. For example, rather than claiming 'Speaker X is talking this way because she is a doctor' (or any other category), or that 'Speaker Y is talking this way because he can't remember events accurately', DP claims might focus on the way being a doctor is made relevant to the interaction by speakers themselves, or on how they talk about past events and orient to their own memories by producing vividly detailed descriptions or, alternatively, vague and imprecise ones. Other validation strategies include attending to deviant cases in order to show whether the claims made are robust or need reworking, and considering the coherence of claims by examining the phenomenon in comparative materials as well as in other analysts' reports on similar features of talk or contexts.

Having spent some time exploring DP's theory and practicalities, we now move on to consider its application to health and clinical contexts and utility for both academics and practitioners.

DP and clinical and health psychology

Over the past ten years, health and clinical psychologists, both academics and practitioners, have looked increasingly to qualitative methodologies, most commonly interview and focus group-based studies, to examine a variety of topics. These include: people's accounts of their health practices (e.g. Radley and Billig, 1996), the organisation of discursive encounters in medical and other institutional contexts (e.g. Maynard, 2003; Middleton, 1996), constructionist approaches to therapy (e.g. Riikonen and Smith, 1997), conversations about health risks, health promotion messages, news reports about health issues, and official documents on health or clinical policy (Lupton, 1992), narrative approaches to medicine (Greenhalgh and Hurwitz, 1999) and the subjective experience of health, ill health and mental illness (e.g. Willig, 2000; Yardley, 1997).

As we have seen, a defining feature of DP is its examination of social practices in real world everyday and institutional settings. Within DP and CA, health and clinical-relevant work focuses on the fine-grained analysis of conversational encounters in specific contexts and examines the sequential patterns in such interactions and their implications. Not only do these kinds of data provide an insight into daily practices, they also complement the different perspective on research – what kinds of knowledge we can obtain, and so on – that DP provides (Potter, 2003). In the area of health or clinical psychology, such data are particularly useful for examining how participants' constructions of health matters are managed in interaction. The examples we provide illustrate how DP can be used to explore how people request help at the doctor's, how speakers manage sensitive issues in AIDS counselling, and constructions of healthy eating in mealtime interaction.

Requesting help at the doctor's

Our first example is taken from Gill, Halkowski and Roberts (2001), and is concerned with the way in which subtle 'hints' are made by a patient as a way of requesting an HIV test. This is a rather delicate situation as the patient may be seen as doing the 'doctor's work', or trying to diagnose themselves. In the extract below the patient (Pt) broaches the issue as the doctor (Dr) starts to look through the patient's health history form.[3] This section of talk is taken from around the middle of the consultation session,

---

[3] Note that in Gill *et al*'s paper they show how non-verbal detail, such as gaze orientation and shuffling papers, are also used to manage this activity. Here we focus on the verbal only.

after talk about migraines and an ear problem. The patient's medical notes show that she has had a hysterectomy and bladder repair some years ago.

Extract 1: VTG/migraine trouble 13

1 Dr: .hh Alright uh- hu- let's see- So: = uh > l:emme just look-<

2 (0.5)

3 Pt: One uh [thuh things that's always worried] my kids-

4 Dr: [look through some things here]

5 Pt: .hh uh:: about that I (ws-) also had blood transfusions

6 °when I had (.) thee hysterec[tomy°]

7 Dr: [Mm hm?]

8 Dr: Mm hm

9 Pt: >°An they said°< did you ever get tested for AIDS

10 Didju ever get tested fe(h)r A(h)I(h)DS y(h)a [kn(h)ow?] .hh

11 Dr: [.hh]

12 Dr: We[ll?]

13 Pt: [No:?] I never got teste(h)d for AI::DS [y(h)a] kno:w,

14 Dr: [ptch]

Gill *et al.* (2001) highlight four main ways in which the patient manages the issue of having an AIDS test: downplaying the urgency of the concern, reporting a particular circumstance, avoiding ownership, and using a question to elicit an answer. Let us examine each of these in turn. First, the issue is raised in the middle of the consultation. The patient had an opportunity to broach it earlier, but delaying talk about it avoids appearing overly concerned about it. Second, the patient reports a circumstance – having had blood transfusions during a hysterectomy operation – without directly saying that she may have AIDS. That is, she provides the means by which the doctor can formulate the implications of this circumstance himself. Again, this allows the patient to avoid looking like she is jumping to conclusions.

The third way in which the issue is managed is through talking about the patient's children as being the 'concerned party'. Through footing shifts (Goffman, 1981) where the speaker removes him/herself as being the source of the talk, she avoids 'owning' the concern; rather, this is portrayed as something that her children are worried about. Finally, the use of the reported question, 'did you ever get tested for AIDS?' (lines 9 and 10), makes an answer relevant here. Indeed, the doctor himself invites such an answer ('well', line 12), to which the patient replies. This reported question-answer then sets up the AIDS test as being relevant here (having not had one already, and given the previous talk about blood transfusions), without the patient appearing to be motivated or overly concerned.

Dealing with sensitive issues in counselling interaction

As we have seen, many health or clinical encounters require a degree of sensitivity, and discursive analyses have allowed researchers to examine how this is achieved or managed in interaction. For example, Silverman (1997) has conducted research into HIV/AIDs counselling and has shown, amongst other things, how and that potentially delicate items are sequentially organized. In the following extract the speakers are engaged in pre-test counselling, in which the client (P) is being asked about risk factors around HIV infection:

Extract 2: DS/UK1 (44–63)

```
 1  C  [.hhh Uhm .hhh d'you know if any of your: your er
 2     partners have been drug users. =Intra[venous drug=
 3  P  [No:.
 4  C  =[users is our main [uhm you- you've never used=
 5  P  [they haven't. [Mm
 6  C  =needles for yourself [(either. = No). .hh I ask=
 7  P  [No:
 8  C  =everybody those questions. =I haven't saved them
 9     [up for you..hhhh Obviously when we're talking=
10  P  [(That's okay yeah).
11  C  =about HIV .hhhh uhm (.) the intravenous drug using
12     population are a population that are at ri:sk.
13  P  Yea[:h
14  C  [Because (.) if they share needles (.) then
15     they're sharing (.) infection with the blood on the
16     needles obvious[ly.
17  P  [Mm hm
```

During an interaction such as the one above, speakers need to manage the potential risk that they might be blamed for their situation (i.e. that it was the client's 'fault' they became infected) and also the negotiation of identities (such as being a drug user, or associating with people who take drugs). Silverman uses a discursive analysis to show how these issues are managed through discursive items such as 'prefaces' and 'category descriptions' in their talk. On line 1, for example, C prefaces her question with 'd'you know'. This avoids the more direct question: 'have any of your partners been drug users', which may suggest that P would *knowingly* associate with people in this category. The 'd'you know' thus shifts the focus slightly, and manages this delicate question.

Silverman also demonstrates how category descriptions are used – often accompanying delays and prefaces – to manage sensitive issues. The category 'partner' (line 2) is more subtle than, for example, 'lover' or 'boyfriend', in that it doesn't imply sexual contact as readily as the latter two categories. When C then asks a more direct question about P herself (lines 4–6) the question is in the negative form, where the preferred answer (Pomerantz, 1984) is a confirmation of the question. Alongside the justification of asking the question (lines 6–9) by C, this also helps to counter the implication that C might suspect that P was the sort of person who would engage in intravenous drug use.

Defining health in mealtime talk

Our final example is taken from an everyday setting: the family mealtime, drawing on data collected by Wiggins. Within health psychology, a great deal of research has focused on measuring people's attitudes towards food and changing eating habits. However, questionnaire-based work on food preferences misses the social aspect of such behaviours and fails to explore their situated occurrence. Our example illustrates how DP can be used to examine the management of healthy eating alongside inter-actional concerns. In the extract below Dave, the father, is being questioned about how he has not eaten his 'greens' by his 21-year-old daughter, Jo. Also present at the meal is the mother of the family, Mary, and the family dog:

Extract 3: SKW/ E2a-M2 (593–655)

```
 1  (2.0)
 2  Jo:   → you haven't eaten your ↑greens:
 3  Dave:  its r:abbit °food° (0.6) I've ate en↑ou:gh of it
 4  ↓thanks:
 5  (4.0)
 6  Dave:  I'd end up ↓looking like a ↑rabbit >wouldn't ↑I<
 7  ((sound of clattering plates))
 8  (2.4)
 9  Dave:  and then you'd be chasing me ↑wouldn't you=
10  ((as if spoken to dog))
11  Jo:   → =it's got ↑vitamins in tho'
12  Dave:  I've ↑ate a lot of ↓it (0.6) 'ave the ↓rest if
13  you [want it
14  Mary:  [not 'alf of it
15  (0.4)
16  Dave:  I ↓'aven't >I've had< more than 'alf of it↑
```

17 Mary: >°no you haven't°<

18 Dave: I 'a<u>ve</u> (0.6) (en<u>ou</u>gh, ye<u>a</u>h) ((*comical, deep voice*))

19 (1.0)

20 Mary: your <u>d</u>aughter's <u>m</u>aths: is getting ↓better and

21 yours: is getting ↑worse

22 (1.4)

23 Dave: par↑don ((in distance – leaves table/room))

24 (1.2)

25 Mary: I said your <u>d</u>au:ghter's <u>m</u>aths: is getting <u>better</u>

26 and <yours is getting: ↑w<u>o</u>rse>

27 (5.0)

A DP approach is used here to examine how the speakers negotiate what counts as 'healthy' food, and what they *should* be eating as a result. In the extract above, Jo points to the nutritional value of the food as being a reason for eating it, despite Dave's claim that it is 'rabbit food' (line 3). This is achieved through the 'tho'^' on line 11, which disregards the previous counter-claims by Dave, and constructs the vitamin content as being more important.

Note also how the 'healthy eating' talk is being used here not so much as advice or information about what Dave should eat, but rather it holds him accountable for his behaviour in this setting. We can see this not only through Jo's talk, but also through the way in which this is managed by Dave and Mary. The conversation turns to the *quantity*, rather than the quality, of food eaten as being the issue at stake. There is also the subtle negotiation of who has the *right* to tell another person how much (or what) they should be eating; remember this is the daughter accusing her father.

In this brief extract, then, we can see how a number of issues could be teased apart through using a more detailed and discursive approach to the interaction. By examining how the conversation is structured and constructed, we can gain an insight into how speakers manage identities, expectations and requirements about eating, and their identities within a family setting.

Concluding comments

Our examples show how we can use discursive techniques, orienting to participants' talk, examining sequences and organization, and so on, to examine how particular activities are achieved. As Potter (1998) has noted, the value of this kind of analysis is that it allows us to examine how interaction is structured and, therefore, made sense of, in particular ways. For example, interaction involves managing identities, rights to knowledge and attending to one's accountability and all this may be analysed for how it is achieved. If we can see more clearly *how* this is done, then we are in a better position to inform or change practices, and to have a greater understanding of our social and cultural construction of health.

Further reading

The following texts provide clear discussions of discursive psychology and/or some consideration of its value to health and clinical psychologists and practitioners:

Edwards, D. and Potter, J. (1992). *Discursive Psychology*. London: Sage.

Murray, M. and Chamberlain, K. (eds) (1999). *Qualitative Health Psychology: Theories and Methods*. London: Sage.

Potter, J. (1998). Qualitative and discourse analysis. In A. S. Bellack and M. Hersen (eds) *Comprehensive Clinical Psychology*. Oxford: Pergamon.

References

Antaki, C. (1994). *Explaining and Arguing: The Social Organization of Accounts*. London: Sage.

Antaki, C. (1999). Interviewing persons with a learning disability: how setting lower standards may inflate well-being scores. *Qualitative Health Research*, **4**: 437–54.

Antaki, C. and Widdicombe, S. (eds) (1998). *Identities in Talk*. London: Sage.

Austin, J. L. (1962). *How to do Things with Words*. London: Oxford University Press.

Beach, W. A. (2000). Inviting collaborations in stories about a woman. *Language in Society*, **29**: 379–407.

Billig, M. (1987). *Arguing and Thinking: A rhetorical approach to social psychology*. Cambridge: Cambridge University Press.

Bruner, J. (1986). *Actual Minds, Possible Worlds*. London: Harvard University Press.

Buttny, R. (1993). *Social Accountability in Communication*. London: Sage.

Edwards, D. (1995). Two to tango: script formulations, dispositions, and rhetorical symmetry in relationship troubles talk. *Research on Language and Social Interaction*, **28**(4): 319–350.

Edwards, D. (in press, a). La psicología discorsiva (Discursive psychology). In L. Iñiguez (ed.) *Análisis del Discurso: Manual para las Ciencias Sociales (Discourse Analysis: Manual for the Social Sciences)*. Barcelona: Edicions de la Universitat Oberta de Catalunya.

Edwards, D. (in press, b). Analyzing racial discourse: The discursive psychology of mind-world relationships. In H. Van Den Berg, M. Wetherell and H. Houtkoop (eds) *Analyzing Interviews on Racial Issues*. Cambridge: Cambridge University Press.

Edwards, D. and Mercer, N. (1987). *Common Knowledge: The developing of understanding in the classroom*. London: Methuen and Co.

Edwards, D. and Middleton, D. (eds) (1990). *Collective Remembering*. London: Sage.

Edwards, D. and Potter, J. (1992). *Discursive Psychology*. London: Sage.

Edwards, D. and Potter, J. (2001). Discursive psychology. In A. McHoul and M. Rapley (eds) *How to Analyse Talk in Institutional Settings: A casebook of methods*, pp. 12–24. London and New York: Continuum International.

Edwards, D. and Potter, J. (in press). Discursive psychology, mental states and descriptions. In H. te Molder and J. Potter (eds) *Talk and Cognition: Discourse, cognition and social interaction*. Cambridge: Cambridge University Press.

Garfinkel, H. (1967). *Studies in Ethnomethodology*. Englewood Cliffs, NJ: Prentice Hall.

Gergen, K. J. (1973). Social psychology as history. *Journal of Personality and Social Psychology*, **26**: 309–320.

Gilbert, G. N. and Mulkay, M. (1984). *Opening Pandora's Box: A sociological analysis of scientists' discourse*. Cambridge: Cambridge University Press.

Gill, V. T., Halkowski, T. and Roberts, F. (2001). Accomplishing a request without making one: a single case analysis of a primary care visit. *Text*, **21**(1/2): 55–81.

Goffman, E. (1981). *Forms of Talk*. Oxford: Blackwell.

Greenhalgh, T. and Hurwitz, B. (1999). Narrative-based medicine. *BMJ*, **318**: 48–50.

Harré, R. and Gillett, G. (1994). *The Discursive Mind*. London: Sage.

Hepburn, A. (2003). *An Introduction to Critical Social Psychology*. London: Sage.

Heritage, J. (1984). *Garfinkel and Ethnomethodology*. Cambridge: Polity Press.

Jefferson, G. (1984). Transcript notation. In J. M. Atkinson and J. Heritage (eds) *Structures of Social Action: Studies in Conversation Analysis*, pp. ix–xvii. Cambridge: Cambridge University Press.

Lupton, D. (1992). Discourse analysis: A new methodology for understanding the ideologies of health and illness. *Australian Journal of Public Health*, **16**(2): 145–150.

Maynard, D. (2003). *Good News, Bad News: Conversational order in everyday talk and clinical settings*. University of Chicago Press.

Middleton, D. (1996). A discursive analysis of psychosocial issues: talk in a 'parent group' for families who have children with chronic renal failure. *Psychology and Health*, **11**: 243–260.

Neisser, U. (1982). *Memory Observed: Remembering in naural contexts*. Oxford: Freeman.

Parker, I. (1989). *The Crisis in Modern Social Psychology, and How to End It*. London: Routledge.

Parker, I. (2002). *Critical Discursive Psychology*. New York: Palgrave Macmillan.

Pomerantz, A. (1984). Agreeing and disagreeing with assessments: some features of preferred/dispreferred turn shapes. In J. M. Atkinson and J. Heritage (eds) *Structures of Social Action: Studies in conversation analysis*, pp. 57–101. Cambridge: Cambridge University Press.

Potter, J. (1998). Qualitative and discourse analysis. In N. Schooler (ed.) *Comprehensive Clinical Psychology: research methods*, vol. 3. Amsterdam: Elsevier Press.

Potter, J. (2003). Discourse analysis and discursive psychology. In P. M. Camic, J. E. Rhodes and L. Yardley (eds) *Qualitative Research in Psychology: Expanding perspectives in methodology and design*. Washington: American Psychological Association.

Potter, J. and Hepburn, A. (2003). 'I'm a bit concerned': Early actions and psychological constructions in a child protection helpline. *Research on Language and Social Interaction*.

Potter, J. and Wetherell, M. (1987). *Discourse and Social Psychology: Beyond attitudes and behaviour*. London: Sage.

Radley, A. and Billig, M. (1996). Accounts of health and illness: dilemmas and representations. *Sociology of Health and Illness*, **18**(2): 220–240.

Rapley, T. J. (2001). The (art)fullness of open-ended interviewing: Some considerations on analysing interviews. *Qualitative Research*, **1**(3): 303–333.

Riikonen, E. and Smith, G. M. (1997).*Re-imagining Therapy: Living conversations and relational knowing*. London: Sage.

Sacks, H. (1992). *Lectures on Conversation*, vol. I, edited by G. Jefferson. Oxford: Blackwell.

Sacks, H., Schegloff, E. A. and Jefferson, G. (1974). The simplest systematics for the organisation of turn taking in conversation. *Language*, **50**: 697–735.

Shotter, J. (1993). *Conversational Realities: Constructing Life Through Language*. London: Sage.

Silverman, D. (1997). *Discourses of Counselling: HIV counselling as social interaction*. London: Sage.

Speer, S. A. (2002). Natural and contrived data: A sustainable distinction? *Discourse Studies*, **4**(4): 511–526.

Speer, S. and Potter, J. (2000). The management of heterosexist talk: Conversational resources and prejudiced claims. *Discourse and Society*, **11**: 543–72.

Vygotsky, L. S. (1978). *Mind in Society: The development of higher psychological processes*. London: Harvard University Press.

Wetherell, M. (2001). Themes in discourse research: The case of Diana. In M. Wetherell, S. Taylor and S. J. Yates (eds) *Discourse Theory and Practice: A Reader*. Buckingham: Open University Press.

Wetherell, M. and Potter, J. (1992). *Mapping the Language of Racism: Discourse and the legitimation of exploitation*. Hemel Hempstead: Harvester Wheatsheaf.

Widdicombe, S. and Wooffitt, R. (1995). *The Language of Youth Cultures*. Hemel Hempstead: Harvester Wheatsheaf.

Wiggins, S. (2003). Good for you: Generic and individual healthy eating advice in family mealtimes. *Journal of Health Psychology* xx-xx

Willig, C. (2000). A discourse-dynamic approach to the study of subjectivity in health psychology. *Theory and Psychology*, **10**(4): 547–570.

Wittgenstein, L. (1953). *Philosophical Investigations*. Oxford: Blackwell.

Yardley, L. (ed.) (1997). *Material Discourses of Health and Illness*. London: Routledge.

Chapter 13

Experimental methods in clinical and health research

Andy P. Field and Graham C. L. Davey

There are, broadly-speaking, two approaches that can be taken to answer research questions or to try to find evidence to support theories in clinical and health psychology. The first is to observe what naturally happens. This is, we administer some measures (or observe some behaviour) that capture certain mood states or psychological constructs relevant to the research question at hand. Typically we then correlate these measures or observations to see whether they are, statistically-speaking, related (for a range of techniques see Miles, this volume). This is known as *cross-sectional* or *correlational* research. Some examples of this type of research are the findings that disgust sensitivity is related to self-reported fears (Davey, 1994), that eating disorders are related to low self-esteem and perfectionism (Hewitt *et al.*, 1995) or that shyness is related (rather unsurprisingly) to social phobia (Heiser *et al.*, 2003). The alternative is to actively manipulate some aspect of the environment and observe the effect it has on some variable of interest. This is known as *experimental research* and some examples of this are the findings that social phobics selectively attend to angry faces (Mogg *et al.*, 2004), that negative information about novel animals makes children avoidant of them (Field and Lawson, 2003), or that obsessive-compulsive-like behaviours can be induced in people without obsessive compulsive disorder simply by manipulating their mood and the task instructions (Startup and Davey, 2001; Davey *et al.*, 2003). This chapter looks at experimental methods and why they are important in clinical research. We begin by looking at how experiments allow causal inferences and end by looking at how such causal inferences are essential in clinical psychology to unearth the mechanisms that drive abnormal behaviour.

Why are experiments important?

Correlational research and causal inference

In correlational research we either observe natural events (such as facial interactions between a mother and child) or we take a snapshot of many variables (such as administering several questionnaires, each measuring a different aspect of personality, at the same point in time, to see whether certain personality characteristics occur in the same people at that moment in time). The good thing about this kind of research is that it provides us with a very natural view of the question we're researching: because the researcher is not influencing what happens they get measures of the variables that should be free of *experimenter bias* (that is, bias introduced by the experimenter being there). This kind of research normally, therefore, has some *ecological validity*, which means that the findings are meaningful within the everyday environment. However, this kind of research does not allow causal inferences to be made. For example, we might find (using appropriate measures) that teenage condom use is related to percep-tions of risk from unsafe sex. It is tempting to assume that attitudes to risk cause teenagers to use condoms: however this inference is invalid. There are two problems:

1 Direction of causality: although 'common sense' may lead you to conclude in the above example that attitudes to risk cause condom use, it is equally valid to conclude that condom use causes attitudes to risk. This isn't a ridiculous idea: if a person never uses a condom and catches an STD or produces an unwanted child this may well change their risk perception about unsafe sex. However, even if it doesn't make sense logically, the direction of causality cannot be determined from correlational research. Imagine we went to a pub and measured blood alcohol lev-els and how drunk people were, and found a relationship between the two. Much as logic dictates that increased blood-alcohol levels cause drunkenness it would be equally valid to conclude that being drunk causes blood-alcohol levels to rise. In the clinical examples above, this means that we don't know whether disgust sensi-tivity causes fear or fear causes disgust sensitivity, and whether perfectionism causes eating disorders or eating disorders lead to perfectionism.

2 The tertium quid: This refers to the possibility another variable exists that has an effect on both the proposed cause and the outcome. So, there may be a variable (such as anxiety) that causes both condom use and increased risk perception from unsafe sex. Likewise, disgust sensitivity and fear might both be caused by a more general variable such as behavioural inhibition or oversensitivity to anything alien.

This is the major limitation of correlational research. However, if we can't make causal inferences from correlational research then how can we?

Identifying causes

The issue of causality has been long-debated by philosophers and methodologists (see Field and Hole, 2003 for a brief history). Much of current experimental methodo-logy stems from the ideas of two philosophers: David Hume (1748, 1739–40) and John Stuart Mill (1865). Hume started the ball rolling by proposing three criteria to infer cause and effect:

1 Contiguity (cause and effect occur close together in time);

2 The cause must occur before an effect does; and

3 The effect should never occur without the presence of the cause.

There are some problems with these ideas (some of which we've already seen). For a start, contiguity is not essential: we can probably all think of examples when we've had something to eat that has made us sick the following day. Now the food is certainly the cause of the illness, yet the illness happens some time later and can be a powerful reinforcer of avoidance behaviour (Garcia and Koelling, 1966). Therefore, cause and effect need not be contiguous.

The observation that cause should precede effect is important, though, because it takes a step beyond mere correlation between variables measured at the same point in time. As such, it goes some way to solving the 'direction of causality' problem. However, this criterion does not rule out the tertium quid: there could still be another variable that influences both the apparent cause and the effect. Finally, the problem with the effect never occurring without the cause is that effects can have multiple causes. Even Hume himself was aware of the difficulties of assuming causality from these three conditions and he believed that the inference to causality was a psychological leap of faith and not one that was logically justified (see Field and Hole, 2003).

Mill (1865) developed Hume's ideas to describe three conditions necessary to infer cause:

1 Cause has to precede effect;

2 Cause and effect should correlate;

3 All other explanations of the cause-effect relationship must be ruled out.

As you can see, the first condition is 'borrowed' from Hume. The second condition is also similar to Hume's criteria; however, Hume merely said that the effect should not occur without the cause, whereas Mill took this a step further to suggest a correlation is important. However, perhaps Mill's most important contribution was to add the third condition, which essentially says 'kill the tertium quid'! To verify that the third criterion is true, Mill proposed three methods:

1 The method of agreement: an effect should be present when the cause is present.

2 The method of difference: when the cause is absent the effect will be absent also.

3 The method of concomitant variation: when the two previous relationships are observed, causal inference will be made stronger because most other interpretations of the cause-effect relationship will have been ruled out.

Put simply, all Mill is saying here is that the correlation between cause and effect should be perfect: it is not good enough to have a correlation, that correlation should be perfect in that cause always leads to effect and absence of cause always leads to absence of effect.

Manipulating causes

Field and Hole (2003) sum up Mill's ideas by saying that the only way to infer causality is through comparison of two controlled situations: one in which the cause is present and one in which the cause is absent. These situations should be identical in all senses except the presence of cause. This forms the basis of experimental methodology (although the situation is rarely as simple as having only two conditions). The simplest experiment involves two conditions: one in which the proposed cause is present (an *experimental group* or *condition*), and one in which that cause is absent (a *control group* or *condition*). You then measure the effect that you're predicting and if the proposed cause is actually a cause then there will be a difference between the groups in the outcome measured. So, the emphasis is on *systematic manipulation* of the proposed cause.

For example, Field and Lawson (2003) wanted to look at the effect of negative information on children's behaviour towards novel animals (some Australian marsupials). Rachman (1977) had suggested that negative information was a viable pathway through which phobias develop. Although adult phobics did report remembering receiving negative information in childhood, this did not mean that this information caused their phobia. Field and Lawson manipulated the proposed cause (negative information) by giving children negative information about one animal (proposed cause present) and no information about another (proposed cause was absent). After the information they took various measures of their fear beliefs, but also asked children to place their hands in some touch boxes that the children believed contained the animals about which they'd heard information. Children were more reluctant to place their hand in the box containing the animal about which they'd heard negative information than the box containing the animal about which they'd been given no information (the boxes both contained toy animals, not the real thing!). This illustrates Mill's ideas: by comparing two situations, one in which the proposed cause is present and one in which the proposed cause is absent, differences in responses (in this case avoidant behaviour) can only be due to the information given. The cause preceded effect: when the cause was present, avoidance occurred, and when cause was absent avoidance didn't occur. Therefore, we can conclude that the negative information caused the avoidance.

Why are experiments important for developing theories in clinical psychology?

So far we've looked at how experimental methods allow causal inferences to be drawn whereas cross-sectional methods do not. We now turn our attention to look at why these causal inferences are important for developing strong theories of psychopathology.

Building theories on the basis of experimental manipulation – the best approach

In almost all fields of science, theories are about how things work; and things work because of causal relationships between the elements that make that thing into a dynamic process. As we have described previously, the best way to infer causal relationships – and therefore the best way to build theories – is to manipulate the supposed causes of an effect, and build up a model of what is being explained in terms of these causal relationships. As we have also explained, this involves setting up experimental conditions in which the putative cause is present, and comparing these with control conditions where the putative cause is absent.

In clinical psychology, such experiments have allowed us to understand a number of features of psychopathology. For example, it is now well known that anxiety states are significantly related to how an individual will process information – and especially information about threat and danger. In particular, anxious individuals have been shown to preferentially allocate attention to threatening stimuli and threatening information (Mathews and MacLeod, 1994; Eysenck, 1997; Mogg and Bradley, 1998), and this information processing bias appears to maintain hyper-vigilance for threat and maintain their anxious state. Two particular procedures have been important in identifying this information processing bias, the emotional Stroop procedure (e.g. Mathews and MacLeod, 1985; Watts, McKenna, Sharrock and Trezise, 1986) and the attentional probe task (e.g. MacLeod, Mathews and Tata, 1986). In the former procedure, participants are presented with individual words in coloured ink. Some of these words are threat-relevant (e.g. death) and others are emotionally neutral (e.g. carpet). The participant has to name the colour of the ink as rapidly as possible. Most Stroop studies indicate that individuals suffering anxiety take longer to name the colour of threat-relevant words than do non-anxious individuals, suggesting that their attention has been biased towards processing the threatening word rather than its colour (see Mathews and MacLeod, 1994 for a review). In the attentional probe task, participants are presented with a threat word and a neutral word in different locations on a computer screen. A probe stimulus then appears in the location formally occupied by one of the words, and the participant has to detect this location as rapidly as possible. Participants with high levels of anxiety show more rapid detection of probes in the location previously occupied by the threat word – suggesting that their attention had been selectively biased towards the threat word (e.g. Bryant and Harvey, 1997; Bradley, Mogg, White, Groom and de Bono, 1999).

These experimental studies suggest there is a link between anxiety and how an individual will process information about threats, but they do not indicate the *direction* of the relationship because most of the studies tend to have been carried out in between-subject designs (comparing anxious participants with non-anxious participants) where neither variable has been experimentally manipulated. So, does anxiety cause the information processing bias, or is the information processing bias a source of anxiety? The way to unequivocally discover the direction of this relationship is to independently manipulate either anxiety or the way that people process information, and see whether these manipulations do have an effect on the other variable. Recent studies that have attempted to experimentally induce information processing biases in non-clinical populations have suggested that attentional and interpretative biases for threat may indeed have a causal effect on experienced anxiety and the processing of future information (Mathews and MacLeod, 2002). These studies have shown that experimentally induced processing biases for threat will not only cause congruent changes in state anxiety, but also tend the individual to interpreting new information in a threatening way (Mathews and Mackintosh, 2000; Mathews and MacLeod, 2002; Hertel, Mathews, Peterson and Kintner, 2003).

Because studies of the relationships between anxiety states and information processing have tended to use these stringent experimental methods, they have given rise to robust theories of how anxiety influences information processing and influences the acquisition and maintenance of anxious psychopathology (Williams, Watts, MacLeod and Mathews, 1997; Mogg and Bradley, 1998). These studies are now forming the basis of training procedures which can alleviate such biases in anxiety sufferers (e.g. Mathews and MacLeod, 2002; Hertel, Mathews, Peterson and Kintner, 2003).

Building theories on correlational data – the seductive, but hazardous, route!

A poor alternative to conducting a tightly controlled experiment is to investigate whether your putative cause is indeed related to the putative effect using a correlational design. If a significant correlation is found between measures of your putative cause and effect, then this does provide evidence that is *consistent* with your theory – but it by no means confirms or proves your theory.

It is tempting to undertake correlational studies in clinical research (usually utilising questionnaire methodology) for a number of reasons:

1 Access to clinical populations is often restricted and difficult to obtain,

2 There are important ethical issues in doing research with people suffering distressing disorders – especially if the research might make their symptoms worse, and

3 Such individuals are often undergoing treatment or therapy, which may make the results of particular studies difficult to interpret.

Because of factors such as these, it is tempting to use the least invasive research method, and correlational studies using questionnaire methodology often appear to provide such a compromise. However, such studies should only be the first step to confirming the existence of relationships between variables, and the nature of these relationships needs to be subsequently pursued wherever possible using experimental methodology.

Davey (2003) has described at least two problems with theory building in circumstances where the relationships between supposed causes and effects have not been thoroughly experimentally verified and have tended to be based primarily on data from correlational studies.

First, for the past 10 years, research on the role of disgust in psychopathology has burgeoned and recent review articles have proclaimed disgust as the 'forgotten emotion of psychiatry (sic)' (Phillips, Senior, Fahy and David, 1998), and studies have implied that the disgust emotion is a significant causal factor in animal phobias, obsessive-compulsive disorder, blood-inoculation-injury phobia, and eating disorders (Davey and Bond, 2005). To be sure, disgust is certainly *experienced* in these disorders, but the majority of research has been correlational in nature and what few experimental studies there are in the literature have so far failed to provide real convincing evidence that disgust has any precipitating or causal function. Jumping from correlation to causation is one thing, but the issue here is that the design of many correlational studies on disgust may provide inaccurate and misleading evidence on which to build theories of the role of disgust in psychopathology. First, many studies have failed to use properly balanced designs in which predicted disgust-relevant psychopathologies are compared with suspected disgust-*irrelevant* psychopathologies (see Davey and Bond, 2005). Because anxiety and disgust are closely related emotions, studies which do not include disgust-irrelevant control comparisons do not provide differential predictions that would rule out the implication of anxiety as a mediating variable – thus, rendering the findings relatively trivial. When studies have included disgust-irrelevant psychopathologies, some have begun to reveal significant relationships between disgust and those psychopatholologies that would *not* have been predicted a priori (e.g. between disgust and situational phobias, height phobia and claustrophobia) (Muris, Merckelbach, Schmidt and Tierney, 1999; Davey and Bond, 2005). Furthermore, many studies have not taken *any* measure of trait or state anxiety. Thus, they will inevitably be unable to determine whether any relationship between disgust and psychopathology measures is independent of levels of anxiety (e.g. Arrindell *et al.*, 1999). It is quite clearly possible that elevated disgust levels may be a consequence of the effects of anxiety raising levels of all negative emotions, and we have yet to rule out the possibility that disgust per se has *no* causal role in psychopathology. The defining evidence, of course, will come when experiments that have manipulated disgust levels show that this manipulation significantly elevates measures of psychopathology, and that other factors that might be related to disgust (e.g. anxiety) can be ruled out as the causes of this effect.

Second, by the very nature of the sub-discipline, much of the theorising in clinical psychology has been developed using constructs derived from clinical experience. Such constructs have a validity through the fact that the clinician commonly experiences a set of characteristics within a particular clinical population. The usual practice is then to develop a tool or instrument to measure the construct, and subsequently to identify how the construct relates to clinical symptoms, usually using a correlational methodology. Unfortunately, quite often, these constructs can detract from attempting to elucidate the cognitive and psychological mechanisms that underlie a disorder, confuse descriptions of symptoms with causes and consequences of the symptoms, and generally set off unproductive chains of research (Davey, 2003). In anxiety research alone, constructs that are still actively used to 'explain' anxious psychopathology include: 'Not just right experiences (NJREs)' (Coles *et al.*, 2003), intolerance of uncertainty (Buhr and Dugas, 2002), and inflated responsibility (Barrett and Healy, 2003). All are used in contexts where the construct is assumed to give a better insight into the psychological characteristics of certain disorders (e.g. NJREs) or have some explanatory purpose (e.g. intolerance of uncertainty, inflated responsibility). Apart from a few exceptions, such constructs are linked to symptoms of psychological disorders using correlational methodologies.

Davey (2003) discusses the example of NJREs as an instructive one in this context. Individuals with OCD frequently report uncomfortable sensations of things not being quite right, and they will continue with their ritualistic compulsions until this feeling has gone. Coles *et al.* (2003) report that preliminary investigation of this construct reveals that NJREs are correlated with OCD features but not with features of other domains of psychopathology, that NJREs may represent a specific form of perfectionism, and that compulsions may represent attempts to relieve the anxiety caused by NJREs. Quite possibly. But in creating constructs such as this, researchers need to ask a series of very important questions: (1) does the construct merely re-describe the symptomatology of OCD (and so cannot be a cause of the symptoms)? (2) Is the construct (and its experience by the client) simply a trivial, epiphenomenal consequence of the mechanisms underlying OCD (e.g. are NJREs themselves caused by other factors which are the real causes of OCD)? And (3) Does the construct really help in any way to explain the *causes* of the psychopathology? None of the answers to these questions can be easily found in correlational analyses, and active manipulation of important variables in an experimental context is necessary to tease out such answers. So at this stage, to say that the construct of NJREs is helpful in explaining OCD is going well beyond the data, and possibly leading researchers on unproductive research paths.

Summary and conclusions

In this chapter we have tried to show you the benefits of experimental methodology when applied to clinical problems. We have shown how philosophical ideas about identifying causes and effects have been translated into empirical paradigms through the idea of control groups and systematic manipulation of proposed causes. We have also illustrated some of the limitations of building theories on correlation work and how experiments can be a useful way to identify mechanisms that cause clinical problems. The benefit of knowing such mechanisms is that they can be manipulated in therapy. Of course, this is a one-sided picture and experiments have their limitations too. Although the rigours of experimental work allow firm statements about cause and effect to be made the findings may be limited to the controlled laboratory environment and may not translate to the real world. The predictably trite conclusion is that there is a place for both approaches, but we hope to have convinced you that experimental work is essential for good theory-building.

References

Arrindell, W. A., Mulkens, S., Kok, J. and Vollenbroek, J. (1999) Disgust sensitivity and the sex difference in fears to common indigenous animals. *Behaviour Research and Therapy*, **37**, 273–280.

Barrett, P. M. and Healy, L. J. (2003) An examination of the cognitive processes involve din childhood obsessive-compulsive disorder. *Behaviour Research and Therapy*, **41**, 285–299.

Bradley, B. P., Mogg, K., White, J., Groom, C. and de Bono, J. (1999) Attentional bias for emotional faces in generalized anxiety disorder. *British Journal of Clinical Psychology*, **38**, 267–278.

Bryant, R. A. and Harvey, A. G. (1997) Attentional bias in posttraumatic stress disorder. *Journal of Traumatic Stress*, **10**, 635–644.

Buhr, K. and Dugas, M. J. (2002) The intolerance of uncertainty scale: psychometric properties of the English version. *Behaviour Research and Therapy*, **39**, 931–945.

Coles, M. E., Frost, R. O., Heimberg, R. G. and Rheaume, J. (2003) 'Not just right experiences': perfectionism, obsessive-compulsive features and general psychopathology. *Behaviour Research and Therapy*, **41**, 681–700.

Davey, G. C. L. (2003) Doing clinical psychology research: What is interesting isn't always useful. *The Psychologist*, **16**, 412–416.

Davey, G. C. L. and Bond, N. (2005) Using controlled comparisons in disgust psychopathology research: The case of disgust, hypochondriasis and health anxiety. *Journal of Behavior Therapy and Experimental Psychiatry*, in press.

Davey, G. C. L., Startup, H. M., Zara, A., MacDonald, C. B. and Field, A. P. (2003) Perseveration of checking thoughts and mood-as-input hypothesis. *Journal of Behavior Therapy and Experimental Psychiatry*, **34**, 141–160.

Eysenck, M. W. (1997) *Anxiety and Cognition: A unified theory*. Hove, England: Erlbaum.

Field, A. P. (2005) *Discovering Statistics Using SPSS*, 2nd edn. London: Sage.

Field, A. P. and Hole, G. (2003) *How to Design and Report Experiments*. London: Sage.

Field, A. P. and Lawson, J. (2003) Fear information and the development of fears during childhood: effects on implicit fear responses and behavioural avoidance. *Behaviour Research and Therapy*, **41**, 1277–1293.

Garcia, J. and Koelling, R. A. (1966) Relation of cue to consequence in avoidance learning. *Psychonomic Science*, **4**, 123–124.

Heiser, N. A., Turner, S. M. and Beidel, D. C. (2003) Shyness: relationship to social phobia and other psychiatric disorders. *Behaviour Research and Therapy*, **41**, 209–221.

Hertel, P. T., Mathews, A., Peterson, S. and Kinter, K. (2003). Transfer of training emotionally biased interpretations. *Applied Cognitive Psychology*, **17**, 775–784.

Hume, D. (1739–40) *A Treatise of Human Nature* (ed. L. A. Selby-Bigge). Oxford: Clarendon Press, 1965.

Hume, D. (1748). *An Enquiry Concerning Human Understanding*. Chicago: Open Court Publishing Co., 1927.

MacLeod, C., Mathews, A. and Tata, P. (1986) Attentional bias in emotional disorders. *Journal of Abnormal Psychology*, **95**, 15–20.

Mathews, A. and Mackintosh, B. (2000) Induced emotional interpretation bias and anxiety. *Journal of Abnormal Psychology*, **109**, 602–615.

Mathews, A. and Macleod, C. (1985) Selective processing of threat cues in anxiety states. *Behaviour Research and Therapy*, **23**, 563–569.

Mathews, A. and MacLeod, C. (1994) Cognitive approaches to emotion and emotional disorders. *Annual Review of Psychology*, **45**, 25–50.

Mathews, A. and MacLeod, C. (2002) Induced processing biases have causal effects on anxiety. *Cognition and Emotion*, **16**, 331–354.

Mill, J. S. (1865). *A System of Logic: Ratiocinative and Inductive*. London: Longmans, Green.

Mogg, K. and Bradley, B. P. (1998) A cognitive-motivational analysis of anxiety. *Behaviour Research and Therapy*, **35**, 297–303.

Mogg, K., Philippot, P. and Bradley, B. P. (2004) Selective attention to angry faces in clinical social psychology. *Journal of Abnormal Psychology*, **113**, 160–165.

Muris, P., Merckelbach, H., Schmidt, H. and Tierney, S. (1999) Disgust sensitivity, trait anxiety and anxiety disorders symptoms in normal children. *Behaviour Research and Therapy*, **37**, 953–961.

Phillips, M. L., Senior, C., Fahy, T. and David, A. S. (1998) Disgust – the forgotten emotion of psychiatry. *British Journal of Psychiatry*, **173**, 373–375.

Rachman, S. (1977) The conditioning theory of fear acquisition: a critical examination. *Behaviour Research and Therapy*, **15**, 375–387.

Watts, F. N., McKenna, F. P., Sharrock, R. and Trezise, L. (1986) Color naming of phobia-related words. *British Journal of Psychology*, **77**, 97–108.

Williams, J. M. G., Watts, F. N., MacLeod, C. and Mathews, A. (1997) *Cognitive Psychology and Emotional Disorders*, 2nd edn. Chichester, UK: Wiley.

Chapter 14

The importance of considering effect size and statistical power in research

David Clark-Carter

Introduction

This chapter will explain why you need to take account of effect size when designing and when reporting research. It will give an effect size for each of the standard statistical tests which health and clinical psychologists employ. In addition, it will look at the need to consider statistical power when choosing a sample size for a study and how statistical power can help to guide the advice which you can give when discussing future research.

What is an effect size?

Imagine that you have created an intervention which is designed to reduce the worry which psoriasis sufferers experience. You wish to test your intervention and so you randomly assign half a sample of sufferers to an intervention condition and half to a control condition. After the period of the intervention you test all your participants on the Penn State Worry Questionnaire (PSWQ). You screen the data and conclude that a between-subjects t-test is the appropriate test of your hypothesis that the intervention is effective (or, strictly speaking, you test the null hypothesis that the control and intervention groups have the same PSWQ scores).

Imagine that you run the test and the result is statistically significant. What do you conclude? Before I look at what you would conclude I want to look at what exactly the statistical test is telling you. Let us say that the probability you are given for your t-test is $p = 0.03$. This probability is telling you that the result of the t-test (or an even larger t-value) could happen on 3 per cent of occasions when the null hypothesis is true. Nonetheless, despite knowing that your result could occur if the null hypothesis were to be true, because the p-level is less than 0.05 you choose to reject the null hypothesis and conclude that your intervention is effective. However, if someone asked you *how* effective your intervention was, if you relied solely on the information provided by having run the t-test you would not be able to answer. As I will demonstrate later that significant result is dependent, among many other factors, on the size of the effect and the sample size.

Unlike the result of the t-test and therefore the probability, an effect size is largely, mathematically independent of the sample size. I say *mathematically* because any estimate, based on a sample, of what would be true in a population is more accurate the larger the sample. Nonetheless, an effect size is much more independent of sample size than a probability derived from a statistical test. In the design I have been describing, one of the most straightforward effect sizes is Cohen's *d*:

$$d = \frac{\text{mean}_1 - \text{mean}_2}{\text{SD}}$$

where mean_1 and mean_2 are the means of the two groups and SD is a measure of standard deviation. Thus, *d* tells you how much difference there is between the two means, *in terms of standard deviations*. This latter aspect is important because it takes account of the nature of the measure being used, whereas the difference between the means alone would not allow for this. In this way, different studies which have used different sample sizes and different measures of worry can be compared; looking at statistical significance alone would not permit this.

Both the American Psychological Association (2001) in its latest Publications Manual and the journals published by the British Psychological Society now encourage strongly the reporting of effect sizes.

Other examples of effect sizes

Statisticians have devised a number of measures of effect size and even the same design/statistical test can have more than one measure of effect size associated with it. Rather than attempt to give an exhaustive description of them, I am going to give one effect size for each type of situation; each one has been chosen because it is the most intuitively understandable.

When looking at the correlation between two variables then *r* (Pearson's product moment correlation coefficient) can itself be treated as a measure of effect size. When you move from comparing two levels of an independent variable, as in the worry example above, to situations where you would use an analysis of variance (ANOVA) then η^2 (eta-squared) is an appropriate measure of effect size. The equation for eta-squared is:

$$\eta^2 = \frac{\text{sum of squares of treatment}}{\text{total sum of squares}}$$

What η^2 tells you is the proportion of the overall variance in scores which can be attributed to differences in scores between the levels of the independent variables. Thus if you extended the worry example to include a control group and two intervention groups then η^2 would tell you how much of the variation in scores could be attributed to the difference between the groups.

In regression you are trying to predict one variable, for example worry, from one or more other variables, for example, severity of psoriasis and measures of coping strategies. Here

R^2 is a measure of effect size; like η^2 it tells you about the proportion of variance in the variable to be predicted which is accounted for by the predictor variables.

Finally, when you are dealing with nominal (or categorical) data such as gender and smoking status, you might use χ^2 to test for differences in proportions of smokers between the two genders. Here w can be used as an effect size, where w is found from:

$$w = \sqrt{\frac{\chi^2}{N}}$$

and N is the overall sample size.

Criteria for judging the size of an effect

Jacob Cohen (1962, 1988) championed the use of effect size by psychologists and others in the behavioural sciences. He reviewed research which had used particular statistical techniques and identified what would constitute small, medium or large effects for each measure of effect size. Thus, for d 0.2, 0.5 and 0.8 would be small, medium and large effects respectively. For r and w the equivalents are 0.1, 0.3 and 0.5. For η^2 they are approximately 0.01, 0.06 and 0.14 and for R^2 they are approximately 0.02, 0.13 and 0.26. Using Cohen's guidelines it is possible to classify the result of a particular study in terms of small, medium and large effects.

This should not be confused with clinical importance; what constitutes an important effect will obviously depend on the situation so that a small effect could be important if life and death were involved, while in another context a result would have to be above a large effect to be important.

Can I get my statistical package to report the effect size?

I am going to stick to SPSS for the answer. It does not provide Cohen's d. It routinely reports r and R^2 for the appropriate tests. You can ask it to provide η^2 but it will only be the same as the version I have shown when the analysis is a one-way between-subjects ANOVA. It calculates what is called partial eta-squared which involves an adjustment to the standard η^2. However, for the one-way between-subjects analysis the adjustment is not made. For the other designs I would recommend calculating η^2 yourself rather than relying on partial η^2. In the case of the effect size for χ^2 (w), you can request a statistic which will be the same as w as long as either there are only two rows or two columns in the table you are analysing. With that restriction, phi (for a two by two table) or Cramér's phi (for more than a two by two table) will be the same as w. Confusingly, SPSS calls it Cramer's V. (This is possibly because of historical reasons about the way characters used to be printed.)

What is statistical power?

If you reject your research hypothesis (or some would say, fail to reject the null hypothesis) then you may be committing what has come to be known as a Type II error: rejecting a research hypothesis when it is true. Statistical power is the probability that you will avoid a Type II error.

Why is statistical power important?

If you don't have a reasonable level of statistical power, then the result of your statistical test is likely not to be significant. In other words, you won't have given your hypothesis a reasonable chance of being supported. This will be true however big the effect size of your study. Cohen and others have recommended that as a minimum we should aim for power of 0.8. There is a direct link between statistical power and the probability of a Type II error. If power is 0.8 then the probability of a Type II error (1 – power) is 0.2. Typically in psychology and many other disciplines we set a probability of 0.05 as the critical level for judging whether a result is statistically significant. In other words, we are willing to risk making a Type I error (rejecting the null hypothesis when it is true) if the probability of our result is 0.05 or less. The question then arises as to why the level we are willing to risk a Type II error is four times that which we are willing to risk a Type I error. In fact these levels are not set in stone and they depend on the relative importance of committing either of the two types of error. Thus, there will be situations when we wish the risks of committing either error to be equal and so we could set power at 0.95 and thus the danger of committing a Type II error at 0.05.

How can I try to improve the statistical power of my test?

There are many factors which influence the statistical power of a test. However, many of these will be determined by the nature of the research hypothesis being tested, the measures being used and the design of the study. Nonetheless, once all those features have been chosen there are two remaining aspects which are critical: the effect size and the sample size. The first is not really under our control, but once we have a figure for it we can determine the sample size which will give us the level of statistical power which we seek.

What magnitude of effect should I be seeking?

The simple answer is: it depends on the situation. I will describe three possible routes to deciding on an effect size to put into the power calculations. The first and preferable method is to look at previous relevant research. If you are fortunate then the researchers will have reported the effect sizes from their studies. However, if they haven't it is still possible to use descriptive statistics which have been reported to work out an effect size. Thus, if means and standard deviations have been reported then you could calculate Cohen's *d*. It is at this point that you often realise just how bad the reporting of results in many papers is.

A second approach is to use the information from your pilot study to work out an effect size. Bear in mind, however, what I said earlier about sample size. If your pilot study has only been conducted on a relatively few people then the effect size you calculate from their data may be rather inaccurate as an estimate of the effect in the population.

The third approach, in the absence of previous appropriate research, is to decide what effect size would be a minimum below which you wouldn't be interested. You could decide this in two ways. One would be to refer to Cohen's guidelines and say that if the effect was below a medium effect size then it wouldn't be of interest. Accordingly, you would choose to have a sample size which gave adequate power if the result were to be a medium effect size. The alternative would be to start from the point of view of clinical importance. Thus, to return to the worry example, you might say that unless your intervention can reduce the mean worry score by at least four points you are not interested. Then using the norms for the test, you could calculate the Cohen's d which would result if you did manage to reduce worry by such an amount.

How can I calculate statistical power?

Once you have determined the design of your study – between-subjects or within-subjects – the statistical test you are going to use, whether the test will be one or two tailed, what critical level you are going to use for deciding whether the result will be statistically significant (usually 0.05), the effect size you are seeking and the level of power which you want to achieve then you can choose the sample size to give you that level of power. This can be done either by referring to power tables (see for example Clark-Carter, 1997; Cohen, 1988; Kraemer and Thiemann, 1987) or using computer programs (for example Gpower – Erdfelder, Faul and Buchner, 1996).

To illustrate the point I am going to continue with the worry example. I wish to test my intervention and I'm going to have a control group and an intervention group – a between-subjects design. I predict that my intervention will reduce worry; in other words, I have a directional hypothesis and so can use a one-tailed test. Given the nature of the measure and the design I am going to use a between-subjects t-test. I want to reduce worry by at least four points on the scale. I find, from Fortune, Richards, Griffiths and Main (2002) that the test had a standard deviation of 8.8. Therefore, the effect size d would be 0.45 (or just under a medium effect size according to Cohen). I want to achieve power of 0.8. I can now put those calculations into a computer or use them to enter the appropriate power table. This tells me that I would need 64 people in each group to achieve that level of statistical power.

It is worth noting what effect requiring a higher level of power has on the necessary sample size. To achieve power of 0.9 with a medium effect size of $d = 0.5$ one would need 70 people in each group and for power of 0.95 one would need 90 people in each group.

What if there is a restriction on the number of participants available?

In such a situation you can turn the process on its head and calculate what effect size would yield the required level of power for the available sample size. For example, if I had access to a maximum of 32 participants then for the same design I would have to achieve an effect size of 0.9 (above what Cohen identified as a large effect size) if I were to achieve power of 0.8.

Statistical power and ethics

It may seem an odd thing to say but statistical power is an ethical issue. There is little point in running a study with so few participants that even if the effect size was relatively large the result is highly likely to be found not to be statistically significant. You will have wasted the time of your participants and possibly exposed them to psychological risks unnecessarily. Similarly, if you involve many more participants than would be required to provide an adequate level of power you will be wasting people's time and exposing them to unnecessary psychological risk. It is not surprising then that in recent years ethics committees have become much more aware of statistical power. Accordingly, it is no longer possible to pluck a sample size out of the air: you will have to justify the sample size on the basis effect size and power considerations.

What should I do if the result of my study is not statistically significant?

In the absence of effect size and statistical power all you had to go on was statistical significance. With them, if your result is not statistically significant, you can use the effect size which you have obtained to calculate what sample size would be necessary in future research to obtain a required level of power. Imagine that we carried out our intervention study and that the result was not statistically significant. We calculate the effect size and find that instead of being 0.45, as we had hoped, it was only 0.3 (or a reduction of 2.64 in the mean worrying score). At this point we have a choice over what we recommend. If we consider that the reduction is too small then we would recommend amending the intervention to try to achieve a larger effect. On the other hand, we might decide that if the reduction we found could be consistently achieved then it would be worth applying such an intervention. We would recommend replicating the study but we could calculate that 140 people would be needed in each group to achieve power of 0.8. In this way we could give specific advice for future research. It would stop the temptation to write that if we had used more participants we might have achieved significance. Such a statement is a tautology; if you use enough participants even the most trivially small result can be statistically significant if you use a two-tailed hypothesis (Cohen, 1988).

What happens if my research hypothesis is that there is no effect?

Sometimes researchers have an explicit hypothesis that there is no difference between two groups, for example that there will be no difference between two interventions. Sometimes there is an implicit hypothesis of no difference, for example when a preliminary test is run to check that males and females don't differ on some measure before combining their results to form a single larger sample. The logic of what I have described so far is that if you had a small sample size and therefore low statistical power then your two groups may very well be shown not to be statistically different, but that would hardly mean that they were not in fact different. Accordingly, to defend yourself against the claim that you have failed to find a difference simply because your study was underpowered you need to adopt a different strategy. One approach is to decide on an effect size which you would consider small enough that if the groups only differed by that amount then they could be treated as sufficiently similar for your purposes. You could back this up by choosing a power level of 0.95 (and thus a probability of committing a Type II error of 0.05) and use a sample size which would achieve that level of power.

It is for this reason that a number of tests which are routinely employed by psychologists and others are problematic. A goodness of fit test such as the one-group χ^2 or the χ^2 which comes from structural equation modelling (SEM) is used to check whether the data fit a hypothetical model. In the case of goodness of fit it might be testing whether the distribution is normal. If the sample is small then the result is likely not to be significant and there is then the danger that the conclusion is drawn that the data fit the model well. However, there is the opposite danger that a large sample size will show even a small difference between model and data as being significantly different and so lead to an erroneous conclusion of a poor fit. SEM packages supply a range of fit indexes which help to deal with this problem.

A similar issue arises over preliminary tests of the assumptions of tests and explains why many people do not recommend their use. As an example, Levene's test is routinely reported as a check on whether two samples have sufficiently similar variances (homogeneity of variance) to allow the use of a standard between-subjects t-test. However, if the samples are small then quite marked differences between the variances may not show up as significantly different, while if the samples are large enough even a small difference between them could be found to be significant. For this reason many people recommend the use of rules of thumb which have come from simulation studies designed to test the effect of certain sizes of difference in variance on the veracity of the probability provided by the *t*-test.

Summary

During the design phase of a study decide on a size of effect which you predict or a minimum value that would be worth finding. Choose a minimum level of statistical power below which you would not want to go. Find the sample size which would be necessary to achieve that level of power for the effect size. When reporting your results always report the size of the effect. If the result is not statistically significant calculate the sample size which would be necessary to achieve your required level of power if the study were to be repeated and use that information to guide the advice you give over future research.

References

American Psychological Association (2001) *Publication Manual of the American Psychological Association*, 5th edn. Washington, DC: American Psychological Association.

Clark-Carter, D. (2004) *Doing Quantitative Psychological Research: A student's handbook*. Hove: Psychology Press.

Cohen, J. (1962) The statistical power of abnormal-social psychological research: a review. *Journal of Abnormal and Social Psychology*, **65**, 145–153.

Cohen, J. (1988) *Statistical Power Analysis for the Behavioral Sciences*, 2nd edn. Hillsdale, New Jersey: Lawrence Erlbaum Associates.

Erdfelder, E., Faul, F. and Buchner, A. (1996) Gpower: A general power analysis program. *Behavior Research Methods, Instruments, and Computers*, **28**, 1–11.

Fortune, D. G., Richards, H. L., Griffiths, C. E. M. and Main, C. J. (2002) Psychological stress, distress and disability in patients with psoriasis: Consensus and variation in the contribution of illness perceptions, coping and alexithymia. *British Journal of Clinical Psychology*, **41**, 157–174.

Kraemer, H. C. and Thiemann, S. (1987) *How Many Subjects? Statistical power analysis in research*. London: Sage.

Chapter 15

Reliability

Susanne Hempel

Reliability – what is it and what is it for?

The information about the reliability of a test or measure can tell me whether this test or judgement is accurate, whether its results are dependable and whether when I use the test, it will lead to consistent and reproducible results. The reliability of a test or a judgement refers to the question of whether the results are repeatable if I use the test or ask for the judgement again.

Reliability is a concept that is most important in measurement generally, and psychometric testing specifically.

Psychometric testing and measurement

Much psychological research is about assessing and quantifying characteristics of a person and differences between people. In other words, it is about measurement.

Measurement commonly happens in one of two ways in clinical and health psychology. We can construct psychometric tests – we can ask the person we are interested in about where they sit on the construct (see Darcy, this volume). Alternatively, we can ask other people to rate them, perhaps after reading a transcription of an interview (see Fylan, this volume).

Very often in clinical and health psychology, we are interested in theoretical constructs like *quality of life*. These abstract concepts have to be translated into something that we can measure. We need to design a test that gives us an indication of the construct of interest. We want to represent construct characteristics with test scores. Different scores in a test should represent differences between people – if a person scores differently on two occasions, then this should represent a real change in the person, i.e. after some form of therapy. We are hoping that the test scores represent a true score, and so show what the people behind the test scores are really like. However, we have to assume that we make errors when we measure theoretical constructs (or anything else) in a test.

The reliability of a test can be expressed in terms of classical test theory. In these terms, reliability is defined as the proportion of the total variance that is due to true variance. When defining reliability in the framework of classical test theory we deal with the implications of this specific theory. Classical test theory is not the only test theory; an alternative item response theory (IRT) offers a different approach (see Santor, this volume; Embretson and Reise, 2000), but the majority of psychometric tests are still designed following the classical test theory principles.

Classical test theory

Classical test theory is a measurement theory that is used to examine data from psychometric tests, and helps to communicate the quality of a test. Parts of the theory are formulated as axioms going back to Gulliksen (1950). The mathematical derivatives within the theory were promoted by Lord and Novick (1968). Measurement error is a central issue in this test theory – random errors that can distort a test result. The main axioms concern the nature of measurement errors and the assumption of a 'true' score.

We want to represent the characteristics of a person and point out the differences between people with test scores. Different scores in a test should represent differences between people or real changes in a person. Differences in test scores could also be due to random errors, e.g. person A misunderstood the question and has therefore a different score from person B. In the sense of the total variance of the test, the reliability indicates how much of this is due to true differences, and all the rest must be error. The reliability indicates how accurately the test reflects true scores, and true differences, and not just measurement error.

Classical test theory stresses the fact that measuring involves measurement error. If a test consists of only one item, like only one question to assess how *healthy* someone is, the probability is high that some of answers of some people to this question are errors, for example, because people will interpret the question of health differently – some may consider mental aspects of health (I am feeling depressed, therefore I am unhealthy); some may consider physical aspects (I am feeling depressed, but I don't have a cold, therefore I am healthy); some may consider long term aspects (I have a cold, but I don't have arthritis, osteoporosis nor asthma, therefore I am healthy); the others may consider short term aspects (I have a cold, therefore I am unhealthy). Complex issues need to be translated into more than one question; therefore more indicators are necessary to come to an accurate assessment. Psychometric testing involves the construction of scales – more than one item is constructed to assess a difficult construct (see Santor, this volume).

Measurement theory provides us with mathematical derivatives that prove practical test construction issues, i.e. that a longer test is a more reliable test. With a larger sample of items, it is to be expected that a more adequate measure of a person can be obtained. Intuitively, one might argue that with every item also a source of measurement error is added to the test. However, the measurement error axiom assumes that the expectancy value of the errors is zero – that is the mean error is zero. That means if an infinite number of people is tested, all errors will cancel each other out – not every single person will misunderstand the questions in the same way. So with a longer test, and errors cancelling each other out, the true part of the test will increase with each new (and comparable) item. While the error variance doubles, the true variance quadruples and so the proportion between true and error variance improves with more items.

The way that the reliability of a test increases is described by the Spearman-Brown prophecy formula, given by:

$$r^*_{xx} = \frac{Nr_{xx}}{1 + (N - 1)r_{xx}}$$

Where r_{xx} is the reliability of the test, r^*_{xx} is the predicted reliability of the test, and N is the proportion of items in the new test, relative to the old test. For example, if we have a test with 20 items, and a reliability of 0.7, and we want to know what the reliability would be if we were to increase the number of items to 40, we use $r_{xx} = 0.7$, and $N = 2$. We would therefore find that the predicted reliability is 0.82.

The formula can be rearranged to ask how much longer we need to make a test, in order to achieve a certain level of reliability.

$$N = \frac{r^*_{xx}(1 - r_{xx})}{r_{xx}(1 - r^*_{xx})}$$

For example, if we have a test with five items, and a reliability of 0.5, and we would like to have the reliability equal to 0.8. If we calculate this we find that $N = 4$, meaning that we will need to make the test four times longer, i.e. 20 items long, to achieve a reliability of 0.8.

Measures of reliability

Several methods have been proposed to measure reliability, some are test orientated and some are rater orientated. The method will measure the reliability in a specific sample, which in itself is an estimate of the test reliability in the population.

The first cluster of methods is entirely test based. We want to know how reliable a test is, so we need tests to measure the reliability. There are many different ways: the parallel test method, the test-retest and a group of internal consistency methods, which cover several approaches.

Other ways of testing for reliability are rater orientated. They do not concentrate on the measure but on people – raters who are judging targets.

Measure orientated

Measure orientated reliability tests cover different aspects of reliability, namely equivalence, stability and consistency. They assess slightly different sources of measurement error. Traub (1994) provides a comparison of test orientated reliability measures.

Parallel test

Some test constructors provide two parallel version of a test. In this case, both tests should be applied simultaneously to see whether they come to the same results.

Both tests use a selection of items that are designed to measure the construct in question, so both selections should come to similar results. The higher the correlation between the two tests, the higher the reliability. Parallel test reliability scores assess the equivalence of both parallel tests. Parallel tests provide information about the selectiveness of an item sample that has to be chosen from an infinite number of possible items. Items are measures for theoretical constructs. Each item will cover a slightly different aspect of the construct and I hope that the selection of items that I choose for my scale will cover the content of the construct well. If two parallel tests, designed to assess the same construct, come to widely different results for a person, the equal covering of the construct content has obviously failed.

Parallel versions of tests are rare, one reason being the difficulty of producing adequate parallel versions. The items created need to be very similar, or a very similar sample of items needs to be included in both versions. This is less difficult when dealing with ability measures: mathematical problems that differ in the numbers but refer to the same mathematical task can be produced easily. For health, personality, or attitude tests however, it is very hard to produce two sets of questions that are completely alike in their content coverage. A distinction is made between two forms of parallel test – parallel and strictly parallel tests: a strictly parallel assessment assumes equal variance, equal error variance, and equal means across items.

If a parallel test is available for a test, it can be used in follow up studies without the main problems discussed under test-retest reliability approaches, in the next section. However, for this quality of interchangability, a parallel test reliability of 0.90 should have been obtained for the test versions (Kline, 1998).

Test-retest

A more common method is the test-retest reliability. For this, the test would be applied at one point and then applied again after some time.

When stable features of a person are assessed, the test should come to the same results both times. This is usually measured by a correlation between the two test outcomes over all participants. This procedure will test the stability aspect of the reliability. The test-retest reliability estimate can demonstrate the generalisability of the test scores over different test occasions by assessing test performance stability.

There are typical problems when the same test is applied again, depending on whether an ability or traits, attitudes or states are assessed. In the case of ability tests, some people might have learned or remembered what they were asked in the test before. This is a typical carryover effect: the question in the first test influences the answer in the second test (Kaplan and Saccuzzo, 2001). In measures of health behaviour, personality or attitude test two types of effect may occur. First, we may find that people remember their previous answer, and repeat it – thus increasing the measured reliability of the measure, but the increase would be an artefact, not real. The second problem is that many measures related to health and clinical psychology are not stable – people's scores may have changed, and we falsely interpret this as a lack of reliability.

To interpret a test-retest reliability it is important that we know the period of time between the tests – these should always be reported.

An alternative to the test-retest method that has become used increasingly commonly in the medical literature is the limits of agreement method (Bland and Altman, 1986). They suggest that the correlation coefficient is inappropriate, as the two measures can have considerable disagreement, and yet still correlate highly. Instead they suggest that the confidence intervals of the agreement between the measures be calculated – that is, given a certain value of the measure at time 1, what would the expected measure at time 2 be? (Although see also Streiner and Norman, 2003, for a different view of the Bland and Altman method.)

Internal consistency

Another cluster of methods are the internal consistency methods. Here the reliability is measured within the original study, within one single presentation of the test. As this method does not require additional administration of the test or of a parallel test it is a comparable easy way of obtaining a reliability measure. The rationale to check for internal consistency within the test is that every single item of a scale was designed to be a test of the construct. Therefore, the items should show consistency.

Split half

One way of measuring internal consistency is called the Split Half method. The test will be applied and then split into two halves and scored separately. The next step is to see whether both halves come to the same result. Both halves measure the same construct, so the closer the results match, i.e. the higher the correlation between the test halves' results, the better.

The main problem with a split half method is how to split the test. How can two equal halves be created? The arbitrary assignment of items can create halves that differ from each other in their specific content selection. An even-odd division of the test is the easiest approach. But also if I let a computer choose randomly which item belongs to which half, how do I know that this is the best solution?

It should be noted that the correlation coefficient between the two halves over each participant is in this case not the reliability of the test but of a test of half the length and therefore should be adjusted using the Spearman Brown formula (already mentioned).

Corrected item total correlation

Another method is called corrected item total correlation. Each item on the test should correlate with the test total, so we can examine the item total correlations, to ensure that each item is correlated with the total, and that each item is therefore contributing to the test. However, the item-total correlation is biased, because the scale total was calculated from all items, including the item that we are testing. Because of this problem it is preference to use the corrected item-total correlation, that is the correlation between an item and the test score calculated without the item under test.

A high corrected item total correlation indicates that the item is closely related to the content that the scale represents and that the item is better than others at predicting the scale score. A low correlation between an item and the scale suggests that the item measures something conceptually different from the scale. When this occurs during the scale construction process, this item would be considered for removal from the scale.

When reporting the corrected item total reliability some authors present the results for all items, or indicate the average corrected item total correlation for all items of the scale.

Inter-item correlation

A simple method to assess the reliability of a test is to look at the correlational pattern among the items of a test.

Again, here the test can be applied once and then analysed in term of the relations between the items in the test. Assume a scale measuring *self-esteem* with the items 'feeling useless', 'being inadequate' and 'satisfied with one self'. Throughout the test applicants, did someone who said they are feeling 'absolutely' useless also say that they are 'absolutely' inadequate and also 'not at all' satisfied with themselves? And someone who said that they feel 'not at all' useless, did they also say that they are 'not at all' inadequate and 'absolutely' satisfied with themselves? With this method, the correlations of all items with each other will be computed, to see how close the items are related.

Inter-item correlations usually show small to moderate effect sizes (see Clark-Carter, this volume). Again, a very low level of correspondence or even negative correlations between items indicates that there is a lack of coherence in the scale. However, very high correlations can indicate the redundancy of items. If two items are so similar that their correlation approaches 1, one might replace the other entirely, provided it is not needed for other reasons.

Coefficient alpha

The most common reliability measure is called Coefficient Alpha or Cronbach's Alpha (α), introduced by Cronbach (1951). The coefficient can theoretically range from zero to one and a higher value of alpha is indicative of a more reliable test.

There are a number of different ways of thinking about alpha – one of the most useful is that it is the average of all of the possible split half correlations that can be applied to a test. A second way to consider it is as the (lower bound) estimate of the correlation between the true underlying trait score, and the score as measured by a test.

There is common agreement that alpha coefficients should be above 0.70, although it should be noted that this means that approximately 50 per cent of the variance in the measurement is true variance, and 50 per cent is error variance. If very important decisions depend on the test, a value of 0.90 is preferably according to Cronbach (1990), although Kline (1993) suggests that if alpha is above 0.9, it probably measures a construct so narrow that it is not actually theoretically interesting. The values of alpha in tests measuring constructs such as intelligence tend to be higher than those measuring psychological morbidity, or personality – it is much easier to come up with a test which is a pure and accurate measure of mathematical ability than it is to come up with a test that is a true and accurate measure of anxiety.

Cronbach's alpha can also be used to describe items, to evaluate items or as a criterion to select items in a scale construction process. A longer scale is more reliable (as we have already discussed), therefore adding an item to a scale should increase the reliability. If the overall alpha drops, it means that the item is important for the scale. But if alpha goes up when an item is removed, the scale is actually better without the item, the item should be removed.

Rater orientated

All of the above-mentioned test situations assumed no possible interference through the person applying the test – the only interaction that took place was between the person and the paper and pencil that they used to answer the questions. Other reliability measures are explicitly test scorer or rater orientated and they assess the test scorer reliability and inter-rater agreement. Under some circumstances, the person administering and scoring the test might have to be assessed as a source of measurement error. In other cases, the reliability of raters' judgements needs to be assessed.

In the first case, the objectivity of a test is assessed. The objectivity of a test is the independence of the test from test situation and test administrator. Some tests also involve an amount of judgement. The answers in a test might need to be scored or open answers might have to be judged. This involves a interpretation on the side of the test scorer (who may or may not be the administrator, or interviewer). In this case, the agreement between two test scorers should be assessed. A test is objective if two scorers come independently to the same test result for each participant when interpreting the test. The results of both scorers should be compared, i.e. test results scored by different test administrators or scorers should be correlated over a number of targets, to estimate the scorer reliability for the test. Traditionally, psychometric tests are highly standardised, to ensure the independence of the test from the test situation and test applicator, and scorer differences should not occur.

In the second case, the reliability of a rater's judgement is tested. Whenever more than one rater gives a judgement about a target, the agreement between the raters can be assessed. If the judgement is highly subjective and dependent on other factors than the target's performance, different observers will come to widely different results about a target. Research in this area has focused on personality assessment and the models formulated by Kenny (1991) to analyse variables that explain why raters come to different judgements (i.e. Shrout, 1993).

The data format decides which reliability coefficient is adequate – is the judgement given in the form of categorical data or continuous data on rating scales. Tinsley and Weiss (2000) give a detailed overview on inter-rater reliability and agreement, including how to separate the concepts.

Categorical judgements

We might want to know whether two people picked the same category when assessing someone or something. Besides this raw agreement between raters that can be counted over all cases, people are usually interested in a chance-free estimate of the agreement. A coefficient is needed that takes into account that two people pick the same category simply by chance. The probability increases the fewer categories there are.

To analyse the chance-corrected agreement between raters, Cohen's Kappa is usually applied. McGinn, Guyatt, Cook and Meade (2002) discuss further methods for clinical use.

Kappa

Cohen's kappa (κ) is a method to analyse chance-corrected agreement between two raters (Cohen, 1960), who can judge an individual to be in one of two categories (e.g. hospitalise versus don't hospitalise; depressed or not depressed).

Two observers could potentially agree 100 per cent of the time. If their performance is entirely chance, they will come to the same judgement 50 per cent of the time. If we find that they actually agree 75 per cent of the time, they are half way between chance and perfection, so the kappa value will be 0.50. The 75 per cent agreement is 25 per cent of the possible further 50 per cent agreement between two raters. Under some circumstances, there might be access to the judgement of more than two raters. How the chance-corrected agreement between more than two raters can be analysed is demonstrated by Fleiss (1971).

There are also some attempts to take partial agreement between raters into account (Cohen, 1968; Landis and Koch, 1977). This might be seen as appropriate if there are several categories raters could chose from and some raters chose a similar category, but not the same (i.e. class II and III which is more similar that class I combined with class IV). In some situations, the categories might have a natural order which could be translated into a rating scale, in which case the intraclass correlation (see below) should be analysed.

Ideally, raters should reach an agreement of above 0.75; values below 0.40 indicate poor agreement (Fleiss, 1981). Maclure and Willett (1987) give more guidance on reporting and evaluating kappa coefficients.

Continuous ratings

Often in clinical and health psychology, more than one rater has used a rating scale to assess someone or something and we want to estimate the agreement in their judgements. This might be a rating scale ranging from 'very low' to 'substantial'. Here a specific type of correlation coefficient, an intraclass correlation, is appropriate.

Intraclass correlation

Intraclass correlations (ICC) measure the agreement between raters who judge the same targets on a rating scale with continuous data points rather than distinct categories.

There are slightly different inter-class correlations that have to be chosen for the individual cases: there are different coefficients depending on who is rating whom. In one hospital, a group of doctors might do all the diagnostic assessment for all patients. In another context, different pairs of raters might provide the information about the targets. Another issue is whether the specific reliability for specific raters should be evaluated or an estimate for a random selection of raters is wanted (i.e. in a test manual). Shrout and Fleiss (1979) provide guidelines for choosing the appropriate coefficient, another useful reference is McGraw and Wong (1986).

Reliability and its relationship to other test criteria

Objectivity is essential for reliability. If two people do not come to the same conclusion when they both apply the test on the same person, it cannot be expected that the test is reliable. If the test is not reliable, so prone to measurement error, it cannot be expected that the test will show a good correlation with external criteria (see also Kline, 2000).

The relation between reliability and validity is not straightforward. On the one hand, reliability is necessary for validity. Reliability is easy to measure and relatively easy to improve, so people tend to maximise it. But a high reliability does not mean that the test is valid. The reliability can be excellent, but that does not answer the question: does the test measure what it is supposed to measure? A problem with the focus on reliability is that optimising reliability and validity is, in parts, incompatible (Loevinger, 1954). With reliability, we want homogeneous items, they should correlate with each other, they should be highly correlated with one total score or they should load on the same factor in a factor analysis. By doing that, information might be lost that is needed for validity – we might end up with a very narrow test, which measures one particular aspect of (say) quality of life very well, but ignores the very broad construct that is quality of life. Reliability is sometimes called the 'poor person's validity' – it is much easier to achieve reliability of a scale than validity, and it is much easier to show reliability than validity – as already discussed, very high reliability (a coefficient alpha above 0.9) may indicate that the applicability of a scale is too narrow for useful application.

Reliability in the applied context

Most psychological constructs represent continuous data. We want to know how *painful* a procedure or how *depressed* someone is. In many applied contexts however, people are interested in categorical data with distinct cut-off points. For diagnostic tests, it is often important to know whether a specific test value means that the person is likely to have the disease in question or not, so the diagnostic accuracy is essential. In this case, we need to know the sensitivity and the specificity of a test when we are talking about test accuracy (see Santor, this volume). This is also a question of validity – does the test measure what it is supposed to measure. The reliability of the test will influence the amount of correct and incorrect clinical decisions that are made with the test (Charter and Feldt, 2001).

The information about the reliability of a test gives also useful information about the precision of a specific test score. Assume that we have measured someone's *intelligence* and our test score is 110. Now we want to know whether this test score represents the true *intelligence* of a person or how far out my measurement is from the real *intelligence* of that person. For this, the standard error of measurement gives concrete answers for individual cases.

Standard error of measurement

To calculate the standard error of measurement, the standard deviation of the test is multiplied with the root of the result of 1 minus the reliability. This allows us to calculate the confidence interval around the test score – we know in what range the true score of a person is likely to be found. (Note that in item response theory, the idea of standard error of measurement is slightly different – this description refers only to classical test theory.)

In the example of an observed test score of 110, we have to add the z-score for a chosen confidence interval times the standard error of measurement. If the reliability of a test is 0.90 and the standard deviation be is 10, the standard error of measurement is equal to 3.16. The lower bound of a 95 per cent confidence interval would be 110 minus a z-score of 1.96 times 3.16, which equals a test score of 104. The upper bound of a 95 per cent confidence interval would be 110 plus 1.96 times 3.16, which equals a score of 116. So we know that with a high probability the true test score will be between test scores of 104 and 116.

This is important information; whenever we want to decide with a test whether a person who has a different test score before and after a treatment has really changed or not. Other applications of this are the decision whether two people are likely to really differ from each other or whether someone with a certain test score is likely to be really below or above a fixed cut-off score of clinical relevance. With increasing reliability, the standard error of measurement is reduced, which narrows down the confidence interval for the true score.

Summary

Reliability indicates how reliable and accurate a measure is. Seen in the context of psychometrics and classical test theory in which it was developed, it indicates how much true differences, or variance, are in all the variance my test produces.

There are many methods to estimate reliability. These can be test or rater orientated. Test orientated measures are the parallel test method, assessing equivalence, test-retest reliability, which looks for stability, and methods that all look for consistency. Internal consistency measures include the Split Half method, the corrected item total measure, the Inter-item correlation and most importantly the coefficient alpha on scale level which can even be analysed for each item, predicting the scale alpha if a specific item was removed from a scale. Rater orientated measures include Cohen's kappa and intraclass correlations depending on the data level.

Finally, reliability was considered in its relationship to other test criteria and in the applied context and the use of the Spearman-Brown Formula and the Standard Error of Measurement was presented.

Further reading

Charter, R. A. (2003). A breakdown of reliability coefficients by test type and reliability method, and the clinical implications of low reliability. *Journal of General Psychology*, **130**, 290–304.

Cronbach, L. J. (1990). *Essentials of Psychological Testing*, 5th edn. New York: HarperCollinsPublishers.

Kaplan, R. M. and Saccuzzo, D. P. (2001). *Psychological Testing: Principles, applications, and issues*, 5th edn. Stamford: Wadsworth.

Nunnally, J. C. and Bernstein, I. H. (1994). *Psychometric Theory*, 3rd edn. New York: McGraw-Hill.

Traub, R. E. (1994). *Reliability for the Social Sciences. Theory and applications*. Thousand Oaks: Sage.

References

Bland, J. M. and Altman, D. G. (1986). Statistical methods for assessing agreement between two methods of clinical measurement. *Lancet*, Feb 8, 307–310.

Charter, R. A. and Feldt, L. S. (2001). Meaning of reliability in terms of correct and incorrect clinical decisions: The art of decision-making is still alive. *Journal of Clinical and Experimental Neuropsychology*, **23**, 530–537.

Cohen, J. (1960). A coefficient of agreement for nominal scales. *Educational and Psychological measurements*, **20**, 37–46.

Cohen, J. (1968). Weighted kappa: Nominal scale agreement with provision for scaled disagreement or partial credit. *Psychological Bulletin*, **70**, 213–220.

Cronbach, L. J. (1951). Coefficient alpha and the internal structure of tests. *Psychometrika*, **16**, 297–333.

Cronbach, L. J. (1990). *Essentials of Psychological Testing*. New York: HarperCollinsPublishers.

Embretson, S. and Reise, S. P. (2000). *Item Response Theory for Psychologists*. Mahwah, NJ: Erlbaum.

Fleiss, J. (1971). Measuring nominal scale agreement among many raters. *Psychological Bulletin*, **76**, 378–382.

Fleiss, J. (1981). *Statistical Methods for Rates and Proportions*. New York: Wiley.

Gulliksen, H. (1950). *Theory of Mental Tests*. New York: Wiley.

Kaplan, R. M. and Saccuzzo, D. P. (2001). *Psychological Testing: Principles, applications, and issues*. Stamford: Wadsworth.

Kenny, D. A. (1991). A general model of consensus and accuracy in interpersonal perception. *Psychological Review*, **98**, 155–163.

Kline, P. (1993). *The Handbook of Psychological Testing*. London, Routledge.

Kline, P. (1998). *The New Psychometrics. Science, psychology and measurement*. London: Routledge.

Kline, P. (2000). *A Psychometrics Primer*. London: Free Association Books.

Landis, J. R. and Koch, G. G. (1977). The measurement of observer agreement for categorical data. *Biometrics*, **33**, 159–174.

Loevinger, J. (1954). The attenuation paradox in test theory. *Psychological Bulletin*, **51**, 493.

Lord, F. M. and Novick, M. R. (1968). *Statistical Theories of Mental Test Scores*. Reading, MA: Addison-Wesley.

Maclure, M. and Willett, W. C. (1987). Misinterpretation and misuse of the kappa statistic. *American Journal of Epidemiology*, **126**, 161–169.

MacGinn, T., Guyatt, G., Cook, R. and Meade, M. (2002). Diagnosis: Measuring agreement beyond chance. In G. Guyatt and D. Rennie, *Users' Guides to the Medical Literature. A manual for evidence-based clinical practice*. Chicago, IL: JAMA.

McGraw, K. O. and Wong, S. P. (1986). Forming inferences about some intraclass correlation coefficients. *Psychological Methods*, **1**, 1, 30–46.

Shrout, P. E. (1993). Analyzing consensus in personality judgments: A variance components approach. *Journal of Personality*, **61**, 769–788.

Shrout, P. E. and Fleiss, J. L. (1979). Intraclass correlations: Uses in assessing rater reliability. *Psychological Bulletin*, **86**, 420–428.

Streiner, D. and Norman, G. (2003). *Health Measurement Scales*. Oxford, UK: Oxford University Press.

Tinsley, H. A. and Weiss, D. J. (2000). Interrater reliability and agreement. In: H. E. A. Tinsley and S. D. Brown *Handbook of Applied Multivariate Statistics and Mathematical Modelling*. San Diego, CA: Academic Press.

Traub, R. E. (1994). *Reliability for the Social Sciences. Theory and applications*. Thousand Oaks, CA: Sage.

Chapter 16

Analysing categorical data

Chris Fife-Schaw

A lot of things in the health domain that we might be interested in understanding and predicting are naturally categorical. Despite the tone of some statistics books this isn't a problem or a limitation but a feature of the real world. People either have illness X or they don't. They attend clinic appointments or they don't. They die from an illness, an accident or some other cause. These things do not usually represent underlying continua or dimensions but true categories that people either belong to or do not.

You are probably already familiar with the χ^2 test for contingency tables which is used when you are looking at the relationship between two variables, both of which are categorical. This test assesses the null hypothesis that the two variables are independent of one another. If we reject that hypothesis we are saying that the variables are indeed related to one another. If one of the variables can be regarded as a predictor variable (possibly an independent variable) and the other an outcome (a dependent variable) then we can suggest a predictive relationship might exist. I'm being slightly cautious here because, as with correlations, showing that there is an association does not necessarily 'prove' a causal relationship. Nevertheless the χ^2 test is a very useful one when you are trying to predict values of categorical variables.

The χ^2 test is effective when you have one potential predictor and one outcome, but what do you do when you have several potential predictors? What do you do if one of these predictors is continuous rather than categorical? Addressing these questions is the focus of this chapter.

Logistic regression

Much of the chapter will focus on this very flexible and popular technique for predicting binary categorical outcomes. There are procedures for dealing with cases where there are more than two categories in the outcome variable and these are discussed briefly later in the chapter.

Typical problem scenarios

1 You would like to predict whether someone will fall into one category or another. An example might be that you run a drug rehabilitation unit and you have a feeling

that you can predict whether someone will attend follow-up sessions or not. Potential predictors might include level of education, presence of other psychiatric problems, the sex of the person etc. There are two kinds of question that you could ask if you had access to patient records. You could ask which variables are good at predicting attendance/drop-out. If you knew the answer to this question, could you then make predictions about the attendance of new clients? If you could, then you might then be able to devote resources to encouraging attendance among those most at risk of dropping out.

2 You would like to run a multiple regression analysis because you want to know if a number of potential predictor variables actually do predict the value of a continuous outcome variable. For example, you might believe that the more depressed a patient is the longer it would take for them recover from a hip replacement operation. You might also reasonably expect that time to recovery is related to age and that the older the patient the longer recovery will take. If your interest is in the relationship between depression and time to recovery ideally you would like to know what this relationship is independently of, or after you have controlled for, age. If your variables are normally distributed you can consider using multiple regression. But what do you do if time to recovery is not normally distributed and is badly skewed, kurtotic or even bimodal? If you are prepared to turn your continuous dependent variable (DV) into a categorical one you may still be able to answer this question (an alternative is to use survival analysis – see Watson, this volume).

In general terms logistic regression has a number of aims and purposes. These are:

◆ to predict a binary outcome or group membership from scores on other variables

◆ to assess the importance of particular predictors in predicting outcome/group membership

◆ to test competing models of the 'causes' of the outcome or group membership

◆ as an alternative to discriminant function analysis when distributional (parametric) assumptions of that test are not met

◆ as an alternative to multiple regression if distributional assumptions are not met and it makes sense to collapse a continuous DV into a dichotomous one

◆ predict the group membership of new cases.

Logistic regression's great advantages are that it can be used with continuous and/or categorical predictors and, with a couple of caveats, the distributional properties of the variables are not particularly important. For this reason logistic regression has gradually replaced discriminant function analysis as the most often used analysis for dealing with predicting binary categorical outcomes.

How it works

I like to think of logistic regression as being bit like multiple regression accept that instead of trying to predict your respondents' raw scores you are trying to predict the 'odds' of their being in one category of the outcome variable rather than the other. The odds of an event occurring is the ratio of the probability that an event will occur to the probability that it will not occur:

$$\text{Odds} = \frac{\text{Prob(that it will happen)}}{\text{Prob(that it will not happen)}}$$

For example, the odds of getting a 'head' on a single toss of an unbiased coin are $0.5/0.5 = 1$. The odds of drawing a spade from a pack of playing cards are $0.25/0.75 = 0.3333$. Don't confuse this technical definition of 'odds' from everyday usage that usually refers to what are technically probabilities. We are talking about predicting odds of category membership here, not probabilities.

Why try to predict odds of category membership rather than the more simple probability of category membership? The reason is really mathematical, but it turns out that you can make an equation that looks rather like the traditional linear multiple regression equation if you try to predict the logarithm of the odds of category membership. This is called a *logit* or the *log of the odds*. Although we try to minimise the amount of mathematical material in this book this next bit might help some readers follow what is going on. If it doesn't, just accept that the main idea is to create a linear combination of predictor variables that will do the best possible job at predicting (the log of) the odds of category membership.

The probability $(\hat{Y}_i)$ that a given case/person (i) is in one of the given categories is given by the formula:

$$\hat{Y}_i = \frac{e^u}{1 + e^u}$$

where $u = A + B_1 X_1 + B_2 X_2 + \cdots + B_k X_k$, '$k$' is the number of predictors and the Xs are the predictor variables themselves.

The formula for 'u' looks like a multiple regression equation. After a bit of relatively simple algebra you can show that:

$$\ln\left(\frac{\hat{Y}_i}{1 - \hat{Y}_i}\right) = u = A + B_1 X_1 + B_2 X_2 + \cdots + B_k X_k$$

This is the logarithm of the probability of one outcome ($\hat{Y}$, being in one group) divided by the probability of the other outcome ($1 - \hat{Y}$, being in the other group). This is the *logit* or the *log of the odds*. Note that $\hat{Y} + (1 - \hat{Y}) = 1$, which is the sum of the probabilities is one as there are only two possible outcomes.

The computer programme picks on values for A and all the Bs that maximise the likelihood (probability) of making the correct prediction (most packages use maximum likelihood estimation, the details of which need not worry us). Each person has scores on each 'X' predictor variable so you (or rather the computer) can work out the log of the odds for each person you can then find the exponential (antilog) of this and make a prediction about which group each case belongs to. In other words a prediction about the level of the dependent or outcome variable.

Goodness of fit

Depending on how good your predictors actually are at predicting the outcome, the predictions of category membership will differ from the actual observed memberships so it becomes important to ask whether the predictions are good enough to warrant the use of the logistic regression model.

Though many textbooks do not mention this, when we do an ordinary regression analysis we are implicitly trying to 'fit' the data to a linear regression model. At a simple level, the degree to which these data fit the model is given by the R^2 figure. If R^2 is found to be relatively small we conclude that we have not accounted for much variance in our outcome measure and other things, things not included in our model, must account for the remaining variance. (Alternatively it could be that the regression model is not the right mathematical model to represent the data though you do not often see this possible conclusion discussed in the psychological literature.) We can also look at the importance and significance of individual predictors to see if we could do without them and potentially simplify the model.

In logistic regression we are trying to do the same thing, but this time the model is not the simple linear regression one but the logistic model in the equations above. The simplest indicator of fit is to compare the predicted with observed category memberships. There is a predicted group membership calculated for each person based on their values on the predictor variables (the Xs). This is compared with the actual observed group membership and the number of correctly predicted cases, expressed as a percentage, gives an indication of how well the model works.

Remember, if you have two groups with about half the cases in each, then getting percentage correctly classified figures close to 50 per cent is not very impressive at all – you are not doing much better than tossing a coin to make the predictions. Ideally you would like to see figures well above 60 per cent and if you were intending to base important clinical decisions on the outcome of such an analysis, figures much closer to 90 per cent. Most packages will give you a table of predicted vs. observed group memberships and this percentage correctly classified figure.

Model comparison (simplified a bit)

The percentage of people correctly classified is useful, but it doesn't tell you whether this figure is better than chance. Ideally we would like a statistical test so that we could have some confidence that we were doing better than tossing a coin. This is done in logistic regression by comparing models.

To work out whether a model containing predictors (the Xs) works better than a model that contained only a constant (just A and no Bs or Xs) the statistical programme will calculate the log-likelihoods for each model (i.e. models with and without predictors):

$$\text{Log-likelihood} = \sum_{i=1}^{n}[y_i \times \ln(\hat{y}_i) + (1 - \hat{y}_i) \times \ln(1 - \hat{y}_i)]$$

For reasons that are to do with parsimony many statistics packages report -2 times the log-likelihood ($-2LL$) and base their model fitting on this instead of the raw likelihoods. The difference between the two is that the $-2LL$ has a χ^2 distribution such that:

$$\chi^2 = (-2LL \text{ for model with predictors}) - (-2LL \text{ for model with no predictors})$$

If this χ^2 is significantly different from zero (the degrees of freedom will depend on number of predictors) then the model with predictors in it is better than the constant only model – in some sense the data fit the model with predictors better.

You can use the same logic to compare models with additional potential predictor variables in them. If a model with an additional predictor produces a significant change in χ^2 then a model with that predictor in it would fit the data better. This is the same as saying the new, added predictor does indeed help improve the prediction of the outcome (and the same as hierarchical multiple regression – see Miles and Shevlin, 2001).

Importance of each predictor

You can run several logistic regressions comparing the impact on log-likelihood of models with and without each predictor as noted above. Like multiple regression you get estimates of the values of the constant (A) and the regression weights (the Bs). If the data fit a model then the B regression weights tell you what effect a unit increase on the predictor would have on the logit, the log of the odds.

These regression weights have standard errors and the regression weight divided by its standard error gives you a figure that can be used to test whether the variable has a statistically significant (non-zero) effect on the predictions. Sometimes this figure is called the Wald statistic in logistic regression, but it functions much like a z-value.

$$W_k = B_k / SE_k$$

'Exp B', or the 'odds-ratio', shows the increase in the odds of being in one category (the response category scored '1' vs. the reference category scored '0') if the value of the predictor increases by one unit. This is a little difficult to understand at first since this is about the effect a variable has on the *odds* of being in a category. If the odds are very small to start with increasing them by a factor of 2, say (an Exp $B = 2$) is less impressive than if the odds were considerably larger to start with. Nevertheless this figure means that for every one unit increase in predictor variable, assuming all other variables are held constant, the odds double. When the Exp B figure is less than one the odds reduce so a value of 0.8 means that the odds of being in a category drop by 20 per cent when the predictor increases by one unit.

Example: predicting who will have had an STD

This is an example based on work done by Alison Westwood on the sexual behaviours of 92 poor young women living in Brazilian *favellas*. Of interest here is an analysis that tries to predict whether a young woman has had experience of a sexually transmitted disease. I have simplified this example a bit for the sake of clarity but we have three candidate predictors that are being thought of as potential risk factors. These are:

1 Reported level of condom use (a quasi-continuous measure),
2 Experience of penetrative anal sex (a simple yes/no variable), and
3 Whether they are studying for a qualification (again a yes/no variable).

The outcome variable is simply whether they report having had an STD. The yes/no variables were coded 0 = No and 1 = Yes.

In this simple model we are interested in a number of questions. First, we want to know if these variables collectively improve our ability to predict whether woman has had an STD above chance levels. Second, there are three sub-hypotheses about whether each of the three potential risk factors actually influences the prediction and in which direction.

When the logistic regression analysis is run we simply ask to compare a model with no predictors with one that contains all three. I ran this analysis in SPSS and to start with the 'constant only', no predictor model is tested. This gives a (−2 times) log-likelihood of 74.641 and because there are no predictor variables it 'predicts' that all cases have never had an STD – which is clearly not very helpful. At the next stage the three predictor variables are added to the equation and the (−2 times) log-likelihood drops to 61.830. The difference between the two log-likelihoods is 74.641 − 61.830 = 12.811 which is the χ^2 figure mentioned above. With 3 degrees of freedom (the number of added predictors) this is significant at the 0.05 level ($p = 0.005$ in fact). This means that the model with the predictors is significantly better than one without and answers our first question with a 'yes' – we can predict who will have had an STD better than chance.

Table 16.1 shows how the case classifications now look.

As you can see, 87.9 per cent of the cases have been correctly classified by this logistic regression model. Bear in mind that without knowledge of these predictors we cannot make a sensible prediction at all and we might just as well flip a coin. This is better than chance and we correctly classify all but three of those without STDs as not having had an STD. Prediction of who had an STD is less impressive but still of interest.

Turning now to the importance of each predictor we need to look at the Wald statistics (SPSS actually reports the square of the Wald statistic) and the odds ratios ($Exp(B)$). The SPSS output is shown in Table 16.2.

Table 16.1 Classification table[a]

Observed			Predicted		
			NEWSTD		Percentage
			.00	1.00	Correct
Step 1	NEWSTD	.00	75	3	96.2
		1.00	8	5	38.5
	Overall Percentage				87.9

[a] The cut value is .500

Table 16.2 Variables in the equation

		B	S.E.	Wald	df	Sig.	Exp(B)
Step	CONDUSE	−.050	.209	.058	1	.810	.951
1[a]	ANALSEX(1)	1.800	.697	6.672	1	.010	6.049
	STUDY(1)	−1.660	.830	4.002	1	.045	.190
	Constant	−1.671	.574	8.479	1	.004	.188

[a] Variable(s) entered on step 1: CONDUSE, ANALSEX, STUDY

The variable CONDUSE has a non-significant Wald statistic that suggests that we cannot safely assume that condom use is a predictor of whether these women will have experienced an STD. This might seem odd at first since one of the claims made for condoms is that they protect against STDs. In this case we simply asked how often condoms are used and, of course, this kind of question obscures a number of possibilities including inconsistent use and use with one kind of partner but not others. These women also knew that they were 'supposed' to use condoms and some may have sought to report the socially desirable response.

Note that the odds-ratio for CONDUSE is less than one, which hints that condom use might be a protective factor. Had we obtained a bigger sample the standard error (SE) of the regression weight would probably be smaller and we might have been more confident that the odds-ratio of 0.951 was indeed less than 1. As it is, this effect is very small and we can't be very confident that it is real.

The variable ANALSEX has a significant Wald value and a large odds-ratio (Exp(B)) of 6.049. This means that having experienced anal sex increases the odds of having had an STD by a factor of just over six (a sixfold increase in the odds). Indeed if you look at a simple cross-tabulation of the STD variable and the anal sex variable you see that only 9 out of the 79 (11 per cent) who have not had an STD have had anal sex. Of the 13 who have had an STD, seven (54 per cent) have had anal sex. Clearly this appears to be a major risk factor and is a candidate for focussing on in interventions.

The last variable, STUDY, also has a significant Wald statistic and the odds-ratio of 0.190 suggests that this is a protective factor. Women who are studying, presumably to improve their lot (remember these were all very poor, uneducated women) are considerably less likely to have had an STD. The odds are reduced if you multiply them by 0.190 and this equates to something just over a fivefold reduction in the odds – again, a major effect.

The next step is to investigate why ANALSEX and STUDY are risk and protective factors respectively. The present logistic regression analysis tells us that these factors are important but does not explain the psychological mechanisms underlying their importance – this is the topic for further study, though I'm sure you will have some ideas about these.

This particular logistic regression had a mix of one quasi-continuous and two binary predictor variables. Multi-category predictors (those with more than two categories) could have been used and so indeed we could have been concerned to predict a multi-category outcome. This is covered briefly in the next but one section.

Cautionary notes

As with a straightforward χ^2 test where you have some discrete/categorical predictors (IVs) then the *expected* frequencies in all cells must be greater than one and no more than 20 per cent of cells should have expected frequencies less than five. If this cannot be met then all is not lost – you can accept lowered statistical power or collapse some of your variables' categories to meet these assumptions.

If the distributional assumptions are met for parametric techniques such as discriminant function analysis or multiple regression then these procedures are likely to be more powerful and efficient than logistic regression. As a general principle you should always use the most powerful test available to you.

If you have two predictor variables that are very highly correlated with one another (e.g. $r > 0.8$) the computer algorithms have trouble working out the unique contribution of each variable (the Bs). This is called *multicollinearity* and the normal solutions are:

1 to omit one of the highly correlated variables from the analysis or, if you are unwilling to do this,

2 see if it is possible to form the two variables into a single composite variable, or

3 run two analyses using one predictor each time.

Predicting multi-category outcome variables

Multinomial logistic regression

This is an extension of the logic we have already seen for standard logistic regression analysis to deal with outcome variables that have three or more categories. This analysis has only recently been made available in the major statistics software packages but is potentially very useful for predicting membership of unordered categories. The analysis produces a set of equations (models) rather than just one and there will be as many equations as there are degrees of freedom in the outcome variable (one minus the number of categories). There is an equation to predict membership of each category, though the one to predict the 'last' category is omitted as this is logically dependent on the predictions of the three previous equations. So, as an example, if there are four categories in the outcome variable there will be three equations each with their own *A*s and *B*s and associated inferential statistics and odds ratios. Related analyses are available for ordered categorical (ordinal) variables too. Miles (this volume) explores some of these types of analyses.

Configural frequency analysis (CFA)

This procedure asks whether combinations of variable values occur more or less often than you would expect by chance or some other predetermined set of expectations that would be made if your null hypothesis were true. It is a general and flexible set of procedures that can address a very wide range of research questions, though to date it has not received the attention it perhaps deserves.

Multinomial logistic regression discussed above assumes you have a single dependent variable with a small number of categories. If you have lots of categories or possibly two or more multi-category outcomes that you want to consider simultaneously, multinomial logistic regression gets to be very cumbersome and difficult to interpret. This is when CFA comes into its own (note that 'CFA' is also used to refer to confirmatory factor analysis: that is something quite different – see Shevlin, this volume).

The focus in CFA is on the profile of scores that people exhibit. As a simple introductory example, if you think about the Brazilian sexual health example above each woman had a score on the NEWSTD variable (either a 0 or a 1), the STUDY variable (0 or 1), and the ANALSEX variable (0 or 1). Thinking just about the numbers here there are a range of possible profiles of responses that a respondent might have given thus:

Table 16.3 Profiles of responses to the key variables in the Brazilian sexual health studies

(a) NEWSTD Frequency	(b) STUDY Frequency	(c) ANALSEX	(d) Observed	(e) Expected
0	0	0	36	36.65
0	0	1	4	7.14
0	1	0	34	29.47
0	1	1	5	5.74
1	0	0	5	6.03
1	0	1	6	1.18
1	1	0	2	4.85
1	1	1	0	0.95

The number of people exhibiting each profile is given in column d. The question that CFA answers is whether some of these profiles of responses (the figures in columns a, b and c) occur more often or less often than you would expect if the variables were unrelated to one another. In the jargon of CFA, profiles that occur more often than expected are 'types' and those that occur less often are 'antitypes'. The existence of any types or antitypes suggests that the (null) hypothesis that drove the expectations should be rejected.

In the above analysis the (null) hypothesis driving what we expect is that the variables are unrelated to one another. Given that more people will not have had an STD than have had one we need to acknowledge the marginal frequencies of each variable much as we do with a χ^2 test when calculating expected frequencies. This gives rise to the figures in column e and technically we are doing what is called a first-order CFA. Of the above profiles, the probability of observing six people with the profile '101' given we expect 1.18 people to have this profile if the variables are unrelated to one another, is 0.00000374 – i.e. very low indeed. This profile is people who have had an STD, did not study and had experience of anal sex. This combination of variables occurs more frequently than expected, suggesting that having had an STD is something to do with having experience of anal sex and not studying. The variables are not unrelated.

This example is a very simple one and it tells us what we already knew from the logistic regression. It also tells us something about the combination of these variables that the logistic regression did not tell, namely that when the woman has experienced anal sex *and* does not study there is a high likelihood that they will have experienced an STD.

The value of this technique lies in its ability to deal with multiple multi-category outcomes and multi-category independent variables. Though there are some limitations on sample sizes these are generally less stringent than with rival techniques and, of course, no assumptions about the normality of variable distributions have been made. In the above example we had a single dependent variable (NEWSTD) and two independent variables (ANALSEX and STUDY) though we did not make this explicit in this simple CFA – we just asked if the three variables were related to each other in anyway. In CFA it is possible make the DV/IV distinction explicit at which point the technique becomes known as 'prediction CFA'.

As with the cautionary notes for logistic regression, CFA approaches can involve some categorisation of variables that may contain higher order information (e.g. reducing interval data to categories). This loses statistical power and if the use of an appropriate parametric test were justified, it would be more powerful than the equivalent CFA.

Conclusion

This has been a brief look at a couple of approaches to dealing with the prediction of categorical variables. There are many other approaches that could have been mentioned, such as log-linear modelling, discriminant function analysis, structural equation modelling using MPlus and CHAID (Chi-square Automatic Interaction Detector). All these have their particular advantages and special uses but for the majority of health and clinical psychology prediction problems logistic regression is probably the most readily applicable. I have included CFA here because I believe it to be a much underused but potentially very helpful technique that deserves a wider airing.

Further reading

Long, J. S. (1997). *Regression Models for Categorical and Limited Dependent Variables*. Advanced Quantitative Techniques in the Social Sciences Series, Sage, Thousand Oaks, CA.

Tabachnick, B. G. and Fidell, L. S. (2001). *Using Multivariate Statistics*, 4th edn. Allyn and Bacon, Needham Heights, MA.

von Eye, A. (1990). *Introduction to Configural Frequency Analysis: The Search for Types and Antitypes in Cross-classifications*. Cambridge University Press, Cambridge.

A good and more recent series of articles on CFA appeared in *Applied Psychology: An International Review* volume 45(4). These span from pp. 301–353 and include rejoinders to a lead article by von Eye, A., Spiel, C. and Wood, P.K. called 'Configural frequency analysis in applied psychological research'.

A free download of Alexander von Eye's software that will run CFAs is available from: http://www.dgps.de/fachgruppen/methoden/mpr-online/issue14/art1/article.html

Chapter 17

General and generalised linear models

Jeremy Miles

Introduction

General and generalised (or generalized to the Americans) linear models are ways of thinking about statistics. If you have ever carried out a t-test, ANOVA, or correlation, you have used a general linear model. If you have used a χ^2 test to analyse a contingency table, you have used a generalised linear model (although you might not have realised it).

The general linear model and the generalised linear model are, as you might expect, closely related. The general linear model is a kind of generalised linear model. Statisticians don't like to make life too easy, and so these two are both abbreviated to GLM. Different books, and different statistical packages use the term GLM differently, so you need to watch out – in SPSS, GLM stands for general linear model, in R, GLM stands for generalised linear model. In this chapter, I shall use GLM to refer to general linear models, and GLZ to refer to generalised (or generalized) linear models.

The basis of the GLM and the GLZ is that:

$$\text{data} = \text{model} + \text{error} \tag{1}$$

As a result of doing some research, we have some data, and we want to model that data, in order to understand the process that led to the data. We want the model to be as close to the data as we can, and we want as little error as we can have. We want, in other words, the best model we can have. When a statistician says best, they don't mean the same thing as everyone else: 'best' has a specific meaning. The best model from a statistician's point of view is the model that has the least amount of sampling variance. We don't need to worry about what that means, but we do need to know that in the simplest case the mean is the *best* model, and that the mean is a general linear model (which is therefore a kind of generalised linear model).

The simplest GLM: the mean

For example, consider that we have depression scores, on the HADS, for ten people – these are the data that we want to model. The scores are:

$$1, 4, 5, 6, 6, 7, 7, 8, 11, 12$$

The best model is the mean, and the mean is equal to:

$$(1 + 4 + 5 + 6 + 6 + 7 + 7 + 8 + 11 + 12) / 10 = 6.7$$

Calculating error

We would like to have some measure of how good our model is – how close is our model to the data? We said that data = model + error. If our data are the original scores, and our model (a very simple model) is the mean then the errors are therefore the differences between our model and the data:

We want to have one number to represent the error (rather than a whole set of numbers). We could add up all of the numbers: however, if we do this, we will just end up with zero. Instead, we can square the errors and then add them up

$$(-0.7)^2 + 1.3^2 + 4.3^2 + 5.3^2 + (-5.7)^2 + (-0.7)^2$$
$$+ 0.3^2 + (-2.7^2) + (-1.7)^2 = 92.1$$

(In analysis of variance, this is referred to as the total sum of squares.)

Table 17.1 The data and the difference between the data and the model

Data	Model (Mean)	Error (difference between model and data)
6		−0.7
8		1.3
7		0.3
11		4.3
12	6.7	5.3
1		−5.7
6		−0.7
7		0.3
4		−2.7
5		−1.7

If we divide this figure by N (the sample size; 10) we arrive at the variance (9.21), and if we find the square root of this figure, we will get the standard deviation (3.03), abbreviated to s. However, both of these are referred to as sample values, it is more common to divide by $N-1$ to get a population estimate,[1] which gives a variance of 10.23 and a standard deviation of 3.20. The population estimate of the standard deviation is abbreviated to σ, the lower case Greek letter sigma. (This follows the convention in statistics that Greek letters represent population values, Roman letters represent sample values.)

We can think of the variance or standard deviation as a measure of the amount of error in our model.

Properties of the mean (and GLMs)

The mean has some special and useful properties that we should know about. One of these is, as we have already said, that the mean is the *best* model – it has the lowest sampling variance. If we repeatedly draw samples from the same population, calculate the mean each time, and then calculate the variance (or standard deviation) of those means, it will have a lower variance (or standard deviation) than any other statistic (like the median, or the mode). (This solves what you may have thought of as something as a paradox – you might not have thought of this, because you have better things to think about, but stick with me.) The mean requires a normal distribution to be valid. If the data are normally distributed, the mean, median and the mode are all the same. So, why bother with the mean? Why not use something easier to calculate, such as the mode, or the median. The answer, as we now know, is that the mean is the *best* estimator.

The second useful property of the mean is that it gives us the least error. Whatever value we choose as our estimator will give us more error than the mean, if we count error as the sums of squares (or variance, or standard deviation). The proof of this, presented in a non-mathematical way, is in Judd and McClelland (1989). Because all other values will give higher values for the sum of squares, the mean is the value that gives the least squares – it is therefore called a 'least squares estimator'. Because statisticians don't like things to be that easy, they have developed other kinds of least squares – but the kind that we have is the most ordinary, and therefore it is called an *ordinary least squares* (or OLS) estimator.[2]

---

[1] Calculating the standard deviation and variance using N, rather than $N-1$ gives values that are lower than the population values. This is corrected by using $N-1$.

[2] One reason that we have to abbreviate generalised linear model to GLZ, rather than GLS, as we might expect, is that one of the other types of least squares estimator is the generalised least squares estimator, which is abbreviated to GLS. And statistics is confusing enough, without me adding to it.

Just as we have introduced a new way to think about the mean – that it is a least squares estimator, we can think about other statistical techniques in different ways. You might have come across regression analysis being called a *least squares*, or an *OLS* technique – regression analysis is based on the same principles that we have just described – it attempts to find the best model, by minimising the sum of squares. You might (although it is less likely) have heard of ANOVA models being called OLS models – this is also true, ANOVA models (all of them) are actually regression models, being thought about in a different way. Correlation can also be thought of as a kind of regression model, so this too can be thought of as an OLS technique. All of these analyses are actually examples of the application of the general linear model.

Samples and populations

Before we move on to this let's continue with the mean for a little while and see where else we can get with it. In research we don't just want models of the sample that we analysed. We want to be able to generalise information from that sample to the population from which the sample was drawn. Luckily for us, this is surprisingly straightforward, using OLS estimators.

We first need to calculate the standard error of the distribution. In the case of a single variable, the standard error is given by:

$$se = \frac{\sigma}{\sqrt{N}} \tag{2}$$

A couple of seconds on our calculator tells us that the standard error is 3.20/ 3.16 which is equal to 1.01. We then need to decide what we need to know. There are two different, but related, questions that we can ask about the sample and the population from which the sample was drawn.

First: Is this value of the mean statistically significantly different from some other value.

Second: What is the value of the mean in other samples likely to be?

(Of course, you would hope for a larger sample than 10 before you asked these questions in any real research context, but the principle holds.)

So first, is this different from some particular value?

We might hypothesise that the data are a sample from a population where the depression score on the HADS is 4 or less. In other words, we want to find out the probability of getting a mean score of 6.7 in our sample, if the mean score in the population is 4 or less. To do this, we find the difference between our sample value and our hypothesised value:

$$6.7 - 4 = 2.7$$

And we divide this score by the standard error:

$$2.7 / 1.01 = 2.67$$

This value is t, as in the t-test, and the full formula that we used was:

$$t = d / se \qquad (3)$$

Where d is the difference between the means, and se is the standard error. We then need to find a probability associated with that value of t – how likely are we to get a value of t as high as 2.67, if the null hypothesis (that the population mean is equal to 4) is true. To find this out we can use statistical tables or a computer, to look at the distribution of the t-statistic. This probability is 0.026 – less than the usually accepted 0.05 cut-off, and so in this case we would reject our null hypothesis. It would be a rare event for a sample of size 10 to have a mean of 6.7 if the population mean is 4 or less.

This is not a very informative question to ask – OK, so we have eliminated 4, what about 4.5? Or 10? Or any other value?

The second question to ask is: What is the likely range of the true, or population, value? Whilst this isn't the question that people ask as often in psychological research, in many ways the answer is more informative. To answer this, we need to define 'likely' – we must decide how often we are prepared to be wrong. If, as is often the case, we are prepared to accept a 5 per cent chance (1 in 20) that we are wrong, we use the 95 per cent confidence intervals.

The first stage is to find the critical value for t, for the 0.05 probability (2-tailed), when the sample size is 10. We can use a computer, or look this up in a table, and we find that the critical value is 2.26 (I used the $tinv()$ function in MS Excel, in case you are interested). The confidence intervals are given by the the standard error, multiplied by the critical value and then added to the mean, to get the upper limit, and subtracted from the mean to get the lower limit.

The confidence intervals are given by:

$$\bar{x} \pm t_{\alpha/2} \times se \qquad (4)$$

Where the symbol $\bar{x}$ represents the mean
The lower 95% confidence interval is given by:

$$6.7 - 2.26 \times 1.01 = 4.42$$

The upper 95% confidence interval is given by:

$$6.7 + 2.26 \times 1.01 = 8.98$$

This is usually written as '95% CIs 4.42 to 8.98'.

To make our lives easier, when sample sizes get larger (and more realistic) the critical value for the 95 per cent confidence interval becomes closer and closer to 1.96 – which is so close to 2, that it usually doesn't matter, and a nice round number like 2 makes the arithmetic simpler.

The next model: two groups

Knowing the mean, and making inferences about the mean can be useful, in research we usually want to go beyond making statements about single groups. One of the most common research questions is to compare the mean score of two groups. For example, we might have a sample who have undergone therapy for depression, and a sample who have not.

In the next model we will consider is where we have two groups of individuals, and we want to compare the mean scores on a scale. For example, two groups of five participants each. One group has undergone therapy, and the other acts as a waiting list control group.

The data are shown in Table 17.2, and the mean, standard error and standard deviation are shown in Table 17.3.

If we examine the 95% CIs, there is clearly overlap – the population mean for the control group could be as low as 5.59, the population mean for the therapy group

Table 17.2 Raw data for Example 2

Participant number	Group	HADS – depression score
1.	Control	6
2.	Control	8
3.	Control	7
4.	Control	11
5.	Control	12
6.	Therapy	1
7.	Therapy	6
8.	Therapy	7
9.	Therapy	4
10.	Therapy	5

Table 17.3 Summary statistics for Example 2

Group	N	Mean	SD	SE mean	95% CIs	
					Lower	Upper
Control	5	8.80	2.588	1.158	5.59	12.01
Therapy	5	4.60	2.302	1.030	1.74	7.46

SD – standard deviation; SE – Standard error

could be as high as 7.46. It would seem that we could argue that the groups overlap. However, if we did argue this, we would be wrong.

First, we would be wrong because the probabilities are more complex – remember that the population mean for the therapy group is only as high as 7.46 1 time in 20, and that the population mean for the control group is only as low as 5.59 1 time in 20. If we just used the presence, or absence, of overlap we wouldn't be wrong 1 time in 20, rather we would be wrong 1 time in 400 (20 × 20).

The second reason we would be wrong is because we are interested in the standard error of the difference, and the standard error of the difference is calculated with a sample of 10, not a sample of five. We are not going to worry about the calculation of the standard error of the difference (or other standard errors) from now on – it is rare that you will not be using a computer to calculate them. If you are interested in exploring this further, then you could follow up by looking in the further reading section.

The most appropriate approach to the analysis of these data would be to carry out an independent samples t-test. If we did this we would find that $t = 2.7, df = 8, p = 0.027$. We would therefore reject the null hypothesis that there is no difference between the two groups.

However, we don't just want to know the difference, we want to know the likely size of the difference – how large will the improvement be?

To answer this question, we calculate the 95 per cent CIs, as before. And we find that the 95 per cent CIs of the difference are 0.63 to 7.77. In other words, if we say that the difference between therapy and control is between 0.63 and 7.77, we would be wrong 1 time in 20.

If we think again of:

Equation 1 (repeated)

$$data = model + error$$

We can think of the data of interest being the outcome variable, and the model the effect of treatment. We can represent this as:

$$Y = BX + E \tag{5}$$

In this equation, Y represents the outcome variable – the variable that we are trying to explain – depression scores. X represents the predictor, or independent variables – the treatment. B represents the link between the outcome and the predictor, and E represents error – everything else that explains the outcome variable, that we haven't included within our predictors.

In our example, Y is equal to depression, X the treatment (0 for control and 1 for therapy) and E represents the errors – the difference between the model and the data. We know the value for B – it is the difference between the means – it is 4.2. However, this is not enough to model our data completely – we could only model the difference. We know the difference is 4.2, but the two means could be 0 and 4.2, or 10 and 14.2, or 1000 and 1014.2 (or any other values).

We still want to use $Y = BX + E$, so we need to create a second predictor variable. This predictor we call the constant, and it has the value 1 for every individual (hence, it never changes – it is constant).

Each of the letters Y, B, X and E could represent a set of variables, and this is now the case. We will call our predictor variables x_0 and x_1 (we call the constant x_0, because it isn't a real variable), and we call the parameters of the model b_0 and b_1. (Note that we have switched to lower case variables, because they are single variables, not sets of variables.)

The equation looks like:

$$y = b_0 x_0 + b_1 x_1 + e \tag{6}$$

However, recall that x_0 is just a set of 1s, that multiplying by 1 has no effect. Because of this, it is usually written without the x_0:

$$y = b_0 + b_1 x_1 + e \tag{7}$$

We know the value of b_1 – it's 4.2 (the difference between the means). In the treatment group, x_1 is 0 – in which case, the equation for the treatment group becomes:

$$y = b_0 + e \tag{8}$$

The value of b_0 is therefore the mean of the control group – 4.6.

We can write our equation out in full:

$$\text{Estimated depression score} = 8.8 - 4.6 \times \text{group} + \text{error}$$

And using equation 8, we can calculate a score, based on each person, and an error for each person. The first person was in the control group, and so the expected value for that person is calculated using

$$y_1 = 4.2 - 4.6 \times 0 + e_1$$
$$y_1 = 4.2 + e_1 \tag{9}$$

This gives the actual value for each case, because we have error in the equation. If we remove the error we can write:

$$\hat{y} = b_0 + b_1 x_1$$

Where the hat on the y means that this is a predicted, or estimated, value. We can also express this as population parameters – recall that a roman letter is used for a sample statistic, such as b. A Greek letter is used for a population parameter, so we use the Greek letter β – beta. However, these are only estimates of the population values, so we need to put hats on the βs.

$$\hat{y} = \hat{\beta}_1 + \hat{\beta}_1 x_1$$

It does all get a bit confusing, and people tend to use the different symbols a little interchangeably.

Anyway, back to our model:

We know the real score for the first person, it was 6, so we know the value of e_1 – it is equal to the predicted value – and is therefore the error equal to 2.8. This is the residual, and we can calculate a residual for each person.

We can think of the residuals as the error in the model, and we can do several useful things with those residuals. The first thing that we can do is see how much error we have got, relative to how much error that we had to start with – this will tell us the reduction in error.

If we square each of the residuals, and add them up, we will find the residual sum of squares ($SS_{residual}$), which we might also call the error sum of squares (SS_{error}) – remember that this was the first stage towards finding the variance and standard deviation. This sum of squares is also sometimes called the Sum of Squares within groups (SS_{within}), because it is the variance that exists within each group.

The sum of squares for the residuals we find to be 48.00. We might be interested in what proportion of error we now have remaining, but more important is the reduction in error – specifically, the reduction in error as a proportion of the amount of error that was there in the first place – know as the Proportional Reduction in Error (PRE).

$$PRE = 1 - \frac{SS_{error}}{SS_{error}} \qquad (10)$$

Substituting the numbers, we find:

$$PRE = 1 - \frac{48}{92}$$

$$PRE = 0.478$$

Table 17.4 Predicted score, actual score and differences

Individual	Group	Predicted score	Actual score	Residual
1.	Control	8.8	6	−2.8
2.	Control	8.8	8	−0.8
3.	Control	8.8	7	−1.8
4.	Control	8.8	11	2.2
5.	Control	8.8	12	3.2
6.	Therapy	4.6	1	−3.6
7.	Therapy	4.6	6	1.4
8.	Therapy	4.6	7	2.4
9.	Therapy	4.6	4	−0.6
10.	Therapy	4.6	5	0.4

This value has different names in different statistical techniques. In multiple regression it is R^2, in analysis of variance it is η^2 (eta-squared). If we find the square root of this value, we find the correlation between the two measures, $r = 0.692$.

The statistical significance of this correlation, with a sample size of 10, won't be surprised to find, is $p = 0.027$, the same value as the t-test. And it won't surprise you to learn that we can calculate the standard error of a correlation, and hence the 95 per cent confidence intervals of a correlation (it is more complex, because correlations have a non-normal distribution, so we won't go into it here).

Many people learn in their undergraduate days that a t-test is one technique, and a correlation is another. I hope that this might have (begun) to show you that they are actually one and the same thing – they are both just different ways of using a GLM.

Before we leave this example, we have one more thing to do with sums of squares.

We have considered two sorts of sums of squares – the total and the error. There is a third type – the sum of squares that are explained by the model (SS model). Sometimes these are referred to as the between groups sum of squares (because it is the amount that has been reduced by separating the groups) and sometimes it is called the regression sum of squares.

The easiest way to calculate SS_{model} is simply to find the difference between the other two sums of squares – SS_{model} and SS_{error} must add up to SS_{total}.

$$SS_{model} = SS_{total} - SS_{error}$$

Substituting the values, we find that:

$$SS_{model} = 92 - 48$$
$$SS_{model} = 44.$$

We then use SS_{model} and SS_{total} to calculate a mean squares (MS). We will calculate MS_{model} and MS_{error}. To calculate MS_{model}, we divide MS_{model} by the degrees of freedom associated with the model – the df, in this case, is equal to the number of predictors. We had one predictor variable – therapy, and so $MS_{model} = SS_{model} / 1$, which is equal to $SS_{model} - 44$.

Next we find MS_{error}. This is equal to SS_{error}, again divided by the degrees of freedom. The df for the error are given by N – the number of predictors – 1, which is 8, so:

$$MS_{error} = 48/8 = 5.5$$

Finally, we can find the ratio of these two mean squares, which is called the F ratio, or simply F.

$$F = \frac{MS_{model}}{MS_{error}} \qquad (11)$$

Substituting the values, we find:

$$F = \frac{44}{5.5} = 7.35 \tag{11}$$

The F test is, of course, the test statistic for ANOVA – we use F to calculate the probability of the results, given the null hypothesis. If we find the statistical significance associated with F, for 1 and 8 degrees of freedom, we find that p = 0.027. Additionally, the value for t was 2.7. If we square the value for t, we find that we have the value for F.

$$t^2 = 2.7^2 = 7.35 = F \tag{12}$$

This is always the case – F will be equal to t^2 (where t can be calculated). Again, you may have learned about t-tests, correlations and ANOVA being different things. I hope that this has begun to show you that they are different ways of looking at the same thing. If you only look at the formulae, they appear to be very, very different – this doesn't tell us anything (except perhaps that formulae are difficult to understand). Underneath, they are all the same; they are all OLS models.

(Some people argue that students should learn statistics by examining the formulae, and then they will understand the underlying process. I think the information that we have seen in the preceding section shows that this is not true, and may even be counterproductive. You can stare at, and calculate, as many correlations, t-tests and ANOVAs as you like, and you will probably not realise that the underlying model is the same.)

Multiple regression and the GLM

The principle that we have employed here generalises to a wide range of situations. We had one categorical predictor, and one outcome, but we could have had a continuous predictor – the principle would be the same. We would use:

$$y = b_0 + b_1 x_1 + e$$

And we would find the values for b_0 and b_1 which minimised the sums of the squared residuals. We could calculate a standard error for the b_0 and b_1 parameters, and we could therefore calculate confidence intervals and probability values. We could also calculate a correlation, and an F statistic.

And the principle generalises to the multiple regression case. We simply extend our equation. For two predictors:

$$y = b_0 + b_1 x_1 + b_2 x_2 + e$$

If we want to keep going, we would write the equation as:

$$y = b_0 + b_1 x_1 + b_2 x_2 + \cdots + b_k x_k + e$$

Where k represents the number of variables. The principle is the same – we find the values for the b parameters which minimises error. Again, we find the values for all the parameters that gives the minimum error (the lowest sum of squared residuals). For each parameter we can calculate the standard error, and hence the t-value, and associated probability. The R^2 and F statistics now take on slightly different meanings. In the multiple variable case, R^2 is the correlation between the predicted values and the actual values of the outcome variable. It tells us how well our model predicts our outcome variable. The F statistic and its probability are associated with the R^2 statistic.

ANOVA and the GLM

Analysis of variance is thought of, often taught, and frequently written about as a different technique to multiple regression. But it isn't.

The problem with multiple regression is that to calculate the values of the parameters which do provide the minimum values for the sums of squares is very hard work. (I deliberately avoided telling you about it earlier.) To carry out the analysis, you are required to calculate the inverse of a correlation matrix – with a computer, this is easy. Without a computer, it's not. If you have two predictors, this would be fiddly. If you have three predictors, it would be time-consuming. If you have four predictors it will be boring. And if you have five predictors, it would take you, literally, several days, and possibly weeks.

Luckily for researchers who do experimental research, if you have categorical predictors, and you have a balanced design (that is with equal numbers in each cell), you can approach the problem in a different way – partitioning sums of squares – and it becomes much, much easier. Just because ANOVA looks different to regression doesn't mean that it is different though – we can calculate all of the same statistics in both methods, it's just that because of tradition we don't.

The horror of dichotomising

Researchers who carry out experimental research and analyse it with ANOVA are very familiar with the concept of interaction – as soon as you have more than one categorical predictor in most statistics programs, they will automatically calculate interactions. When researchers have predictor variables that are continuous, rather than categorical, researchers use regression techniques. When they hypothesise interaction effects in these variables, they don't feel comfortable using regression techniques, instead they force their data into an ANOVA framework by splitting a variable into high and low scorers. That way, they can use ANOVA, and they understand interactions in ANOVA. However, dichotomising variables is frowned upon – it is discarding information. I want to ask these people (I do ask these people) why they went to all of the effort of collecting data, using reliable measures, and entering it accurately, when they are going to throw away all that information. If they were researching people aged 16 to 94, they would dichotomise them, and split them in the middle, at 53. Anyone younger than 53 would be called 'young' – the researcher would say, that as far as they are interested, a 16-year old and a 52-year old are the same. And they would say that a 53-year old, and a 96-year old are, as far as their research is concerned, also the same. But, they would be arguing, from the perspective of their research hypothesis, that a 52-year old and a 53-year old are different from one another. I wonder how interesting their research is going to be.

The second argument against dichotomising is that it loses power. You are effectively throwing away about a third of your participants. 'But Jeremy, I have a large sample – I have 150 participants, so that doesn't matter' they sometimes say to me. So I say to them, 'If you could have found equivalent results with 100 participants, if you bothered to analyse the data properly, why did you waste the time of those additional 50 people?' They probably had something better to do than fill in your questionnaire. Why did you waste the money on paper, stamps, envelopes? Why did you waste your time entering it into the computer? (I *know* that they had something better to do.)

Because, I say to them (and this won't surprise you) ANOVA and regression are the same thing – they are aspects of the general linear model – they are the same thing.

GLMs in SPSS

In version 7.5, SPSS threw out its old ANOVA / MANOVA functions[3] and replaced them with GLM functions. This changed the way that what we think of as ANOVA designs were analysed in SPSS.

In this section, I shall briefly demonstrate how ANOVA designs are structured within SPSS, and show the additional information that SPSS can give to us.

A study was carried out looking at a combination of psychotherapy and chemotherapy. There were two predictor variables: drug and psychotherapy. There were therefore four groups: control, drug only, psychotherapy only, psychotherapy + drug. The outcome was a measure of subjective happiness. The data raw data are shown in Table 17.5, and a summary in Table 17.6.

Analysing these data using ANOVA gives the following results: significant effects of therapy ($p = 0.018$), drug ($p = 0.043$) and therapy $\times$ drug interaction ($p = 0.032$). To interpret these results, I could carry out post-hoc tests, or I could look at the parameter estimates from the GLM. In SPSS, I would click on options, and then select parameter estimates. The (slightly edited) output of the parameter estimates is shown below. The variables were coded as $1 =$ treatment, $0 =$ no treatment.

I could analyse these data using a GLM – however, to do this, I need to create a new variable – the interaction term. (SPSS will do this automatically for us, but we are going to do it the long way, to understand what is happening.)

---

[3] Actually, they didn't throw them out, they are still there, if you know how to find them.

Table 17.5 Results of study of effects of therapy and drug on happiness

Therapy	Drug	Happiness
No	No	28
No	No	12
No	No	26
No	No	12
No	No	16
Yes	No	38
Yes	No	30
Yes	No	26
Yes	No	32
Yes	No	35
No	Yes	41
No	Yes	23
No	Yes	28
No	Yes	33
No	Yes	30
Yes	Yes	38
Yes	Yes	32
Yes	Yes	26
Yes	Yes	33
Yes	Yes	30

Table 17.6 Summary of table 17.5

Drug		Therapy group	
		No	**Yes**
No	Mean	18.80	32.20
	SD	(7.69)	(4.60)
Yes	Mean	31.00	31.80
	SD	(6.67)	(4.38)

I have coded the variables as 0 to mean no intervention, and 1 to mean intervention. To create the interaction term, we simply multiply the variables together. 0×0 is zero, 1×0 is also 0, and 1×1 is 1. The four groups get the values that are shown in Table 17.7.

Table 17.7 Values for predictor variables

Therapy	Drug	Interaction
0	0	0
0	1	0
1	0	0
1	1	1

Table 17.8 Parameter estimates

	B	SE	t	Sig.	95% CI	
					Lower bound	Upper bound
Intercept	18.800	2.684	7.004	.000	13.110	24.490
THERAPY	13.400	3.796	3.530	.003	5.353	21.447
DRUG	12.200	3.796	3.214	.005	4.153	20.247
THERAPY * DRUG	−12.600	5.368	−2.347	.032	−23.981	−1.219

SE – Standard error

I can now use either regression or GLM in SPSS (or any other program, although the terminology might differ) to analyse these data – I enter all three as independents in SPSS, or covariates in GLM.

The resulting parameter estimates are shown in Table 17.8.

Recall that we used the equation:

$$Y = BX + E$$

We now have three x's, and three b's. Therefore the full equation looks like:

$$\hat{y} = b_0 + b_1x_1 + b_2x_2 + b_3x_3 + e$$

We can substitute the values into the equation, and get predicted values. The intercept is b_0, which is 18.8, and b_1 is the therapy, which has an estimate of 13.4, b_2 the drug, which has a parameter estimate of 12.2, and b_3 is the interaction effect, which has a parameter estimate of −12.6.

We putting these numbers into the equation, along with the values for the predictors we get:

Control	= 18.8 + 13.4 × 0 + 2.2 × 0 − 12.6 × 0 = 18.8
Therapy only	= 18.8 + 13.4 × 1 + 2.2 × 0 − 12.6 × 0 = 32.2
Drug only	= 18.8 + 13.4 × 0 + 12.2 × 1 − 12.6 × 0 = 31.0
Drug + Therapy	= 18.8 + 13.4 × 1 + 12.2 × 1 − 12.6 × 1 = 31.8

And the predicted values, as we saw previously, are equal to the means for each group.

So what are the advantages of doing this in this slightly more convoluted way? There are three. First, it can help with interpretation. The effects of psychotherapy and chemotherapy were not, in this case, additive – that is, you could not say that taking the drug will make you X amount happier, and therapy will make you Y amount better, therefore taking both will make you $X + Y$ amount better. The effect of the two treatments do not add together, rather they multiply together.

The second advantage of this approach is that it extends very easily to continuous variables. We looked at the parameter estimates in order to get a prediction for the different groups, but really, we looked at the values that represented those groups. We used those values to calculate a predicted value for a person that had those values of the predictors. There is no reason that those predictors could not have been continuous variables – we could have looked at the effect of a drug for people of different ages, for example. We could have looked at the effect of psychotherapy for people with different initial levels of depression. The model easily extends to cope with more sophisticated models, and theory. We can include three-way and higher interactions, and we can include continuous variables in them. We can include non-linear effects, and these non-linear effects can also be included in interaction terms.

Before we finish this section, I did say that I was going to tell you the easy way to calculate the interaction terms in the GLM function in SPSS. First, if all of the predictors are categorical they can be entered into the 'fixed factors' box; SPSS will automatically calculate interaction variables and provide parameter estimates for them. If any of the predictors are continuous these should be entered into the covariates box. Then click on the 'model' button. Click on the 'Custom' button at the top, and you can add any combination of main effects and interactions. To add a main effect, click on the variable on the left, and then click on the button to move it to the right. To add an interaction, click on any two (or more) variables and then click on the button – this will add an interaction variable to the model (without you going to the effort of calculating it). The model window is shown in Figure 17.1, with drug and therapy as categorical predictors and age as a continuous predictor.

The generalised linear model

Useful as the GLM is, there are occasions when it cannot be used. The technique assumes normal distribution (of the residuals) and a continuous scale of measurement for the outcome variable. If these assumptions are not satisfied (as they are not, in many cases) the model is not valid, and cannot be used.

Luckily, the generalised linear (GLZ) can come to the rescue. The GLZ is a generalisation of the GLM – it takes the ideas of the GLM and extends them to other situations – you can also think of the GLM as a case of the GLZ. An important difference between

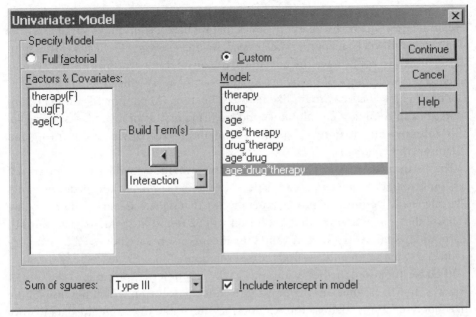

Fig. 17.1 Building interaction terms in SPSS.

the GLM and the GLZ is the *link function*. The link function specifies how we go from the output of the parameter estimates to the predicted value of the outcome variable.

You might not have noticed that we didn't do anything to go from the outcome of the parameter estimates to the outcome variable – and that would be because we didn't. The parameters estimates gave us the predicted value directly – this link is called an identity link.

However there are occasions when this link won't work, and we need to move to a form of the GLZ. These might occur if:

♦ We have a categorical outcome, with two possible values. In this case we would use logistic or probit regression. (See Fife-Schaw, this volume.)

♦ We have a categorical outcome, with three or more possible values. In this case we would use multinomial logistic regression.

♦ We have an ordinal outcome, with three or more possible values. In this we would use ordinal regression (SPSS calls this procedure 'PLUM' – PoLytomous Universal Models).

♦ We have a count or rate variable. These tend to be highly positively skewed and have a lower limit of zero. We would use Poisson regression in this case.

♦ We have time to an event (such as hospital discharge, cure or death). These tend to be highly skewed and have an additional problem known as censoring – the event we are waiting for might not happen. A person may not be cured, or may die of some other condition before they are cured – these are referred to as censored data. (See Watson, this volume).

In these cases we can frequently no longer rely on the least squares estimator – the use of the least squares estimator assumes that we have a continuous variable – if we don't, then this will be inappropriate. Instead, we use *maximum likelihood* (ML) estimators, or MLEs. MLEs have the advantage of considerable flexibility – they can be applied to a wide range of problems, and OLS estimators (which include the mean) can be thought of as maximum likelihood estimators. (Maximum likelihood estimators are also common in exploratory and confirmatory factor analysis – see Shevlin, this volume – and structural equation modelling – see Hoyle, and Bunting and Adamson, this volume.)

The disadvantage of MLEs is their degree of mathematical complexity – they are not as simple to understand as OLS estimators without a reasonable knowledge of things like calculus. ML estimation proceeds iteratively – that is there are no equations that we can use that will guarantee that a solution will be found: instead, to carry out ML estimation, we must try a set of values for the unknowns, see how well they do, try another set, and so on until we find the best solution.

In OLS estimation, the best solution was the solution that minimised the sum of squares. In ML estimation, the best solution is the solution which maximises the likelihood function – that is, it maximises the probability of getting the data that we have, given the model.

A further disadvantage of ML techniques is that they tend to struggle with small samples – the algorithms become less stable, and may stop before they have found the true best model – it is not always easy to diagnose these problems.

One of the most widely used statistical packages – SPSS – does not handle GLZs especially well (at least in the opinion of the author). Where they exist, they are accessed in different ways, and the data sometimes need to be in different formats (logistic regression and probit regression, which are very similar, need to have the data organised very differently). Binary logistic regression, ordinal logistic regression and multinomial logistic regression are similarly accessed via different menu options, and have different options available. Other programs that do have more appropriate GLZ functions include SAS (although if you are not familiar with SAS, this has a very steep learning curve), Stata (which is similar in its menu system to SPSS) and *R*. *R* is a little more challenging than Stata, but will open an SPSS file, and has the advantage of being free and downloadable (www.r-project.org).

Further reading on GLMs

For further information on coding and interpreting different designs and interactions (including repeated measures designs, which we have not touched on, but can still be coded) you can consult Rutherford (2000). For information on interactions with continuous and categorical variables, you can consult a general book on regression, e.g. Miles and Shevlin (2001)or Cohen, Cohen, West and Aiken (2003). Sadly currently out of print now, but a very useful introduction to GLMs is Judd and McClelland (1989). Another book that is useful is Fox (1997) which has a companion text, *An R and S-Plus companion to applied regression* (2002).

In addition, there are two books that deal specifically with interactions in regression: these are Aiken and West (1991) and Jaccard and Turrisi (2003).

Further reading on GLZs

There is a limited range of books on GLZs that do not require considerable depth of knowledge of statistics. Long (1997) and Liao (1994) are amongst the most accessible (although be warned they aren't *that* accessible). For those wishing to delve a little deeper then possibly the most definitive book is McCullagh and Nelder (1999). If you would like to learn more about ML estimation, then consult Eliason (1993).

References

Aiken, L. S. and West, S. G. (1991). *Multiple regression: testing and interpreting interactions*. Newbury Park, CA, Sage.

Aiken, L. S. and West, S. G. (1991). *Multiple regression: testing and interpreting interactions*. Newbury Park, CA, Sage.

Cohen, J., Cohen, P., West, S. G. and Aiken, L. S. (2003). *Applied multiple regression / correlation analysis for the behavioral sciences*, 3rd edition. Mahwah, NJ, Erlbaum.

Eliason, S. (1993). *Maximum likelihood estimation*. London, Sage.

Fox, J. (1997). *Applied regression analysis, linear models, and related methods*. Thousand Oaks, CA, Sage.

Jaccard, J. and Turrisi, R. (2003). *Interaction effects in multiple regression*, 2nd edition. Thousand Oaks, CA, Sage.

Judd, C. M. and McClelland, G. H. (1989). *Data analysis: A model comparison approach*. New York, Harcourt Brace Jovanovich.

Liao, T. F. (1994). *Interpreting probability models: logit, probit, and other generalized linear models*. London, Sage.

Long, J. S. (1997). *Regression models for limited and categorical dependent variables*. London, Sage.

McCullagh, P. and Nelder, J. A. (1999). *Generalized linear models*. Boca Raton, Florida, Chapman & Hall.

Miles, J. N. V. and Shevlin, M. E. (2001). *Applying regression and correlation*. London, Sage.

Rutherford, A. (2000). *Introducing ANOVA and ANCOVA: A GLM approach*. London, Sage.

Chapter 18

Survival analysis

Peter Watson

Introduction

Time to an event is an important outcome in many studies. Examples include: age when an event occurred, time taken to recall an event, time to recovery from a disease, and (less happily) time to death. For example, we could ask what factors influence the length of stay in hospital. To do this we would need an idea of what characteristics relate to length of stay and data on these characteristics of individuals, possibly from a longitudinal study, together with information about their length of stay.

Censoring

The measures of time we are concerned with are measures of duration time or 'time to' an event occurring. One common feature of such times is that the event we are waiting for doesn't actually happen in the observation period. For example, the person isn't discharged from hospital in the period of the study, or the person suffers complications unrelated to the condition that we were interested in. In these circumstances we don't know the actual duration times – we don't know how long they would have stayed in hospital, if we had waited, or they hadn't had the complications. However, unlike most missing data, we do usually have some information concerning the missing event time. The most common piece of information we know is the time by which the event could *not* have occurred. For example, the memory wasn't recalled within a set time or the person is still known to be alive by a particular date.

This feature is regarded as a special case of missingness, known as censoring. Censoring can be of two types: the usual form is right censoring when we know the time by which the event of interest hadn't occurred. (Less frequently we have left censoring when we know a time by which the event must have occurred e.g. a childhood accident was known to have occurred before a certain time.) The analyses described in this chapter assume unobserved duration times are right censored. We also assume censoring occurs at random.

It is not a good policy to simply analyse known duration times because most observations tend to be right censored – these will typically have longer duration times than the reported ones (e.g. if all we know is that a person was known to be alive when they were 80, we know that they will be older than 80 when they die). Any analyses on complete duration times would tend to be biased towards shorter durations and give an incomplete view of the data.

Using censored times representing lower, or upper, bounds on the time of interest reduces bias. Survival analysis is an umbrella term for techniques that model a mixture of complete and censored duration times. The techniques are mainly used in medical research but also have applications to the social sciences.[1]

In this chapter we will introduce two special functions which are particularly useful in describing duration times because they take censoring into account. We then compare these functions graphically across different participant groups and assess their association with hypothesised grouped and continuous duration time predictors using a regression approach.

Ideas will be illustrated using data from the longitudinal study of cognitive ageing in the elderly by Rabbitt *et al.* (1993). The sample comprised 3572 healthy community volunteer residents in Manchester and Newcastle. They were assessed on a range of cognitive tests examining memory, verbal and fluid intelligence. The ages of participants at their time of testing were between 50 and 93 years. Gender and socio-economic group (OPCS, 1980), were also recorded.

Death certificates were obtained for 465 (13.0 per cent) of these. Details of interest from the certificates include the age at which they died, the date and cause of death. (Right) censoring occurs if there is no death recorded on that person. If a death has occurred the duration time represents age at death. If a death hasn't occurred the duration time represents the person's age at a specific date (censor point) taken to be the date at which we started checking the death status of participants (that is, whether or not a death had been recorded). People were followed up for a period of between 4.5 and 11 years.

The aim of the analysis is to explore the association of the cognitive tests and demographic characteristics with age at death.

Functions of duration time

Duration time is usually assessed indirectly using special functions to utilise information from censored times. Two of the most popular are outlined below.

The survival function

This measure defines the chance of a randomly selected person who has still to experience an event at a given time having a duration time at least as long as that specified time. In the Rabbitt study this corresponds to the probability of a randomly selected person surviving to a given age. Since all the participants were alive at the youngest recorded

---

[1] Right censoring occurs in longitudinal studies of disease survival where the patient is either lost to follow up, or (inconveniently for both the patient and the researcher) dies for some other reason.

age, 50, the function declines from a value of one towards zero. The survival function at a particular time is cumulative because it pools information from times greater than or equal to that particular time.

We estimated two widely used forms of survival function from the Rabbitt data using ages and numbers of censored observations and deaths at these ages. The Kaplan–Meier survival function (Kaplan and Meier, 1958) is a continuous measure evaluated at each age individually. If all the observations at the oldest age represent deaths, the Kaplan–Meier survival function at this and all subsequent ages equals exactly zero. If the largest age has at least one censored value (i.e. age of death equals at least the largest age) the survival function value at this age will be greater than zero.

An actuarial life table approach (Cutler and Ederer, 1958), on the other hand, requires the grouping of ages into bands and is evaluated for each band of ages. This is particularly appropriate if the duration time is less precisely measured. For example, if duration time represents time spent in day care and is checked every three months then the point at which someone left day care might only be known to within a three-month period.

Kaplan–Meier and life table estimates may be plotted for separate predictor groups. They do not, however, directly take into account relationships between survival function and its predictors. We use other methods of estimating survival functions when assessing the effect of predictors.

One common strategy (the Cox regression model – see page 241) for estimating functions of duration time, age in the case of the Rabbitt data, is based on the values of predictors such as memory score.

Figure 18.1 shows estimates of survival functions for a person with average memory score using the Cox model separately in the two locations of residence (Newcastle and

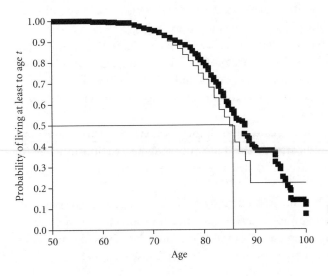

Fig. 18.1 Estimated survival functions in Newcastle (dashed line) and Manchester (full line).

Manchester) in the Rabbitt study. Notice, as with the Kaplan–Meier estimate, that these survival functions are evaluated at individual ages rather than for age groups.

Age percentiles may be read off from the survival curve that corresponds to different likelihoods of living at least to a particular age. In this way, a survival function value can be mapped to a duration time, in this case age of death. For example, the median age is regarded as a good average measure of duration. The survival function at the median age equals a half. This, therefore, represents the age when half the sample is expected to have died. Reading off from Figure 18.1 gives a median age in the mid-eighties in the two locations of residence for a person with average memory.

We might expect median age in this study to be higher than the general population, given the relatively high socio-economic status of the volunteers and the fact that participants in the study may represent a hardier group than the general population since they were required to have survived to at least 50 years of age to enter the study!

The hazard function

The other commonly used function of duration time is the hazard function. In this chapter the hazard of dying at a particular age is the estimated rate, or risk, of death at that age amongst individuals who were known to have lived to at least that age. The hazard is estimated using the method described by Link (1984) and directly incorporates the effect of predictors. There is also a life table estimate of hazard based on age bands which does not (Gehan, 1969).

It is common to graph the cumulative hazard. Cumulative hazard at age t is the sum of the rates of death at ages less than or equal to t. One reason for graphing the cumulative hazard rate is clarity, especially if hazard is evaluated at individual ages. Graphs of continuous hazards tend to be spiky because death rates are only non-zero at ages where at least one death has occurred. The change in slope of the cumulative hazard at a particular age shows the magnitude of the death rate at that age. The steeper the rate of increase at an age of death the higher the death rate at that age.

Hazard functions for different memory scores are plotted in Figure 18.2. For illustrative purposes average death rates per age are plotted for five year age bands between 50 and 94 years and a six year bands between 95 and 100 years. The hazards were estimated using the Cox regression model discussed on page 241 which can directly adjust hazards for predictor values.

The functions suggest the rate of death tends to increase with age. This is consistent with theories such as that indicated by the 'bath tub-shaped' distribution (see for example, Kalbfleisch and Prentice, 1980) which suggests rate of death increases over the later years.

In addition, causes of death in the Rabbitt study could be grouped into deaths from heart disease, malignancy and other (e.g. trauma, infection, suicide). Such cases are called competing risks since each cause is 'competing' against the others to bring about death. In these cases it may be more natural to model each cause separately.

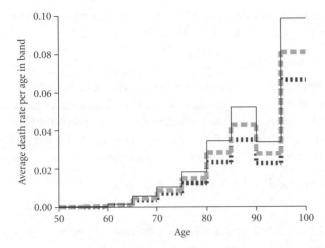

Fig. 18.2 Estimated rate of death for mean memory score (full line), memory score one standard deviation above the mean (long dashed line) and memory score two standard deviations above the mean (short dashed line).

Cox's proportional hazards model

We now consider assessing the relationship between duration time functions and other individual's traits in more detail. For example, we may be interested in the joint effect of location of residence, socio-economic group, gender and cognitive performance on predicting death rate.

If we have a continuous outcome variable and a number of predictor variables (which may be correlated) we use a multiple regression analysis (see Miles, this volume). This can tell us the effect of each predictor, controlling for the other predictors. The regression models used in modelling survival functions have specific features appropriate to modelling duration times. First, they incorporate information available from censored observations. Second, they can accommodate predictors that vary over time. Examples of predictors that vary over time include a participant showing a learning effect on a particular test and changes in salary or standard of living over a period of years. Such predictors are discussed in the section on Time varying predictors. As well as these specific advantages survival regression models can assess predictor relationships with duration time functions adjusted for other terms in the model, and also fit interactions between the predictors – in just the same way as multiple regression analysis (see for example, Miles and Shevlin, 2001).

There are several forms of regression models which relate characteristics to duration time. The regression model which we consider is the popular Cox proportional hazards model (Cox, 1972) which may be fitted in major statistical packages such as SAS and SPSS.

The Cox model's prime purpose is to assess the unique relationship between a set of predictors such as socio-economic group and gender and the hazard of a duration time such as age at death. It does this by taking into account the chronological ordering of the deaths rather than the actual age of death (and is therefore a distribution-free approach since the age of death is considered as a rank variable).

Proportional hazards assumption

The Cox model expresses the death rate at a particular age as a function of an underlying, or baseline, hazard of dying which varies with age and a factor, which adjusts this hazard for values of the predictors. This is illustrated in the formula below which defines the Cox model where B is the regression coefficient relating a memory score to hazard and the letter 'e' is the value of e, which is used as the basis for natural logarithms.[2]

$$\text{Death rate for score at age t} = \text{baseline rate of death at age t}$$
$$\times e^{B \times \text{score}} \qquad (18.1)^3$$

It follows from formula 18.1 that baseline hazard represents the rate of dying associated with a zero score. In our analysis memory score was centred around its mean – that is the mean of all scores was subtracted from all the scores, so the mean score becomes zero – this makes the results easier to interpret. Because the baseline hazard is the hazard when the score of the predictor is zero, the baseline hazard represents the average score. The exponential term adjusts this rate for particular values of non-average memory scores.

It follows from formula 18.1 that the *ratio* of a pair of death rates at any age depends only on the values of memory score and not on age.

$$\text{Hazard ratio of score 1 relative to score 2 (any age)}$$
$$= e^{B \times (\text{score 1} - \text{score 2})} \qquad (18.2)$$

The ratio of hazards in formula 18.2 compares death rates associated with two memory scores. In particular, the ratio of any pair of hazards corresponding to two different memory scores is the same for all ages. This means that two people with different memory scores at different ages have the underlying rate of death at these ages adjusted by an amount which depends only on their memory scores and not their ages.

This feature is called the proportional hazards assumption. It follows that the profiles of the hazard function of duration time are the same arbitrary shape for different values of each predictor. A limitation of many other regression approaches is their assumption of hazard function having a specific shape.

The proportionality of hazards can be checked first by plotting baseline hazard (or more usually cumulative baseline hazard) functions over time in different groups.

---

[2] i.e. is equal to (approximately) 2.718 – however, you don't need to know this, because your calculator or statistics package does.

[3] If you are familiar with logistic regression analysis, or consult Fife-Schaw, this volume, you will see similarities between this function and the logistic regression function.

Cumulative baseline hazards can be converted into baseline survival functions and vice-versa. The cumulative baseline hazard functions, corresponding to the survival functions in Figure 18.1, look roughly parallel. That is, rate of death varies in the same way with age in the two locations. Death rate goes up by an increasing amount with age in both.

A more formal test of proportionality of hazard with age in the locations of residence is the testing of the interaction between age and location on hazard function. This term can be fitted as an extra predictor, in the same way as it would in a regression analysis (see Aiken and West, 1991; Jaccard and Turrisi, 2003; Miles and Shevlin, 2001). Some packages (including SPSS) will calculate the interaction term for you automatically. There is no evidence to suggest the presence of a significant location by age interaction ($z = 1.86$, $p = 0.06$) hence we could conclude the location hazards vary proportionally with age.

If the hazard ratio of the two locations varies with age then the two locations should be modelled separately. If this is the case comparisons cannot be made between the locations but the relationship between death rate and other predictors which satisfy the proportional hazards assumption can still be assessed using separate baseline hazard functions for each location. Further details can be found in Kalbfleisch and Prentice (1980).

Log-linearity

An important property of the Cox model is that the association between hazard of dying over the age range and its predictors is log-linear. Figure 18.2 illustrates log-linearity graphically by plotting the hazard of dying associated with five year age bands between 50 and 94 years and a six year age band (to include the largest duration time of 100 years) between 95 and 100 years for standardised memory scores. This was produced using the Cox model with standardised memory score as predictor of death rate. Standardised scores are formed from raw scores by subtracting the score mean and dividing by the score standard deviation.

The Cox model measures the association between standardised memory scores and hazard by the regression estimate, B. This estimate is plugged into formula 18.1 to adjust the baseline hazard, representing average score, for individuals one and two standard deviations above mean memory score. Note the ratio for a pair of hazard functions in Figure 18.2 is the same for all ages illustrating the proportional hazards assumption. The relationship between differences in hazard function of two individuals at the same age based on their memory scores is illustrated in formula 18.3 where B is the Cox model regression estimate for memory on hazard:

Difference in logged hazards at any age = B × difference in memory scores

(18.3)

The above relationship is termed log-linear since a linear function of the scores represents a difference in *log* hazards. This means ratios of hazards or equivalently differences in logged hazards are both equal for the same difference in scores. The difference between unlogged hazards, on the other hand, does vary for the same difference in scores. For example, in Figure 18.2 the difference across the age range between hazards representing memory scores one and two standard deviations above the mean is smaller than the difference in hazards for mean memory and a score one standard deviation above mean memory score even though the difference in scores is one standard deviation in both cases.

One advantage of using a log-linear model as opposed to a linear one is the estimated death rate is never negative in a log-linear model but is if a linear model is fitted (the same is also true for logistic regression – see Fife-Schaw, this volume). Since death rate at a given age is the outcome and also never negative, a log-linear model is more interpretable than an unlogged linear one.

Interpreting the Cox model

This section illustrates the interpretation of Cox regression coefficients.

The Cox model predicts the death rate at a particular age. Each predictor, however, represents a ratio of two hazards hence regression coefficients represent hazard ratios. In this study for dichotomous predictors the hazard ratio can be thought of as comparing the hazard of death in one group (e.g. Newcastle) to the hazard of death in the other (e.g. Manchester). For socio-economic group (SEG) there are more than two levels, and so dummy coding is used to represent the groups (with pooled SEG 4 and 5 group used as the reference category). These are consequences of using dummy variables which are used in regressions to represent categorical predictors (see, for example, Cohen and Cohen, 1983).

For standardised memory scores the hazard ratio represents the ratio of the death rate for a score one standard deviation higher compared to the rate associated with the original score. If raw scores are used then the hazard ratio represents the death rate with a score one unit higher to the rate with the original score. A hazard ratio of one indicates the rate of death is the same for one predictor value relative to the other, suggesting no relationship between the predictor and rate of death.

Table 18.1 features Cox model regression coefficients, B hazard ratio, its 95 per cent confidence interval, a z statistic and its p-value. Gender, socio-economic group (SEG) and location of residence are categorical whereas standardised memory is continuous.

The z statistics and their p-values suggest memory and gender are statistically related to hazard of death. Hazard ratios are obtained by exponentiation of regression coefficients (B). To calculate the hazard ratio for being male (rather than female) we find $e^{0.65}$, also written as exp(0.65).[4] Using a calculator, I find that exp(0.65) = 1.92, telling me that risk of death in males is 1.92 times that of females (controlling for other

---

[4] Be careful when using logs and exponentials – it is sometimes not clear whether your calculator or statistics program is using logs with a base of 10, or logs with a base of e (natural logs). In statistics, when we say log, we usually mean natural logs.

Table 18.1 Relationship between rate of death and predictors using the Cox model

Predictor	B	Hazard ratio	95% CI hazard ratio		Z	P
			Lower	Upper		
Male	0.65	1.92	1.72	2.11	6.52	<0.001
SEG 1 and 2	−0.09	0.91	0.78	1.07	−1.19	0.23
SEG 3N	0.02	1.02	0.85	1.23	0.21	0.83
SEG 3M	0.18	1.19	0.96	1.48	1.61	0.11
Newcastle	−0.11	0.90	0.70	1.09	−1.06	0.29
Memory	−0.07	0.93	0.91	0.95	−7.82	<0.001

predictors). I already know that this is statistically significant, but I should also be interested in the 95 per cent confidence intervals – that is the likely values in the population. These range from 1.72 to 2.11 – so the true value in the population is likely to fall between these two values.[5]

Interpretation of the memory scores is very similar. If memory score increases by one standard deviation rate of death changes by $e^{-0.07}$, or 0.93. Multiplying by a number lower than 1 of course decreases the hazard. Note that negative values of B (with corresponding hazard ratios less than one) indicate a smaller death rate either for that particular group or for increasing values of cognitive score.

We could additionally examine interactions between sets of predictors by creating extra terms (Cohen and Cohen, 1983) and compare more than one predictor simultaneously (e.g. the three SEG predictors) using a chi-square test rather than a z statistic (see for example, Hosmer and Lemeshow, 1999).

Time varying predictors

On page 243 we presented an interaction term between age and location to test the proportional hazards assumption. This was a time dependent variable since it depended on duration time, age.

Predictors related to duration time vary over time within an individual. For example, an individual's ability may change over time or their income rise with inflation. It would be useful if one could update the individual's data to reflect these changes. This would give a more precise measure of his or her status at a particular age.

In the Rabbitt data, for example, one might consider updating a person's test score to reflect their decline in cognitive ability with ageing, however, since we do not have these follow-up data any updating must statistically estimate change in test scores with age.

....

[5] Note that the confidence intervals are not symmetrical.

Let's consider the relevance of updating to the Cox model. When an age is found where death occurred the data of the person(s) who died at that age are compared to the data of people who lived to that age. By allowing test scores, for example, to vary with age we are able to statistically match test scores for the age of death. This means test scores are estimated at each age where death occurred using scores obtained at age of test and an estimate of rate of decline with age. This applies to all people who lived to that age. These comparisons form the basis of the estimation of the Cox model. A decline in cognitive performance with age can be specially incorporated into the Cox model by declaring the cognitive scores to be time varying predictors and specifying the rate of decline estimated from a simple linear regression of test score on age.

Table 18.1 results included linear adjustments of memory score for the ageing process on memory. The relationships of all predictors with rate of death are changed, though not substantially in this case, by allowing for cognitive decline with age even if these predictors are assumed to be constant over time. Nonlinear change in cognition with ageing could also be adjusted for, if necessary, by fitting a term representing the square of age, for example.

Odds ratios

Another useful measure of the relationship between a predictor and hazard is the odds ratio. This is estimated using logistic regression, rather than a specialist survival regression model. The associated hazard is the probability of being a known death, rather than a death rate taking any non-negative value. This alternative hazard is estimated using duration time periods, rather than individual time points as in this chapter. The periods are coded dichotomously to reflect whether the event of interest has occurred (Allison, 1982).

The odds ratio differs from the hazard ratio, estimated earlier using the Cox model, in not explicitly taking the order in which deaths occur into account. In fact, it makes no assumptions of when a person died. This method can be laborious since data often need to be reformatted prior to analysis. It is particularly useful when events are known only to have occurred in a given interval e.g. period of unemployment ended in the third quarter of the year.

Acknowledgements

The author is grateful to Professor Patrick Rabbitt for permission to use the ageing data and to David Ryder for his help and encouragement.

Further reading

Allison, P. D. (1982). Discrete time methods for the analysis of event histories. In S. Leinhardt, ed. *Sociological Methodology*, pp. 61–97. Jossey-Bass, San Francisco (relatively straightforward).

Allison, P. D. (1984). *Event history analysis: regression for longitudinal event data*. Sage, London (short; relatively straightforward).

BMDP statistical software manual volume 2 (1992). University of California Press, Oxford (relatively straightforward; examples).

Cox, D. R. and Oakes, D. (1984). *Analysis of survival data*. Chapman and Hall, London (a classic; bit mathematical).

Hosmer, D. W. and Lemeshow, S. (1999). *Applied survival analysis: regression modeling of time to event data*. Wiley, New York (comprehensive; relatively straightforward).

Kalbfleisch, J. D. and Prentice, R. L. (1980). *The statistical analysis of failure time data*. Wiley, New York (a classic; mathematical).

Parmar, M. K. B. and Machin, D. (1995). *Survival analysis: a practical approach*. Wiley, New York (accessible with examples).

Pezzullo, J. C. (1999). *Analysis of survival data*. http://www.statisticstutors.com/links.html (free to use software).

Singer, J. D. and Willett, J. B. (2003). *Applied longitudinal data analysis: Modeling change and event occurrence*. Oxford University Press, Oxford (accessible with examples).

Yamaguchi, K. (1991). *Event history analysis*. Sage, London (accessible with examples).

References

Aiken, L. S. and West, S. G. (1991). *Multiple regression: testing and interpreting interactions*. Newbury Park, CA, Sage.

Cohen, J. and Cohen, P. (1983). *Applied multiple regression/correlation analysis for the behavioral sciences*, 2nd edition. Lawrence Erlbaum, Hillsdale, NJ.

Cox, D. R. (1972). Regression models and life tables (with discussion). *J. R. Stat. Soc. B*, **34**, 187–220.

Cutler, S. J. and Ederer, F. (1958). Maximum utilization of the life-table method in analyzing survival. *J. Chronic Dis.*, **8**, 699–713.

Gehan, E. A. (1969). Estimating survivor functions from the life table. *J. Chronic Dis.*, **21**, 629–644.

Jaccard, J. and Turrisi, R. (2003). *Interaction effects in multiple regression*, 2nd edition. Thousand Oaks, CA, Sage.

Kaplan, E. L. and Meier, P. (1958). Nonparametric estimation from incomplete observations, *J. Amer. Statist. Assoc.*, **53**, 457–481.

Link, C. L. (1984). Confidence intervals for the survival function using Cox's proportional hazards model with covariates. *Biometrics*, **40**, 601–10

Miles, J. N.V. and Shevlin, M. (2001). *Applying regression and correlation*. London, Sage.

Office of Population Censuses and Surveys (1980). *Classification of occupations*. London, HMSO.

Rabbitt, P. M., Donlan, C., Bent, N., McInnes, L. and Abson, V. (1993). The University of Manchester age and cognitive performance research centre and north east age research longitudinal programmes 1982 to 1997. *Zeitschrift Gerontology*, **26**, 176–183.

Chapter 19

Exploratory and confirmatory factor analysis in clinical and health psychology

Mark Shevlin

A very brief history of factor analysis

Factor analysis could be described as a method of reducing a large number of observed variables to a smaller number of latent, or unobservable, variables. This definition may not be self-explanatory, but everyone is a competent factor analyst. We factor analyse data every day without knowing it. For instance, imagine that you were asked to describe one of your friends. You may say, 'Jane likes talking to people, she likes going to lively places, she does not like being alone, she likes meeting people, and likes going to parties.' However, you are more likely to say, 'Jane is an extrovert.' What you have done is reduce a larger number of observable characteristics to a single unobservable construct, or factor. It is this type of *latent* variable that psychologists are generally interested in. As psychologists we are not generally interested in manifest, directly observable characteristics of people such as height, eye colour, and finger length (although some of us are). Psychologists are more interested in latent unobservable constructs that cannot be directly measured such as anxiety, depression, intelligence, or psychoticism.

The basic idea behind the statistical method of factor analysis and the intuitive method of factor analysis that we use is the same – covariation. Covariation refers to the degree that variables are associated (more technically a correlation coefficient is a standardised covariance). If variables covary strongly, or have a high correlation, it is considered that they reflect the same thing. To take an extreme example, consider a researcher who weighed a group of people and recorded the weights in pounds, kilograms, and grams. These three different measures would be highly correlated; indeed they should all show perfect positive linear correlations. They are all highly correlated because they are all measuring the same thing – weight. Similarly an individual's self-report on talkativeness, how much they enjoy meeting new people, how much they dislike being alone, how much they like meeting people, and like going to parties should be highly correlated because they all reflect the dimension of extraversion.

To understand the historical and philosophical underpinnings of factor analysis we *could* begin 2000 years ago with the work of Plato and Hippocrates (Hägglund, 2001).

However, we can leap forward to 1904 to the work of Charles Spearman to get an idea of the principles and thinking behind modern day factor analysis. Spearman collected data from school children in London on various abilities such mathematics, discrimination of pitch, English, Classics and French. He found that scores on all these abilities were positively correlated, the correlations ranging from $r = 0.40$ to $r = 0.83$. He further found that if these correlations were corrected for measurement error then the correlations were all close to one. As mentioned before, if a group of variables are all highly correlated then it suggests that they are measuring the same thing. In this case Spearman considered this single latent construct to be general intelligence or g. Subsequent work by Godfry Thompson and Cyril Burt extended this original idea. They retained the general factor of intelligence but also included specific, or group, factors. They found that the single factor of general intelligence did not always fully explain the covariation among tests of ability. For example, because g did not explain the covariation between scores on a picture completion task, a picture arrangement task and a maze task, a specific factor was introduced to explain this group of tests. In this case the additional factor may be labelled a 'broad spatial factor'. All the previous psychologists retained a factor representing general intelligence. Louis Leon Thurstone broke from this tradition and replaced Spearman's g with multiple factors. Using factor analysis Thurstone analysed about 60 tests and found seven primary mental abilities such as verbal ability, numerical ability, memory, reasoning, and perceptual speed.

Although factor analysis started off in the field of mental abilities, its use has expanded beyond this. Personality theorists have used factor analysis extensively to test their models. The idea behind the use of factor analysis is that a broad range of trait-descriptive words in the English language can be reduced to a smaller number of latent variables that represent the major dimensions of personality. Similar to the aforementioned investigations into mental abilities, many of the findings in the area of personality appear to be somewhat contradictory. Hans Eysenck (1991) claimed that three super-factors (extroversion-introversion, neuroticism, and psychoticism) are sufficient while Cattell (1981) proposed 16 factors. Alternatively McCrae and Costa (1996) support a five-factor model with extraversion, agreeableness, conscientiousness, neuroticism, and openness as the major dimensions of personality.

A closer look at the factor analysis model

Factor analysis is a statistical model. By 'model' we mean an approximation or simplified representation of a particular phenomenon. In the case of factor analysis we are trying to model the relationship between the latent variable of interest and the observed variables that we use to measure it. This model can be represented as:

$$x = \lambda \xi + \delta$$

In this equation the x represents the observed variable. The observed variable can have many forms in psychological research. It may be a questionnaire item, a reaction time measure, a physiological measurement, or a score on a test. The ξ (ksi) represents the latent construct that is being measured, such as anxiety or IQ. The defining feature of this variable is that it is a latent unobservable variable being indirectly measured by x. Commonly psychologists do not make the distinction between observed and latent variables. For example, the summed scores of all the items that comprise a scale, for instance the Beck Depression Inventory, are often used to reflect the construct of depression. It should be noted that this summed score is only a fallible, indirect measure of depression. Bollen and Lennox (1991) neatly describe this: '. . . a common practice is to calculate the sum of equally weighted items to form a composite stand in for the latent variable . . . The linear composite is not equivalent to the latent variable' (pp. 309–310). Although the observed and latent variables are not equivalent, they are related. The equation explicitly states that the latent variable causes the observed variable – the strength of the association is denoted by λ (the Greek letter lambda). In this context this regression coefficient is known as a factor loading. It is highly unlikely that the relationship between the latent (ξ [ksi]) and observed variable (x) is perfect. Therefore there will be some variation in x that is not explained by ξ. The unexplained variance is denoted as δ (delta), and is commonly referred to as error variance, measurement error, or unique variance. This simple model can also be represented as a diagram. In Figure 19.1 this model is presented using the conventions of path diagrams. Notice the similarity between this equation and the regression equation:

$$y = bx + e$$

In Figure 19.1 the circle represents the latent variable, or factor. In this example the factor is depression. The box represents the observed variable, in this example the responses to the item 'My mood is generally low'. The arrow represents a causal pathway. From the diagram it should be clear that the model is making some strong assumptions. First, that the latent variable 'causes' responses to the observed variable. It is assumed therefore that if depression increases there will be a subsequent increase in the observed variable, that is, the item will be endorsed more strongly. Second, the model assumes that the causal pathway between the latent variable and the observed variable is not perfect. Put simply it states that all our measures are fallible indicators of the constructs we are attempting to measure. It has been long established and accepted that in the sociobehavioural sciences that '. . . all measurement is befuddled with error' (McNemar, 1949). Therefore, the third assumption is every observed variable will

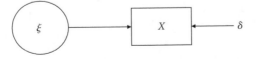

Fig. 19.1 A basic measurement model.

contain measurement error, represented as δ. This measurement error is assumed to be comprised of both a random and systematic component. The random component can be attributable to chance occurrences such as selecting the wrong category on the response format. The systematic component arises because the question may tap factors other than the intended factor. In this case people may endorse the question 'My mood is generally low' for reasons other than being depressed. The question may be tapping transient mood or responses to situational effects, rather than depression per se. Both these sources of variation are assumed to be independent of the latent construct.

In essence Figure 19.1 represents the factor analytic model, but in a form that is not familiar to psychologists. This particular model may be unfamiliar because it has only one observed variable. Measures employed by psychologists typically use multiple items. There are many reasons for this. For instance, it is impossible to measure a complex multifaceted dimension such as depression, or any other psychological construct, using only one item. Generally measures of depression attempt to cover the all the salient aspects of depression. In addition, multiple items tend to increase the reliability of measurement. The use of multiple items, or indicators, can be easily accommodated within the factor analytic framework. Imagine that we now have four items that are designed to measure depression. The original equation can now be written as:

$$X = \Lambda\xi + \delta$$

The only difference is that there are four x variables representing the four items, four factor loadings (λ) in a matrix denoted by Λ, and a vector of error variances (δ) representing the measurement error associated with each item. There is still only one latent variable that we can call depression. Diagrammatically this equation can be presented as shown in Figure 19.2.

Figure 19.2 shows that we now have multiple indicators of the latent construct of depression. The process of factor analysis involves estimating values for each of the factor loadings and error variances. These values are derived from the correlations among

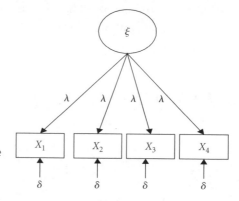

Fig. 19.2 Diagram of multiple indicators and a single latent variable.

the four observed variables. The technical issues involved in the process of estimation will be addressed later. Generally the factor loadings can range from ± 1, the sign of the loading reflecting whether the item is reverse scored. Invariably, high factor loadings are desirable as that suggests that there is a strong association between the latent variable and the observed variables that are being used to measure it.

How can health and clinical psychologists use factor analysis?

Over the years factor analysis has been used for many purposes. However, psychologists generally use the technique for data reduction or during the process of scale validation.

Researchers can sometimes collect a lot of data using questions that are not theoretically derived. For instance, a psychologist may notice that individuals who have experienced some form of traumatic event tend to exhibit certain types of behaviours and cognitions. It may be noticed that such people tend to actively avoid reminders of the traumatic event and that they suffer from intrusive thoughts about the incident. The researcher may then develop a number of questions that reflect such behaviours and cognitions. If 20 questions were developed and administered to a sample of participants the researcher will be left with a lot of data to make sense of. At this point the psychologist may want to use factor analysis to simplify, or reduce the complexity of, the data. The process of factor analysis may reveal that the items cluster into two groups. Unfortunately factor analysis cannot tell us what the factors actually are; this is where the psychologist has to use their knowledge of psychological theory to label the resultant factors. One group of items that load on the first factor may be similar, such as 'I thought about it when I didn't mean to' or 'Pictures about it popped into my mind'. This factor could be labelled intrusion. The other group of items that load on the second factor may also be similar, such as 'I tried to remove it from memory' or 'I stayed away from reminders of it'. This factor could be labelled avoidance. The result of the factor analysis is that the psychologist can now better understand the nature of the data collected as it is presented in a more psychologically meaningful, and simpler, way. At this point a word of caution should be issued: factor analysis should *not* be used to guide theory. Factor analysis is merely a tool by which hypotheses drawn from theory can be tested. In 1948 Thurstone noted the usefulness of factor analysis but also was clear about its place in the research process: 'Factorial methods will be fruitful in the advancement of psychology only in so far as we use these methods in close relation to psychological ideas' (p. 408).

A related reason for using factor analysis is that of test validation. There is a plethora of psychological scales purporting to measure a huge range of psychological constructs. On many occasions these scales are used without adequate checks that they are measuring what they state they are measuring. Factor analysis allows the psychologist to make basic checks that the scales are performing as they should do. Take for example a measure of posttraumatic stress disorder, the Impact of Event Scale (IES) (Horowitz, Wilner, and Alvarez, 1979). Horowitz developed this 15-item scale to measure the two factors of intrusions and avoidance. Factor analytic studies have been used to assess the dimensionality of the scale. Most studies have reported factor analytic solutions that are similar to the structure suggested by Horowitz (Zilberg, Weiss, and Horowitz, 1982; Robbins and Hunt, 1996: Shevlin, Hunt, and Robbins, 2000), although some studies have reported a one factor (Hendrix, Jurich, and Schumm, 1994) or multi-factor solution (Andrews, Shevlin, and Joseph, 2004).

Exploratory factor analysis

In recent years there has been a distinction made between two alternative methods of factor analysis. The distinction relies upon your reason for conducting the factor analysis in the first place, but more importantly the way you conduct the analysis. If you have a large and unwieldy data set and want to simplify the data, exploratory factor analysis will generally be used. Alternatively, if you have collected data and you want to test that it conforms to a particular structure, confirmatory factor analysis is the most appropriate tool. Bollen (1989) noted that the distinction is commonly more apparent than real, in that in many exploratory factor analyses the goal is to confirm an a priori structure while confirmatory methods can be used in an exploratory fashion. The following description of both methods may elucidate the differences, but only close critical inspection of published factor analytic studies will reveal when one masquerades as the other.

Exploratory factor analysis

Exploratory factor analysis (EFA) can be accomplished using any standard statistical package such as SPSS, Minitab or Systat. This section will present an exploratory factor analysis conducted on eight items from the Impact of Event Scale. Four items were designed to measure intrusion, and four designed to measure avoidance. The factor analytic process involves three stages: extraction, rotation, and interpretation. The actual analysis is not based on the raw data, rather it is based on the correlation matrix of the observed variables (in this case the intercorrelations among the eight items).

The first part of the EFA process is extraction. This simply means determining the number of factors that best explains the pattern of correlations. The guiding principle is that of parsimony: to find the minimum number of factors that explain as much of the variation as possible in the observed variables. If too many factors are extracted we end up with a complicated solution with factors that explain too little variance and are of no psychological consequence (or even worse are attributable to sampling error). If too few factors are extracted then we are failing to adequately explain our data. So how do we determine the optimal number of factors? A detailed answer could probably fill this entire book and still cause disagreement!

Let's run with the default option in SPSS, which is to use eigenvalues. The question you are going to ask is 'What on earth is an eigenvalue?' Well, first you should know that when conducting a factor analysis a program will begin by sequentially extracting as many factors as there are observed variables, or items. The first factor will be used to explain, or extract, the maximal variance, and the remainder of the variability will be left to be explained by the second factor. This is similar to the Thurstone method of analysis described above, where the remainder of variance left over from g was used for specific, or group factors. The third factor will then extract, or explain, the remainder of the variance and the process continues until all the factors have been extracted. So in this instance the procedure will extract eight factors and have calculated factor loadings for every item on every factor throughout the process. If you can remember from earlier, the higher the factor loading the better, as that indicates that there is a strong association between the latent variable and the observed variables that are being used to measure it. If I now say that an eigenvalue is the *sum of the squared factor loadings for a given factor*, it may make more sense. The eigenvalue associated with each factor gives us an idea of how much variance in the observed items it has explained, and it follows that we want factors that explain a lot of variance. Therefore our decision on the number of factor to retain (remember we want to retain the smallest number of factors that explain the most variance in the observed variables) could be based on the eigenvalues. The higher the eigenvalue for a factor, the higher its association with all, or a specific group, of items. Although it sounds arbitrary, and it actually is, it is common practice to retain those factors with eigenvalues greater than one. In fact most programs will do this for you as their default. After the process of extraction the programme will only report statistics for factors with eigenvalues greater than one.

The first part of the output from the factor analysis procedure in SPSS shows the results of the extraction of factors, which will look something like Table 19.1.

Table 19.1 Initial eigenvalues for factor analysis of the Impact of Event Scale

Factor	Initial eigenvalues		
	Total	% of variance	Cumulative %
1	3.582	44.769	44.769
2	1.246	15.577	60.346
3	0.730	9.125	69.472
4	0.700	8.755	78.227
5	0.502	6.280	84.507
6	0.449	5.612	90.118
7	0.418	5.231	95.349
8	0.372	4.651	100.000

From this table there are only two factors with eigenvalues greater than one, suggesting two meaningful factors. This is what we would have expected as the items were designed to tap the two factors of intrusion and avoidance. The '% of variance' column indicates how important each factor is in terms of explaining the variation in the observed measures. The first factor accounts for almost 45 per cent of the variance and the second for almost 16 per cent. Together these two factors account for just over 60 per cent of the variance, as can be seen from the 'Cumulative %' column. This result should be considered acceptable as the factors are accounting for more variance than the random or systematic sources of variation.

At this stage of the analysis SPSS has decided, on the basis of eigenvalues, how many underlying dimensions can best explain the correlation matrix – in this case two. If there is only one factor that meets this criterion you have arrived at a unidimensional solution. If there is more than one factor extracted you have to decide on a method of rotation. Rotation simply means that SPSS will attempt to achieve a simple structure, that is, minimize the magnitude of cross-factor loadings. If we consider the example above, there were items that measured intrusion and items that measured avoidance. Rotation simply maximises the factor loadings for the items that measure intrusion on the intrusion factor, and maximises the factor loadings for the items that measure avoidance on the avoidance factor. It does this by you selecting either an orthogonal or oblique solution. This is where some psychology knowledge comes into play. An orthogonal solution (for example varimax) forces the factors to be uncorrelated. Alternatively, an oblique solution can be requested (for example, direct oblimin) that allows the factor to be correlated. The interfactor correlation can be estimated by SPSS. Hopefully, at this stage in the analysis you will have some informed decision whether the factors should be correlated or uncorrelated. For example, Eysenck proposed a biological/physiological basis for each of his proposed three dimensions of personality. Each biological/physiological system was independent in terms of function, so he chose an orthogonal solution so that the statistical model represented his psychological model. Similarly, your choice of rotation should be based on the theoretical nature of the psychological constructs that you are examining. For the data we are using it is expected that the two factors will be correlated, as both intrusion and avoidance are thought to be symptoms associated with one condition, namely posttraumatic stress disorder. Therefore, we have chosen to use an oblique rotation (direct oblimin). There is considerable controversy about the use of orthogonal versus oblique rotations – orthogonal rotations, especially varimax, are popular, because they tend to give solutions that are more easily interpreted, however many argue that they are inappropriate – Cattell has argued that 'there are no orthogonal rotations in nature'.

The final stage of the factor analytic process is interpretation. This is accomplished by examining the structure matrix. This matrix shows all of the factor loadings,

Table 19.2 Structure matrix for factor analysis of the Impact of Event Scale

	Factor	
	1	2
Q1 Pictures about it popped into my mind	0.690	0.433
Q2 I thought about it when I didn't mean to	0.774	0.459
Q3 Other things kept making me think about it	0.715	0.359
Q4 I had dreams about it	0.782	0.514
Q5 I tried not to think about it	0.420	0.661
Q6 I avoided letting myself get upset when I thought of it	0.226	0.450
Q7 I tried not to think about it	0.360	0.530
Q8 I stayed away from reminders of it	0.477	0.826

indicating the association between each observed measures, or items, and each of the factors. The structure matrix is presented in Table 19.2.

From the structure matrix it is clear that the first four items have factor loadings that are higher for factor 1 than factor 2, that is, they load on factor 1. Similarly, items 5 to 8 load more strongly on factor 2 than factor 1. The question is 'What are factors 1 and 2?' SPSS, or any other statistical package, will not label the factors. It is the person in front of the computer that (hopefully) knows about psychology, and it is their job to determine what the factors actually represent. It is necessary to look for patterns of similarity of meaning between items that load on a particular factor. In essence you are looking for what is common among a set of items that load on a factor. In this case the job is relatively easy, because we know what each item was designed to measure. The first four items refer to involuntary intrusive cognitions and so could be labelled 'Intrusion'. The last four items all refer to active evading reminders and so could be labelled 'Avoidance'. You should be warned that not all solutions will be as readily interpretable as this example. In this case each item loads strongly on only one factor, this is called simple structure. Clearly items that load on two or more factor are problematic, but not uncommon.

At this stage in the analysis we know that there are two factors, Intrusion and Avoidance. The factor correlation matrix in Table 19.3 shows the nature of the relationship between the two factors. In this case the factors are positively related, and the correlation is moderate ($r = 0.579$). This means that if you score highly on the Intrusion sub-scale then you are also likely to score highly on the Avoidance sub-scale.

If factors are very highly correlated this can be indicative of higher order factors. In the same way that factors attempt to explain the variation and covariation in observed measures, second-order factors can be used to explain the variation and covariation among first-order factors.

Table 19.3 Factor correlation matrix

Factor	1	2
1	1.000	0.579
2	0.579	1.000

Confirmatory factor analysis

The aim of both exploratory and confirmatory factor analysis (CFA) is the same – to represent a large number of observed variables as a smaller number of latent variables, or factors. The main distinction is that CFA is a hypothesis testing and theoretically driven approach. Take, for example, the analysis reported above. Previous research findings have consistently reported a two-factor solution for data from the Impact of Event Scale so there is a testable hypothesis that the variation and covariation of the items could be explained by two factors. Furthermore, some items were designed to explicitly measure intrusion and other designed to measure avoidance. On the basis of this we could propose a specific model and determine if the sample data is a suitable description of it. This is the idea of model fit: if in 'reality' there are two factors, Intrusion and Avoidance, this should generate sample data that is consistent with a two-factor model. This would mean that the proposed model should be consistent with the sample data. If this is the case then we should fail to reject the proposed model. Alternatively, if in reality there were three factors, for example some items tapped the dimension of hyperarousal, then the sample data should not be consistent with this and subsequently fail to explain a two-factor model. This ability of CFA procedures to explicitly reject proposed models represents the notion of falsification (Popper, 1968) whereby those models that fail to explain, or fit, the data are rejected. Bollen (1989) describes this as 'model-data consistency' (pp. 66–72).

Figure 19.3 shows a typical CFA model based on the eight Impact of Event Scale items.

In Figure 19.3 the eight observed variables, or items, are represented as boxes $(x_1 - x_8)$. The first four observed variables $(x_1 - x_4)$ were designed to measure the intrusion (I) factor, shown as a circle, and so they load only onto the intrusion factor. Note that there are no cross-factor loadings. Unless specified in the model all cross-factor loadings are zero. The same structure is proposed for the avoidance items. The last four observed variables $(x_5 - x_8)$ load only onto the avoidance factor (A). The double-headed arrow between the factors represents the correlation between the factors. The error variance associated with each observed variable is represented by δ. During the process of CFA a value for each element, or parameter, of the model will be estimated.

The adequacy of this model to explain the sample data can be judged using the many fit indices that are now available when using structural equation modelling software

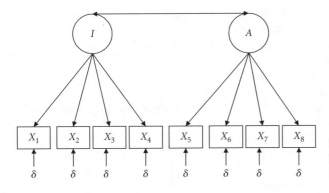

Fig. 19.3 A typical CFA model based on the eight Impact of Event Scale items.

such as LISREL 8 (Jöreskog and Sörbom, 1999). On the basis of these indices a decision to reject or fail to reject the proposed model can be made. This ability to use objective, statistically based information to assess the quality of a factor analytic solution is the primary benefit of CFA over its exploratory predecessor. In addition, current CFA appliances allow the analyst to: include parameters such as correlated errors, constrain parameters to be equal, test the invariance of a proposed model across different groups, assess the temporal stability of models, deal effectively with non-normal data, and introduce factor means.

Conclusion

Hopefully this chapter has provided a relatively pain free overview of factor analysis and how it can be used by health psychologists. The information presented here is far from being definitive or comprehensive, indeed it could be described as a whirlwind visit to a vast and varied land. There is a huge literature on the technical aspects of factor analysis and it's applications that can be daunting for the less statistically orientated reader.

Further reading

For a gentle introduction to exploratory factor analysis I suggest the relevant chapters in Hair, Anderson, Tatham, and Black (1998) and Tabachnick and Fidell (1996). Schumacker and Lomax (1996) and Maruyama (1998) provide accessible introductions to confirmatory factor analysis.

References

Andrews, L., Shevlin, M., and Joseph, S. (2004). Alternative factor models of the Impact of Event Scale: A case for the multidimensionality of intrusion and avoidance. *Personality and Individual Differences*, **36**, 2, 431–446.

Bollen, K. A. (1989). *Structural Equations with Latent Variables*. New York: Wiley.

Bollen, K. and Lennox, R. (1991). Conventional wisdom on measurement: A structural equation perspective. *Psychological Bulletin*, **110**, 305–314.

Cattell, R. B. (1981). *Personality and Learning Theory*. New York: Springer.

Eysenck, H. J. (1991). Dimensions of personality: 16, 5, or 3? Criteria for a taxonomic paradigm. *Personality and Individual Differences*, **12**, 773–790.

Hair, J. F., Anderson, R. E., Tatham, R. L., and Black, W. C. (1998). *Multivariate Data Analysis*, 5th edn. Prentice-Hall: Upper Saddle River.

Hendrix, C. C., Jurich, A. P., and Schumm, W. R. (1994). Validation of the Impact of Event Scale on a sample of American Vietnam Veterans. *Psychological Reports*, **75**, 321–322.

Horowitz, M., Wilner. and Alvarez, W. (1979). Impact of Event Scale: A measure of subjective stress. *Psychosomatic Medicine*, **41**, 209–218.

Hägglund, G. (2001). Milestones in the history of factor analysis. In R. Cudeck, S. H. C. du Toit, and D. Sorbom (eds) *Festschrift in Honor of Karl G. Jöreskog*, pp. 11–39. Chicago, IL: Scientific Software International.

Jöreskog, K. G. and Sörbom, D. (1999). *LISREL 8.3*. Chicago, IL: Scientific Software International, Inc.

Maruyama, G. M. (1998). *Basics of Structural Equation Modeling*. Thousand Oaks, CA: Sage Publications.

McCrae, R. R. and Costa, P. T., Jr. (1996). Toward a new generation of personality theories: Theoretical contexts for the five-factor model. In J. S. Wiggins (ed.) *The Five-factor Model of Personality: Theoretical Perspectives*, pp. 51–87. New York: Guilford.

McNemar, Q. (1949). *Psychological Statistics*. New York: Wiley.

Popper, K. R. (1968). *The Logic of Scientific Discovery*. London: Hutchinson.

Robbins, I. and Hunt, N. (1996). Validation of the IES as a measure of the long-term impact of war trauma. *British Journal of Health Psychology*, **1**, 87–90.

Schumacker, R. E. and Lomax, R. G. (1996). *A Beginner's Guide To Structural Equation Modeling*. Mahwah, NJ: Lawrence Erlbaum Associates.

Shevlin, M., Hunt, N. and Robbins, I. (2000). A confirmatory factor analysis of the Impact of Event Scale using a sample of World War Two and Korean War veterans. *Psychological Assessment*, **12**, 414–417.

Tabachnick, B. G. and Fidell, L. S. (1996). *Using Multivariate Statistics*, 3rd edn. New York: Harper Collins.

Thurstone, L. L. (1948). Psychological implications of factor analysis. *American Psychologist*, **3**, 402–408.

Zilberg, N. J., Weiss, D. S., and Horowitz, M. J. (1982). Impact of Event Scale: A cross-validation study and some empirical evidence supporting a conceptual model of stress response syndromes. *Journal of Consulting and Clinical Psychology*, **50**, 407–414.

Chapter 20

Applications of structural equation modelling in clinical and health psychology research

Rick H. Hoyle

Structural equation modelling (SEM), also referred to as causal modelling, latent variable modelling, LISREL, and covariance structure analysis, is a statistical technique for modelling associations among variables. Although the same could be said of more familiar techniques such as multiple regression analysis and factor analysis (see Shevlin, this volume), SEM is more flexible and general than these techniques. Indeed, techniques such as correlation, regression, analysis of variance, and factor analysis can be construed as special cases of SEM. That is, any analysis that could be accomplished using one of these techniques could be accomplished (with the same result) using SEM. In this chapter, I provide a conceptual overview of SEM, followed by a presentation of several categories of hypotheses for which SEM is particularly well suited. The focus of the chapter is applications of potential interest to researchers in clinical and health psychology. Broader treatments that include information about implementation and interpretation can be found in a growing number of volumes, chapters, and articles that range from relatively non-technical (e.g., Anderson and Gerbing, 1988; Crowley and Fan, 1997; Hox and Bechger, 1998; Hoyle, 1991, 1995; Kline, 1998; Pugesek, Tomer, and Von Eye, 2003; Raykov and Marcoulides, 2000; Schumacker and Lomax, 1996) to challenging (e.g., Bollen, 1989; Kaplan, 2000; Marcoulides and Schumacker, 1996).

Overview

SEM derives its name from the fact that the statistical procedure involves the derivation of an optimal solution to a set of equations that imply a specific structure underlying a set of covariances. By *structure*, I mean a set of associations that is more useful, interesting, and parsimonious than the set of $2(p-1)$ zero-order associations conveyed in the covariance matrix itself. For instance, a multiple regression equation with three predictors implies a structure underlying the six covariances among four variables. Specifically, one of the four variables is an outcome, and the other three are predictors assumed to be causally associated with the outcome but not causally associated with each other. Although this simple model is no more parsimonious that the covariance matrix because it requires the estimation of 10 parameters (three variances of predictors, three covariances among predictors, three regression coefficients, and a residual), the same number of unique elements in the covariance matrix (including variances), it is more interesting and potentially more useful. Unlike traditional multiple regression analysis, which can be used to estimate one equation with one outcome variable, SEM can be used to simultaneously estimate multiple dependent equations that include equations specifying directional associations among multiple outcome variables.

An additional advantage of SEM over multiple regression analysis for modelling the structure of a set of covariances is the capacity to model the predictors and outcomes of interest as latent variables (Bollen, 2002). An underappreciated assumption of multiple regression analysis is that variables are measured without error. The full implementation of SEM does not carry this assumption. Instead, multiple, fallible measures of constructs, *indicators*, can be used to model theoretical variables that correspond more closely to the constructs of interest than any single measure. This modelling is accomplished by partitioning variance in indicators into a portion shared with the remaining indicators of the construct, the *latent variable* (i.e., factor, as in factor analysis), and a portion not shared with the remaining indicators of the construct, the *uniqueness*. These latent variables then serve as predictors and/or outcomes in structural equations, ensuring that coefficients reflecting the associations between constructs are not contaminated by measurement error. SEM integrates multiple regression analysis and factor analysis, extending the capabilities of each by allowing for simultaneous estimation of potentially large sets of equations.

Path diagram

A convenient and informative means of depicting a model to be analysed using SEM is the *path diagram* (McDonald and Ringo Ho, 2002). An example appears in Figure 20.1. This path diagram includes all the elements necessary for depicting even the most complex models. The ellipses represent latent variables, sources of influence not measured directly. The model illustrates two types of latent variables. The large ellipse, labelled *F1*, corresponds to a substantive latent variable, or factor. The smaller ellipses, either labeled u_i, for uniqueness, or e_i, for error, correspond to unexplained variance. The uniquenesses are that portion of variance in the indicators not shared with the remaining indicators and, therefore, not attributable to *F1*. The errors are that portion of variance in outcomes not accounted for by predictors as specified in the model. For instance, e_6 is variance in x_6 not accounted for by *F1* and x_4. The lines represent association. Straight lines represent directional association, and curved lines represent non-directional association, or correlation. The asterisks represent unknowns, *free parameters*, to be estimated from the data. These parameters are of three types. Parameters associated with *exogenous variables* – those variables, latent or observed,

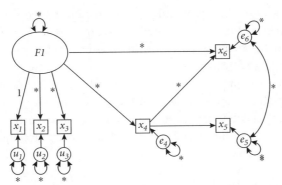

Fig. 20.1 Path diagram illustrating elements of a model. Squares represent observed variables and circles represet latent variables. The large circle represents a substantive latent variable, or factor, and the small circles represent either uniquenesses (u_i) or errors of prediction (e_i). Curved lines of which both ends point to the same variable represent variances, and those that point to two variables represent covariances. Straight lines indicate directional influence. Asterisks indicate parameters to be estimated.

not explained in the model (i.e., that have no straight line pointing toward them: $F1$, u_1–u_3, and e_4–e_6) – represent variances. Parameters associated with straight lines are regression coefficients or, in the case of arrows running from a latent variable to its indicators, factor loadings. Finally, parameters associated with curved lines between two variables are covariances or, if standardised, correlation coefficients.

An important characteristic of the model shown in Figure 20.1 is that certain paths that could have been included were not. For instance, there is no path from $F1$ to x_5. Implicitly, this path is accompanied by a *fixed parameter*, one that has been set to a pre-determined value (in this case, 0). Also, there are no covariances between uniquenesses, meaning these parameters were implicitly fixed at 0 as well. Fixed parameters in the form of excluded paths are desirable in a model, for they contribute to parsimony. They also can explain the inadequacy of a poor fitting model. Hence, when processing path diagrams, it is important to take note of paths that haven omitted, indicating that the accompanying parameters have been set to 0.

One additional feature of the model in Figure 20.1 bears mention. Notice that the directional effect of $F1$ on x_6 takes two forms in the model. The model indicates that $F1$ has a *direct effect* on x_6 as indicated by the horizontal path along the top of the diagram. In addition, the model indicates that $F1$ has an indirect effect on x_6 through x_4. That is, x_4 serves as an intervening variable through which the effect of $F1$ on x_6 is transmitted.

Measurement model

At a general level, the model depicted in Figure 20.1 includes two types of hypotheses. Ignoring x_4, x_5, and x_6 and associated paths and variances, we are left with a model focused specifically on the measurement of $F1$ using x_1, x_2, and x_3. Such models, termed *measurement models*, frequently are the sole focus of an application of SEM (for a review, see Hoyle, 1991). The defining feature of measurement models is that the only directional paths are between latent variables and their indicators. Although in the case of multiple latent variables a covariance between two or more latent variables might be posited, no attempt is made to infer causality or directionality in the association between latent variables. Variants of the factor analysis model (e.g., principal axis, principal components) are measurement models. Desirable measurement models are those in which each latent variable is uniquely and adequately represented by three or more indicators.

Structural model

The second type of hypothesis in the model depicted in Figure 20.1 concerns the directional associations between variables that are not indicators of latent variables. As with measurement models, such *structural models* can be the sole focus of an application of SEM. For instance, if only x_1 were available as a measure of $F1$, the model would include no latent variables but still could be used to evaluate the non-measurement-oriented directional paths in the model. Although such a model might seem to forfeit the benefits of SEM and suffer from the same unattainable measurement assumptions of multiple regression, it has the desirable quality of permitting the simultaneous estimation of direct and indirect effects on multiple outcome variables.

Structural models with latent variables

The most desirable applications of SEM includes both measurement and structural models. Indeed, the strongest application of SEM to the model shown in Figure 20.1 would include multiple indicators of x_4, x_5, and x_6, with all directional paths running between latent variables. Such models maximize the benefits of SEM as a flexible, comprehensive approach to modelling associations among a set of variables.

Measurement hypotheses

In describing specific hypotheses that can be tested by SEM, I first describe hypotheses about the indicators of latent variables. Because a considerable amount of attention has been devoted to these applications (e.g., Hoyle, 1991, 2000; Marsh and Hocevar, 1985), I review them only briefly, citing more detailed treatments in the literature.

Reliability

At the most fundamental level of adequacy, measures of a latent variable must assess the variable in a stable and consistent fashion. Both stability and internal consistency can be evaluated using SEM, although SEM offers no clear improvement over more straightforward approaches to evaluating internal consistency (e.g., coefficient alpha).

Stability

The path diagram in Figure 20.2 depicts a measurement model in which latent variable *F1* was assessed on two occasions using the same three-item measure. The path diagram illustrates two advantages of SEM over the typical strategy of correlating a simple composite from the two assessments to evaluate stability. First, note that the curved line, which represents the correlation between $F1_a$ and $F1_b$, is between latent variables, from which measurement error has been removed. Second, note that a curved line runs between the uniqueness associated with each indicator of *F1* at Time 1 and the same indicator of *F1* at Time 2. Those paths account for the associations between identical indicators at the two occasions that are not attributable to the association between the substantive latent variables $F1_a$ and $F1_b$. For instance, if a questionnaire item designed to measure a symptom of depression also engenders socially desirable responding, then a correlation between responses to the item on two occasions can be attributed to both stability of the symptom report and stability of socially desirable responding. For that reason, stability estimates that derive from the simple correlation between multiple assessments of a measure are biased. The extent or the direction of the bias is difficult to ascertain because of the attenuating effects of measurement error within occasion and because of inflation that is due to covariation between uniquenesses between occasions. The evaluation of stability is enhanced by removing both sources of bias–unreliability and correlated uniquenesses – before estimating the test-retest correlation.

Internal consistency

Internal consistency concerns the degree to which variance in the indicators of a construct can be attributed to the latent variables required to explain the covariances among the indicators. To the extent that the covariances among indicators can be attributed to a single latent variable (presumably the latent variable they were intended to measure), traditional measures of internal consistency such as coefficient alpha are

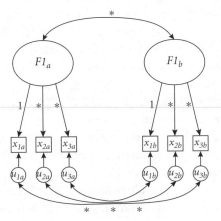

Fig. 20.2 Measurement model for evaluating stability of *F1* over time. (Note: variance paths associated with latent variables and uniquenesses have been omitted to improve readability.)

valid and to be preferred because of their widespread use (Cortina, 1993). If all of one's analyses are to be carried out using SEM, then fairly simple formulas are available for estimating internal consistency using parameter estimates from a measurement model (Werts, Linn, and Jöreskog, 1974); an example can be found in Bagozzi's (1993) study of measures of positive emotions.

A virtue of SEM over traditional approaches to estimating internal consistency is the capacity to evaluate the consistency of the associations between a set of indicators and the latent variable they represent. Referring back to Figure 20.2, that evaluation concerns whether the paths that run from each latent variable to its indicators are of equivalent strength. Although such equivalency is not mandatory, it is a desirable characteristic of a measure (Nunnally, 1978). Because specification of measurement models can include constraints on the relative magnitudes of parameter estimates, it would be possible to estimate the measurement model depicted in Figure 20.2 imposing the constraint that all path coefficients from $F1_a$ to its indicators are equal. If the adequacy of that model is no worse that the adequacy of a model in which the path coefficients are free to vary, then there is a basis for inferring that the contribution of the latent variable to each of its indicator is equivalent.

Validity

The question of validity is a multifaceted one that involves the evaluation of the internal characteristics of a measure as well as its associations with other measures. SEM is well suited for evaluating both.

Factorial validity

Factorial validity refers to the degree to which the measure of a construct conforms to the theoretical definition of the construct. For instance, if theory holds a construct to be unidimensional (e.g., g theories of intelligence), then any measure of the construct should be unidimensional as well. Similarly, if theory holds a construct to be multifaceted, perhaps hierarchical in nature (e.g., theories that conceptualize intelligence in terms of specific abilities), then a valid measure of the construct should conform to that structure. Thus, hypotheses about factorial validity derive from questions about the number of factors (i.e., latent variables) that underlie a set of indicators, the associations among those factors, and the contribution of the factors to the indicators. Such hypotheses traditionally have been evaluated using factor analysis or principal components analysis; however, the inability to place restrictions on those models limits their effectiveness for testing hypotheses relevant to factorial validity (Mulaik, 1987). Because of the hypothesis-testing capabilities of SEM, multiple hypotheses about the structure of a measure can be evaluated directly and unequivocally as variations of the measurement model. For instance, it is possible to compare statistically the adequacy of single- and multifactor measurement models. A variety of detailed treatments of the techniques and strategies involved in using SEM to evaluate hypotheses about factorial validity have been published (e.g., Hoyle, 1991; Morris, Bergan, and Fulginiti, 1991).

Construct validity

Once the factorial validity of a set of indicators has been upheld, an important second set of questions concerns the associations between the underlying construct and other constructs. Although the evaluation of construct validity often is portrayed in informal terms as an exploration of the associations between a new or reconceptualized construct and established constructs, it is best viewed as a focused, hypothesis-testing endeavor in which specific associations are posited and tested (Hogan and Nicholson, 1988). Because the hypotheses concern associations among variables, they involve formulation and evaluation of a structural model. Because they assume that the internal structure of the variable is understood and well represented, they also should involve formulation and evaluation of a measurement model. Thus, structural models with latent variable are preferred when evaluating construct validity because they require formal statements of hypotheses about within- and between-construct associations and provide a context for simultaneously evaluating all aspects of the validity of a measure.

The most straightforward application of SEM to the evaluation of construct validity involves two steps: (a) obtaining support for a measurement model of the latent variables that account for the associations among a set of indicators, and (b) either correlating criterion variables (preferably modelled as latent variables) with the focal latent variables or regressing the focal latent variables onto criterion variables. When the correlations among criterion variables are moderate to high, the regression approach is to be preferred because it evaluates the unique association between each criterion and the latent variables of interest (e.g., Hoyle, 1991).

SEM also can be used to evaluate validity hypotheses inherent in multitrait–multimethod (MTMM) designs (Campbell and Fiske, 1959). In the MTMM design, each measure is influenced by three sources, a trait factor, a method factor, and error. The potential advantages of SEM over simple visual inspection or other statistical means of evaluating MTMM data include the ability to obtain clear estimates of the contribution of method and trait variance to the total variance in a measure and compare statistically a variety of specific ways in which those sources influence a measure (Widaman, 1985). Marsh and Grayson (1995) provide an excellent overview of MTMM analyses using SEM, including strategies for overcoming the challenges unique to this application (Kenny and Kashy, 1992).

Uniquenesses

Because uniquenesses are explicitly modeled as latent variables in measurement models, hypotheses about their associations with other variables can be evaluated using SEM. To the extent that uniquenesses comprise only random error, they are, by definition, unrelated to other uniquenesses or other variables in a model. Recall, however, that uniquenesses comprise all variance in an indicator not shared with *all* other indicators of the latent variable to which it is assigned. It is not uncommon for a portion of this variance to be systematic (i.e., nonrandom) and, therefore, potentially correlated with other uniquenesses or variable in the model.

Correlated uniquenesses

I have already presented one form of correlated uniquenesses in the measurement model for evaluating stability, shown in Figure 20.2. These autocorrelations are expected due to the design that generated the data and, therefore, require no theoretical justification or explanation. More commonly, correlated uniquenesses are introduced into a measurement model in order to improve the fit of the model. For instance, considering only the latent variable for $F1_a$ in Figure 20.2, assume that x_{1a} and x_{2a} share something in common that they do not share with x_{3a}. This commonality is not captured by $F1_a$ and because the covariance between u_{1a} and u_{2a} is implicitly fixed at 0, the model does not fully account for the x_{1a} and x_{1b} covariance. Adding a curved arrow between u_{1a} and u_{2a} would add a free parameter to the model and potentially result in a dramatic improvement in fit. In addition to the potential improvement in fit, a virtue of adding correlated uniquenesses to a measurement model is that such a move can reveal unexpected and possibly problematic sources of covariance among indicators. The drawback to adding correlated uniquenesses is that such a move is almost always post hoc and rarely is accompanied by a satisfactory explanation for the correlation. Thus, the likelihood that the correlation is idiosyncratic to the sample and, therefore, not likely to replicate, is high.

Specific effects

A second hypothesis that involves uniquenesses concerns specific effects, the association between a uniqueness and an observed or latent variable elsewhere in the model. Returning to Figure 20.1, there might be reason to believe that not all of the non-random variance in x_1 is captured by $F1$ and that some portion of this uniqueness is related to x_4, x_5, or x_6. This association might be represented by a curved or directional arrow between u_1 and x_4, x_5, or x_6. The effect is considered specific because it involves variability in x_1 that is not shared by the remaining indicators of $F1$. Hypotheses about specific effects have proven particularly interesting in research on the effects of drug use (e.g., Newcomb, 1994). Although the latent variable polydrug use might account for shared variance in the frequency of individual drug use and predict various important outcomes, it also is likely that additional non-random variability in the reported use of specific drugs predicts various outcomes. As with hypotheses about correlated uniquenesses, hypotheses about specific effects often are post hoc and, therefore, subject to Type 1 error. Either class of associations could be specified a priori; however, each involves a prediction that suggests an understanding of the process under investigation and a knowledge of one's data that is rare in psychological research. Thus, when associations involving uniquenesses are 'discovered' in sample data, replication is a must (MacCallum, Roznowski, and Necovitz, 1992).

Measurement invariance

Among the most overlooked measurement hypotheses in clinical and health research are those concerning the invariance of a construct across groups or time. The question of measurement invariance concerns the degree to which a construct as represented by a set of indicators has the same meaning for different groups or for a single group at different points in time. The issue of measurement invariance is a profound one because the comparison of scores between groups or over time when those scores represent qualitatively different constructs is meaningless.

The various degrees of measurement invariance can be described with reference to a hypothetical measurement model such as the one depicted in path diagram form in Figure 20.3. In the path diagram, x_1–x_6 are indicators, measured separately for groups a and b. According to the model, commonality among the indicators can be attributed to two latent variables, $F1$ and $F2$. Associated with each latent variable and uniqueness is a variance, v. r indicates the covariance between $F1$ and $F2$. The *s indicate factor loadings, or the slope parameter in the equations regressing indicators on factors. The constant, c, permits the estimation of means (e.g., M_{F1a}) and intercepts (the +s). To avoid clutter, the *s and +s are not subscripted; however, estimates of each are free to vary from their counterparts in the model. The definition of invariance in this

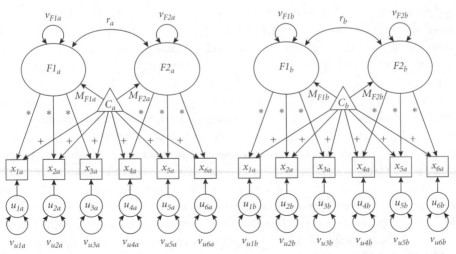

Fig. 20.3 Path diagram showing hypothetical factor structure and parameters to be tested for equivalence across groups or time.

context is statistical equivalence of estimates of a given parameter across the two groups (e.g., $v_{F1a} = v_{F1b}$). Any parameter shown in the path diagram (plus any covariances between error terms) can be tested for invariance.

The following levels of invariance typically are evaluated (Bollen and Hoyle, 1990; Widaman and Reise, 1997):

1 *Configural invariance*, or invariance of form (Jöreskog, 1971), is the most rudimentary form of invariance and concerns the number of sources of commonality, latent variables, evident in a set of indicators and the pattern of association between the indicators and latent variables (i.e., zero and nonzero loadings). In Figure 20.3, this hypothesis is evident in the specification of two *F*s with indicators x_1-x_3 loading on *F1* (and not *F2*), and indicators x_4-x_6 loading on *F2* (and not *F1*) for both *a* and *b*. Absent configural invariance, evaluations of other aspects of invariance are not meaningful.

2 *Weak metric invariance* assumes that factor loadings are equal across groups or time. That is, each of the six *s in the model for each group in Figure 20.3 is equal to its counterpart in the model for the other group.

3 *Strong metric invariance* adds the restriction of equality of intercepts, the +s in Figure 20.3. As stated by Widaman and Reise (1997), 'If strong [metric] invariance holds, group differences in both means and variances on the latent variables, which represent the constructs in psychological theories, are reflected in group differences in means and variances on the measured variables' (p. 295).

4 *Strict metric invariance* assumes identical reliabilities across groups, tested by constraining item unreliabilities, uniquenesses (e.g., v_{u1a}), to be equal across groups or time.

If the hypothesis of strong metric invariance is at least partially supported, then invariance hypotheses concerning the latent variables, hypotheses that typically are of more substantive than methodological interest, can be tested. These include tests of latent variable variances (e.g., $v_{F1a} = v_{F1b}$), covariances (e.g., $r_a = r_b$), and means (e.g., $M_{F1a} = M_{F1b}$).

Invariance of the full set of loadings and intercepts for items in a composite is unlikely, particularly when the number of items is large. In such cases, the items must evince at least partial invariance in order for the composite to be useful for comparisons across groups or time (Byrne, Shavelson, and Muthén, 1989). Minimally, the scale of the latent variable must be defined equally across groups or time points. Such partial invariance is established when the loading and intercept of one item are fixed to define the units and set the origin of the latent variable, and equality constraints are tenable for the loading and intercept of at least one other item. In such cases of minimal metric invariance, comparisons must be of structured means in the contact of a measurement model (e.g., M_{F1a} and M_{F1b}, as in Figure 20.3) as opposed to raw score means (Salzberger, Sinkovics, and Schlegelmilch, 1999).

I now move away from a focus on hypotheses that primarily are tested in the context of measurement models to a focus on hypotheses that require specification of a structural model. In each case, I assume that independent, dependent, and intervening variables are modeled as latent variables, although the hypotheses can be tested using observed variables.

Structural hypotheses

At the most basic level, hypotheses tested within the structural portion of a model are similar in form to hypotheses that might be tested in the general linear model (GLM; see Miles, this volume) framework (e.g., multiple regression, analysis of variance). For instance, referring back to Figure 20.1, the structural equation that expresses the hypothesis for x_6 is,

$$x_6 = {}^*F1 + {}^*x_4 + e_6,$$

where the variable names correspond to those in Figure 20.1 and the $*$s are parameters equivalent to regression coefficients in a multiple regression analysis. Two key differences between the SEM and GLM approaches is apparent in this model. First, $F1$ is modeled as a latent variable. Second, in addition to the structural equation for x_6, structural equations for x_4 and x_5 are estimated simultaneously. These features coupled with the capacity to test hypotheses about parameters typically not evaluated in GLM analyses, make the SEM approach highly desirable for many hypothesis tests in clinical and health psychology.

Hypotheses about mean differences

Hypotheses tested in the structural portion of a model typically refer to the magnitude and direction of associations among variables rather than group differences; however, for certain hypotheses about group differences, SEM might be preferred over traditional techniques such as t test or ANOVA. Using SEM, more detailed and complex hypotheses about group differences can be tested than can be tested using GLM approaches.

There are two strategies for comparing means in a structural model. The first involves introducing into a structural model a variable (or set of variables) that reflects variability in group membership – a strategy similar to introducing dummy coded variables into regression models (Cohen, Cohen, West, and Aiken, 2003). The second strategy, which is an extension of the between-groups analysis of measurement invariance, involves simultaneously estimating separate, at least partially invariant, measurement models for comparison groups (see Aiken, Stein, and Bentler, 1994, for a direct comparison).

Dummy variable approach

ANOVA is a special case of the regression model. For instance, a two-factor ANOVA can be estimated as a multiple regression equation by creating $k - 1$ dummy variables for each factor and one or more multiplicative terms that correspond to the ANOVA tests of interaction (Cohen *et al.*, 2003). Similarly, dummy variables can be introduced into structural models (recall that the regression model is a structural model) as a means of testing between-groups hypotheses. The simplest version of this strategy would involve a single outcome variable, either latent or observed, and, as a predictor, a two-level dummy variable with values 0 and 1. The unstandardised estimate of the association between the two variables would correspond to the difference between the two groups on the outcome. Most structural models are considerably more complicated than that, and therefore, the introduction of dummy variables into a model may be considerably more involved. Cohen *et al.* provide a detailed discussion of creating and evaluating effects of dummy variables in regression models, which can be generalised to the structural model. In structural models that include only observed variables, the dummy variable approach to group comparisons is the only approach possible.

Multigroup model approach

An alternative to the dummy variable approach is the multigroup model approach, which involves simultaneously estimating the same model for two or more groups and testing the equality of estimates of particular parameters between groups. When the outcome variables are modeled as latent variables, the test involves constraining latent means (e.g., M_{F1a} and M_{F1b} in Figure 20.3) to be equal and evaluating whether this constraint leads to a deterioration in model fit. If model fit deteriorates, indicating that the equality constraint is not tenable, then the implication is that the latent means are different. This strategy is referred to as *structured means analysis* and, as described earlier, requires at least partial strong metric invariance. Importantly, if anything less than full strong metric invariance is evident in the measurement model, structured means analysis is the only valid approach to comparing means on the construct represented by the latent variable.

A somewhat different set of hypotheses for which multigroup structural models are particularly well suited concerns between-group differences in the patterns of associations among independent and dependent variables. Such hypotheses refer to structural invariance, and correspond to moderator hypotheses, which are described in the next section. Returning to the model in Figure 20.1, it is possible to test the hypothesis that the association between $F1$ and x_4 is different between two groups. This hypothesis can be evaluated in conjunction with a test of measurement invariance that investigates whether the latent structure of $F1$ as represented by x_1–x_3 is the same for the two groups.

Mediation and moderation

The structural hypotheses discussed to this point involve only direct and unqualified associations between variables. Many hypotheses of interest to clinical and health researchers concern indirect effects and the boundary conditions of direct and indirect effects. SEM can be used to considerable advantage for testing such hypotheses (Hoyle and Robinson, 2003).

Mediation hypotheses concern the degree to which a direct effect (e.g., the $F1$–x_6 effect in Figure 20.1) can be explained by one or more intervening variables, or mediators (e.g., x_4 in Figure 20.1). To the extent that a demonstrable direct effect significantly declines when indirect effects through putative mediators are added to the model, the mediators are plausible explanations for the direct effect (Baron and Kenny, 1986). SEM is the most efficient and least problematic statistical approach to testing mediation. Because of the capacity to simultaneously estimate multiple equations and include latent variables, SEM (a) avoids problems of over- and underestimation of mediated effects by controlling for measurement error (Hoyle and Kenny, 1999), (b) permits isolation of the direct effect by allowing inclusion of problematic third variables in the model (Bollen, 1989), and (c) permits estimation of models that include multiple mediators (e.g., Shadish and Sweeney, 1991) and combinations of mediated and moderated effects (Baron and Kenny, 1986).

Hypotheses about moderation concern the magnitude of an effect, direct or indirect, at different levels of a variable believed to qualify the effect (Hoyle and Robinson, 2003). In ANOVA, moderation is tested as a matter of course in the form of interaction effects. Such effects are not typically included in multiple regression models but can be through the creation of product terms between predictors and putative moderators (Aiken and West, 1991). In the SEM context, tests of moderation hypotheses that involve observed variables only are accomplished in the same manner as in multiple regression analysis. Tests of moderation hypotheses that involve latent variables are more challenging, requiring the specification of a product latent variable that is non-linear in loadings and uniquenesses (Kenny and Judd, 1984).

Tests of moderation in designs typical of research in clinical and health psychology are inherently low in statistical power (McClelland and Judd, 1993). This disadvantage is compounded when product terms are created from variables measured with error, resulting in attenuated estimates of effects (Busemeyer and Jones, 1983). If the number of indicators of the latent variables can be held to four or fewer, then SEM is a viable strategy for overcoming the ill effects of measurement error in tests of moderation. An additional advantage of testing moderated effects using SEM is the ability to examine the mediation of such effects or to model product terms as mediators. Hoyle and Robinson (2003) describe and illustrate these promising applications.

Hypotheses involving time

Among the most appealing applications of SEM are those that take advantage of repeated observations of a sample over time (i.e., longitudinal, or panel, data). The most straightforward models of this sort are *autoregressive models*. In these models, a set of variables (observed or latent) are modelled at two or more points in time. Directional paths run from variables at each observation to variables at subsequent observations (typically only between adjacent observations). These paths are either autoregressive paths, which run from one observation of a variable to the next observation of the same variable, and cross-lagged paths, which run from each variable to other variables at subsequent observations. An important feature of these models is that all variables are modeled at each observation. This feature permits the removal of stable variance from outcomes via the autoregressive paths, ensuring that significant cross-lagged paths reflect only the directional effect of a predictor on an outcome (Hoyle and Robinson, 2003).

An alternative strategy for modelling repeated observations of a sample is *latent growth curve modelling*, by which trajectories of means are modelled and potentially included as predictors or outcomes in structural models (Duncan, Duncan, Strycker, Li, and Alpert, 1999). Models of latent growth require at least three, preferably four, repeated observations on a sample. As with trend analysis in repeated measures ANOVA, one can model up to $k - 1$ trajectory shapes (e.g., four observations would allow fitting of linear, quadratic, and cubic trajectories). In some applications, *unconditional models*, determining the best-fitting trajectory for one or more samples is the primary focus. Slope and intercept terms in these models are latent variables, for which a variance is estimated. If the estimated variance for a slope parameter is near zero, then the sample-wide slope estimate applies equally well to each individual in the sample. If the variance is nonzero, then the latent variable can be treated as an outcome in a *conditional growth model*. In these models, other variables (observed or latent) – typically time-invariant – are used to explain variance in the growth parameters (slopes and intercepts).

An innovative application of SEM combines autoregressive and latent growth modelling in an autoregressive latent trajectory (ALT) model (Bollen and Curran, 2004). Although this model can be estimated with as few as three repeated observations, the ideal design would include at least five. A strength of this model is the simultaneous and integrative approach to modelling associations and trajectories over time.

Caveats

Like all statistical strategies, SEM has strengths and limitations. To review, the primary strengths are:

- ◆ the capacity to model constructs as latent variables, thereby obtaining disattenuated estimates of effects;
- ◆ the capacity to test complex and subtle hypotheses regarding the latent structure of sets of indicators;
- ◆ the simultaneous estimation of multiple equations potentially involving multiple independent, intervening, and dependent variables in either latent or observed form.

These features make for a rich and flexible context within which to test hypotheses typical of clinical and health research.

When considering the use of SEM, these advantages must be weighed against a number of limitations. Unlike ordinary least squares, by which estimates are obtained in most applications of the GLM, maximum likelihood, the most frequently used estimator in applications of SEM, assumes large samples (Bollen, 1989). No simple formula can be offered for determining how many observations are necessary for valid estimation using maximum likelihood. Simulations suggest that under ideal conditions (reasonably normal distributions, well-specified model) samples of as few as 100 are large enough for valid estimates (e.g., Hoyle and Kenny, 1999). The condition of data typical of clinical and health research is rarely ideal; hence, larger samples are recommended. Samples of 200–400 are adequate for most applications, with larger models requiring larger samples.

An additional concern is the distribution of variables. Although SEM does not differ from other statistical models in the assumption that variables are normally distributed, the influence of nonnormality on the validity of SEM analyses is somewhat more complex. When sample size is large and a model accounts well for a set of data, the impact of nonnormality is no worse than for ANOVA or multiple regression. However, when sample size is small (i.e., less than 400) and a model does not evince a near-perfect fit to a set of data, the ill effects of non-normality on estimates and standard errors are magnified (Curran, West, and Finch, 1996). Fortunately, well-performing corrections to maximum likelihood estimates are available that allow for the use of SEM when distributions of variables are significantly nonnormal (Satorra and Bentler, 1988). A final concern involves interpretation, specifically inferences regarding causality. As noted at the beginning of the chapter, SEM is sometimes referred to as causal modelling. This is unfortunate, because SEM suffers most of the same limitations of other statistical models with regard to causal inference. This is because the ability to infer causality is tied most fundamentally to research design, not statistical analysis. Indeed, sophisticated statistical analyses cannot overcome a flawed or limited research design. That is not to say that statistical analyses are unimportant to the inferential process. Rather, it is to say that even the most sophisticated statistical model does not provide a basis for inferring causality apart from considerations about the manner in which the data were gathered. Thus, firm causal inferences from applications of SEM, which often are based on quasi- or non-experimental data, are rarely justified. As such, any SEM results that are portrayed in causal terms should be evaluated carefully – not in terms of statistical criteria but with regard to fundamental criteria of research design.

A related concern is the direction of influence between two variables that are associated. It is important to acknowledge that, although a model that specifies a particular direction of influence might fit well, it often is the case that a model can be found that fits equally well with the direction of influence running in the other direction. Indeed, it can be shown that, in many cases, many of the arrows in a model can be reversed without altering the fit of the model to the data (MacCallum, Wegener, Uchino, and Fabrigar, 1993). Because only one model can, in reality, be the 'true' model that generated the data, it is important to keep in mind that the evaluation of the statistical adequacy of a model is an evaluation of the consistency of the model with a particular set of data, not with reality (Bollen, 1989; Cohen *et al.*, 2003). It is also important to consider the statistical adequacy of alternative models that are conceptually inconsistent with the model being evaluated to determine whether that model is unique in its ability to account for the observed data rather than one of several models that account for the data equally well (MacCallum *et al.*, 1993).

At their core, these concerns are no different for SEM than for statistical procedures more typical of clinical and health research such as ANOVA and multiple regression. Yet, because of the standard use of large-sample estimators and the flexibility in model specification, the potential for misuse and misinterpretation is greater. The best advice for would-be users of SEM is to evaluate the condition of their data, taking the necessary steps to ensure the integrity of estimates and fit indices, and to limit inferences to those that the study design can support. When used in this responsible manner, SEM offers a compelling alternative to traditional statistical models for testing hypotheses in clinical and health psychology research.

Acknowledgements

During the writing of this chapter, the author was supported by grants R01-DA12371 and P20-DA017589 from the National Institute on Drug Abuse.

References

Aiken, L. S., Stein, J. A. and Bentler, P. M. (1994). Structural equation analyses of clinical subpopulation differences and comparative treatment outcomes: Characterizing the daily lives of drug addicts. *Journal of Consulting and Clinical Psychology*, **62**, 488–499.

Aiken, L. S. and West, S. G. (1991). *Multiple regression: Testing and interpreting interactions*. Thousand Oaks, CA: Sage Publications.

Anderson, J. C. and Gerbing, D. W. (1988). Structural equation modeling in practice: A review and recommended two-step approach. *Psychological Bulletin*, **103**, 411–423.

Bagozzi, R. P. (1993). Assessing construct validity in personality research: Applications to measures of self-esteem. *Journal of Research in Personality*, **27**, 49–87.

Baron, R. M. and Kenny, D. A. (1986). The moderator-mediator variable distinction in social psychological research: Conceptual, strategic, and statistical considerations. *Journal of Personality and Social Psychology*, **51**, 1173–1182.

Bollen, K. A. (1989). *Structural equations with latent variables*. New York: Wiley.

Bollen, K. A. (2002). Latent variables in psychology and the social sciences. *Annual Review of Psychology*, **53**, 605–634.

Bollen, K. A. and Curran, P. J. (2004). Autoregressive latent trajectory (ALT) models: A synthesis of two traditions. *Sociological Methods and Research*, **32**, 336–383.

Bollen, K. A. and Hoyle, R. H. (1990). Perceived cohesion: A conceptual and empirical examination. *Social Forces*, **69**, 479–504.

Busemeyer, J. R. and Jones, L. D. (1983). Analysis of multiplicative combination rules when the causal variables are measured with error. *Psychological Bulletin*, **93**, 549–562.

Byrne, B. M., Shavelson, R. J. and Muthén, B. (1989). Testing for the equivalence of factor covariance and mean structures: The issue of partial measurement invariance. *Psychological Bulletin*, **105**, 456–466.

Campbell, D. T. and Fiske, D. W. (1959). Convergent and discriminant validation by the multitrait-multimethod matrix. *Psychological Bulletin*, **56**, 81–105.

Cohen, J., Cohen, P., West, S. G. and Aiken, L. S. (2003). *Applied multiple regression/correlation analysis for the behavioral sciences*, 3rd edn. Mahwah, NJ: Erlbaum.

Cortina, J. M. (1993). What is coefficient alpha?: An examination of theory and applications. *Journal of Applied Psychology*, **78**, 98–104.

Curran, P. J., West, S. G, and Finch, J. F. (1996). The robustness of test statistics to nonnormality and specification error in confirmatory factor analysis. *Psychological Methods*, **1**, 16–29.

Crowley, S. L. and Fan, X. (1997). Structural equation modeling: Basic concepts and applications in personality assessment research. *Journal of Personality Assessment*, **63**, 508–531.

Duncan, T. E., Duncan, S. C., Strycker, L. A., Li, F. and Alpert, A. (1999). *An introduction to latent variable growth curve modeling*. Mahwah, NJ: Erlbaum.

Hogan, R. and Nicholson, R. A. (1988). The meaning of personality test scores. *American Psychologist*, **43**, 621–626.

Hox, J. J. and Bechger, T. M. (1998). An introduction to structural equation modeling. *Family Science Review*, **11**, 354–373.

Hoyle, R. H. (1991). Evaluating measurement models in clinical research: Covariance structure analysis of latent variable models of self-conception. *Journal of Consulting and Clinical Psychology*, **59**, 67–76.

Hoyle, R. H. (ed.) (1995). *Structural equation modeling: Concepts, issues, and applications*. Thousand Oaks, CA: Sage Publications.

Hoyle, R. H. (2000). Confirmatory factor analysis. In H. E. A. Tinsely and S. D. Brown (eds) *Handbook of applied multivariate statistics and mathematical modeling*, pp. 465–497. New York: Academic Press.

Hoyle, R. H. and Kenny, D. A. (1999). Sample size, reliability, and tests of statistical mediation. In R. H. Hoyle (ed.) *Statistical strategies for small sample research*, pp. 195–222. Thousand Oaks, CA: Sage Publications.

Hoyle, R. H. and Robinson, J. I. (2003). Mediated and moderated effects in social psychological research: Measurement, design, and analysis issues. In C. Sansone, C. Morf, and A. T. Panter (eds) *Sage handbook of methods in social psychology*, pp. 213–233. Thousand Oaks, CA: Sage Publications.

Jöreskog, K. G. (1971). Simultaneous factor analysis in several populations. *Psychometrika*, **36**, 409–426.

Kaplan, D. (2000). *Structural equation modeling: Foundations and extensions*. Thousand Oaks, CA: Sage Publications.

Kenny, D. A. and Judd, C. M. (1984). Estimating the nonlinear and interactive effects of latent variables. *Psychological Bulletin*, **96**, 201–210.

Kenny, D. A. and Kashy, D. A. (1992). Analysis of the multitrait-multimethod matrix by confirmatory factor analysis. *Psychological Bulletin*, **112**, 165–172.

Kline, R. B. (1998). *Principles and practice of structural equation modeling*. New York: Guilford Press.

MacCallum, R. C., Roznowski, M. and Necovitz, L. B. (1992). Model modifications in covariance structure analysis: The problem of capitalization on chance. *Psychological Bulletin*, **111**, 490–504.

MacCallum, R. C., Wegener, D. T., Uchino, B. N. and Fabrigar, L. R. (1993). The problem of equivalent models in applications of covariance structure analysis. *Psychological Bulletin*, **114**, 185–199.

Marcoulides, G. A. and Schumacker, R. E. (eds) (1996). *Advanced structural equation modeling: Issues and techniques*. Mahwah, NJ: Erlbaum.

Marsh, H. W. and Grayson, D. (1995). Latent variable models of multitrait-multimethod data. In R. H. Hoyle (ed.) *Structural equation modeling: Concepts, issues, and applications*, pp. 177–198. Thousand Oaks, CA: Sage Publications

Marsh, H. W. and Hocevar, D. (1985). The application of confirmatory factor analysis to the study of self-concept: First and higher order factor structures and their invariance across age groups. *Psychological Bulletin*, **97**, 562–582.

McClelland, G. H. and Judd, C. M. (1993). Statistical difficulties of detecting interactions and moderator effects. *Psychological Bulletin*, **114**, 376–390.

McDonald, R. P. and Ringo Ho, M.-H. (2002). Principles and practice in reporting structural equation analyses. *Psychological Methods*, **7**, 64–82.

Morris, R. J., Bergan, J. R. and Fulginiti, J. V. (1991). Structural equation modeling in clinical assessment research with children. *Journal of Consulting and Clinical Psychology*, **59**, 371–379.

Mulaik, S. A. (1987). A brief history of the philosophical foundations of exploratory factor analysis. *Multivariate Behavioral Research*, **22**, 267–305.

Newcomb, M. D. (1994). Drug use and intimate relationships among women and men: Separating specific from general effects in prospective data using structural equation models. *Journal of Consulting and Clinical Psychology*, **62**, 463–476.

Nunnally, J. C. (1978). *Psychometric theory*, 2nd edn. New York: McGraw-Hill.

Pugesek, B. H., Tomer, A. and Von Eye, A. (eds) (2003). *Structural equation modeling: Applications in ecological and evolutionary biology*. Cambridge University Press: Cambridge, England.

Raykov, T. and Marcoulides, G. A. (2000). *A first course in structural equation modeling*. Mahwah, NJ : Erlbaum.

Salzberger, T., Sinkovics, R. R. and Schlegelmilch, B. B. (1999). Data equivalence in cross-cultural research: A comparison of classical test theory and latent trait theory based approaches. *Australasian Marketing Journal*, **7**, 23–38.

Satorra, A. and Bentler, P. M. (1988). Scaling corrections for chi-square statistics in covariance structure analysis. *1988 Proceedings of the Business and Economics Statistics Section of the American Statistical Association*, 308–313.

Schumacker, R. E. and Lomax, R. G. (1996). *A beginner's guide to structural equation modeling*. Mahwah, NJ: Erlbaum.

Shadish, W. R., Jr. and Sweeney, R. B. (1991). Mediators and moderators in meta-analysis: There's a reason we don't let dodo birds tell us which psychotherapies should have prizes. *Journal of Consulting and Clinical Psychology*, **59**, 883–893.

Werts, C. E., Linn, R. L. and Jöreskog, K. G. (1974). Interclass reliability estimates: Testing structural assumptions. *Educational and Psychological Measurement*, **34**, 25–33.

Widaman, K. F. (1985). Hierarchically nested covariance structure models for multitrait-multimethod data. *Applied Psychological Measurement*, **9**, 1–26.

Widaman, K. F. and Reise, S. P. (1997). Exploring the measurement invariance of psychological instruments: Applications in the substance use domain. In K. J. Bryant, M. Windle, and S. G. West (eds) *The science of prevention: Methodological advances from alcohol and substance abuse research*, pp. 281–323. Washington, DC: American Psychological Association.

Chapter 21

Some statistical and graphical strategies for exploring the effect of interventions in health research

Gary Adamson and Brendan Bunting

A substantial portion of health research involves assessing the effectiveness of intervention programmes: where the term 'intervention' refers to any situation in which researchers are interested in assessing the effect of a treatment on a number of individuals, over a given period of time. The treatment could be, for example, the administration of a drug that is assumed to alleviate the symptoms of a disorder such as asthma; or alternatively, it could be a cognitive therapeutic programme thought to reduce alcohol misuse. In such interventions, researchers are mainly interested in assessing the efficacy of the treatment, but one important aspect of demonstrating treatment efficacy is that the health problem should otherwise persist in the absence of treatment – that is if individuals don't undergo the intervention the problem or disorder remains. In the classic approach for assessing the efficacy of an intervention there is generally an intervention group who receive the treatment and a control group who don't; with only pre-test and post-test treatment scores recorded. This scheme enables the researcher to assess the efficacy of the treatment and to demonstrate that members of the control group remain relatively unchanged in the absence of treatment. An extension of this design is presented diagrammatically in Figure 21.1. In this instance, the research design is extended to allow for examination of maintenance of treatment effect at two further time periods. This type of research design is often referred to as a 'repeated measures' because the same participants provide responses on a specified number of occasions, but it also has a between-subjects component, as there are different participants in the intervention and control groups. When there are elements of both 'repeated' and 'between' measures the research design is commonly referred to as a 'mixed' design.

Participants are randomly assigned to one of two groups – an intervention group and a control group (in most cases, although this might be two intervention groups, or more than two groups). Participants are then measured, on a number of occasions over time. Depending on the design and hypotheses, these measurements may be over the course of hours, days or years. For some types of analysis, it is necessary that participants are measured at the same time points (although these do not need to be equally

$$O_1 \quad X_1 \quad O_1 \quad O_1 \quad O_1$$
$$O_1 \quad X_0 \quad O_1 \quad O_1 \quad O_1$$

$$\xrightarrow{\hspace{2cm} \text{Time} \hspace{2cm}}$$

Fig. 21.1 Representation of an intervention design with a Treatment group (X_1) and a Control group (X_0) and observations (O_1) at four time points.

spaced), however this is not required. It may be necessary to record the data when the participant next has an appointment, and this might vary. In addition, participants may miss measurement occasions.

The overarching aim of this design is of course to demonstrate that any change in the participants in the intervention group relative to the control group is due to the treatment. This is a strong research design since it permits assessment of the three major criteria for establishing cause and effect relationships, which are: (a) changes in the outcome measure should fluctuate as a function of changes in the treatment – this is known as the *covariation principle*; (b) changes in the outcome measure are preceded by the treatment – this is known as the *temporal precedence principle*; and (c) the treatment is the only reasonable cause of changes in the outcome measure – known as the *no plausible alternative explanation principle*.

Perhaps a concrete example of the design will help convey its advantages. Let's suppose that we want to assess if a behavioural therapy session is effective in terms of increasing length of exposure (in seconds) to a perceived adverse stimulus in phobic patients.[1] One hundred and fifty phobic patients are randomly assigned to either the 'intervention' group (i.e. receiving behavioural therapy treatment) or the 'control' group (no treatment) with seventy-five patients in each group. For the first (baseline) observation ('O_1'), which is pre-intervention, all patients are presented with an image of the adverse stimulus; and the time taken before the patient requires verbally that the stimulus be withdrawn is recorded in seconds, which is labelled 'time to withdrawal'. The next step in the sequence of events is that the patients in the intervention group undergo a behavioural therapy session. This involves a therapist introducing patients to a relaxation technique, which is hypothesised to help them deal with their phobia. Patients in the control receive no such treatment throughout the duration of the study. In the next observation, which is immediately post-intervention, all patients are presented with the same stimulus and time to withdrawal is again recorded in the same manner. Exactly the same measurement procedure is followed for two further observations, and time to withdrawal recordings are made in each of these observations. The time period between observations is held constant for each individual patient throughout the sequence of events. This is a robust experimental design, at least when compared to a design which involves responses being taken from different individuals at

---

[1] Please note that this is a contrived scenario for illustrative purposes only and the associated data were simulated.

different observations (independent subjects). Inter-individual differences would arise in a situation where different individuals respond on the various occasions. In this repeated measures design, the same individual responds on each occasion within each of the conditions. The advantage of this is that we are controlling for differences between individuals, since the data is obtained from the same individuals. One consequence is that the unexplained source of variance in the analysis is likely to be reduced because we don't have error arising from individual differences across observations. This is a fairly simple design and only one of many possible alternative configurations to assess treatment efficacy, but it nevertheless permits exploration of a number of interesting questions, which include:

◆ Has the randomisation procedure been effective i.e. are the distributions for the control and intervention groups equivalent in terms of time to withdrawal at the pre-intervention observation?

◆ Are the distributions of time to withdrawal scores for the control group and intervention group different over time?

◆ If change is evident for the intervention group, what is the pattern or rate of change in relation to post-intervention maintenance?

◆ Is there change in the control group over time?

◆ Is the rate of change or growth the same for all participants in the intervention group?

◆ What shape best describes the rate of growth for the intervention group?

To answer these questions some thought needs to be given to the type of data derived from this intervention design, and importantly, the relationships between the individuals' data at the various time points. As with any statistical analysis, one should begin by looking at descriptive statistics and use graphical representations in an attempt to get a good 'feel' for the data.

Table 21.1 provides summary statistics for the intervention and control groups. There are clear differences between the two groups in terms of the means and standard deviations, which to reiterate, reflect time to withdrawal in seconds following presentation of a perceived adverse image for our phobic patients. The means relating to the intervention group increase over the first three time points and drop slightly at the final time point, which suggests that the behavioural therapy has a positive effect. In contrast, the means for the control group remain fairly constant over the four observations, although there are some fluctuations in the mean time to withdrawal. Interestingly, the standard deviations for the intervention group decrease substantially across the observations, while the standard deviations for the control group do not show much change over the four observations. It is always good practice to plot the distributions in order to visually inspect the shape and relationships among the distributions. Figure 21.2a plots the means and standard deviations for both groups, and the same data are plotted in Figure 21.2b using boxplots.

Table 21.1 Descriptive statistics

	Intervention group				Control group			
	Time 1	Time 2	Time 3	Time 4	Time 1	Time 2	Time 3	Time 4
Count	75	75	75	75	75	75	75	75
Mean	42.67	57.28	61.61	60.50	42.62	39.95	42.79	41.99
SD	15.89	9.89	8.81	8.27	15.44	16.01	14.21	15.48
Median	46.11	56.84	61.49	60.24	41.12	41.54	42.74	41.49
Range	68.86	45.71	42.22	45.15	63.84	71.06	67.14	81.44

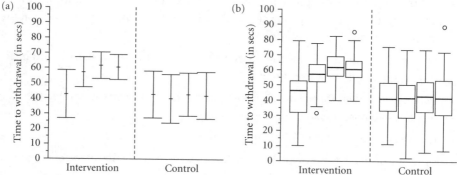

Fig. 21.2(a) and (b) Distributions for the groups across the four observations.

The means and standard deviations plot in Figure 21.2a is perhaps the most commonly used format for displaying distributions, but this hides a lot of information and we would generally not recommend its use. For example, it implies that all the distributions are symmetrical, but this may not be the case since the error bars simply represent plus and minus one standard deviation; and besides, this information can easily be derived from Table 21.1. From the information in Figure 21.2a it is *not* possible to assess the shape of each distribution in terms of skewness or kurtosis, or to examine the presence of outliers (i.e. aberrant or unusual values). In contrast, Figure 21.2b makes use of boxplots, which provide a method of assessing the distributions and they provide better visual insights into the nature of the data. Conventionally, boxplots are based on the 'five number summary', namely the median, upper and lower quartiles, and the maximum and minimum values (see Tukey, 1977). The box represents the interquartile range, which contains 50 per cent of the values, and the bold line intersecting this box depicts the median value of the entire distribution. The whiskers are the lines that extend from the box to the highest and lowest values, excluding outliers. Outliers are classified into two categories, mild and extreme. Mild outliers are generally defined as cases with values greater than 1.5 times the interquartile range (usually signified in the boxplot by a circle). Extreme outliers are cases with values that are three times greater than the interquartile range (usually signified by an asterisk). It is evident from these boxplots that across all the observations the distributions are roughly symmetrical, perhaps with the exception of the pre-intervention condition for the intervention group, which is very slightly negatively skewed relative to the median location. Moreover, there are a few mild outliers in some of the distributions, which sometimes can have an adverse effect on subsequent statistical analysis, so the data analyst needs to be wary of such cases. Neither of these graphical formats, however, provides information about the performance of each individual across the four observations. While in many forms of statistical analysis we are often interested only in assessing summaries for group trends, on such occasions as interventions it is frequently important to consider and explore the impact of the treatment across individuals, since it is always possible that the intervention may or may not be equally effective for all participants. One form of graphical presentation that facilitates examination of individual trends is the profile plot; examples of which are given in Figures 21.3a and 21.3b.

These profile plots show the actual value obtained from each individual at each of the four time points for the intervention and control groups separately, with a line joining the four time points for each individual. This type of graph is frequently useful, particularly when there are relatively few participants. However, as the number of participants increase the graph becomes cluttered and the trend across observations can become somewhat unclear. Nevertheless, this graph is often valuable for gaining a general impression of the character of the trend for individuals across the observations. In this instance, there appear to be clear differences between the patterns of the results for the intervention group (Figure 21.3a) and the control group (Figure 21.3b). The intervention group scores increase over time, while the control group scores appear somewhat erratic.

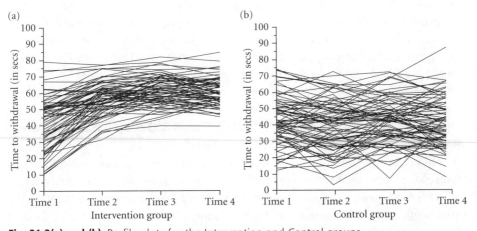

Fig. 21.3(a) and (b) Profile plots for the Intervention and Control groups.

It is considered good practice to visually explore data using graphs to obtain insights into the pattern of the relationships across individuals and between groups. Indeed such graphs might point to the type of analysis required, but obviously they do not provide estimates of statistical significance. The remainder of this chapter will look at some statistical procedures or models that can be applied to data derived from intervention designs such as that described previously.

Gain scores

One common method used to analyse scores from an intervention study is simple 'gain scores'. Gain scores are usually derived by subtracting an individual's pre-test scores from her/his post-test scores. If, as with the current data, one expects that the post-test scores will be greater than the pre-test scores, the gain scores would be positive, whereas a negative gain score would indicate that the pre-test score was greater than the post-test score. Recall that in our data we have three sets of post-test scores, so potentially for the intervention group alone we could calculate three sets of gain scores, and likewise, three sets of gain scores for the control group. To test the statistical significance of any one set of gain scores, the researcher could perform a one-sample t-test to assess if the gain scores differ significantly from zero. Note that if gain scores were around zero for the intervention group this would indicate that the intervention was unsuccessful and as for the control we would expect scores to be around zero. In fact, calculating gain scores for any one group and then performing a one-sample t-test is equivalent to performing a paired-samples t-test on the pre-test and post-test scores, making the calculations of gain scores in this instance unnecessary. The question arises though, given the structure of our design, as to which pre-test and post-test scores to assess, since we have three sets of post-test scores for the intervention – and indeed three for the control group as well. We also need to consider differences in performance across the intervention and control groups, which can be achieved by calculating gain scores for each group and then performing an 'independent samples' t-test to test for mean differences across the two groups. So, with gain scores there are potentially quite a large number of pairs of scores we could test using either a paired or independent samples t-test, which would inflate the likelihood of committing Type I errors – i.e. rejecting the null hypothesis when it is true.

Another major problem associated with gain scores is that they fail to take into account the covariation or correlation between individuals over the time periods. Consider the data presented in Table 21.2. It is obvious that the sets of scores for 'Time 1' and 'Time 2' have the same mean value and the same variance; but each individual score has changed from Time 1 to Time 2. Our onclusion from examining the gains scores alone would be that there is no difference between the scores. Of course, this is correct for the mean difference, yet there is perfect negative correlation between the two sets of scores from Times 1 and 2, which is not taken into account in this form of statistical modelling. While the data in Table 21.2 are extremely unlikely to occur in

Table 21.2 Calculating gain scores

Respondent	Time 1	Time 2	Gain scores
1	16	19	3
2	17	18	1
3	18	17	− 1
4	19	16	− 3
Mean	17.5	17.5	0

reality, it nevertheless conveys the potential pitfalls in using gain scores to analyse data from repeated measures or intervention designs.

Analysis of variance models

Another statistical model that is frequently applied to data from intervention studies is repeated measures analysis of variance (ANOVA). Again, like the gain scores method, the main concern of repeated measures ANOVA is, in essence, to test for statistically significant differences among the mean scores across the various time periods for a single group. The main advantage of this type of model over the gain scores approach is that it controls for the likelihood of obtaining Type I errors due to multiple pairwise comparisons.

However, the ANOVA approach primarily seeks to assess the extent to which the means differ across the repeated observations and between groups, and in many situations this may not be an optimal choice for us. Frequently, when we reflect, our only interest may not be in the mean differences. The pattern of correlations/covariances across time may also be important. Do the correlations or covariances appear to be similar across groups? Do the correlations indicate a weakening across occasions or treatment levels? The variance may be equally important: if the study involves an intervention where we expect change to have occurred, should we not expect the variance to change along with the means and possibly the correlations/covariances? If the treatment is having a positive effect on everyone and in turn creating a clustering around a given point, is it not then of interest to know that the variance is reducing across occasions or conditions? In Figures 21.4a and 21.4b we have used a matrix scatterplot to examine the relationships between the four time points for each of the individuals in the groups separately. This plot is useful as it permits inspection of how the distributions covary at the individual level across the time points.[2] For example, by simply looking at the last column of plots for the intervention group we see that the distributions appear to become gradually more tightly clustered over time. The choice of a statistical model with which to analyse the data from intervention designs should not be driven solely

[2] Be sure that the scaling is same across all plots within the matrix.

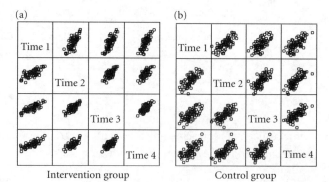

Fig. 21.4(a) and (b)
Distributions for the groups
across the four observations.

by the desire to assess point estimates (i.e. the means): due consideration needs to be given to covariances/correlations of the distributions.

Structural equation modelling

An alternative approach to the more conventional methods mentioned previously is structural equation modelling (SEM). SEM is useful in many contexts because it enables the researcher to describe and test the appropriateness of theoretical models (in a statistical sense) by assessing if the data obtained from a study fits the statistical model proposed by the researcher (see Hoyle, this volume, for more information on SEM). As such, SEM is primarily a confirmatory approach that facilitates testing of specifically tailored research hypotheses in terms of examining the distribution of, for example, the variances, covariances and means. The extent to which a hypothesised model fits the data is then assessed by various fit statistics and indices. In this section we describe a statistical model that is formulated in line with our expectations, given the structure of the design used in our study. To begin, our data contains 12 covariances, six for the intervention and six for the control group, which provide information about the relationship between individual scores across the four time points. The data also consists of eight means and eight variances, four for each group; and these provide information about the most typical response and extent of spread of the distributions for each of the four time points. These characteristics present us with very many possible points for comparison across and within the groups. However, statistical assessment of such characteristics should only be made where they are directly related to the hypotheses formulated by the researcher. Indeed, in any research, statistics should primarily be used to check the veracity of our claims regarding what is happening within the data, and therefore it is essential that the researcher should dictate which aspects of the data require examination and the form that this examination should take. A key task for any researcher, particularly in the SEM context, is to bring order and meaning to the myriad of possible options that is potentially available.

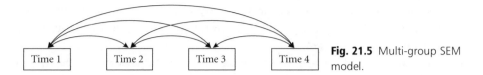

| Time 1 | Time 2 | Time 3 | Time 4 |

Fig. 21.5 Multi-group SEM model.

Figure 21.5 shows the four time points and the covariances between each pair of time points, which are represented by lines with doubled headed arrows, and of course, there is a variance and a mean associated with each of the time points. In this instance we use a multiple group approach, which allows us to assess the appropriateness of the model across and within the control and intervention groups. That is to say, by using a multiple group approach we can determine the extent to which our hypothesised model fits the data from both groups simultaneously, with one set of fit statistics produced – even though we may place different restrictions across the groups.

There are a number of expectations that we might have in relation to the data derived from our study and we could impose a number of constraints that reflect our expectations. First, because individuals were randomly assigned to the intervention or control group and as scores at time point one are pre-intervention, we would expect that the means and variances across both groups would be the approximately the same – with any difference attributable to random fluctuations. Consequently, in this multi-group model we would begin by constraining the means and variances to be the same across the groups at time point one. Second, we would also expect that individuals in the control group would not change significantly across the four time points because they did not receive the treatment. Therefore, for the control only, we have constrained the means and variances to be the same across the remaining time points. Finally, we would expect that the covariances between each of the time points would be the same for the control group, since we expect that each bivariate relationship should remain fairly stable across the four time points. In line with this expectation the covariances in the control group were constrained to be equal. When these constraints are imposed it is clear that the model describes the data very well: the hypothesised model resulted in a χ^2 goodness of fit value of 10.3, $df = 11$, $p = 0.51$ which is indicative of good model fit.

While the hypothesised model fits the data very well, it would be useful in this instance to establish that the variances, covariances and means in the intervention group actually do differ substantially. This can be assessed by constraining each of these estimates to be equal in the intervention group. When these restrictions are imposed the model is rejected as indicated by the chi-square goodness of fit statistic: $\chi^2 = 89$, $df = 20$, $p < 0.00001$, and from this we can infer that collectively, the means, variances, and covariances are different within the intervention group across the time points. However, if only the variances for the intervention are constrained to be equal, and the covariances and means are set free to be estimated, the model does fit the data ($\chi^2 = 15$, $df = 13$, $p = 0.294$); from this result we can conclude that the variances across the time points for the intervention group are approximately equivalent. For completeness, when the means, and then covariances, were sequentially restricted both these models were rejected.

In sum, this set of results suggest that the randomisation of participants to the control and intervention groups was successful in achieving equivalent groups and that there was no significant change in 'time to withdrawal' for the control group across the four time periods. In contrast, the intervention group appear to change substantially across the time periods both in terms of means and the covariances, while the variances remain fairly constant for post intervention distributions.

Latent growth model

So far in this chapter we have considered a number of conventional statistical models, together with fixed effects structural equation models. While in many situations these methods are effective, they sometimes impose unreasonably restrictive assumptions, and they may also result in a loss of statistical power, together with producing biased parameter estimates (Curran and Muthén, 1999; Muthén and Curran, 1997). Moreover, and perhaps most importantly, these models generally fail to provide the researcher with an adequate description of the likely growth trajectory or change in individuals' responses over time, and they also fail to assess the variability associated with this overall change in participant's profiles (Curran and Muthén, 1999). An innovative approach for assessing change over time has been realised with the introduction of latent growth models, sometimes referred to as random coefficient modelling (McArdle, 1987, 1988, 1989; Muthén and Curran, 1997; Willet, 1991). The latent growth approach is advantageous because it permits examination of individuals' profiles in terms of two latent variables, which are usually labelled the *intercept* and *slope*. The former captures the initial status of the individual when they approach the intervention programme, and the latter is an estimate that describes the pattern of growth (or otherwise) resulting from the participant's interaction with the intervention programme – subsequent to initial status – i.e. individuals' growth trajectories over time. The variability associated with, and relationship between, these latent constructs provide information on how individuals differ with respect to both their initial status and their pattern of growth.

Prior to considering the specification for a latent growth model and fitting it to our data, we decided to perform casewise regressions for all individuals. This was achieved by simply regressing the four observed scores for each individual on the numbers 0, 1, 2, 3 – where the latter represents a linear growth across the four time periods. A regression line was fitted to each individual's data using ordinary least squares (OLS) regression and the resulting intercept and slope estimates were stored.

To illustrate this procedure, we have shown the data for two individuals in Table 21.3. For each of these individuals, we calculate a regression equation, using time (1, 2, 3, 4) as the predictor, and the score as the outcome. These two individuals are shown plotted

Table 21.3 Data for casewise regression

	Time				Intercept	Slope
	1	2	3	4		
Person 1	46	52	57	53	45.5	2.6
Person 2	60	55	62	55	60	−0.8

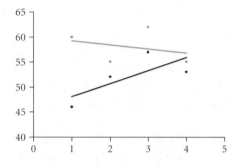

Fig. 21.6 Data from Table 21.3, with lines of best fit. The black line represents Person 1, the grey line represents Person 2.

in Figure 21.6, with the lines of best fit plotted. Notice that this now gives us two new statistics for each person – an intercept, representing their starting point, and a slope, representing their average change over each time point.

While these estimates are most likely biased, they should nevertheless be useful in terms of providing a general notion of what is going on in the data; but perhaps more importantly, this simple approach will help us to describe and explain some of the salient aspects of the latent growth method. To facilitate explanation of the characteristics associated with latent growth models we have plotted each individual's slope against their intercept for the intervention and control groups separately in Figure 21.7.

The filled dots in Figure 21.7 represent the relationship between individuals' intercepts and slopes for the intervention group, and the open dots represent those for the control group. There are a number of interesting aspects in this scatterplot. First, the distribution of the data values on the vertical axis provides a visual impression of the typical slope and the variation of the slopes across individuals in the intervention and control groups. This shows how individuals differ in terms of their growth trajectories over the four time periods. It is notable that, in general, the intervention group have substantially larger slopes than the control group. Indeed, the average slope for the intervention group is slightly more than five, which means that for every time period the time to withdrawal increases by slightly more than five seconds. Therefore, over all four time periods the average increase for the intervention group would be around 17 seconds. In contrast, the slope for the control group is fairly close to zero, which indicates that the change in time to withdrawal time for this group remains relatively unchanged over the four time periods. Second, the distribution of the intercepts, which

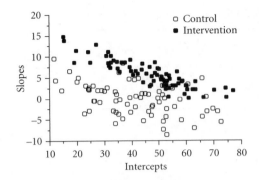

Fig. 21.7 Scatterplot of the relationship between individual's slopes and intercepts, using OLS.

to reiterate is initial status of all individuals pre-intervention (i.e. at time point one), are plotted along the horizontal axis. Based on these OLS regression estimates the average intercept for the intervention group is around 46 seconds and the control approximately 42, with the standard deviation of about 15 for both groups, which suggests that there is substantial variability in the initial status of individuals at pre-intervention. In addition to the variance and means of the slopes and intercepts, we are also interested in the covariance or correlation between them. Such information tells us whether the individuals within the groups perform differently. For example, as shown in Figure 21.7 the correlation between the slopes and intercepts for the intervention group is strong and negative. This suggests that those individuals who have low pre-intervention scores (i.e. small intercepts) increase more rapidly (relatively large slopes) and individuals who have large intercepts have relatively small slopes. For the control group the correlation is rather weak and slightly negative. In sum, Figure 21.7 is useful for it graphically presents the aspects of the data that we are interested in assessing using latent growth models, namely, the average intercept and variation of the intercepts, the average slope and the variation of the slopes, and the relationship between intercepts and slopes. In addition, rather than fitting a linear relationship between the intercepts and slopes as we did for Figure 21.7, the advantage of using latent growth model is that it will estimate the shape of the growth trajectories for the individuals in our sample.

Figure 21.8 is a path diagram which details the form of the model used in latent growth analyses. As mentioned above it contains two latent variables, the intercept and slope, and there are four observed variables, time one through to time four.

A multiple group approach was used to estimate the appropriateness of the latent growth model across both the intervention and control groups simultaneously, although different constraints were placed on each of the groups. In latent growth models the paths leading from the intercept latent variable to the observed variables are fixed to one and this specification is invariant across groups. This specification captures the average intercept or initial status for each group, together with the variance of the intercept. The paths leading from the latent variable slope to the observed variables may be specified in a number of ways to represent the expected growth across time points.

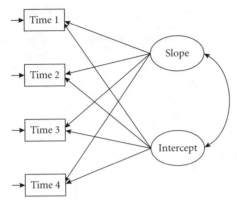

Fig. 21.8 Unconditional latent growth model (multi-group).

For example, if we expected a linear growth across time points we would fix the first path to 0 and subsequent paths to 1, 2, and 3; or alternatively to get the same result we could set the first to 0 and subsequent paths to 0.333, 0.666 and 1. If quadratic growth was expected over the four time periods the paths could be set to 0, 1, 4, and 9 and tested. In regard to the current data we decided to fix the first path to 0 and the last path to 1 and to allow paths two and three to be estimated for the intervention group. As for the control group, we expected that the slopes would be flat with no change, so we set the paths to 0, 1, 1, and 1 for this group. When this model was fitted to the data it had a $\chi^2 = 20.480$, $df = 14$, $p = 0.116$, which is indicative of a good model fit. Given that the model fits the data, it is then appropriate to consider the estimates associated with the latent variables. All the estimates, including the fixed paths, are listed in Table 21.4.

The intercept estimate, which represents the initial status of the average participant, is significant for both groups. This indicates that both groups, at the pre-intervention stage, have on average time to withdrawal times that differ significantly from zero. Moreover the standard deviation of the intercepts are also significant for both groups, which indicates that there is significant variability in each of the groups intercept distributions: signifying that some individuals have relatively low time to withdrawal scores, while others have relatively high scores. The slope estimate for the intervention group is statistically significant, which indicates that the slope for the intervention group differs significantly from zero. The standard deviation associated with this estimate is also significant, which shows that there is substantial variability in the slopes for individuals in the intervention group. For the control group both the estimate of the slope and its standard deviation is non-significant. This result illustrates that the control group slope does not differ significantly from zero, that is, it is relatively flat and the non-significant variability of slopes suggests that all individuals' slopes are closely clustered around the zero slope. The negative correlation between the intercepts and the slopes for the intervention group is statistically significant. This indicates that those individuals with low pre-intervention time to withdrawal scores (small intercepts) have relatively large rates of growth or steep trajectories (large slopes) – i.e. they benefit substantially from

Table 21.4 Estimates from the unconditional latent growth model

Estimate	Intervention group	Control group
Intercept	42.623*	42.620*
SD of the intercept	14.804*	12.996*
Slope	17.969*	−1.047
SD of the slope	7.883*	3.584
Correlation of intercept and slope	−0.986*	−0.183
Intercept at Time one	1†	1†
Intercept at Time two	1†	1†
Intercept at Time three	1†	1†
Intercept at Time four	1†	1†
Slope at Time one	0†	0†
Slope at Time two	0.828*	1†
Slope at Time three	1.043*	1†
Slope at Time four	1†	1p 292

* denotes a statistically significant estimate at $p < 0.01$.

† denotes a constrained or fixed path. SD – Standard deviation.

the intervention; and those individuals with relatively large intercepts have shallower slopes – they benefited less form the intervention. The correlation between the intercepts and slopes for the control group is non-significant. This result for the control group shows that is no relationship between individuals' pre-intervention score and their rate of growth (or lack of it) for the post-intervention scores. Finally, in relation to the estimates for the paths leading from the slope to the Time 2 and Time 3 observed variables, these were found to be 0.828 and 1.043 respectively. Noting that the paths for Time 1 and Time 4 were constrained to 0 and 1 respectively, this gives an overall growth rate for the intervention group of 0, 0.828, 1.043, and 1 across the four time points. Interpretation of these estimates, in this instance, is rather straightforward: the first and last time points are constrained to 0 and 1, therefore, the estimates for each of the intervening time points can be considered as proportional or percentage increase in overall growth (i.e. the slope) from initial status (i.e. the intercept value).

The statistical model described in this section (Figure 21.8) is usually referred to as an unconditional latent growth model because there are no predictor variables incorporated in the model that might help explain the variance and covariance of the latent intercept and slope. That is, latent growth modelling also allows the researcher to introduce additional explanatory variables, which can be used to assess the extent to which participant characteristics influence their respective trajectory. For example, variables such as participant's gender, age and self-esteem could be assessed in regard to the influence they have on the participant's growth throughout the duration of the intervention programme. In total, the latent growth approach enables the researcher to answer a variety of research questions, which relate to individual's progress as a result of participating in an intervention programme.

Final remarks

In this chapter we provided a brief overview of some common and some not so common methods for assessing data from interventions and have pointed to some associated advantages and disadvantages. We have also tried to cover some graphical methods for visualising and exploring data. This is in line with our belief that the data analyst should never rely solely on the 'black box' approach to draw conclusions about data. We also readily acknowledge that there are a number of limitations in our treatment of this large and complex area. Indeed, we have only considered one type of intervention design, when there are many alternative configurations. Moreover, in some instances, but particularly in relation to the latent growth curve modelling, we have only touched on the potential applications of this type of statistical model. The body of knowledge in this area continues to grow steadily, although we do feel we have provided a good starting point for the unfamiliar reader. Our final hope is that the reader will find this chapter helpful and will be inspired to undertake further reading – many of the papers listed in the reference section will be useful in this quest.

Further reading

Good introductions to this area are: Little, Schnabel and Baumert (2000) and Duncan, Duncan, Strycker, Li and Alpert (1999) or Singer and Willett (2003).

References

Curran, P. J. and Muthén, B. O. (1999). The application of latent growth curve analysis to the testing of developmental theories in intervention research. *American Journal of Community Psychology*, **27**, 567–595.

Duncan, T. E., Duncan, S. C., Strycker, L. A., Li, F. and Alpert, A. (1999). *An introduction to latent growth curve modelling: concepts, issues and applications.* Mahwah, NJ: Erlbaum.

Little, T. D., Schnabel, K. U. and Baumert, J. (2000). *Modeling longitudinal and multilevel data.* Mahwah, NJ: Erlbaum.

McArdle, J. J. and Epstein, D. (1987). Latent growth curves within developmental structural equation models. *Child Development*, **58**, 110–133.

McArdle, J. J. (1988). Dynamic but structural equation modeling of repeated measures data. In J. R. Nesselroade and R. B. Catell (eds) *Handbook of multivariate experimental psychology*, 2nd edn, pp. 561–614. New York: Plenum Press.

McArdle, J. J. (1989). Structural modeling experiments using multiple growth functions. In R. Kanfer, P. Ackerman and R. Cudeck (eds) *Abilities, motivation, and methodology: The Minnesota Symposium on Learning and Individual Differences*, pp. 71–117. Hillsdale, NJ: Erlbaum.

Muthén, B. O. and Curran, P. J. (1997). General longitudinal modelling of individual differences in experimental designs: A latent variable framework for analysis and power estimation. *Psychological Methods*, 2, 371–402.

Singer, J. D. and Willett, J. B. (2003). Applied longitudinal data analysis: Modeling change and event occurrence. New York: Oxford University Press.

Tukey, J. W. (1977). *Exploratory data analysis*. Reading, MA: Addison-Wesley.

Willett, J. B. (1991). Measuring change: the difference score and beyond. In H. J. Wallerg and G. D. Haetel (eds) *The international encyclopedia of educational evaluation*. Oxford, England: Pergamon Press.

Chapter 22

Meta-analysis

Andy P. Field

Until relatively recently research evidence was assimilated and evaluated by discursive literature reviews. A typical review would entail the author collating articles on a given topic (for example, do antidepressants make people less depressed?), summarising them and placing some kind of subjective weight on their findings. They might then, if you're lucky, conclude something about the topic of interest: perhaps that certain kinds of antidepressants initially make people more depressed, whereas others do not. Sometimes these are referred to as 'tick-counting reviews' or 'vote-counting reviews' – the reviewer counted the ticks or votes in each column (significant result/non-significant result).

These reviews are still common; however, they have the obvious flaw that even the most discerning of researchers could give particular importance to studies that others might believe to be relatively less important. This can sometimes lead to quite long and heated debates in which different researchers reach different conclusions from the same literature (e.g. researchers at a drugs company believing that the available evidence fully supports the efficacy of their antidepressants whereas a clinician thinking about using the drug disagrees). Meta-analysis rose out of a desire to objectify literature reviews using statistics. In short it is used to discover how big an effect actually is and what factors moderate that effect.

Effect sizes

What is an effect size?

When you read an empirical paper, the first question you should ask is 'How important is the effect obtained?' When carrying out research we collect data, carry out some form of statistical analysis on the data (for example, a t-test or ANOVA) which gives us a value known as a *test statistic*. This test statistic is then compared to a known distribution of values of that statistic that enables us to work out how likely it is to get the value we have. If it is very unlikely that we would get a test statistic of the magnitude we have (typically, if the probability of getting the observed test statistic is less than 0.05) then we attribute this unlikely event to an effect in our data (see Field, 2005). We say the effect is 'statistically significant'. This often leads to the misconception that when our test statistic is not statistically significant (the probability is greater than 0.05) that there is 'no effect'. In fact, there is always an effect, it's just that some effects are small and others are large (see Cohen, 1990; Field, 2005). As such, to answer the question 'How important is the effect obtained?' that you should be asking yourself as you read a paper, it's not the statistical significance that you should look at but the effect size.

An effect size is simply an objective and standardised measure of the magnitude of observed effect. The fact that the measure is standardised just means that we can compare effect sizes across different studies that have measured different variables, or have used different scales of measurement. So, an effect size based on the Beck depression inventory could be compared to an effect size based on levels of serotonin in blood.

Effect size measures

Many measures of effect size have been proposed, the most common of which are Cohen's, d, and Pearson's correlation coefficient, r (although there are others such as odds ratios; see Clark-Carter, this volume, for further discussion of effect sizes).

Cohen's d is based on the standardized difference between two means:

$$d = \frac{M_1 - M_2}{\sigma}$$

So, you simply subtract the mean of one group from the other and then standardise this difference by dividing by σ, which is the sum of squared errors (i.e. take the difference between each score and the mean, square it, and then add all of these squared values up) divided by the total number of scores.

Pearson's correlation coefficient, r, is simply a standardised form of the covariance between two variables. The covariance is given by:

$$\text{cov}(x, y) = \frac{\sum_{i=1}^{n}(x_i - \bar{x})(y_i - \bar{y})}{N - 1}$$

So, for a given case of data, you take the score on variable x and subtract from it the mean score on variable x, you then do the same for variable y and multiply these two values together (known as the *cross-product*). You do this for each case of data and add them all up to give you the top half of the equation. You then divide by the number of cases minus 1, which in effect gives us an average cross-product. To standardise this value we simply divide by the standard deviation of each variable multiplied together:

$$r = \frac{\text{cov}_{xy}}{s_x s_y}$$

Many of you will be familiar with the correlation coefficient as a measure of the strength of relationship between two continuous variables: however, it is also a very versatile measure of the strength of an experimental effect.[1] It may be difficult for you to reconcile how the correlation coefficient can also be used in this way; however, this is only because students are often taught about it within the context of non-experimental research. Although I don't want to get into it now (see Field, 2005 if you're interested), trust me that r can be used to express differences between means and this is the measure that I prefer because it is constrained to lie between 0 (no effect) and 1 (a perfect effect) and is familiar to almost all students and researchers.

R can be easily obtained from several common test statistics. For example, when a t-test has been used r is a function of the observed t-value and the degrees of freedom on which it is based:

$$r = \sqrt{\frac{t^2}{t^2 + df}}$$

When ANOVA has been used and an F-ratio is the test statistic, then when there is 1 degree of freedom for the effect, the following conversion can be used:

$$r = \sqrt{\frac{F(1, -)}{F(1, -) + df_{error}}}$$

In which $F(1, -)$ is simply the F-ratio for the effect (which must have 1 degree of freedom) and df_{error} is the degrees of freedom for the error term on which the F-ratio is based. So, imagine you saw in a paper 'the short-term effect of breast enlargements on self-esteem was significant, $F(1, 36) = 6.82$, but the long-term effect was not significant'. The effect size for the short term benefit of breast enlargements on self esteem would be:

$$r = \sqrt{\frac{6.82}{6.82 + 36}} = 0.4$$

The reason the degrees of freedom for the effect need to be 1 is simply because this means that 2 things are being compared. It's difficult to interpret effect sizes for complex effects involving lots of groups because you have no idea which groups contribute to the effect. So, it is best to calculate effect sizes for focused comparisons such as comparisons of two groups or interactions with only 1 degree of freedom.

Finally, r can be calculated from the probability value of a test-statistic. First, you must convert the probability into a z-score using tabulated values of the normal

---

[1] In fact, d and r can be converted approximately using the following equation: $r = d / \sqrt{d^2 + 1/(pq)}$ in which p is the proportion of participants in the first group and q is the proportion of participants in the second group. To make the conversion the opposite way (again this is approximate) it is simply: $d = 2r/\sqrt{1 - r^2}$.

distribution (see Field, 2005), and then simply divide the resulting z by the square root of the total sample size on which it is based:

$$r = \frac{z}{\sqrt{N}}$$

Why are effect sizes useful?

Effect sizes are useful because they provide an objective measure of the importance of an effect. It doesn't matter what effect you're looking for, what variables have been measured, or how those variables have been measured: we know that a correlation coefficient of 0 means there is no effect, and a value of 1 means that there is a perfect effect. Cohen (1992, 1988) has made some widely accepted suggestions about what constitutes a large or small effect:

• $r = 0.10$ (small effect): in this case, the effect explains 1 per cent of the total variance.

• $r = 0.30$ (medium effect): the effect accounts for 9 per cent of the total variance.

• $r = 0.50$ (large effect): the effect accounts for 25 per cent of the variance.

We can use these guidelines to assess the importance of our effects (regardless of the significance of the test statistic). However, r is not measured on a linear scale so an effect with $r = 0.4$ isn't twice as big as one with $r = 0.2$.

Finally, the effect size in the sample is not actually that interesting: it is the size of the effect in the population that is important. However, because we don't have access to this value, we use the effect size in the sample to estimate the likely size of the effect in the population (see Field, 2001).

Principles of meta-analysis

As scientists, we measure effects in samples to allow us to estimate the true size of the effect in a population to which we don't have direct access (Field and Hole, 2003). Imagine I were interested in knowing the effect of cognitive behavioural therapy (CBT) in treating eating disorders. There is a true effect that CBT has, but I don't have access to that true effect because I cannot collect data from the entire population of people with eating disorders. Instead I use the small sample available to me (perhaps from my clinic and some other local clinics; see Buchanan and Coulson, this volume), I assume that this sample is representative of the population of interest and use the effect in my sample to estimate the true effect that CBT has. The chances are that lots of other clinicians will also be interested in the effects of CBT on eating disorders, and they too have used samples to estimate the size of the effect that CBT has. Meta-analysis is based on the simple idea that we can take all of these individual studies, quantify the observed effect in a standard way and then combine them to get a more accurate idea of the true effect in which were interested. We saw in the previous section that we express effects in a standard way using effect sizes.

The first step in meta-analysis is to search the literature for studies that have addressed the same research question. So, we would conduct searches to attempt to find all studies that had used these approaches (e.g. the ISI Web of Knowledge, PubMed, PsycInfo) to search for articles that have tested the effects of CBT on eating disorders. We might also search relevant conference proceedings, hand-search relevant journals (in case the electronic searches missed anything), search the reference sections of the articles that we have found, and consult people we consider to be experts in the field – all of this is an attempt to avoid the file drawer problem (which we will discuss later on).

It may make sense to have some kind of systematic criteria for including studies (for example, CBT is a term that could be applied to a variety of interventions, you might reasonably restrict your analysis to more specific forms of CBT), or to reject studies that are methodologically weak. However, in doing so, unless you formulate a precise set of criteria you may well be introducing subjective bias into the analysis. It is also possible to classify studies into groups, for example methodologically strong or weak, and then see if this variable moderates the effect size; by doing so you can see whether methodologically strong studies (by your criteria) differ in effect size to the weaker studies.

Once you have collected your articles, you need to find the effect sizes within them, or calculate them for yourself. Articles may not report effect sizes, or may report them in different metrics; your first job is to get effect sizes for each paper that represent the same effect and are expressed in the same way. If you were using r this would mean obtaining a value for r for each paper you want to include in the meta-analysis. The main function of meta-analysis is to estimate the effect size in the population (the 'true' effect) by combining the effect sizes from a variety of articles. Specifically, the estimate is a weighted mean of the effect sizes. Although it isn't the primary concern of meta-analysis, the probability of obtaining that mean can also be computed: we can see whether the average effect size is statistically significant. Meta-analysis can also be used to estimate the variability between effect sizes across studies (the *homogeneity of effect sizes*) and to explain this variability in terms of moderator variables (see Field, 2003a). For example, we might find that CBT including group therapy produces a larger effect size for improvement in eating disorders than CBT without a group component.

Types of meta-analysis

There are two ways to conceptualise meta-analysis: fixed effects and random effects models.[2] These models differ not only in the theoretical assumptions that underlie them, but also in how the mean effect size and its significance are computed.

---

2 There is actually a mixed model too, but for simplicity I'll ignore it.

The fixed-effect model assumes that all studies in a meta-analysis come from a population with a fixed average effect size: studies in the meta-analysis are sampled from a population in which the average effect size is fixed (Hunter and Schmidt, 2000). The alternative assumption is that the average effect size in the population varies randomly from study to study: studies in a meta-analysis come from populations that have different average effect sizes, so, population effect sizes can be thought of as being sampled from a 'superpopulation' (Hedges, 1992).

Statistically speaking, the main difference between fixed- and random-effects models is in the amount of error. In fixed-effects models there is error introduced because of sampling studies from a population of studies (see Figure 22.1). This error exists in random-effects models but in addition there is error created by sampling the populations from a superpopulation (see Figure 22.2). So, calculating the error of the mean effect size in random-effects models involves estimating two error terms, whereas in

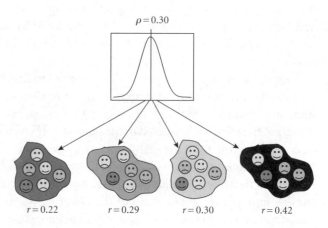

Fig. 22.1 Diagram representing the fixed-effects conceptualisation of meta-analysis. The population has an average effect size that is fixed (.3), and studies taken from the population will have similar (but not necessarily the same because of sampling error) effect sizes to that of the population.

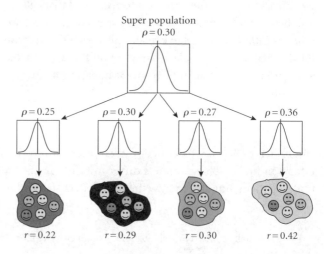

Fig. 22.2 Diagram representing the random-effects conceptualisation of meta-analysis. Each study is taken from a population in which the mean effect size is variable: so, it can be thought of as if each study is taken from a population, that itself is taken from a 'superpopulation'.

fixed-effects models there is only one error term. As we shall see, this has some implications for computing the mean effect size.

Doing a meta-analysis

Although there are many variations on how to do meta-analysis, I will explain two of the most popular (see Field, 2001, 2003b).

Hedges and colleagues' method

In this method (Hedges and Olkin, 1985; Hedges and Vevea, 1998), effect sizes are first converted into a standard normal metric (using Fisher's r-to-Z transformation) before calculating a weighted average of these transformed scores. Fisher's (1921) r-to-Z transformation is described below in which r is the correlation coefficient from study i:

$$z_{r_i} = \frac{1}{2} \text{Log}_e \left(\frac{1 + r_i}{1 - r_i} \right) \tag{1}$$

which has an approximate normal distribution with mean, $\bar{z}_r$, and variance $1/n - 3$. The transformation back to r is simply:

$$r_i = \frac{e^{(2z_i)} - 1}{e^{(2z_i)} + 1} \tag{2}$$

In the fixed-effect model, the transformed effect sizes are used to calculate an average in which each effect size is weighted by the inverse within-study variance of the study from which it came (for correlation coefficients the sample size, n, minus three):

$$\bar{z}_r = \frac{\sum_{i=1}^{k} w_i z_{r_i}}{\sum_{i=1}^{k} w_i} = \frac{\sum_{i=1}^{k} (n_i - 3) z_{r_i}}{\sum_{i=1}^{k} (n_i - 3)} \tag{3}$$

in which k is the number of studies in the meta-analysis.

This average is used to calculate the homogeneity of effect sizes: the squared difference between each study's observed transformed r and the mean transformed r (calculated above) is used. To account for the variance of each study these differences are weighted by the variance. The resulting statistic Q has a chi-square distribution with $k - 1$ degrees of freedom:

$$Q = \sum_{i=1}^{k} (n_i - 3)(z_{r_i} - \bar{z}_r)^2 \tag{4}$$

If you wanted to apply a fixed effects model you could stop here. However, as we've seen there is another conceptualisation, which is the random effects model. To calculate the random-effects average effect size, the weights use a variance component that incorporates both between-study variance and within-study variance. The between-study variance is denoted by τ^2 and is simply added to the within-study variance. The weighted average in the z metric is, therefore:

$$\overline{Z}_r^* = \frac{\sum\limits_{i=1}^{k} w_i^* z_{r_i}}{\sum\limits_{i=1}^{k} w_i^*} \tag{5}$$

in which the weights (w_i^*) are defined as:

$$w_i^* = \left(\frac{1}{n_i - 3} + \tau^2 \right)^{-1} \tag{6}$$

The between-study variance can be estimated in several ways (Hedges and Vevea, 1998; Overton, 1998), however, Hedges and Vevea use Q (which we came across earlier), k, and a constant, c:

$$\tau^2 = \frac{Q - (k - 1)}{c}$$

where the constant, c, is defined (for correlation coefficients) as:

$$c = \sum\limits_{i=1}^{k} (n_i - 3) - \frac{\sum\limits_{i=1}^{k} (n_i - 3)^2}{\sum\limits_{i=1}^{k} (n_i - 3)} \tag{7}$$

If τ^2 is negative then it is set to zero (because the variance between-studies cannot be negative). Having calculated τ^2, it is used to calculate the weights, (w_i^*), which in turn are used to calculate the mean effect size (5). This average effect size must be converted back to the r metric before being reported.

Finally, it is useful to construct confidence intervals for the mean effect size. Confidence intervals are limits constructed such that a certain percentage of the time (usually 95 or 99 per cent) the true value of the population statistic of interest will fall within these limits. So, a 95 per cent confidence interval for a mean effect size can be thought of like this: if we'd done 100 meta-analyses, calculated the mean effect size and then calculated a confidence interval for that mean then for 95 of these meta-analyses, the confidence intervals we constructed would contain the true value of the mean effect size in the population (see Field, 2005 for a more detailed explanation). To calculate these confidence intervals we need to know the standard error of the mean effect size:

$$SE(\overline{z}_r^*) = \sqrt{\frac{1}{\sum\limits_{i=1}^{k} w_i^*}} \tag{8}$$

which uses the weights we've already calculated.

The confidence interval around the average effect size is easily calculated using the standard error and the two-tailed critical value of the normal distribution (which is 1.96 for the most commonly used 95 per cent confidence interval). The upper and lower bounds are calculated by taking the average effect size and adding or subtracting its standard error multiplied by 1.96:

$$CI_{\text{Upper}} = \bar{z}_r^* + 1.96SE(\bar{z}_r^*) \tag{9}$$

$$CI_{\text{Lower}} = \bar{z}_r^* - 1.96SE(\bar{z}_r^*) \tag{10}$$

These values are again transformed back to the r metric before being reported.

Hunter and Schmidt method

Although this method's greatest virtue (Hunter and Schmidt, 1990) is its emphasis on isolating and correcting for sources of error such as sampling error and reliability of measurement variables, it is dealt with here in only its simplest form. Unlike Hedges' method the untransformed effect-size estimates, r, are used to calculate the weighted mean effect size, and the weight used is simply the sample size, n:

$$\bar{r} = \frac{\sum_{i=1}^{k} n_i r_i}{\sum_{i=1}^{k} n_i} \tag{11}$$

Hunter and Schmidt (1990) argue that the variance across sample effect sizes consists of the variance of effect sizes in the population and the sampling error and so the variance in population effect sizes is estimated by correcting the variance in sample effect sizes by the sampling error. The variance of sample effect sizes is the frequency weighted average squared error:

$$\sigma_r^2 = \frac{\sum_{i=1}^{k} n_i (r_i - \bar{r})^2}{\sum_{i=1}^{k} n_i} \tag{12}$$

The sampling error variance is calculated as:

$$\sigma_e^2 = \frac{(1 - \bar{r}^2)^2}{\bar{N} - 1} \tag{13}$$

in which, $\bar{r}$ is the average effect size, and $\bar{N}$ is the average sample size. The variance in population effect sizes is estimated by subtracting the sampling error variance from the variance in sample effect sizes:

$$\hat{\sigma}_\rho^2 = \sigma_r^2 - \sigma_e^2 \tag{14}$$

Hunter and Schmidt recommend correcting this estimate for artefacts (see Hunter and Schmidt, 1990) and then constructing credibility intervals. These intervals are based on taking the average effect size and adding or subtracting from it the square root of the estimated population variance multiplied 1.96 (for a 95 per cent interval):

$$\text{Credibility Interval}_{\text{Upper}} = \bar{r} + 1.96\sqrt{\hat{\sigma}_\rho^2} \tag{15}$$

$$\text{Credibility Interval}_{\text{Lower}} = \bar{r} - 1.96\sqrt{\hat{\sigma}_\rho^2} \tag{16}$$

These credibility intervals will, by definition, be larger than standard confidence intervals (see Hall and Brannick, 2002). If confidence intervals are required (rather than credibility intervals) these can be obtained by using the standard error of the mean effect size, which is the square root of the variance of sample effect sizes divided by the number of studies in the meta-analysis, k:

$$CI_{\text{Upper}} = \bar{r} + 1.96\sqrt{\frac{\sigma_r^2}{k}} \tag{17}$$

$$CI_{\text{Lower}} = \bar{r} - 1.96\sqrt{\frac{\sigma_r^2}{k}} \tag{18}$$

Problems with meta-analysis

Publication bias and the 'file drawer' problem

Publication bias refers to the fact that significant findings are more likely to be published than non-significant findings both because researchers do not submit them (Dickersin, Min and Meinert, 1992) and reviewers may tend to reject manuscripts containing them (Hedges, 1984). It is sometimes known as the 'file drawer' problem, because non-significant research is more likely to end up in the researchers file drawer than in a journal (Rosenthal, 1979). This bias can be substantial, for example, Greenwald (1975) has estimated that significant findings were eight times more likely to be submitted than non-significant ones and Sterling (1959) reported that 97 per cent of articles in psychology journals reported significant results. The effect of this bias is that meta-analytic reviews are likely to overestimate mean effect sizes (and their significance) because they might not include unpublished studies, in which effect sizes would have been small (Shadish, 1992, reports that unpublished research can have effect sizes half the value of comparable published research).

Artefacts

Effect sizes are influenced by the quality of the research and quality precision of measurement of variables. The error in the measurement of variables will vary across studies: one study might have used a very reliable and well-respected questionnaire (such as the Beck Depression Inventory) whereas another uses one created by the authors with few known psychometric properties. In addition, correlational research studies can vary in the range of scores elicited from participants (*range variation*), these differences in the range of scores elicited will affect the resulting effect sizes. In its simplest form meta-analysis doesn't take account of the measurement reliability, range differences, or the general quality of research. Although Hunter and Schmidt (1990) have suggested statistical techniques for correcting for measurement error and range variation, many researchers either do not apply these corrections or apply them incorrectly (Schmidt and Hunter, 1996). Given that artefacts contribute to differences in effect sizes, as I've suggested earlier, an alternative approach is to use 'quality of research' as a moderator variable to test whether the effect size is significantly different in 'well-conducted' and 'badly-conducted' studies.

Misapplications of meta-analysis

There are theoretical (Field, 2003a,b; Hunter and Schmidt, 2000; National Research Council, 1992) and empirical (Barrick and Mount, 1991) grounds to believe that the majority of real-world data reflect the random-effects conceptualisation of meta-analysis. However, the choice of model depends not only on the assumptions about the true state of the world, but also on the type of inferences that the researcher wishes to make. Hedges and Vevea (1998) argue that fixed-effect models are fine if the goal is to draw inferences only about the studies included in the meta-analysis: however, if the goal is to generalise beyond the studies in the meta-analysis then random-effects models are more appropriate.

Arguably, social scientists are more likely to want to generalize beyond the studies included in the meta-analysis and so random-effects models should be used (see Field, 2003a,b; Hunter and Schmidt, 2000). Despite this, fixed-effects models are routinely applied. Even in highly regarded journals such as *Psychological Bulletin* this error is frequently made: Hunter and Schmidt (2000) found 21 examples of meta-analytic studies using fixed-effects models and none using random effects models.

The consequences of using fixed-effects models on random-effects data are an overestimation of the estimate of the mean effect size and its significance. Hunter and Schmidt (2000) predict that the usual Type I error rate of 5 per cent error rate will increase to between 11 and 28 per cent, and Field (2003a) showed with simulations that error rates increase to anywhere between 43 and 80 per cent in certain circumstances.

Errors in the methods

The final issue is whether the methods themselves yield accurate estimates. Johnson, Mullen and Salas (1995) compared the Hedges–Olkin (fixed-effect), and Hunter–Schmidt (which is arguably random-effects) meta-analytic methods by manipulating a single data set and concluded that the Hunter and Schmidt method reached more conservative estimates of significance than other method. However, there were some problems with this study (see Field, 2001; Schmidt and Hunter, 1999) and Field (2001) found that when comparing random-effects methods, the Hunter–Schmidt method yielded the most accurate estimates of population effect size across a variety of situations (see also Hall and Brannick, 2002). Neither method controlled the Type I error rate when 15 or fewer studies were included in the meta-analysis, but Hedges' random-effects method controlled the Type I error rate better than the Hunter–Schmidt method when 20 or more studies were included. In a more recent set of simulations, Field (2002) demonstrated that the results of comparisons between the methods depended somewhat on how the simulations were run and specifically the shape of the superpopulation from which effect sizes were sampled. Hedges' method performed better than the Hunter–Schmidt method as the superpopulation deviated from normality. One general finding is that neither method was accurate when fewer than 20 studies were in the meta-analysis.

Objections to meta-analysis

Finally, it should be mentioned that some authors have objected to the whole concept of meta-analysis. Eysenck (1978, 1994) has been a vocal critic of meta-analysis, calling it 'an exercise in mega-silliness' (1978). Eysenck suggests that meta-analysis has a number of problems. One of the advantages of meta-analysis, according to its advocates, is that subjective judgments are avoided – all studies can be included – regardless of how poor the quality of the study. Eysenck (1994, p. 789) suggests

> A good review is based on intimate personal knowledge of the field, the participants, the problems that arise, the reputation of different laboratories, the likely trustworthiness of individual scientists, and other partly subjective but extremely relevant considerations. Meta-analysis rules out any such subjective factors. It can be done by simply feeding the published results to a computer and coming up with an effect size.

He also suggests that meta-analysis is often an oversimplification – we try to condense a complex multivariate effect into a simply univariate effect. Interventions may have complex effects, on a range of different variables, which may interact with other factors – e.g. when looking at the effects of passive smoking, we cannot ignore genetics, personality or stress. Meta-analysis is prone to 'adding apples and oranges'. A meta-analysis carried out by Smith, Glass and Miller (1980) examined the efficacy of psychotherapy for treating neuroses, and concluded that there was strong evidence that psychotherapy was effective (a result that came to the opposite conclusion of Eysenck's [1965] review). Eysenck suggests that in this review 'neither treatments, nor patients, nor end-points were remotely comparable'. Eysenck would argue that it is hard to interpret an effect size that is made up of so many disparate groups.

Summary

This chapter has given you a whistle-stop tour of meta-analysis, a statistical technique for assimilating research findings. We've seen that effects can bet expressed in terms of standard measures known as effect sizes. These effect sizes can be combined to try to estimate the true size of effect in the population. It is also possible to see if effect sizes vary across studies. Although we haven't covered this in detail, we saw that we can also try to explain effect size variability by factoring in moderator variables (interested readers should read Field, 2003a). Finally we have looked at a selection of ways in which bias can be introduced into a meta-analysis. This should, I hope, give you a good foundation to build upon in carrying out a meta-analysis of your own.

References

Barrick, M. R. and Mount, M. K. (1991). The big five personality dimensions and job performance: a meta-analysis. *Personnel Psychology*, **44**, 1–26.

Cohen, J. (1988). *Statistical power analysis for the behavioural sciences*, 2nd edn. New York: Academic Press.

Cohen, J. (1990). Things I have learned (so far). *American Psychologist*, **45**, 1304–1312.

Cohen, J. (1992). A power primer. *Psychological Bulletin*, **112** (1), 155–159.

Dickersin, K., Min, Y.-I. and Meinert, C. L. (1992). Factors influencing publication of research results: follow-up of applications submitted to two institutional review boards. *Journal of the American Medical Association*, **267**, 374–378.

Eysenck, H. J. (1965). The effects of psychotherapy. *International Journal of Psychiatry*, **1**, 97–178.

Eysenck, H. J. (1978). An exercise in mega-silliness. *American Psychologist*, **33**, 517.

Eysenck, H. J. (1994). Meta-analysis and its problems. *BMJ*, **309**, 789–793.

Field, A. P. (2001). Meta-analysis of correlation coefficients: a Monte Carlo comparison of fixed- and random-effects methods. *Psychological Methods*, **6**, 161–180.

Field, A. P. (2003a). The problems in using fixed-effects models of meta-analysis on real-world data. *Understanding Statistics*, **2**, 77–96.

Field, A. P. (2003b). Can meta-analysis be trusted? *The Psychologist*, **16**, 642–645.

Field, A. P. (2005). *Discovering statistics using SPSS*, 2nd edn. London: Sage.

Field, A. P. and Hole, G. (2003). *How to design and report experiments*. London: Sage.

Greenwald, A. G. (1975). Consequences of prejudice against the null hypothesis. *Psychological Bulletin*, **82**, 1–20.

Hall, S. M. and Brannick, M. T. (2002). Comparison of two random-effects methods of meta-analysis. *Journal of Applied Psychology*, **87**, 377–389.

Hedges, L. V. (1984). Estimation of effect size under non-random sampling: the effects of censoring studies yielding statistically insignificant mean differences. *Journal of Educational Statistics*, **9**, 61–85.

Hedges, L. V. (1992). Meta-analysis. *Journal of Educational Statistics*, **17**, 279–296.

Hedges, L. V. and Olkin, I. (1985). *Statistical methods for meta-analysis*. Orlando, FL: Academic Press.

Hedges, L. V. and Vevea, J. L. (1998). Fixed- and random-effects models in meta-analysis. *Psychological Methods*, **3**, 486–504.

Hunter, J. E. and Schmidt, F. L. (1990). *Methods of meta-analysis: correcting error and bias in research findings*. Newbury Park, CA: Sage.

Hunter, J. E. and Schmidt, F. L. (2000). Fixed effects vs. random effects meta-analysis models: implications for cumulative knowledge in psychology. *International Journal of Selection and Assessment*, **8**, 275–292.

Johnson, B. T., Mullen, B. and Salas, E. (1995). Comparison of three major meta-analytic approaches. *Journal of Applied Psychology*, **80**, 94–106.

National Research Council (1992). *Combining information: Statistical issues and opportunities for research*. Washington, DC: National Academy Press.

Overton, R. C. (1998). A comparison of fixed-effects and mixed (random-effects) models for meta-analysis tests of moderator variable effects. *Psychological Methods*, **3**, 354–379.

Rosenthal, R. (1979). The 'file drawer' problem and tolerance for null results. *Psychological Bulletin*, **86**, 638–641.

Schmidt, F. L. and Hunter, J. E. (1999). Comparison of three meta-analysis methods revisited: An analysis of Johnson, Mullen, and Salas (1995). *Journal of Applied Psychology*, **84** (1), 144–148.

Shadish, W. R. (1992). Do family and marital psychotherapies change what people do? A meta-analysis of behavioural outcomes. In T. D. Cook, H. Cooper, D. S. Cordray, H. Hartmann, L. V. Hedges, R. J. Light, T. A. Louis and F. Mosteller (eds) *Meta-analysis for explanation: a casebook*, pp.129–208. New York: Sage.

Smith, M. I., Glass, G. V. and Miller, T. I. (1980). *The benefits of psychotherapy*. Baltimore, MD: Johns Hopkins Press.

Sterling, T. C. (1959). Publication decisions and their possible effects on inferences drawn from tests of significance – or vice versa. *Journal of the American Statistical Association*, **54**, 30–34.

Index